CURRENT GOOD PRACTICES
AND NEW DEVELOPMENTS IN
PUBLIC SECTOR SERVICE
MANAGEMENT

COMMONWEALTH SECRETARIAT

Commonwealth Secretariat
Marlborough House
Pall Mall
London SW1Y 5HX
United Kingdom

© Commonwealth Secretariat
September 2002

Published by the Commonwealth Secretariat.
Designed by Something Big Ltd
Printed in the United Kingdom by Abacus Direct
Wherever possible, the Commonwealth Secretariat uses paper
sourced from sustainable forests or from sources that minimise
a destructive impact on the environment.

Copies of this publication can be ordered direct from:
The Publications Manager,
Information and Public Affairs Division,
Commonwealth Secretariat,
Marlborough House,
Pall Mall, London SW1Y 5HX
United Kingdom
Tel: +44 (0)20 7747 6342
Fax: +44 (0)20 7839 9081
Email: r.jones-parry@commonwealth.int

Price: £18.50
ISBN: 0-85092-712-9

Website:
www.thecommonwealth.org

Contents

Acknowledgements

Introduction

1.0 Making the Most of Staff

6.0 Improving the Management of Finance

7.0 Improving Policy Making

Appendix

Acknowledgements

This publication is the product of some remarkable co-operation and some very generous assistance from experts who have given their time and knowledge as a signal of their commitment to the improvement of the public service in the Commonwealth.

The original edition was co-ordinated and authored by Nick Manning, currently Senior Advisor with the Public Sector Group at the World Bank. Other contributors to the first edition included Jane H. Cole, Cecil Wonham, Greg Covington, Sir Kenneth Stowe, Francis Plowden of Coopers and Lybrand, London and the Institute for Development Policy and Management at the University of Manchester. Their significant contributions to the first edition have in large part formed the foundation for this second edition.

The Commonwealth Association for Public Administration and Management (CAPAM) and the Commonwealth Secretariat are grateful to the late Dr. Sam Agere, former Special Adviser on Management and Development in the Commonwealth Fund for Technical Co-operation, and former independent Public Sector Management Consultant, based in Harare, Zimbabwe, for undertaking the update. Dr. Agere put together most of the important themes and topics that have been on the agenda for most of the conferences, seminars, workshops, and roundtables since 1996 when the last Portfolio was prepared.

Special thanks are due to Dr. Carolyn Johns, Assistant Professor in the Department of Politics & School of Public Administration at Ryerson University, Toronto, Canada, who compiled the numerous abstracts for CAPAM's Practice Knowledge Centre, the majority of which formed the basis upon which this update was prepared. Dr. Johns also contributed to the Introduction to the Portfolio and editing of the final draft.

Special thanks to Nick Manning, Peter Frost (Senior Special Advisor, the Commonwealth Secretariat), Gordon Draper (Director of International Development, CAPAM), and Mohan Kaul (Director General, Commonwealth Business Council), who all acted as reviewers of the second edition and provided expert input ensuring the production of a high quality product.

Thanks are also due to Art Stevenson (the Executive Director of CAPAM), Gillian Mason (Director of Programming and Marketing at CAPAM) and Randi Glass (Conference Manager/Accountant at CAPAM) who tirelessly assisted in the co-ordination of the consultants involved in this exercise and who made the final production of this publication possible based on CAPAM's desire to share current resources and thinking on public service management.

Finally, thanks are due to Bill Robins, Public Sector Consultant, who authored several of the new sections in the Portfolio and edited the transcripts.

Although in compiling this publication, every attempt has been made to retain the accuracy of the contributors, presenters, authors, reports, etc., the final responsibility for any errors or inaccuracies rests with the author.

Foreword

Since the production of the Commonwealth Portfolio in 1996, there have been many meetings of the Commonwealth Heads of Government and various workshops, seminars and roundtables held by public service practitioners, scholars and researchers, politicians and non-government organisations in an effort to improve the delivery of services to the public. From these meetings and conferences various ideals and values for improving the public service were proposed such as the Rule of Law, Just and Honest Government, Public/Private Sector and Civil Society Partnerships. The role of practitioners has been, amongst other objectives, to translate such ideals into workable and practical solutions and guidelines for implementation. As a result, various attempts and initiatives have been made to institutionalise activities and programmes of action into the administrative machinery of the public sector as a whole.

The Commonwealth Association for Public Administration and Management (CAPAM) has been able to provide access to some of the contemporary thinking and current public management practices to public service managers, scholars and researchers throughout the diverse Commonwealth. The themes that have been selected have been debated at various conferences and workshops held and supported by CAPAM, one of whose objectives it is to share these experiences with others in the field of public management. All the themes provide reflections on agendas which inform many approaches to the modernisation or revitalisation of public service machinery so that it has the capacity and capability to deliver public services more efficiently and effectively.

This publication contains a wealth of information derived from a purposeful and rich compilation of data and information, and the author's own experience as an executive official in the public service and his extensive research and advisory services to many countries in the Commonwealth. Some of the articles and passages have been extracted from publications in CAPAM's Practice Knowledge Centre, reports from presentations and seminars and conference reports. Acknowledgements have been made in each case.

This update to the 1996 Portfolio continues to provide a framework for building and sustaining effective public service organisations based on the experiences of senior public sector managers throughout the Commonwealth. The second edition is a combination of original sections from the first edition and several new sections (indicated in italics in the Table of Contents) including:

- capacity building of management development institutes;
- top executive management development programmes;
- strengthening anti-corruption measures;
- promoting good governance;
- strengthening Cabinet decision making;
- management of government transitions;
- improving partnerships, featuring a subsection on the New Partnership for Africa's Development (NEPAD)
- e-government; knowledge management, financial management, auditing and e-government; and political and administrative roles and responsibilities

Introduction

1   A Guide to the Portfolio

This update to the 1996 Commonwealth Portfolio is intended to serve as a guide to good managerial and organisational design practices in areas of topical concern to senior public service officials and politicians in the Commonwealth. It is hoped that the material reflects current thinking and developments in public sector management and administration, and in the delivery of services to citizens. The Portfolio is based on the assumption that sharing experiences within a framework of similar values in Commonwealth countries is an important contribution to continuous improvement and learning in public service development. The format is designed to provide practitioners rather than external experts with the ability to drive the debate on good practices in public service management.

The areas covered in the Portfolio include traditional public service management concerns such as accountability and improving policy implementation but also more recent areas of concern such as e-government, knowledge management and partnerships. Since performance improvement is a continuous process, and as perceptions of good practices shift over time, the Portfolio does not aspire to be the last word on its selected topics. This is the first update of the Commonwealth Portfolio and it is anticipated that updating will be an ongoing process producing future editions.

The Portfolio update is designed to provide a companion resource to the first edition published in 1996 by CAPAM and the Commonwealth Secretariat. It is designed as a convenient resource for senior public sector officials and a quick reference on a number of important management topics. Although the sections are written and organised based on the recognition that management topics are integrated, sections have been written to also be used as reference material. Building on the first Portfolio, the content summarises the key principles underpinning good practice in seven sections: staff performance, efficiency, service quality, partnerships, managerial effectiveness, financial management and policy making. As outlined in the Table of Contents, some of the existing sections have been updated and several new sections have been added to cover topics such as governance, managing government transitions, e-government, and knowledge management.

Within each section, the content describes current good practices under specific sub-headings. Each section begins with a background section providing an overview of current thinking on the given topic and includes definitions of key concepts and terms. Each section generally includes the following subsections:

The context for change: a description of the pressures on existing systems, policies and management practices and the measures and reforms taken which are perceived to improve and solve the problems.

Reasons for Caution: a warning note concerning the risks and uncertainties involved in making changes.

Achieving Change: some insights into the typical steps or stages in implementing improvements seen across the Commonwealth.

Examples of Change: selected indications of Commonwealth countries where such changes or new initiatives have taken place.

Other Useful Materials: a short list of related resource materials referenced in the section or available from other sources such as the Commonwealth Association for Public Administration and Management's (CAPAM) Practice Knowledge Centre (see Appendix).

In some sections additional subtitles are included to highlight specific developments related to the topic or simply to organise the above subsections by using further section titles.

The Portfolio update is also designed to be used as a companion resource with Public Service Country Profiles also published by the Commonwealth Secretariat. The sections in the Portfolio provide material on current good practices and brief examples of countries which are leaders or experienced with good practices across the Commonwealth. The material in the Public Service Country Profiles provides more detailed information for more specific comparisons on selected management topics and public sector reform initiatives. Together the two documents can be used as a basis of benchmarking to compare activities and best practices across different national settings.

This Introduction to the Commonwealth Portfolio Update is organised into three parts. The first part introduces the context for change in the Commonwealth through an overview of the governance and public service management environment. This section lays the foundation for a more detailed discussion of the ways and means of promoting good governance in subsequent sections.

The second part of the Introduction deals in more detail with current approaches to the promotion of good governance and the implications for public service management, organisations and citizens. This part of the Introduction highlights the varied experiences, trends and good practices across the Commonwealth in both developed and developing countries using a framework that outlines the spectrum of reform programmes.

The third part contains reflections and observations on the economic and administrative reforms implemented in developing countries in the last decade for the purpose of learning from past mistakes and charting the way forward.

II The Context for Change in the Commonwealth: Governance and Public Administration

Governance may be seen as the process through which decisions are made in societies. It encompasses elements relating to how a country is governed and how its affairs are administered and managed. The central importance of governance to the latest developments and thinking in public administration across the Commonwealth is clearly reflected in the visions, missions and agendas declared by the Commonwealth Heads of Governments at their biennial meetings.

The Harare Declaration of 1991 set a course of action for the promotion of democracy, good governance, respect for human rights and the rule of law. This vision has been reaffirmed at subsequent meetings and provides the backdrop for much of the current activity on governance in the Commonwealth. A decade later, Commonwealth countries are still committed to work with vigour on the following areas.

- the protection and promotion of political values;

- equality for women;

- universal access to education;

- continuing action to bring about the end of apartheid and the establishment of a free, democratic, prosperous South Africa;

- the promotion of sustainable development and the alleviation of poverty;

- extending the benefits of development within the framework of respect for human rights;

- the protection of the environment;

- action to combat drug trafficking and abuse and communicable disease; and

- help for small Commonwealth states in tackling their particular economic and security problems.

Many of these remain outstanding governance and public policy challenges have been reiterated as important areas requiring public service reform. At the conclusion of the Commonwealth Heads of Government meeting in Durban, South Africa in November 1999, the Commonwealth Heads of Government issued the "Fancourt Commonwealth Declaration on Globalisation and People Centered Development."

The Declaration states:

> "The greatest challenge therefore facing us today is how to channel these forces of globalisation for the elimination of poverty and the empowerment of human beings to lead fulfilling lives."

In pursuit of this, the Heads affirmed the following:

> "We believe that the spread of democratic freedoms and good governance, and access to education, training and health care, are key to the expansion of human capabilities, and to the banishment of ignorance and prejudice. Recognising that good governance and economic progress are directly linked, we affirm our commitment to the pursuit of greater transparency, accountability and the rule of law and the elimination of corruption in all spheres of public life and in the private sector."

There appears to be an emerging consensus that the movement towards good governance must include initiatives to strengthen the institutions of government and civil society with the objective of making governments more accountable; more open and transparent; more democratic and participatory while promoting the rule of law. Public service management is a key component of moving the good governance agenda forward. Governance processes and related public service management challenges are shaped by a number of environmental forces. The following are some of the forces impacting on good governance and public service reform.

Globalisation

Although definitions of globalisation are varied, at a worldwide level globalisation may be seen to relate to economic interdependence across countries which is being facilitated by the increasing flow of goods and services, capital and know-how across borders. Globalisation is being driven by factors that include:

- an increasing number of countries are embracing the free market ideology;
- the acceptance of the World Trade Organisation and its principles and rulings;
- technological advance which includes information technology; and
- the opening of borders to trade, investment and technology transfers.

For many developing countries lacking strong governance institutions and the technology and skills base to harness globalisation the impact could be disastrous. While globalisation has brought economic reward to some in many countries, it has been characterised by economic and financial crisis, a widening of the gap between rich and poor, and social instability. While globalisation could serve to integrate, it has demonstrated a powerful capacity to marginalise. These forces demand governance approaches that embrace transparency, accountability and stakeholder participation in policy debates.

Information Technology

Information technology will continue to be one of the leading drivers of change and change management in the 21st century. All sectors of civil society have moved to embrace IT advances to increase efficiency and effectiveness. Some governments are attempting to ensure a basic level of access for all citizens and this could include programmes in schools as well as community-based access programmes.

The significance of information technology is evident in the significant role the Chief Information Officer (CIO) is now playing in organisational change and management in both the public and private sectors. CIO's are now taking responsibility for knowledge management, information systems strategy, standard setting and best practices in IT management and development.

Demand for Citizen and Community Empowerment

Technology now makes it feasible for governments to seek citizens' views on a wide range of issues and citizens are increasingly demanding access to government information and decision-making processes. Policy making must become more inclusive. Citizens want and expect efficient and effective performance from their governments. People also see a need for a strong civil society where citizens:

- are aware and informed;
- understand their rights and responsibilities;
- behave as active citizens in the family and community;
- show solidarity, generosity and mutual respect towards fellow citizens;
- participate in local associations and organisations to work on a common agenda;

- demonstrate assertive, caring and ethical leadership;
- are enabled and encouraged to connect with public institutions and officials; and
- are not passive, apathetic or self-centred.

A recent survey of how Canadians perceive the services that their government provides identified the following as critical drivers that determine service quality: timeliness, knowledge, competence, courtesy, comfort, fair treatment and outcome.

Questioning Existing Political/Parliamentary Systems

Related to the demand for citizen and community involvement is the growing scepticism and cynicism with respect to existing political and parliamentary systems. This question of trust also extends to the public service and other contexts of governance. The time has come to move away from the adverserial style towards finding ways for parties to work together, finding consensus rather than conflict. Focusing on problem solving rather than point scoring, looking for common ground rather than operating territorially and acting out of political vengeance and intolerance.

Ecological Concerns

Ecological issues are now recognised as being among the most critical challenges of our age. In addressing these concerns some governments are now insisting on environmental impact studies for all major investments. Environmental audits are increasingly being utilised by both private and public sector organisations.

Diversity Issues

Within countries, governments are challenged to ensure that all groups feel a sense of inclusion. Issues of race, ethnicity, gender, age, religious and sexual orientation are all elements that need careful attention and policies and practices that foster inclusion.

III Towards Good Governance: Responses Across the Commonwealth

Institutions in civil society have been responding to the challenges that the new governance environment creates. Responses to these environmental forces have been varied across the Commonwealth but common developments are evident on some fronts. Attempts to move towards good governance across the Commonwealth have lead to spheres of convergence in a number of areas.

The New Public Administration

Discussions and research from senior public executives across the Commonwealth identify similar pressures driving public service reform and similar responses to these pressures. The development of New Public Administration, or New Public Management, has been used to describe many of the public service reform responses in Commonwealth countries. The Commonwealth Association for Public Administration and Management (CAPAM) has identified a number of components and values of the new public administration, which include:

- providing high quality services that citizens value;
- increasing autonomy for public service managers;
- the reduction of central agency controls, devolution and decentralisation;
- establishing performance assessment of both organisations and individuals;
- improving the development of human and technological resources;
- developing partnerships with the private sector and non-government organizations; and
- using citizens' charters and identifying service standards for public service agencies.

The new public administration has also recognised the need to focus on the interface between the political and administrative spheres of government. The separation of policy making and oversight, and implementation and service delivery are central features of the new public administration. The clarification of roles and the development of appropriate relationships are critical in this interface.

Developments in the Non-Government Organisation (NGO) Sector

The growing number and role of NGOs is also viewed as a central pillar of good governance across the Commonwealth. A number of regional workshops and pan-Commonwealth seminars formulated an action plan for continuing to strengthen and understand the relationships between government and non-government organisations based on six main recommendations:

1 the distinctive purposes and activities of NGOs and the vital roles they play in the development process should be recognised and promoted;

2 formal mechanisms should be established through which NGOs could participate in official policy making as part of open governmental processes;

3 legal frameworks and regulatory mechanisms should be developed which reflect the increasingly diverse nature, scope and purposes of NGOs in contemporary society;

4 civil society demands ethical conduct, accountability and transparency from both governments and NGOs;

5   action should be taken to strengthen the capacity of NGOs to achieve their objectives, maintain their values and discharge their responsibilities; and

6   action should be taken to improve the viability and sustainability of NGOs.

Local Government Perspectives

Governance and public service management issues at the local level have also brought local governments to the forefront of change and reform initiatives across the Commonwealth. The Commonwealth Local Government Forum, at its meeting in Edinburgh in 1997, confirmed the growing recognition throughout the Commonwealth for greater democracy, decentralisation and good governance at local levels. It recommended some of the following good practices and roles for local governments:

- an active role in the promotion of sustainable economic and social development;
- strategies to ensure environmentally sustainable development;
- cost effective provision of quality services to the community via a range of service provision options;
- transparent and open government with close involvement of the community and the adoption of participatory decision-making processes;
- development of effective management and communications capabilities;
- commitment to the development of internal council capacity including training;
- good employment and industrial relations practices;
- implementation of equality of opportunity policies;
- emphasis on addressing the needs of the poor and disadvantaged groups in the community;
- respect for local democratic processes;
- adoption of innovative institutional reforms designed to improve accountability; and
- debate and discussion on models of governance.

Rethinking Political and Parliamentary Systems

Related to the governance issues of demands for citizen engagement and questioning of existing political and parliamentary systems, some Commonwealth countries have now begun to rethink their parliamentary structures and processes. The impetus for this also comes from concerns about representativeness and the need to facilitate a more inclusive political culture and policy-making process. The electoral and voting system is one element being reviewed in some countries. There are also concerns about the fundamental operations and powers of Parliament. The issues of training for parliamentarians and local government councillors has also been raised.

Parliaments and local government are also being challenged to be more accountable and open. The political and parliamentary systems. therefore, need to be the drivers of change and facilitate inclusion.

Evolving Management Thought

One other stream of convergence has been the evolution in management thought and practices. The concept of continuous improvement is very central to the quality management approach in many Commonwealth countries. Another stream of management thought which resonates with new governance principles, has been the concept of the learning organisation. The concept of a learning organisation identifies the following as critical disciplines:

- Personal mastery: this discipline causes a focus on personal vision and a reflection on the self and how our individual behaviour impacts on others;

- Mental models: this discipline of reflection and inquiry skills is focused on developing an awareness of the attitudes and perceptions that influence thought and interaction;

- Shared vision: this focuses on developing the shared vision of the future and the principles and guiding practices to get there;

- Team learning – group interaction; and

- Systems thinking: in this discipline people learn to better understand interdependency and change

The challenge of becoming a learning organisation goes beyond the provision of training and development.

Some Common Elements

Across the Commonwealth in both developed and developing countries there are some common threads that link the responses to environmental pressures in the new governance context. These elements are central features of the movement towards good governance, as well as core elements of the new public administration. These elements are:

- **People centredness:** There is a clear concern with focusing on people issues and ensuring they are the focal point for development. At the national level this is manifested in concerns about poverty eradication, while at the organisational level this is concerned with citizen engagement;

- **Holistic:** This is manifested in the discipline of the need for more comprehensive frameworks, as well as more comprehensive reform agendas;

- **Inclusion:** All the spheres of convergence point to the absolute essential of stakeholder participation and involvement. This points to the importance of mindsets that value diversity, and the need for institutional frameworks that facilitate full involvement and participation;

- **Shared visions:** The concept of the learning organisation explicitly focuses on the importance of shared vision;

- **Accountability:** An element of the reform agenda for all sectors is the importance of accountability;

- **Openness:** This element also underscores the importance of known systems and procedures for decision-making as well as the need for public access to information.;

- **Performance focused:** An increased focus on outputs and outcomes, and a move away from traditional concerns with inputs;

- **Continuous learning:** The Learning Organisation Model argues that a commitment to continuous improvement and human resource development is the only way to ensure ongoing organisational success and effectiveness;

- **Ethics and values:** A central feature of good governance and the new public management is the need for clear ethical principles; and

- **Partnering and leadership:** Recognition of new network forms of governance, the concept of stewardship and the need for all sectors to work in partnership.

These common responses are evident across both developed and developing countries in the Commonwealth. However, there are many challenges remaining depending on the path to economic and administrative reform taken and the state of public service management in many countries. In the discussion that follows, the concept of good governance and its implications on various parts of society and state will be explored in more detail. A brief review of the type and nature of the economic and administrative reforms in Commonwealth countries will be made with a view to learn from past experience. The review also helps to avoid mistakes that have been made in the past and to develop new ideas, innovations and improved ways and means of delivering public services to citizens through the critical analysis of the methods and approaches used. Observations from the past decade of public sector reforms in Commonwealth countries provide an important baseline for future pursuits of good governance principles and practices.

IV The Types and Characteristics of Economic and Administrative Reforms in Commonwealth Countries

Many countries in the Commonwealth are, and have been, implementing economic and administrative reforms of one type or another in response to the environmental forces associated with the changing governance context. The implementation of these reforms exhibits peculiar features and characteristics that reflect on the nature of the State and the role of governments in societies. The tactics and strategies that are used are a symptom of the strength and weakness of the State, reflect the dominance of external influence and in some cases show that the state is or is not in control of its own resources. In analysing these reforms it is possible to differentiate between those countries that show a heavy dominance of external influences and those that determine their own policies. To some degree it is also possible to clearly distinguish the countries that have been responsible in formulating their own policies from those in which policies for reform are externally determined and financed. The purpose of the reform, the strategies and instruments used, the pace and costs of the reform vary in accordance with the ownership of policy formulation, political will and commitment and the extent to which countries control their own resources and are therefore not dependent on external sources.

For the purpose of this Introduction to the Portfolio, comparisons are made between those countries whose reform programmes were dominated by economic considerations from those that placed emphasis on human resources. There is an assumption in this analysis that some countries have placed equal emphasis and attention on both the economic and human resource considerations with the appropriate mix, while the majority have emphasised economic imperatives. In general, there has been a heavy concentration on economic and financial reforms with less attention being paid to human resources management. Accordingly, many countries have tended towards elements of human resource management approaches as an afterthought or as a consequence of the financial and economic reforms but not as a priority.

The framework in this section attempts to outline the reform responses along a spectrum with economic factors as determinants at one end of the spectrum and human resource factors at the other. Summaries of specific factors for each of these approaches are outlined below for the following: purpose of reform, type and range of programmes, mechanisms used, and impacts on the behaviour of senior public service managers. The analytical framework can also be used to more fully describe and assess economic and administrative reforms in any Commonwealth country based on general observations. Some of these observations become particularly clear when the objectives of the reform have not been achieved. What is evident from this analysis is that those States which use elements from both approaches seems to have better results in terms of public service reform and moving towards good governance.

Purpose of Reform

In many developing countries in the Commonwealth, the emphasis has been more on economic reforms with less attention paid to human resources. This is a reflection of the dominance of the push factors for reform such as economic imperatives e.g. debt settlement, deterioration of economic performance and the dire need for financial assistance irrespective of conditionalities imposed by those who provide financial assistance.

Economic ←————————————————→ **Human Resources**	
• Reduction of budget deficit and liberalisation of trade; • Removal of controls; • Encourage private enterprise; • Privatise public enterprise; • Achieve fiscal and monetary discipline, removal of subsidies; • Elimination of black market; • Less government;	• Improve service delivery; • Make services affordable, acceptable and available; • Prompt responsiveness to the needs of the people; • Better government;

The drivers of economic and administrative reform have also had some distinct approaches depending on whether the reforms were initiated and driven using a "top-down" approach, which does not include debate or discussion on the merits of the reform, or a more "bottom-up" approach which focuses more on reform of human resources.

In analysing the characteristics, purpose and assumptions of the economic and administrative reforms, it is possible to differentiate between those countries that own and control the reforms and those that do not. This distinction is related to the origin, initiative or source of the reforms and whether it is externally or internally determined. Taking into account all these distinctions, it is evident that most developing Commonwealth countries have had their reforms initiated from external sources as conditionalities for assistance.

Economic – Supply Side ←————————→ **Human Resources – Demand Side**	
• Quantitative • Statistical • Control direction • Structural • Conditionality • Time limit • Externally determined • Profit-making	• Qualitative • People centered • Process/Ownership • Management • Homegrown • Own pace • Internally determined • Improved knowledge and skills base • Evaluation programmes

Type and Range of Programmes

The response to governance challenges has taken many different forms across the Commonwealth. In some cases, countries have used a number of the following programmes in both State-wide and more targeted initiatives to implement economic and public service reforms.

Economic ←——————————————————→ **Human Resources**

• Cost reduction	• Human Resources Development
• Downsize Civil Service	• Performance Management Systems
• Commerclalisation programme	• Clarity of goals for reform
• Privatisation programme	• Develop Citizens Charter
• Deregulation	• Improve morale of Civil Servants
• Decentralisation	• Improve delivery systems
	• Customer care

Mechanisms Used

Following the observation that many Commonwealth countries have focused primarily on financial and economic reforms and deemed human resource approaches a secondary priority, the mechanisms used more commonly fall on the economic end of the spectrum. The type of reform imposes the choice of instruments to be used in the reform process and the methodologies and tools used to achieve the economic and financial goals. In many cases, the mechanisms used to implement economic and administrative reforms have been varied but generally include a mix of the following, depending on the focus and emphasis of the reform programme.

Economic ←——————————————————→ **Human Resources**

• Budget control	• Performance Appraisals Systems
• Redundancy schemes	• Performance Agreements
• Accounting Instructions	• Training Policy & Career Planning
• Joint Ventures/Partnerships	• Reward Systems
• Legislation	• Develop code of conduct
• Directives	• Procedures manual
• Hierarchical structure	• Records and Information Management Systems
	• Improve conditions of Civil Servants

Behaviour Patterns for Permanent Secretaries & Public Service Managers

Following the observation that the factors at the economic end of the spectrum have received more priority for policy makers in Commonwealth countries, it is not surprising that certain behaviour patterns and expectations of Permanent Secretaries and senior public service managers stem from this approach. The type of reform, therefore, also imposes the behavioural pattern of those who manage the reform. The dominance of economic approaches encourages certain behaviours and accountability frameworks for those holding senior public service positions, especially when they have not been involved in the policy formulation process and have received directives from their superiors. The outcome has resulted in less of a focus on human resource management functions and values.

Economic ⟵──────────────────────⟶ **Human Resources**

• Impersonal	• User-friendly
• Distant	• Proximity
• Inaccessible	• Accessible
• Plan	• Communicative
• Organise	• Consultative
• Control	• Participative
• Administrator	• Leader/manager
• Apex of pyramid	• Base of pyramid
• Master/directing	• Servant of people

This framework also allows for some specific observations related to countries in the Commonwealth. There are some countries that have used elements of both approaches and determined their own path towards reforms that promote good governance, and there are other countries which have followed one end of the spectrum more closely than the other.

- In most developed countries of the Commonwealth such as Australia, Britain, Canada and New Zealand, due emphasis has been placed simultaneously on both financial and human resources. The reforms have been determined and initiated from within rather than externally, are seen as a necessary process of change and are owned by the countries themselves.

- In the African Region, Botswana stands out as one country that has initiated, owned and implemented reforms at its own pace without much external pressure. It has placed emphasis on the development and management of human resources while at the same time efficiently managing the economy. It has regarded the reform as a process of change and not as an event which is given a time frame and other conditionalities.

- Within the developing Commonwealth and outside the Southern African region, Malaysia and Singapore have placed a lot of emphasis on human resources while at the same time efficiently managing the economy. These two countries designed their own reforms and determined on their own time frame within which reforms have to be implemented. Essentially, they own the reform process.

V Observations on Reform in Developing Countries of the Commonwealth

The general observation that countries have used a mix of the two approaches with an emphasis on the economic drivers and factors, however, is in contrast to reform responses in most developing countries in the Commonwealth. Public service reform programmes, emphasising economic factors, have been applied most extensively in the OECD member countries of the Commonwealth. The impact of public service reform based on the principles of the new public administration has been less evident and profound in developing countries. Although the new context of governance and appeal of the new public administration has broadened the menu of managerial choice and reform approaches within the public sector, there is also evidence that its implementation can be more difficult in developing countries.

The efforts associated with the new public administration and reforms have focused to an even larger degree on the economic end of the spectrum in developing countries and the implications have been very partial. In the past decade, the impact of economic and administrative reforms on developing countries has been felt primarily through development agencies and structural adjustment programmes.

Considering the importance of these reform initiatives on structural adjustment programmes, the impact they have on the lives of the citizens and the financial and social costs to the country, it is surprising to note that very few studies have been conducted to determine whether or not they achieve the desired results. Both the countries that have implemented the economic reforms as well as the donors that have recommended or imposed the conditionalities for reform have not committed human and financial resources to evaluate the impact of the reforms. This is surprising since this should be an ongoing exercise before further changes are made and funds committed for an extension of the programme.

Despite this seeming lack of commitment for evaluation of these fundamental economic and administrative programmes, a few studies have been conducted by the United Nations Development Programme, and the European Centre for Development Policy Management and Public Policy at the University of Birmingham. They have revealed the following weaknesses:

- The envisaged cost savings on downsizing the Civil Service fell far short of expectations. In some cases, the costs escalated, thereby leaving the major problem unresolved;

- There was an absence of institutional provision for co-operation between the two major Ministries responsible for reform, i.e. the Ministry of Finance and the Ministry of the Public Service. In still other instances, the Ministry of Finance reached an agreement with the International Financial Institutions without the knowledge of, or consultation with, the Ministry responsible for personnel, even in matters of redundancy and administrative reforms. There was great emphasis on saving financial costs at the expense of human costs;

- The reform process was very much dependent on top-down direction and external stimuli. In some countries, external forces dominated the form of change and were not well understood by those who were to implement the reform programme. The absence of a team approach in managing the reform left a vacuum in which the donor could effectively influence the pace and direction of the change process;

- There was an absence of a training policy that would facilitate and equip relevant human resources with adequate skills and knowledge to implement a new programme which had never been experienced before and in which they did not participate in formulating. The budget for reform did not include training. In the few instances where training was mentioned in policy reform documents, it was not made relevant to meeting the needs of Civil Servants, management and those who were to supervise the change process. It was assumed that once policy was formulated, the Civil Servants would simply obey the instructions and implement the policy whether they understood it or not. This is a traditional approach to policy development which is incapable of meeting the current demands and needs of a highly politicised public.

- The management development training institutions were not involved in the policy formulation and were equally ignored in both the implementation of the programme and in training public service managers in preparation for such a fundamental and structural change in society;

- The reduction in the cost and size of the Civil Service alone did not result in the automatic achievement of efficiency, effectiveness, responsiveness and increases in productivity. Consequently, the reduced Civil Service and budgetary allocations did not improve the delivery of services such as health, education, agriculture and overall performance in administration. With reduced budgetary allocations, agricultural extension services were severely curtailed, as there was limited allocation for staff to travel to deliver the relevant agricultural inputs necessary to increase food production. The same can be said about teachers and nurses;

- The reforms to structural adjustment programmes envisaged savings from cost-cutting measures. The savings were expected to be ploughed back into the system to improve the wages for Civil Servants. However, the new systems of incentives and employee motivation were not consolidated into the reform programmes and adjustment conditions and budgetary restrictions constrained improvements in salaries/wages and incentives. Since there were no savings, some countries proceeded to freeze the salaries of Civil Servants, thereby reducing their morale and performance. This was done without negotiation or consultation. One of the consequences of such a freeze in wages was the strained relationship between the State and public service staff associations. This often resulted in strikes or other forms of industrial action being taken by the loyal Civil Service. Furthermore, staff associations, in their negotiations with the State on wage increases, did not use the costs savings as a criterion but rather the increase in the cost of living and the devaluation of the currency, which resulted in the decline of their purchasing power;

- Economic and administrative reforms were introduced at a time when there was a noticeable decline in the performance of the Civil Service and when the weak capacities of the State administrative machinery had been observed. Various commissions, which had been set up to improve the performance of the Civil Service, prior to the economic reforms, had indicated many weaknesses of the different Ministries in the delivery of service to the people. Critics of the reform programme have wondered why the State would expect a weak administrative system to implement very complex and fundamental reforms in which it did not have the capacity, know-how and commitment.

- The environment of political instability, social unrest, political interference in Civil Service administration, economic mismanagement and highly institutionalised corruption, largely contributed to a degeneration of the entire public service system. Such systems could not be expected to reform themselves with success.

A more recent evaluation indicates that there seem to be three likely explanations for why public service reforms under the banner of "new public administration" and "new public management" have delivered less in developing countries than initially claimed.

1   Public expectations of government in developing countries are fundamentally different that those found in developed Commonwealth countries. The populations are less homogenous and the concern about public service from a "customer" perspective is less evident as public expectations are lower. Also, the discontent at a local level is not with public service provision but more commonly with donor conditionalities.

2   Discontent with traditional public service disciplines and values as a condition favourable to public service reform based on economic factors has also generally been absent in developing countries. The assumption that a Civil Service culture based on hierarchy, budget discipline, authoritative accountability, and clear standards of behaviour as a foundation for reform is problematic and has made reforms more unpredictable in developing countries where informal administrative behaviour and corruption are still realities.

3   The marginal nature of economic and administrative reforms in developing countries has also hindered the impact of these reforms. Even in developed countries these impacts are debatable and difficult to assess. In the context of the economic performance and public services available in many developing countries the impact of reform programmes is not even detectable.

Clearly, motivation and capability are important factors in determining the extent and success of economic and administrative reforms in developing countries. Many developing countries remain incapable and unmotivated, with high levels of administrative corruption, little administrative competence, non-participatory governance and high State capture by unrepresentative, specialised interests. In this content, technocratic, economic and public management reforms are doomed.

Even in countries where governments are somewhat motivated and somewhat capable, economic and public service reforms need to address the limitations of these Commonwealth countries. In some cases capacity can be built through raising public expectations, public participation and strengthening local governments. In those countries where there is a civil society filling an accountability role, basic administrative reforms such as budget transparency and financial accountability may be relevant.

Although the reliance on the economic end of the spectrum and reforms associated with the new public administration has had an impact in developed countries in the Commonwealth and on development agencies, the impact in the developing countries has been more limited.

VI Lessons and Challenges

A review of economic and administrative reforms across the Commonwealth indicates that responses to the environmental forces of the new governance context have been multidimensional and varied. Many Commonwealth countries have placed an emphasis on economic types of reforms at the expense of human resource reforms. Those countries that have attempted to integrate the two ends of the spectrum seem to have made more progress in working towards good governance practices. It is also evident that progress related to public service reform has been more limited in developing countries.

The weaknesses and ineffectiveness of the implementation of public service reforms and structural adjustment programmes in many countries reveal the lack of appropriate approaches and strategies to policy development and management. They also demonstrate the lack of involvement of stakeholders, the absence of thorough studies on the nature of the problem to be addressed by the policy measures, the absence of a capacity to manage the policy and, above all, the lack of skills in the policy management process. In more general terms, the State has lacked ownership of the policy measures, thereby giving an impression that reforms were imposed by external forces and that many countries were desperate in accepting the conditionalities of assistance from donors. The conditionalities have exhibited an ideological bias and are exactly identical, whether in a small or a large State or in a poor or rich country, giving rise to the belief that they emanate from one source even if the countries themselves claim that such policies are homegrown.

The lack of understanding of the implications of reforms by policy makers is another significant challenge. The lack of skills and experience in designing policies of such magnitude and the absence of precedents from which to learn and share experiences demonstrate the need to examine some policy models that have been effective in other countries. The emerging best practices in policy management are also drawn from the most experienced and successful policy makers and managers, who tend to be from developed Commonwealth countries and may or may not have the same public service culture and values. This abdication of strategic policy analysis and policy making to external agents such as international financial institutions, donors and international development agencies creates a capacity challenge for many Commonwealth countries.

The implementation of structural adjustment programmes in some developing countries, for example, has demonstrated at least four key issues and problems that are experienced in policy development and management. The issues include:

1 Policy makers do not seem to understand or appreciate their policy environments and the kinds of problems they generate. This is attributed to the social distance between the policy makers and the rest of the population;

2 Policy makers seem to be making choices without adequate information because of the poor articulation of differences between political and administrative roles in the policy process. Often politicians would like to seize the initiative in making certain policies and tend to do so without adequate knowledge of the consequences; a problem that could have been avoided if they had listened to experts;

3 The inability to mobilise adequate resources and the inability to effectively utilise available capacity renders policy making a symbolic exercise. Many interest groups are not always aware of the content of the policy until the implementation process begins; and

4 The policy evaluation mechanism is sometimes deliberately weakened. Policy makers appear not to like to hear that their policies are performing poorly. Hence, previous mistakes remain undetected and uncorrected. At the same time, no meaningful lessons can be learned from past experience within this milieu.

Another important challenge is the institutional decline of the public service in many Commonwealth countries as evidenced by the inability to:

- attract and retain skilled personnel in the Civil Service;

- maintain strong values, ethics and professionalism or eliminate corruption;

- generate, store and disseminate information about the Civil Service itself, the economy and society;

- respond adequately to challenges from the environment, e.g. new economic blocks, new technologies, the effects of globalisation, etc.

From this discussion, it would appear that there is a need for the development of an effective framework for policy development and management capable of analysing problems, formulating intervention strategies and evaluating policy outcomes and impacts. The framework that is developed should be institutionalised and strengthened within the state machinery such as the Cabinet, legislature, Ministries and departments and other agencies of government such as public enterprises and local governments.

The policy framework which focuses on the public sector is an important instrument that facilitates the analysis of the problem or issue to be addressed and identifies key issues and practices that should be considered when developing and managing a policy. It also should assist in improving decision making at all levels in government and should provide an evaluation mechanism which is result-oriented and which provides feedback on the efficiency, effectiveness and performance of public policies and can be critical of reform initiatives and experimental innovations. Consequently, evaluation forms an important part of a wider performance management framework. In essence, the framework must contribute to accountable government. A successful framework is one that is based on collaboration between key participants such as consumers of public policy and other relevant stakeholders. It should be mentioned that frameworks vary from one country to another and depend very much on the political, economic and social conditions which often interact in complex and unforeseen ways in any one country.

Thus, although there are evidently spheres of convergence related to economic and administrative reforms, and movements toward good governance and learning have taken place across the Commonwealth, there are nonetheless some outstanding challenges. The challenges include:

- the need for overarching vision and leadership;

- the need for a comprehensive reform policy framework;

- partnering and new service delivery arrangements;

- communication, citizen engagement, stakeholder involvement and inclusion;

- human resources management approaches being emphasized in reform agendas;

- management of change;

- valuing diversity;

- effective policy co-ordination;

- performance measurement;

- improving the political/administrative interface;

- effectively using accessible technologies; and

- building civil society and local government capacity.

This brief overview only summarizes some of the contextual realities, lessons and challenges facing public service organisations and managers in Commonwealth countries. Lessons and progress towards addressing these challenges through good practices in a number of different management areas are reflected and discussed in more detail in sections of the Portfolio.

The first section of the Portfolio seeks to outline the importance of improvements in the performance of staff, particularly senior and top executives in the public service. This section also examines the role of management development institutions responsible for developing and training human resources. Good practices in performance management and the use of performance appraisal of organisations and individuals are also discussed.

Section 2 attempts to outline how to make government more efficient by examining how governments walk the tightrope between efficiency and accountability in selecting and designing the machinery of government. This section also identifies the obstacles to efficiency and provides some guidance on removing obstacles such as reducing or eliminating corruption in the public sector. The importance of managing change, promoting good governance, strengthening Cabinet decision making and managing government transitions are also reviewed in this section.

Section 3 outlines good practices related to service quality improvements across the Commonwealth. Preconditions such as open government and public reporting are reviewed as well as the importance of quality management frameworks and performance measurement.

Section 4 relates to the improvement of partnerships between the public/private sectors and civil society in the delivery of public services to citizens. This section comprehensively covers the variety and importance of partnerships in the new governance context.

Sections 5 and 6 focus on the important components of making management more efficient including management information systems, e-government, knowledge management and strengthening financial management systems.

The last section of the Portfolio focuses on the necessary improvements in policy making and management processes by examining the political and administrative environments within which policies are formulated and implemented. Suggestions are made on how to strengthen institutions and systems involved in policy development and management as well as how to improve the relationships between the elected leadership and senior leadership of the public service.

Other useful material (2nd edition)

Regional Commonwealth workshop of top and senior public officials held in May 1997 in Nairobi, Kenya.

Commonwealth Advanced Seminar for Public Service Reform organised by the Graduate School of Business and Government Management at Victoria University of Wellington, New Zealand, February 1997.

Robert Dodoo "Best Practices in Public Sector Management" in African Journal of Public Administration and Management vol. X1, No 1 July 1999.

The New Zealand Experience: Reforming the Public Sector for Leaner Government and Improved Performance. Paper presented by Basil Walker at the CAPAM Biennial Conference April 1996.

Draper, G., "Reflections on Governance at the Turn of the Century", paper prepared for the 2000 CAPAM Conference, Cape Town, South Africa, October, 2000.

Manning, N.,"The Legacy of the New Public Management in Developing Countries", International Review of Administrative Sciences Vol. 67, No.2, 2001.

Status Report on Public Sector Reform Programme: Office of Public Sector Reform, Government of Barbados 1999.

1.0 Making the Most of Staff

1.1 Setting the Overall Framework

1.1.1 Achieving/communicating a mission orientation

The mission of a public or private sector organisation captures its overall purposes, what it exists for, and what it intends to achieve within its area of operation and responsibility.

Achieving a *mission orientation* is concerned with establishing a clear sense of direction and commitment within the organisation.

A central feature is the mission statement, which captures the best intentions of the organisation.

However, producing a mission statement is only a stage in the whole process of achieving a mission orientation and gaining commitment to its aims and purposes among managers and staff.

Mission is closely related to other terms concerning the purposes of the organisation, which can be set out in a hierarchy for planning and direction-setting as follows:

- *Vision*: looking ahead to the best possible outcome; where the organisation intends to be in, for example, three or five years time. It is related to policy formulation and, therefore, in government organisations, has a strong political dimension.

- *Mission*: how the organisation intends to operate in order to bring about that vision. This is a primary responsibility of the chief executive or administrative head of the organisation, but should reflect the importance of adaptable and consultative management.

- *Objectives/targets*: more specific achievements, which the organisation hopes to bring about within the mission framework.

- *Key tasks*: what individual units of the organisation need to do.

From here, strategies will be devised to determine what actions the organisation and its component units will take in order to achieve its purposes at various levels; and performance indicators will be devised to determine whether these purposes are being achieved.

The context for change

Mission orientation programmes have increased rapidly in recent years as a direct result of the tighter and more businesslike trends in organisations within the public service. There is an increasing tendency for smaller units and agencies to establish their own mission statements and agendas for change.

The main purposes in establishing a mission orientation are:

- to help managers clarify in their own minds what the business of the organisation is;

- to provide a focus for managers and other staff in meeting organisational goals;

- to stimulate among the staff a sense of membership of the organisation rather than being merely employees; and

- to provide a framework within which to determine targets and more precise objectives.

Mission statements have an important role in the process by providing a specific reference point which can be published and displayed for the benefit of both staff and clients of the organisation.

The process of developing a mission statement, including employees at all levels, is as important as the statement itself.

Reasons for caution

Moves to orient staff and activities towards the achievement of organisational goals will highlight existing institutional weaknesses. A decision to focus on mission must imply a willingness to address challenges, which may include:

- Low morale among staff and its linkages with low levels of remuneration and poor working conditions, overstaffing, understaffing and insecurity of employment;
- high turnover of personnel within the organisation;
- political apathy or lack of top management commitment; and
- strong trade union opposition.

Mission statements are means and not ends. They will not achieve their purpose of providing a "banner" behind which the organisation can "rally" if they are:

- too vague and generalised to have any substantial value;
- too idealistic to have any realistic hope of implementation;
- not felt to be owned by all levels of staff;
- not seen to be owned by top management;
- not regularly reviewed and renewed; and
- not publicised widely.

Organisations within the public service are not autonomous business units. They each contribute to the public service. Enthusiasm for mission definition at unit or ministry level must be consistent with larger strategies.

Achieving change

The preconditions for developing a mission orientation are:

- commitment and active support by top management and political leaders;
- understanding and appreciation within the organisation of client/customer needs;
- a collaborative environment between management, staff and, where relevant, public service unions;
- a determination to monitor performance and provide feedback to all levels through effective communication channels within the organisation; and
- a willingness by top managers and political leaders to set challenging targets which are realistically achievable within the available resources.

When the development of a mission statement is considered to be a useful contribution to the mission orientation, the stages typically included are:

- a meeting between the chief executive (Permanent Secretary, administrative head) and his/her Minister. Where the initiative comes from the executive head rather than his/her political superior, it will be essential to sound out the Minister's views on the organisation's mission, in relation to current policy, planning and vision for the future, before proceeding further;

- staff meetings/workshops at various levels, including top management, to consider what the organisation exists for, and wants to achieve;

- written suggestions for a mission statement from staff throughout the organisation;

- consideration by top/senior management, including the Minister, of outcomes of meetings and written suggestions;

- formulation of a draft statement in clear and concise language;

- testing the draft statement on representative groups of staff and, where these can be defined, consumers;

- refining the draft for final approval by top management and political leaders; and

- publication of the mission statement and incorporating it into all promotional materials.

Mission statements emphasise the responsibilities of managers at all levels to:

- set challenges (expectations for subordinates ensure that all officers understand how their activities contribute towards the mission);

- provide feedback on the organisation's achievement of its mission; and

- value suggestions as to how the mission might be better accomplished.

Examples of change

In *Canada*, over 4,500 employees participated directly in the development of the Agricultural Department's mission statement. At Correctional Service Canada, the mission statement exercise led to over 3,500 concrete proposals from staff, and almost all have been acted upon.

In *Malaysia*, following the introduction of Total Quality Management in the Civil Service in 1992, Government departments are required to formulate vision and mission statements, and these have encouraged managers and staff to be more customer focused.

In the *UK*, a set of objectives published by the Department of Trade and Industry in 1987 has led to individual agencies and businesses within the Department producing their own mission statements.

Other useful material (current as of 1996)

Managing Change in the Public Service – A Guide for the Perplexed. The Task Force on Workforce Adaptiveness. Public Service 2000, Ottawa, 1991 (CAN)

Public Service 2000. A Report on Progress. P. M. Tellier, Clerk of the Privy Council and Secretary to the Cabinet, Ottawa, 1992 (CAN)

Development Administration Circular No. 6, 1991, Guidelines on Productivity Improvement in the Public Service. Malaysia (MAL)

Development Administration Circular No. 1, 1992, Guidelines on Total Quality Management in the Public Service. Malaysia (MAL)

Service Circular No. 4, 1992, Guidelines for the Implementation of the Performance Appraisal System of the Malaysian Public Service (MAL)

1.1.2 Developing a merit culture

Effective public administration needs the continuity and stability provided by a professional and trustworthy body of efficient public servants, concerned with due process, but responsive to changing politically defined priorities. The recognition of *merit* is a fundamental prerequisite of such administration.

Competent public servants are selected, retained and promoted on the basis of qualification, experience and the ability to achieve the organisational objectives of government within a legal and ethical framework. They are not selected, retained or promoted on the basis of creed, colour, caste, wealth, family connections, gender or physical ability (unless the latter is directly related to the nature of the tasks to be performed).

Recognising merit within systems for managing staff recruitment, development, retention, and exit requires the application of two principles: to emphasise capability and achievement, and to deter patronage.

The context for change

Experiences across the Commonwealth emphasise that:

- historically, capability has been under-emphasised in many settings;
- significant patronage is present in some settings; and
- the machinery for deterring patronage can also deter recognition of achievement.

Public service strategies for avoiding patronage and inequity have relied on a highly structured professional career system. Appropriately qualified recruits have followed career paths which are determined to a large degree by the training they have received, and by the length and breadth of their public service work experience. Security of tenure, a regular and sufficient income, provision for retirement, working as part of a team, and an opportunity to serve the public interest, have been seen as adequate incentives for good performance.

Such a system seeks to be fair to every official. However, it provides little motivation for the most able public servants because proven ability to deliver forms but one, frequently small, component of decisions concerning career advancement. The system encourages conformity and, while routine task administration can be an efficient means of harnessing the efforts of lower grade staff, senior managers undertaking more loosely defined strategic activities will be inhibited by inflexible and mechanistic rules.

The challenge for a public service is to ensure that reasonable prospects are available for all public servants, whilst at the same time ensuring in the public interest that the best rise to the top.

The structured public service career systems found in most Commonwealth countries have been founded on specialist training programmes in Public Administration and on service commissions, constitutionally protected from political interference. Where these devices have been successful, the neutrality of the resulting public service systems is widely valued; but the effectiveness of the traditional bureaucracy in achieving the policy aims of reformist governments, and in securing significant productivity improvements in the delivery of services to the public, is increasingly questioned. Public servants' slavish adherence to outdated rules is held to frustrate, or at least to fail to advance sufficiently rapidly, the policies and priorities of the government. Additionally, the systems have shown themselves prone to maintaining the elitism which has characterised many post-colonial public services.

In recent years, more results-oriented approaches have been developed within the public service designed to counter such traditional bureaucracy and elitism. In some settings the concern has been to renew the government commitment to deterring patronage. In other settings, particularly the industrially developed countries of the Commonwealth, human resource management systems have been introduced which emphasise the significance of achieving organisational goals.

Reasons for caution

Changing the public service culture to emphasise the place of achievement within the assessment of merit presents three areas of risk:

1. Divisiveness

An emphasis on the recognition and reward of personal ability and results achieved inevitably risks promoting some degree of divisiveness within the public service, not least by alienating those public servants who are denied such recognition. This unavoidable risk has two particular implications. First, it denotes clearly that flexible reward schemes can only be safely implemented in situations where charges of patronage or undue influence can be firmly rebutted.

Second, it highlights the need for all human resource management developments to be underpinned by a strong and collective sense of mission running through the public service. The ethic of service to the public is not self-generating; it requires careful nurturing and explicit leadership.

2. Opaque appraisal

It is not easy to differentiate fairly between good and poor performers in public service. Many tasks do not have any clearly measurable outputs. Ambiguity is inevitable in situations where economy or efficiency may well be achieved only at the expense of effectiveness or equity. The responsibilities of more senior Civil Servants are complex and changeable to the extent that objective criteria which can be used for assessment can be elusive. At more junior levels, innovative management by individuals risks being disruptive for the service as a whole. Methodological solutions can be found, but they are conditional on sensitive consultations and continuing determination and commitment to change from the highest levels.

3. Tensions between service managers and the service commissions

Changing the role and remit of the service commissions, and devolving greater operational freedom in human resource management to service units, within a broad framework of principles to be followed, brings with it two particular concerns.

The commissions were established to minimise patronage; this is an ever present risk, and reducing the control of commissions over the detail of appointments and promotion presents an opportunity for its resurgence within the public service. Audit systems of sufficient strength are necessary to confirm that operational units maintain adequate consistency in recruitment and retention decisions and practices.

A more subtle risk concerns the change process itself. Experience in many settings indicates that in a period of evolution for service commissions, frequently with complex legal and constitutional implications, roles may become confused. As a result, unproductive battle lines may be drawn between managers and commissioners at worst derailing, and at best delaying, broader strategies for public service reform.

Achieving change

In many Commonwealth countries, the merit principles of emphasising capability and achievement and deterring patronage have been embedded more firmly within the working culture by taking three steps:

- attracting and retaining the best staff;
- removing the worst; and
- identifying organisational goals as a focus for achievement.

These three steps have been taken at each of the key points in the human resource management cycle, as given below.

Emphasise merit in systems for acquiring staff

- devolve responsibilities for recruitment and retention from central control departments to line Ministries and business units, allowing more flexible and locally-determined systems for recruitment;
- develop the role of the service commissions from "quality control" (a mission to inspect and approve the detail of recruitment and promotion practices) to "quality assurance" (a mission to advise on and audit locally-managed processes);
- strengthen measures to guard against discrimination on the grounds of sex, religion, race or other factors irrelevant to ability;
- recruit openly for many positions; and
- provide remuneration at levels closer to that of the private sector.

Encourage merit in staff retention and development

- introduce performance management systems to link clearly-defined organisational objectives to individual work objectives;
- establish performance appraisal systems to ensure that individual officers receive consistent feedback on how their efforts contribute towards the whole;
- link performance appraisal systems with clear incentives ranging from positive endorsement by the supervising officer to (with caution) performance-related pay;
- focus staff training and development programmes more clearly on the need to achieve organisational goals; and
- strengthen codes of conduct.

Emphasise merit in systems for managing staff exit

- introduce different forms of contractual employment, enabling the more prompt removal of poorly performing staff and ensuring that staff expertise relates to changing organisational requirements; and
- increase the risk and decrease the rewards available through corruption.

Examples of change

After five years' experience as pioneers in the development of public service chief executive performance management, officials in *New Zealand* stress the importance of:

- adequately specifying performance expectations in a manner that can be measured or readily assessed;

- adequately monitoring against these specifications during the year so that issues can be dealt with as close to their occurrence as possible;

- undertaking assessment and review, using a procedure that is accepted as fair, and that draws on a broad base of good evidence; and

- undertaking follow-up actions that reinforce good performance and encourage improvement from poor performance.

In *Singapore*, the Personnel Management Steering Committee has introduced a system of potential appraisal, asking, "What is the highest level a person can achieve in his/her career while giving continually satisfactory performance?" Such a policy is employee-centred rather than task-centred, it means that promotion is not based on past performance alone, but also on long-term capability and readiness for higher positions.

Other useful material (current as of 1996)

From Problem to Solution: Commonwealth Strategies for Reform. Managing the Public Service. Strategies for Improvement Series: No. 1. Commonwealth Secretariat, 1995 (ComSec)

Management Advisory Board. Building a Better Public Service. Australian Government Publishing Service, Canberra, 1993 (AUS)

1.1.3 Introducing/improving performance management

Performance management is the means by which public service goals are linked to individual target-setting, appraisal, and development. It provides a strategy for delivering a higher quality service, and for increasing efficiency by enhancing accountability and individual motivation, and improving communication to assist organisational change.

The context for change

Performance management builds on two major themes in public service improvement programmes. Identifying the mission of an organisation within the public service defines its broad objectives and intentions, and encourages a climate in which achievements are measured. Appraising the performance of individuals provides them with feedback and encouragement. Linking the organisational and individual goals within a performance management framework clarifies responsibilities at all levels. In particular, performance management establishes a clear connection between individual effort and organisational performance.

Reasons for caution

Performance management requires a change in thinking on the part of managers, requiring a "cultural change" in the organisation. Honesty and dialogue are fundamental prerequisites. If a more open approach cannot be envisaged, then it may not be worth contemplating the introduction of performance management.

Where performance management has been introduced, one of the consistent ingredients of success has been the ability to respond to the new needs of managers through management development programmes. Effective performance management produces service gains, but it is not without cost.

Achieving change

In general, experience across the Commonwealth indicates that the components of a performance management system are as shown in the diagram below:

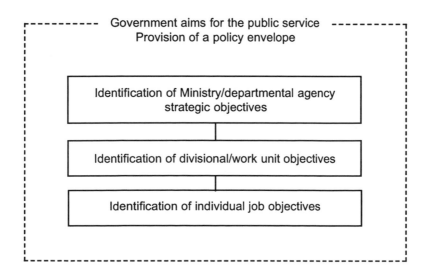

The cycle for managers is as follows:

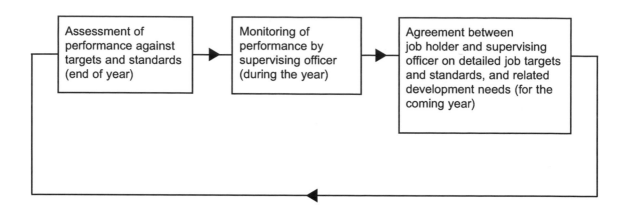

In working to identify objectives from Ministry to work-unit levels, the key areas to consider are:

- the needs of specific "customers" (internal and/or external);
- the "critical success factors" – those things which must be done well in order to meet those needs;
- where the organisation is now in relation to those "success factors";
- what the organisation needs to do to close the gap; and
- specific objectives for the planned period which would assist in meeting those aims.

At top management level, individual objectives are synonymous with the overall organisational objectives identified through the above process. The objectives for other staff will represent an accountable contribution to the achievement of objectives at the level of their unit.

Linking individual targets with organisational objectives may be considered as a seven-step process. Systems must be in place which broadly ensure that these steps are taken for each post. Ideally, target-setting at individual level follows the identification of organisational objectives. Experience suggests that in practice this is not a one-way street, and that examining individual targets contributes to a climate in which organisational objectives are more readily considered.

The Performance Management System

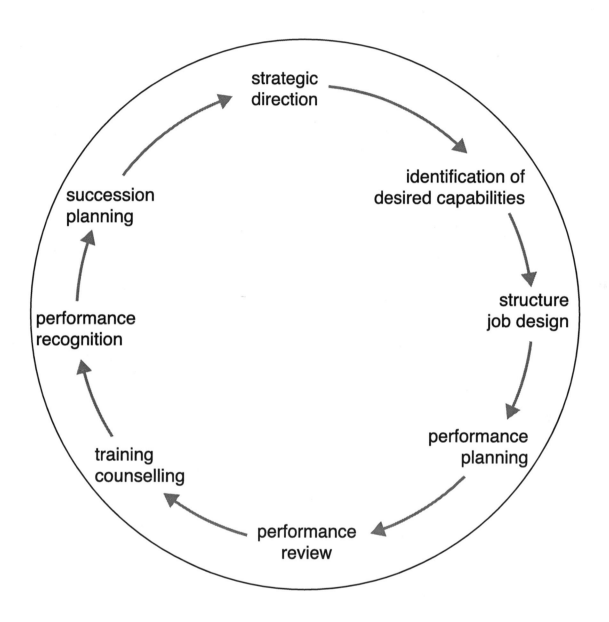

strategic direction

identification of desired capabilities

structure job design

performance planning

performance review

training counselling

performance recognition

succession planning

The Performance Management Cycle

Clarify Organisation
Policy and Objectives

Follow Up
Action Plan

Cascade Clarify Policy and
Objectives to Each Level

Indentify Development
Needs and Action Plan

Agree Objectives for
Each Level

Conduct Formal
Performance Review

Agree Performance
Standards

Continue to Give Feedback
and Performance Support

Monitor and Discuss
Performance Standards

Review Relevance of Objectives
and Performance Standards

Give Feedback and
Performance Support

Conduct Regular
Reviews

Step 1: Clarify purpose of job

Key question: Why does this person's job exist?

Step 2: Define "key result areas" for which the job holder is accountable

Having established the overall job purpose, the next step is to break it down into four to six areas of significant activity, which reflect priorities for the reporting period. For example, in a policy area, the "key result areas" may include: developing an effective research capability; seeing through a significant piece of legislation; running an efficient committee secretariat service.

Key questions:

- Which activities contribute most to organisational performance?

- What are the areas in which this individual has personal responsibility for achieving results?

- What are the areas in which any failure on his or her part may damage the overall performance of the division/branch/section?

- What does this person do that neither their line manager nor the staff reporting to them do?

Step 3: Identify desired objectives for each key result area

There may be more than one objective for each key result area, however, a total of more than 12 objectives for the job becomes unwieldy.

Key question: What does this job holder need to achieve in each key result area?

Step 4: Decide how performance will be assessed

Measures have to be derived for each of the objectives identified. Qualitative measures are clearly the most difficult to develop, and judgement and common sense play an equally important role, provided that managers and staff are in agreement.

Key question: How will we know when this objective has been achieved?

Step 5: Review the objectives

The next stage is to check that objectives work together as a whole.

Key questions:

- Are the objectives compatible/achievable as a whole? Are they compatible with those of other job holders?
- Is there an appropriate balance between work, management and personal development objectives?
- Will they stimulate and motivate, or exhaust and discourage?

Step 6: Monitor and review performance against objectives

Regular monitoring and review is effectively the only means by which objective-setting progresses from a paper-based system to an integral part of the management process.

Key question: Is there a risk that the only time this employee will know how he or she is perceived is at the annual appraisal?

Step 7: Evaluate achievement against objectives

Key questions:

- Were the objectives met to the required standard? If not, to what extent was the job holder responsible?
- Were objectives met within agreed timescales? If not, to what extent was the job holder responsible?
- How were resources used?
- What skills and competencies were demonstrated in the course of working towards objectives?
- What was the degree of personal effectiveness demonstrated by the job holder?
- Were any objectives achieved at the expense of other people/activities? If outside factors intervened, how did the job holder respond?
- Was the overall performance in line with standards set or expected (e.g. for the grade), or did it exceed expectations, or fail to meet expectations?

The collective level of achievement against objectives forms part of the context for determining the following year's organisational objectives, thus forming a continuous performance management cycle.

Examples of change

Recent changes in the public services of many Commonwealth and other countries, including *Australia, Canada, Ghana, Malta, Mauritius, New Zealand, the UK* and *Zimbabwe*, have all stressed the important role of performance management in achieving lasting change. The specific systems adopted have reflected the varying government circumstances, but all have contributed to an enduring change in the attitudes of managers towards clients and achieving value for money.

Other useful material (current as of 1996)

Managing People's Performance. Advice for Managers. Public Service Commission, Canberra, 1994 (AUS)

Performance Management: The Integrated Use of Recognition, Rewards and Sanctions. Australian Government Publishing Service, Canberra, October 1994 (AUS)

Generic Executive Performance Management System. Executive Service. Occasional Paper No. 2. Premier's Department, New South Wales, 1993 (AUS)

Objective Setting in Personal Review. Cabinet Office, London, 1993 (UK)

1.1.4 Human resource information and planning systems

Human resource information and planning systems provide the means for creating a public service workforce of appropriate size and quality to deliver the government's projects and programmes in a cost-effective manner. Overall responsibility for the systems must rest within a central agency of the public service, such as a Ministry of Public Service or a Ministry of Finance; systems with split responsibilities have a poor record of success.

The context for change

Planning for future developments in the public service workforce is a key component in improving the performance of the public service. Strategic planning systems, supported by accurate information, are necessary:

- to monitor and control the growth of the public service establishment in line with financial targets;

- to ensure that existing staff are utilised and deployed in response to development priorities; and

- to instigate strategies in line with priorities for staff acquisition, retention, development and exit.

Reasons for caution

Improvements in human resource information and planning systems are essential. However, experience suggests that there are several risks associated with the development of strategic systems:

- they can be experienced as a "top-down" control system, removing establishment control pressures from local managers;

- they can encourage an attitude of mind in which common sense is undermined by anticipated scientific precision i.e. nothing happens for many years pending the installation of an elaborate planning system; and

- they can be interpreted too narrowly, e.g. they can be seen as a tool for downsizing at the expense of recognising their significance for productivity improvement.

Achieving change

At its centre, a human resource planning and information system provides the mechanism for reconciling three conflicting pressures:

- the forecast of demand for human resources;
- the likely supply; and
- establishment controls.

Commonwealth experience suggests that typically a fully developed system entails the following elements:

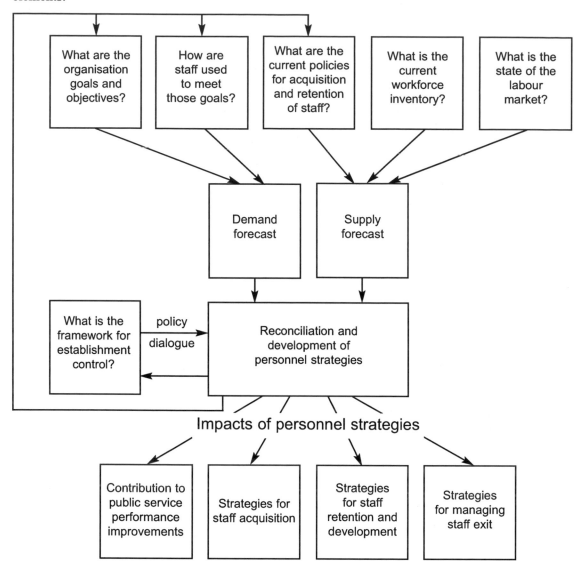

Four key elements within the system are:

1. A workforce inventory information system

An adequate personnel records information system is an essential prerequisite for human resource planning. The information required can be separated into two categories:

(i) Information about people

- numbers and characteristics of employees (age, gender, qualifications, skills, experience);
- location of employees (Ministry/department/unit); and
- acquisition, promotion and exit, including transfers and dismissals.

(ii) Information about posts

- job types and levels;
- numbers, locations, types and levels of established posts, posts filled and vacancies; and
- grade, pay and conditions.

2. An overall framework for establishment control

There are two methods which may be adopted in relation to Ministries/departments/units: stated ceilings may be placed on the number of personnel; or the running costs (i.e. the costs of administering the particular unit excluding transfer payments to beneficiaries and any revenue derived from clients) may be controlled.

Personnel ceilings can be unproductive if they encourage units to subcontract work at added cost. Controlling the running costs is preferable as it can allow some flexibility in terms of how resources are used (including temporary additional staff, contracting-out, planned overtime), while retaining overall control of costs.

3. Demand forecasting

The demand forecast for an occupational group is the number of posts required in a future time period based on the organisational objectives, and is made by:

- identifying an output indicator for an occupational group by selecting from the following range:

  - performance indicators (showing how much output may be expected per employee);

  - time indicators (showing how long is required to complete a task);

  - demographic indicators (showing the number of people served by one employee); and

  - location indicators (showing the number of locations served by one employee).

- checking that the indicator is:
  - quantifiable;

  - readily understood;

  - reasonably consistent over time and between different units;

  - acceptable to staff; and

  - based on readily available data.

- establishing a current value for the indicator which represents the average workload to be expected from a staff member;
- establishing a preferred value for the indicator bearing in mind reasonable efficiency improvements; and
- combining the preferred indicator value with the total level of activity expected to establish the number of staff required in the category.

4. Supply forecasting

The supply forecast is an investigation of current personnel policies for staff acquisition, retention and development, and exit, to assess their potential effect in closing the gap between projected human resource demand and supply. Supply forecasting examines the possible impact of changes in these policies, in the light of labour market conditions on the available workforce. In particular, it examines the impact of policy changes on:

- high rates of staff turnover;
- skills shortages;
- high overtime levels;
- recruitment difficulties; and
- shortage of suitable promoters.

The development of a human resource information and planning system is not a short-term task. Pilot studies and some determination are necessary to disseminate its potential value to managers to move the idea forward. Consensus and, at the very least, extensive dialogue, is essential in an area which requires agreement on the basis of some highly sensitive forecasts and policy judgements. The key questions to be addressed in implementation are:

- What are the objectives for introducing the system?
- Who is ultimately responsible for the elements of the system and for its co-ordination?
- How will the co-operation of all Ministries, departments/units be secured in developing and managing the system?
- What additional specialist support is required, if any, to introduce the system?
- Will the development of the system delay changes which are inevitable?
- What are the current information sources for the system, and how can deficiencies be remedied?

Examples of change

Public service reforms in *Botswana, Canada, Malaysia, Malta* and *the UK* have utilised a strategic approach to human resource planning to put their respective services on a sound financial basis and to improve service delivery.

Other useful material (current as of 1996)

Blueprint for Renewing Government Service Using Information Technology. Treasury Board Secretariat, 1994 (AUS)

A Framework for Human Resource Management in the Australian Public Service. Public Service Commission, Canberra, 1992 (AUS)

Proceedings of the 1992 Public Sector Convention. New Zealand Society of Accountants, 1992, Wellington (NZ)

Manpower Planning in the Civil Service. UK Treasury, London, 1990 (UK)

1.2 Acquisition of Staff

1.2.1 Improving recruitment and retention practices

Recruitment is widely used as an umbrella term to cover two specific elements: recruitment and selection. The recruitment and selection process involves a sequence of activities which, if planned and undertaken fairly and effectively, will enable the organisation to identify and appoint the most suitable candidate for a vacancy.

The recruitment phase covers the stage of the process from the identification of the post to be filled, the completion of the scheme of service (or job description and person specification), to the attraction of suitable candidates who wish to be considered for the post.

The selection phase covers the activities which are used to assess and select the most suitable candidate.

Retention of employees within the organisation is achieved by ensuring that sufficient measures are in place to encourage employees to work and want to continue working for that particular organisation.

The context for change

Sound recruitment, selection and retention are fundamental to the effective performance of the public service. Poor policy, procedures or practice can result in the wrong quality or quantity of recruits, leading to poor individual and organisational performance, low morale, and high levels of absence and turnover.

However, achieving effective recruitment and retention involves balancing the need for consistency in organisational standards with the need for flexibility and "ownership" at local level, and this balance can be difficult to achieve.

Traditionally, in government organisations, recruitment and retention activities have been centrally co-ordinated with a central public services commission, or equivalent, setting or defining policy and assuming responsibility for all activity in this area. Although this approach can be effective in establishing and maintaining standards and in concentrating expertise, it also has limitations.

Potential shortcomings include long delays in making appointments, rigidity, frustration and a failure to meet the operational needs of the employing department or the career needs of individual employees. This can lead to inefficiencies and poor service delivery to the public.

At the opposite end of the continuum, some governments are moving towards the total delegation of recruitment activity to Ministries or departments, with light co-ordination of recruitment policy undertaken at the centre. This approach allows flexibility at local level and an improved "ownership" of decision making and of responsibility for the employees recruited.

However, it too can have drawbacks, such as variations in recruitment standards and in employment terms and conditions. These, in turn, may limit future mobility and development of staff across the public service. Arguably, a reduced independent monitoring function at the centre might also fail to correct unfair or biased practice.

Between these two extremes, the public service in many countries is moving gradually towards the selective devolution to departments of personnel management functions, including recruitment. This is being done within an overall umbrella of centrally-defined policy and standards, and alongside a process of systematic monitoring of practice and results. These strategic functions remain the responsibility of the public service commission or other independent co-ordinating body.

Most commonly, an approach of gradual devolution is followed. Any transition from centralised recruitment towards local recruitment with central quality assurance mechanisms highlights the responsibility of Ministries and departments to improve retention. There is little advantage to recruiting the best if they are not retained within the public service.

Pay and grading issues are generally outside the control of the Ministries and departments – training and understanding of organisational goals, the two key ingredients of job satisfaction, are not.

Successful devolution of personal management functions can result in:

- fewer delays in recruitment;
- a better "match" of candidate and departmental needs;
- greater staff retention and lower staff absenteeism;
- more customer commendations and fewer complaints;
- improved individual and organisational efficiency and productivity;
- improved staff and management morale; and
- greater cost-effectiveness in meeting organisational objectives.

Reasons for caution

Effective change requires a facilitating structure to be established which:

- assists Ministries and departments to focus on their goals as service providers;
- develops commitment across the public service to improvement of the present system; and
- monitors results.

Proposed devolution of decision making to departmental level will represent a major change to the traditional role of the public service commission or equivalent body. Resistance to change should be anticipated and planned for.

Initial limiting factors to be expected and overcome are:

- a lack of relevant personnel management experience and expertise at Ministry/departmental level;
- a lack of capacity at departmental level to undertake new functions;
- procedural inconsistency with variations in organisational standards;
- poor communication between departments; and
- in the short-term, duplication of organisational resources.

Achieving change

Improving recruitment and retention within the public service entails a realignment of the responsibilities of the three key players in public service personnel management: the service commission; the central personnel office; and the line Ministries and departments.

- *Line Ministries and departments* will increasingly take responsibility for selection, appointment and discipline within a framework set by the central personnel office and the service commission.

- *The central personnel office*, where this is separate from the service commission, will increasingly set that framework, translating broad directions from the service commission into detailed guidelines.

- *The service commission* will use a lighter touch in setting the overall regulatory framework, but will increasingly focus its attention on the longer-term issues of professional standards and commitment.

This movement of responsibilities is, at the very least, challenging for all involved and will inevitably bring with it the full diversity of organisational reactions to change. However, it is unlikely that the public service in any setting will find itself completely insulated from the changing climate of public expectations and labour mobility which are forcing a new look at traditional personnel management practices throughout the public sector.

Commonwealth experience suggests that there are ten lessons for the line Ministries and departments, central personnel office, and the service commission, at a time of management change: These are as follows:

1. The only hope of minimising sterile win/lose debates is to ensure that there must be a sense of direction and some strategic targets which all can recognise.

2. Incremental change is more probable than revolution, and even if the revolution happens, that will not be the end of the story – dialogue must be established between the three key players in personnel management.

3. Start sooner rather than later – some movement can be achieved despite the complexity of the constitutional entrenchment of the service commission.

4. Change will be extremely difficult and support will be hard to find – build a constituency for change from the public, from politicians, and from within the public service.

5. No-one wants to build a failure, but it is against all experience to assume inevitable and continuous success. Given the significance of the public service to national development, some attention must be focused on refining the changes, and even on the possibility of retreat where major problems are emerging.

6. Create some sense of safety for all involved by introducing explicit safeguards in advance of the changes.

7. Build line-management capacities – new tasks require new skills and outlooks.

8. The changes in responsibilities imply new tasks requiring a new balance between powers and accountabilities. Develop the avenues of accountability in step with the reforms.

9. Training is no panacea, but all staff must understand the new personnel management arrangements, and the outlook they imply – train the users of the system.

10. Delegation does not leave a vacuum at the centre, there is a strategic gap and the service commissions are in the best position to fill it – encourage the development of a new role for the service commissions in which they are looking beyond the immediate horizon.

Examples of change

The 1986 O&M Review of the *Botswana* Directorate of Personnel, aimed at improving organisational efficiency and making the Government more responsive to clients' needs, has resulted in a shift in personnel responsibility to Ministries and departments. This approach was endorsed by Ministers in 1991, with the Directorate of Public Service Management issuing procedures and guidance manuals to ensure consistency and uniform standards.

Legislation in *New Zealand* in the late 1980s, aimed at improving the efficiency and effectiveness of the Public Service, has emphasised accountability at departmental level for the management of resources and performance. Chief executives now have responsibility for the appointment of all staff to their own departments on the basis of the person "best suited to the position".

In the *UK*, there has been a gradual delegation of responsibility to departmental managers since the 1960s for all recruitment except senior grades and fast-stream entrants. This started in shortage areas, but has extended as the UK Government has emphasised the need for improved management and quality of service in Government. Recruitment advice and expertise is available on a cost-recovery basis through the Recruitment and Assessment Services Agency, although all recruitment must comply with the requirement for "fair and open competition".

Other useful material (current as of 1996)

From Problem to Solution: Commonwealth Strategies for Reform. Managing the Public Service. Strategies for Improvement Series: No. 1. Commonwealth Secretariat, 1995 (ComSec)

Redrawing the Lines. Service Commissions and the Delegation of Personnel Management. Managing the Public Service. Strategies for Improvement Series: No. 2. Polidano, P. and Manning, N. Commonwealth Secretariat, 1996 (ComSec)

Selection: A Guide to Hiring Practices in the State Sector. State Services Commission, Wellington, 1989 (NZ)

1.2.2 Non-discrimination in recruitment

Discrimination in recruitment is unfair and undermines the principle of merit. The personnel management functions that are susceptible to racial, sexual, cultural and other discriminatory biases are:

- recruitment and selection;
- appraisal; and
- promotion.

In this complex and sensitive area, communicating and explaining why non-discriminatory policies should be introduced and implemented are as important as the policies themselves. Senior managers within Ministries and departments have a crucial role to play.

The context for change

In every country, there are minorities who experience discrimination. Racial prejudice is a powerful negative force in recruitment practices. Moreover, a lot of evidence shows that women with similar experience, skills, ability and career motivation to men are still excluded from senior positions. Furthermore, people with disabilities and those from "minority" or "indigenous" cultures are assumed to lack ability.

Recruitment and appraisal processes in the public service must ensure that posts are genuinely open to all, and must assess ability fairly and objectively overcoming stereotype and bias. Attracting previously discriminated groups into public service employment serves little purpose if they will face a hostile climate within it. Reducing discrimination in recruitment must be accompanied by culture change within the organisation.

Non-discrimination is more than a moral imperative for public service. Discrimination means a loss of talent, a loss of diversity, and in particular, a loss of service. The only public service that can serve the entire public is a service which is broadly representative of that public.

Reasons for caution

Challenging discrimination enters sensitive territory and produces strongly emotional reactions. Discrimination within public service employment practices and in dealings with the public is unacceptable. But a highly contentious debate which has shifted the focus from serving the public to institutional in-fighting represents little progress. Determined progress must balance the need for change with the need to engage the support of all parties.

Achieving change

General Approach

Typically, anti-discrimination strategies for the public service can involve three steps:

- legislative action to outlaw discrimination;
- reforms in the recruitment and selection of staff; and
- promotion of attitudinal changes.

Affirmative action goes further than these steps by allowing special measures to be taken to ensure that people with appropriate potential from disadvantaged groups, inside and outside the public service, are identified and appointed with the aim of improving the representativeness of the public service.

Successful strategies for minimising discrimination in the public service are as follows:

- promote the public service as representative of the nation;
- counter resistance with strong arguments for diversity;
- increase awareness by regular training;
- introduce specific selection techniques;
- ensure physical access to all facilities; – set targets and monitor action plans;
- publicise good practice; and
- monitor recruitments, re-gradings, and promotions.

Key issues

Positive/affirmative action

- emphasise that positive action is not positive discrimination; and
- encourage action by managers to motivate a broader range of people to apply for posts.

Advertising

- word adverts carefully to avoid implying preference for a particular group; and
- use additional publications to reach under-represented groups.

Scheme of Service (job description)

- test the "Scheme of Service" for in-built bias;
- avoid overstated requirements which may discourage competent applicants; and
- inform the applicants of the equal opportunity policies and practices.

Person specification

- refer only to those skills and talents which are essential for the job to avoid unconscious bias;
- avoid unnecessary requirements (e.g. age-bands) that restrict access to positions; and
- recognise potential as well as experience.

Interviewing and selection procedures

• focus on factual information rather than impressions;

• ask all candidates the same questions;

• prompt for individual potential, interests and capabilities;

• avoid personal questions about domestic plans and arrangements;

• take all selection decisions as a panel;

• record and retain the basis and reason for selection to allow for subsequent monitoring; and

• make grievance procedures available to all applicants and employees.

Promotion and re-grading

• institute formal appraisal systems;

• publicise promotion posts to all possible candidates; and

• re-grade on the basis of proven ability in the existing job.

Indicators of change

• monitor entry and exit to grades and units;

• assess change through focus groups drawn from the organisation and the wider community; and

• monitor sickness rates, absenteeism and turnover.

Examples of change

Since 1984, the *Australian* Public Service Act has required organisations to develop equal employment opportunity programmes to address the employment inequities of non-English speaking peoples, women, and those with disabilities. Individual organisations have introduced more flexible working, formal appraisal systems, paternity leave and child care.

The Public Services in *India, Jamaica, Sierra Leone* and *Tanzania*, have undertaken research which indicates that women's management skills are no different from those of men. Training to change attitudes and to develop managerial potential has been undertaken.

A gender planning strategy in *Lesotho* has been developed through open and participatory research techniques.

In *New Zealand*, all Public Service Departments are required to submit equal employment opportunities reports to the State Services Commission annually. The Commission is required by law to promote, develop and monitor equal employment opportunities and programmes in each department.

In the Public Service of the former Republic of *South Africa*, 95% or more of posts at all levels were held by whites. By 1995, whites held slightly less than half (48%) of the posts, and at the front line, Africans held the largest percentage (50%) of posts.

Other useful material (current as of 1996)

Parikh, I. J. & Farrell, P. Approaches to Women Managers Training, Commonwealth Secretariat, London, 1991 (ComSec)

Mkhonza, A. P. Managing towards equity in staffing policies. In: Government in Transition: The Inaugural Conference of the Commonwealth Association for Public Administration and Management, Charlottetown, Canada, 28-31 August 1994. Commonwealth Secretariat, 1995 (ComSec)

Employment Equity Reporting Resources Kit, Canadian Management Board Secretariat, Ontario, 1993 (CAN)

The Manager's Deskbook, Treasury Board of Canada, Third Edition (CAN)

Treasury Board Manual, Human Resources volume, Chapter 1-4, 1-5 (CAN)

Into the 90s: Equal Employment Opportunities in New Zealand. Department of Labour, Wellington, 1991 (NZ)

Equity at Work: An Approach to Gender Neutral Job Evaluation. State Services Commission/Department of Labour, Wellington, 1991 (NZ)

EEO: Progress in the Public Service as at June 1993. State Services Commission, Wellington (NZ)

Employment of People with Disabilities: A Code of Practice. Cabinet Office, London. 1990 (UK)

Equal Opportunities for Women in the Civil Service. Progress Report 1992-93. London, 1993 (UK)

Equal Opportunities in the Civil Service for People of Ethnic Minority Origin. Progress Report, 1992-93. London, 1993 (UK)

1.3 Developing/Enhancing Staff Skills and Motivation

1.3.1 Enhancing staff training and development

Broadly, *training* is the planned process by which staff are equipped to carry out their existing tasks; and *development* is the means by which they are prepared for future roles, for increased or wider responsibilities, and to utilise their potential within the organisation.

Training and development are means towards ends, not ends in themselves. Training and development plans must stem from the needs of the business and be measured by the improved business performance which they achieve.

The context for change

Staff training and development is increasingly central to performance improvement strategies in the public service for the following reasons:

- the pace of organisational and technical change is accelerating, requiring staff to assimilate new skills and attitudes throughout their career in the public service;

- the reductions in staff numbers require individuals to be competent in a wider range of skills;

- public expectations of the public service are rising, requiring sharper technical skills and changed attitudes; and

- the continuing pressure for demonstrable efficiency improvements in the public service requires enhanced business planning and strategic change skills at all levels.

Reasons for caution

Training is neither a panacea nor an entitlement created by long service. Training is a potential solution to a business problem. Strategies for enhancing staff training and development which do not critically examine the assistance they will provide to meeting short and long-term business goals waste opportunities.

Disconnected training strategies perpetuate two notions in the public service which restrict its ability to change and respond to altered circumstances.

First, unless a clear link can be established between training inputs on the one hand, and service and strategic outputs on the other, training activities can be seen as "time off for good behaviour" – a period of relaxation away from the daily pressures of the service.

Second, and related, hard-pressed managers will consider training to be a distraction they can ill afford or an indignity they will not suffer.

Both notions highlight the risk of devaluing training activities, removing a significant item from the tool-kit available to a hard-pressed public service at a time of rapid change.

Achieving change

A sound staff training and development strategy has four elements:

1. The strategy embodies a clearly-stated commitment from senior management to develop all employees to achieve business objectives.

    -   This frequently entails a written plan which identifies business goals and targets, and which assesses how employees can be developed to meet those targets.

    -   It requires a clear sense of mission for the organisation, understood widely within the public service.

2. A staff training and development strategy focuses on the needs of new recruits.

    -   Technical competence must be complemented by a detailed understanding of the organisation, its functioning, its objectives, and its culture.

3. The strategy requires the continuing regular review of the training and development needs of employees throughout their employment.

    -   This requires detailed consideration of the business plan.

    -   The identification of realistic training needs must be a core element within the performance appraisal system.

4. The strategy emphasises evaluation to assess achievements, and to improve future effectiveness.

    -   The investment in training, the impact on the competence and commitment of employees, and the use made of skills learned, should be reviewed at all levels against business goals and targets.

Putting the training and development strategy into practice will require:

-   On-the-job training, which will need:
    -   development of institutional knowledge of the processes of the department or agency, and of the broader public service;
    -   experience of related positions, including job rotation;
    -   peer review and discussion; and
    -   regular briefings by management.

-   Formal training through external courses.
-   Professional development, which will require:
    -   access to information on courses;
    -   arrangements for part-time study;
    -   contributions towards fees; and
    -   assistance and encouragement in joining professional associations.

Examples of change

A recent review of training and development policies and objectives in *Canada* recommended a shift in the role of the existing central body to one of co-ordination, with delegation of needs assessment, and training and development provision to departments. There has also been an emphasis on improved monitoring and evaluation of programmes, with the aim of improving the appropriateness and cost-effectiveness of the methods adopted.

In line with the emphasis on the creation of a Total Quality Management culture and the adoption of the "Client's Charter", training in *Malaysia* has been recognised as a vehicle for achieving the knowledge, skills, and necessary values to ensure that the Civil Service "is continuously staffed with highly-skilled and knowledgeable personnel to provide excellent public service".

Recent legislation in *New Zealand* aimed at achieving efficiency in the Public Service has highlighted the need for effective management skills, developed through systematic programmes of management development. New Zealand has already adopted a strong policy of decentralisation of responsibility to departments, but is now recognising the need for a more co-ordinated strategic, service-wide approach to management development, based upon a set of core competencies for a "Public Service Senior Manager". This has led to calls for improved central co-ordination of the process to complement departmental activity.

Other useful material (current as of 1996)

From Problem to Solution: Commonwealth Strategies for Reform. Managing the Public Service. Strategies for Improvement Series: No. 1. Commonwealth Secretariat, 1995 (ComSec)

Jugnauth, A. Human resource management: challenges and opportunities. In: Government in Transition. The Inaugural Conference of the Commonwealth Association for Public Administration and Management, Charlottetown, Canada, 28-31 August 1994. Commonwealth Secretariat, 1995 (ComSec)

Developing People in the Australian Public Service. Report on the Public Service Commission's Human Resource Survey, 1991/92. Public Services Commission, May 1993 (AUS)

The Manager's Deskbook, Treasury Board of Canada, Third Edition (CAN)

Treasury Board Manual, Human Resources volume (CAN)

Report of the Public Service 2000 Task Force on Staff Training and Development (CAN)

Training and Development Canada: Course Calendar (CAN)

Training and Development Canada: Systems Approach to Training (CAN)

The Civil Service of Malaysia – A Paradigm Shift. Chapter 13, pp 678-702, 1993 (MAL)

Education Gazette, Vol. 72, No. 7. Ministry of Education, Wellington 1993 (NZ)

Training Directory, Wellington, 1993 (NZ)

Developing People: The Line Manager's Job. UK Cabinet Office, London, 1993 (UK)

Objective Setting in Personal Review. Development Division, Cabinet Office, Office of Public Service and Science, London, 1993 (UK)

1.3.2 Career Management

Career management strategies aim to provide a path for competent staff through the public service, enabling them to occupy positions which they will find satisfying and in which they will contribute significantly to meeting business objectives. In essence, successful career management combines personal satisfaction with succession planning for positions, ensuring that those positions will be filled by people able to deliver organisational results.

The context for change

Career management strategies provide a positive and rewarding path for competent staff at a time of significant change within the public service.

The conviction that probity and impartiality in the service are best maintained by guaranteeing secure, lifelong employment with progression determined significantly by seniority is fading. This traditional model assumed that promotion would be based on merit that is best assessed by neutral, centralised procedures. It also assumed that employees would spend their entire careers within the public service and that the range of career options and progression possibilities would be fully known at the outset.

This model was altered somewhat by the development of "high-flyer" training and promotion schemes in which particularly talented individuals would be placed on a fast track to more senior positions. The picture has altered more substantially with the introduction of open recruitment schemes which attract applicants from outside the public service for positions at all levels.

These developments, responding to the changes and less secure business circumstances of the public service, represent a major challenge to the career assumptions of many public servants. In this transition period, there is a particular need for strategies which combine opportunities for individual achievement and job satisfaction with an increased focus on meeting the business targets of the public service.

Reasons for caution

The development of career management strategies presupposed that there is the capacity for career planning within the public service; that flexible alternatives to lifelong permanent employment are available, including short-term contracts, secondments, and career breaks; and that expectations can be managed.

Few public or private sector organisations operate a fully developed, comprehensive career management strategy, but where aspects are in place, they rely on a strong culture of realism, and on explicit and well publicised policy statements on management support for career development.

Achieving change

Career management strategies are built on clear policy decisions concerning:

• the use of fixed-term contracts;

• secondments within the public service and to the private and NGO sectors;

• the possibility of career breaks;

- the scope for open recruitment at senior level; and

- the organisational investment to be made in the central personnel management office and, where devolved, in the departmental units.

Realistically, career management strategies will target senior positions in the public service. Stemming from those policy decisions, the career management strategy will have three components:

Component 1: Development of the organisational capacity to plan and manage career paths

In most settings this entails developing capacity within the central personnel management office or, where devolved, in the departmental units to:

• identify senior positions which are key to service improvement;

• assess recruitment trends and likely skill shortages; and

• provide counselling to staff whose career paths could lead them towards key senior positions.

Component 2: Establishment of mechanisms for developing staff in preparation for key senior positions

This requires a coherent policy of management training and an effective performance appraisal procedure. Career counselling is again significant.

Component 3: Improving systems for recruitment of senior staff

Experience indicates that this entails:

- the appropriate use of open recruitment, balancing the need to attract skills from outside the public service with career opportunities for experienced and talented public servants;

- the development of appropriate reward frameworks for senior staff; and

- counselling for potential applicants.

At all stages, career management strategies require the organisational capacity to provide confidential and credible counselling for staff. This is the key to:

- reviewing the options available for "plateaued managers" who are operating competently but are unlikely to be promoted and whose interest and motivation must be maintained; and

- breaking the "glass ceiling" for women and others whose careers may be unfairly restricted.

Examples of change

A Task Force on Management Improvement for the *Australian* Public Service reported in December 1992 that there was a "substantial commitment" to implementing "career planning" in agencies. However, it drew attention to the contradiction between career planning in the sense of mapping out career paths for individuals and the preferred Civil Service approach to promotion via open competition for vacancies.

In the *UK*, a Career Management and Succession Planning Study was carried out by the Efficiency Unit of the Office of Public Service and Science in 1993, which attempted to lay down (and reaffirm) principles of career development for senior Civil Servants, in particular, the "Senior Open Structure". Amongst its recommendations were more explicit selection criteria, published policy statements on career development, a review of "fast-stream" entry, schemes for interchange between the Civil Service and the private sector, selection for promotion more closely tied to achievement, increased emphasis on equal opportunities, and flexibility in contracts of employment.

Other useful material (current as of 1996)

Administrative and Managerial Reform in Government: A Commonwealth Portfolio of Current Good Practice. Proceedings of a Pan-Commonwealth Working Group Meeting held in Kuala Lumpur, Malaysia, 19-22 April 1993. Commonwealth Secretariat, 1993 (ComSec)

Developing People in the Australian Public Service. Report on the Public Service Commission's Human Resource Development Survey, 1991/92. Public Service Commission, May 1993 (AUS)

Career Management and Succession Planning Study. Efficiency Unit, Cabinet Office. HMSO, London 1993 (UK)

1.3.3 Performance appraisal

Performance appraisal is a system by which an individual is guided towards making an effective contribution to the work of the public service.

Performance appraisal systems achieve one or more of the following:

• relate individual performance to organisational goals;

• test competence; and

• contribute towards a climate of open discussion within the public service.

The context for change

At a time of rapid change within the public service, there is an urgent need to ensure that public servants are working effectively as well as efficiently – that they are doing the right things and doing those things well.

This concern is addressed by ensuring that employees understand how their work contributes to the achievement of organisational goals, by ensuring that employees have the skills to make that contribution and, above all, by developing a climate of open discussion in which performance, achievements, and difficulties can be approached openly and supportively.

The traditional annual confidential report system in operation in many Commonwealth countries is inadequate for this purpose. It is subjective, unrelated to corporate objectives, and poorly regarded by employees at all levels and their appraising officers. As it is a closed system, appraisees are provided with feedback on their performance only when it is negative, providing little encouragement or motivation.

Open performance appraisal systems:

• relate individual performance to organisational goals by:
  - identifying personal targets for employees;
  - clarifying the linkages between those targets, the key tasks for the unit or department, and the broader objectives for the service; and
  - providing examples of appropriate behaviours which will assist in meeting those personal targets.
• test competence by:
  - identifying the obstacles faced by the employee in meeting targets;
  - identifying areas where training and other inputs can assist in overcoming those obstacles;
• contribute towards a climate of open discussion within the public service by:
  - providing a closed and safe meeting environment in which the appraisee and the appraising officer can discuss achievements and difficulties openly; and
  - providing an opportunity for managers to receive feedback concerning the systems and procedures in operation in a format which they will not perceive as threatening or undermining.

Reasons for caution

Of the three objectives of performance appraisal, the establishment of a climate of open discussion within the public service is the most significant. Establishing appraisal systems with a narrower emphasis on relating individual performance to organisational goals, and testing competence, run two risks.

First, it can allow a negative perception of the system to develop, with employees reacting suspiciously to a proposal that they feel carries little benefit for themselves.

Second, it may encourage the establishment of further systems for driving improved performance on an inadequately tested base. Performance-related pay, or automatic linkages between appraisal and promotion, are possible strategies to be introduced over time. Both are contentious and require a sound and well-tested system of appraisal, which attracts widespread support across the public service. Hasty moves in this direction, neglecting the overriding goal of establishing a climate of open discussion, can result in the construction of unpopular and managerially time-consuming systems, on the basis of an appraisal methodology which will be the subject of continuing and demoralising methodological dispute.

Achieving change

The development of a performance appraisal system within the public service must be signalled by an unambiguous commitment from senior management to introduce a mechanism which:

- ensures that the work programme of each employee reflects the goals of the unit or division and the overall goals of the Ministry or department;

- ensures that supervisors and employees have a common understanding of the job requirements;

- reviews individual performance against mutually-agreed standards, some of which are specific to that individual, and some general to the level or position;

- provides feedback on performance to employees and identifies training and skill development needs;

- develops a more open and participative environment through improved communication between supervisors and employees; and

- encourages improvement and recognises good performance.

This commitment provides the basis on which the performance appraisal system will be evaluated and owned across the public service.

Most performance appraisal systems require a four-stage annual cycle, as follows:

Stage 1 – Developing the work plan

At this point, the key tasks for the individual are agreed. The individual performance standards for the employee are set out against those key tasks, providing a clear statement of expectations. The key tasks and individual performance standards should as far as possible be agreed by the appraisee and appraising officer.

The identification of the key tasks is facilitated if the unit or department have a clear business plan identifying its broader objectives for the year.

The work plan also includes general performance standards which provide guidance on appropriate behaviours for all employees in the public service or in a particular occupational group.

Stage 2 – Progress review

Although discussions on the employee's performance should be continuous throughout the year, a formal progress review meeting serves to focus minds and to provide an early warning of any emerging difficulties.

Stage 3 – Annual performance review

This provides the opportunity to assess achievements in meeting the individual performance targets, and in meeting the general performance standards. In well-established performance appraisal systems, it is regarded as a sign of failure if an appraisee first learns of management concern about his or her performance at a formal review meeting.

The performance review includes a recognition of any particular contributions made by the employee during the year, recommendations for training and development, and might include some assessment of the employee's career potential.

In terms of best practices across the Commonwealth, many public service organisations have moved from the traditional hierarchical model of performance appraisal where staff are assessed by their immediate supervisors to the more comprehensive 360 degree Developmental Feedback Model. This model is used to provide staff and management with broader input on an individual's performance. Staff members at all levels of the organisation conduct a self-assessment of their performance and receive performance feedback from those they interact with in performing their duties including their peers, clients, subordinates, and superiors. This model of the performance appraisal process is designed to give staff a more balanced perspective of performance for follow-up decision making and for identifying areas for improvement and development.

Hierarchical vs. Developmental Feedback Model

Traditional Hierarchical Feedback Model

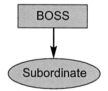

The Developmental (360%) Feedback Model

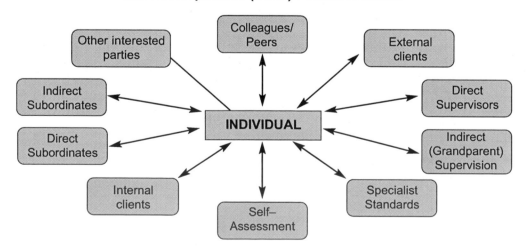

Stage 4 – Decisions

The appraising officer, based on review recommendations which are, as far as possible, agreed with the employee, and in discussion with other managers, must decide on appropriate action.

This may include:

- recognition of good performance and the acknowledgement of a job well done, nomination for special training or other career development opportunities, acting up possibilities, and entry into public service award schemes; and
- responding to unsatisfactory performance, with continuous discussion and mentoring and, in more extreme situations, the development of an individually-tailored performance improvement plan, in collaboration with personnel management staff.

Documentation must be clear, simple, and readily understood.

Examples of change

The Public Services in *Lesotho* and *Zimbabwe* have developed comprehensive performance appraisal procedures and arrangements to train all public servants in their operation.

The *Mauritius* Public Service has introduced a performance appraisal system reflecting the four stages given above.

In *Zambia*, the Annual Performance Appraisal System is being introduced in parallel with the review and restructuring of all Ministries, ensuring that newly-clarified organisational goals are translated into clear performance targets for individual employees.

Other useful material (current as of 1996)

Cherry, N. Appraisal: How to kill it and how to make it work. Public Service Commission. Australian Government Publishing Service, Canberra, 1989 (AUS)

Waldron, L. & Smith, L. Performance Appraisal – Questions and Answers. Public Service Commission Senior Executive Staffing Unit. Occasional Papers. Australian Government Publishing Service, Canberra, 1990 (AUS)

Evaluating Performance Appraisal Programmes in APS Departments and Agencies – Resource Kit. Public Service Commission, Canberra, 1993 (AUS)

Making Performance Appraisal Count. Effective Performance Appraisal for Senior Officers and Senior Executives in the Australian Public Service. Public Service Commission, Canberra, 1994 (AUS)

Managing People's Performance. Public Service Commission, Canberra (AUS)

Service Circular No. 4 1992 and Guidelines for the Implementation of Performance Appraisal System of the Malaysian Public Service, 4 December 1992. Public Service Department, Kuala Lumpur, 1993 (MAL)

Annual Performance Review System for the Civil Service: Guidelines. Government of Mauritius, 1995 (MAU)

Scott, G., Bushnell, P. and Sallee, N., 1990, Treasury, Wellington (NZ)

Trotman, I. & Jones, N. Review of Public Sector Chief Executive Performance in New Zealand. Paper delivered to Australasian Evaluation Society Conference 1993, State Services Commission, Wellington (NZ)

A Guide to Performance Appraisal, Department of Social Security, London, 1993 (UK)

Objective Setting in Personal Review. Executive Summary. Development Division. Cabinet Office (OPSS), London, 1993 (UK)

Annual Performance Appraisal System. Government of Zambia, 1995 (ZAM)

1.3.4 Relating awards to performance

Awards for excellent performance are increasingly employed within the public service. These may or may not have a financial value. Performance-related pay can be the most contentious of the approaches, but has been widely adopted. Public servants, like all other employees, require recognition of their achievements to maintain their motivation in a demanding and fast-changing environment.

The context for change

The use of performance awards has a long history, especially in manufacturing operations, marketing, and, to some extent, top executive remuneration. However, because of increased competitive pressure and the need to tie individual performance more closely to corporate objectives and strategy, their application has spread to other areas, including public sector employment. Although performance awards can take a variety of forms, the most noticeable recent development has been the increasing introduction of performance-related pay.

Performance awards have become a tool in the move away from the static, reactive notion of salary administration towards a more dynamic, strategic approach to rewards management. Bureaucratic payment systems, where people doing the same work are paid the same, are being replaced by more flexible and personalised reward structures which specifically set out to reward an individual's contribution.

Reasons for caution

Performance awards are intentionally divisive in that they single out well-performing individuals. The systems employed to identify individuals for particular recognition must be robust and well respected if they are to have credibility across the public service.

Performance-related pay raises some particular risks:

- *Short-termism*. There is little evidence that extra payments do improve overall performance. Most motivational theories stress intrinsic motivation (i.e. the job itself) rather than extrinsic motivation (money and benefits). Performance-related pay schemes must avoid the risk that employers' long-term targets will be replaced by short-term responses which trigger the rewards.

- *Inappropriate targets*. In setting explicit and well-defined targets, units and departments must avoid the risk of squeezing out broad public interest considerations which are less amenable to target-setting.

- *Weak methodologies*. Performance-related pay can be a contentious development and may be subject to some resistance within the public service. If it is to be credible and sustainable, it must avoid any risk of serious challenge to the performance appraisal methodology which underpins it.

Achieving change

Non-financial performance awards honour and reward public servants who have shown a willingness to make an extra effort in carrying out their duties or who have distinguished themselves in serving the public.

Introducing such awards requires a clear policy statement indicating the intention to recognise particularly meritorious contributions, the range of awards to be provided, and the means by which outstanding contributions are to be identified, including the development of performance appraisal systems.

Non-financial awards may be at departmental level or service-wide, and can cover groups or individuals only. The key to their credibility is that they are associated with recognition from the highest levels of the public service.

Strategies for introducing financial awards, including performance-related pay, require:

- a determination to challenge the perceived right to automatic annual pay increases, irrespective of performance;
- a comprehensive dialogue with staff associations and other representative bodies;
- a full explanation to all affected staff; and
- a sound, tested and credible system for performance appraisal.

Three overall models can be identified across the Commonwealth.

Model 1: Performance-related pay for senior staff

Supported by a performance appraisal system, which recognises the particular responsibility on senior staff to play a leadership role in the public service, performance-related bonuses can be allocated subject to an overall distribution curve which ensures service-wide equity and consistency.

Model 2: Performance-related pay across the public service

Such broad-based systems require a reconsideration of the generally fragmented and over-elaborate grading structures existing within the public service.

Rationalising and reducing schemes of service, and classifying them into fewer broad service classifications, provides an opportunity to:

- emphasise talent, experience and expertise in place of academic qualifications;
- incorporate assessed performance as the key to annual salary progression; and
- develop a performance appraisal methodology which relates to each of the broad service classifications.

Model 3: Devolved performance-related pay

In such systems, departments or agencies are given authority to negotiate pay and pay-related conditions of service and develop locally-appropriate performance-related pay frameworks.

Such delegation requires continuing central control of the total pay bill. Departments and agencies cannot negotiate the total beyond an agreed control total. Delegation also requires a clearly established negotiating remit, agreed between the department and the Ministry of Finance at the outset, which defines the limits of the department's negotiating authority.

Examples of change

In 1990, the *Australian* Government was considering introducing performance-related pay into the Senior Executive Service. However, a Senate Standing Committee concluded "[we] are far from convinced that it is desirable to introduce performance-based pay at all" and suggested a thorough cost-benefit analysis, piloting of various appraisal systems, and ascertaining staff acceptance of performance-related pay prior to implementation.

In 1992, the New Remuneration System was introduced into the *Malaysian* Civil Service in order to overhaul its total reward management system. It formed part of a comprehensive package of reforms and rationalisations and intended to base annual salary progressions on individual performance rather than seniority.

Performance-related pay has been introduced for the top three levels of the *Maltese* Civil Service, linking this to the notion of a three-year "Performance Contract". It is based on the assumptions of fairness and consistency, pay for performance, linking of individual and organisational objectives, participative leadership, and openness.

A Flexible Wage System was introduced into the whole *Singapore* economy in 1986 to attempt to overcome the contradictory pressures of the need for flexibility versus the need for security/stability of earnings. This was extended into the public sector in 1988 whereby variable payments could be made to Civil Servants depending on the performance in the economy. Additionally, the Flexible Wage System sets a guideline maximum of 20 per cent for the variable component of reward.

In the *UK*, the 1994 White Paper, Continuity and Change, proposed an extension to existing delegated pay and grading arrangements in order to establish a clear link between pay and performance. By 1996, responsibility for all staff below senior levels was passed to individual departments and agencies. All pay increases are now made through performance-related pay systems.

Other useful material (current as of 1996)

From Problem to Solution: Commonwealth Strategies for Reform. Managing the Public Service. Strategies for Improvement Series: No. 1. Commonwealth Secretariat, 1995 (ComSec)

The Development of the Senior Executive Service: Performance-Based Pay. Senate Standing Committee on Finance and Public Administration. Australian Government Publishing Service, Canberra, May 1990 (AUS)

Enterprise Bargaining in the New South Wales Public Sector. Guidelines for Chief Executive Officers. April 1993. NSW Department of Industrial Relations, Employment, Training and Further Education (AUS)

The Manager's Deskbook. Treasury Board of Canada, Third Edition (CAN)

Treasury Board Manual. Human Resources Volume, Chapters 1-6 (CAN)

Public Service 2000: The Renewal of the Public Service of Canada. The Government of Canada, 1990 (CAN)

Improvements and Development in the Public Service 1992, Chapter 9, pp 461-464 (MAL)

Development Administration Circular No. 3, 1991 entitled "Public Service Innovation Awards", 1 April 1991 (MAL)

Development Administration Circular No. 2, 1993 entitled "Guidelines for the Award of the Public Service Excellent Service Awards", 27 January 1991 (MAL)

1.3.5 Developing a public service code of conduct

A *public service code of conduct* provides guidance on required behaviour within the service and prescribes required standards of integrity and professional conduct. Such codes relate directly to conditions of employment and legally enforceable regulations.

They differ from codes of ethics, found in many professional organisations, which have an emphasis on self-regulation rather than externally imposed rules of behaviour.

The context for change

At a time of rapid change, when organisational goals are increasingly emphasised and flexibility of process encouraged, codes of conduct are assuming a particular significance. Corruption and disloyalty have always been present to some degree within the public service, but the increasing emphasis on flexibility and entreprenuerism may need some balancing with a clear statement of appropriate conduct.

There is increasing recognition that:

- codes of conduct should be dynamic and not static, reflecting the changing environment and circumstances in which public services work; and

- they should focus on the positive as well as the more negative aspects of conduct, on values and ideals of service which public officers can aspire to, as well as on the bottom line of acceptable conduct, and on discipline and penalties for transgression.

The public services of many Commonwealth countries have recently revised or re-written their codes of conduct, or are in the process of doing so, in order to:

- provide a reference point to which all stakeholders and other interested parties can turn;

- offer assurances to the public that the public service is subject to specified standards;

- provide Civil Servants with clear statements of the standards of behaviour below which they are not expected to fail;

- maintain safeguards within the service at a time of increasing devolution and commercialisation;

- inculcate a sense of discipline, responsibility and integrity in public servants;

- form the basis for effective human resource and management development within the service; and

- provide support for heads of departments in the management of their department, and in their responsibility for the development of their staff.

Reasons for caution

A code of conduct may be necessary, but not sufficient, as a mechanism for maintaining professional standards. One single code cannot cover all aspects of conduct for all groups within the service, and there are a number of cautions to be considered:

- Codes of conduct should not be regarded as "being written in stone". Although some aspects will remain permanent and universal, others will need to be reviewed and amended to meet changing circumstances and relationships.

- Codes of conduct should avoid focusing excessively on negative aspects of behaviour. A clear framework of disciplinary rules and regulations, with appropriate sanctions is important, but does not of itself inculcate positive values.

- A code of conduct must be seen to apply to all levels of the public service.

- A code of conduct for the core public service may require bolstering from consistent and compatible codes of conduct for Ministers and elected representatives, on the one hand, and parastatals, boards and other organisations, on the other.

Achieving change

Recent revisions to codes of conduct for the public service in Commonwealth countries show a concern to develop codes which cover the process of appointment to the service, and the accountability of a public servant while in office, and immediately following dismissal, resignation, or retirement.

Accountability is a very broad term encompassing the duty of a public servant to manage public funds properly, and to discharge duties effectively, in response to government priorities and national needs.

In relation both to the process of appointment and to the subsequent accountability of appointed public servants, codes of conduct generally refer to the need for political neutrality, the duty of public servants to make their best efforts on behalf of the service, and the necessity of avoiding bringing the government or the public service, into disrepute.

More than any other instrument of the public service, codes of conduct are specific to the setting and to the time at which they are introduced. Developing or revising a code of conduct requires three broad policy decisions:

- The legislative or regulatory framework for the code.
    - How is it to be enforced?
    - Is it to be voluntary, enshrined in public service regulations, or placed on a statutory basis?
- The impact on conduct in the public service of political pressures, and of standards of conduct and discipline in other public sector bodies.
    - Is there a need for a code of conduct for Ministers?
    - How should conduct be reviewed in parastatals, boards and other organisations?
- The breadth of the public service code of conduct.

In this latter area the policy decision might be that the code should cover any or all of the areas given in the table overleaf.

Issues which might be covered	Appointments to the service	Accountability in the service
Neutrality	Example: strict emphasis on skills for the job.	Examples: avoidance of political activity and not allowing a perception of political influence; compliance with existing laws; the need to alert senior staff to undue pressure (whistle-blowing).
Best efforts	Examples: need to achieve a representative workforce through recruitment efforts; need to declare any personal interest.	Examples: management of public funds and use of government resources, including vehicles; a concern for service to the public at all times; provision of sound advice to Ministers regardless of personal political affiliations.
Avoiding disrepute	Example: no direct or indirect incentives to appoint unfairly.	Examples: avoidance of negligence/irresponsibility; appropriate dress; confidentiality of government business

Examples of change

The *Malaysian* Government undertook a comprehensive review of the codes of conduct and discipline for Civil Servants in 1991.

A revised Code of Conduct is being developed for the Public Service of *Mauritius* covering: the values and principles of the Civil Service; the obligations of public servants to Government; the need for political neutrality; the importance of service to the public; the need for leadership; the avoidance of conflicts of interest; avoiding bringing the Government into disrepute; the use of Government resources; and the relationships with colleagues.

The *Kenyan* Government has recently revised its Code of Regulations for Civil Servants and is currently working on a new Code of Ethics.

In the *UK*, the Nolan Committee has emphasised the need for a strong code of conduct for Civil Servants compatible with the Code for Ministers.

In *Malta*, on 31 October 1994, a Code of Conduct was released by the Prime Minister replacing previous instructions in the Staff Management Guidelines (ESTACODE).

Other useful material (current as of 1996)

The Twelve Pillars: Values, Norms and Ethics in the Public Service. Government of Malaysia, Kuala Lumpur, 1992 (MAL)

Martin, J. Public Service and the Public Servant. New Zealand State Services Commission, Auckland, 1991 (NZ)

The Civil Service Management Code. Standards of Public Life. Report of the Nolan Committee. HMSO, London, 1995 (UK)

1.4 Managing Workforce Reduction and Exit

1.4.1 Utilising contractual employment

Contractual employment generally refers to employment status which is not full-time, permanent and pensionable, even if it does not involve a specific contract.

Traditionally the vast majority of public service employees have been on permanent and pensionable terms.

The current trend in the public service is towards more flexible working arrangements for at least a substantial minority of employees. This stems partly from the pressure on the public service to develop staffing patterns which can be changed rapidly in response to changing needs. It is also driven by the increasing demand from employees for employment arrangements which fit more comfortably with fast-changing lifestyles.

The context for change

This trend towards employment flexibility represents a response to the needs of both employers and employees.

On the side of public service employers, there is a general need to reduce costs and to downsize the workforce. Flexible contractual arrangements can make savings while avoiding or reducing the need for stark choices between full-time, permanent employment and redundancies.

At the same time, flexible employment arrangements may be more acceptable to some people who do not want to commit themselves to full-time or continuous employment, such as women with young families.

The main forms of variation from full-time, permanent terms of employment are as follows:

Fixed-term contracts. These are made for a specific project or period of time, with defined start and expiry dates. They may be used where the task has limited duration, where there is a short-term need to employ staff for a limited period, or where a programme or unit is being terminated. There is a major movement towards fixed-term contracts for senior staff. Fixed-term contracts may also be used to employ non-nationals or others who for various reasons do not qualify for permanent employment within the public service.

Rolling contracts. These are also for a fixed term, but are "rolled-on" annually for two or three years, and thus offer somewhat longer-term security for the employee. Again, rolling contracts are being increasingly applied to higher-level appointments instead of the traditional full-time, permanent terms.

Part-time employment. These employees are those working less than the standard weekly hours of the grade concerned. Part-time employment is increasing in many public service organisations, offering potential advantage to both employer and employee. Part-time employment may be permanent or temporary. It may also apply to the job, or to the person (e.g. an employee may occupy a part-time post temporarily without sacrificing rights to full-time employment).

Job sharing. This is an example of part-time working where two people share one full-time job, normally by each working one-half of each week.

Seasonal~temporal/casual/standby. These combine elements of both fixed-term and part-time appointments, but are usually for a shorter period. They may be used to cover unexpected increases in workloads, maternity or sick leave, seasonal or recurring increases in workloads.

Consultancy contracts. When specific consultancy services are contracted out, the persons undertaking such services for a government department or other public service organisation are not, and do not become, public service employees.

Reasons for caution

The increase in contractual employment arouses resistance from interest groups and staff associations. Concerns expressed are:

- "flexibility" is a euphemism for reducing job security, threatening full-time jobs and lowering conditions of employment;
- part-time staff are vulnerable to management pressure to produce the same work in less time;
- women tend to be further discriminated against and segregated into a limited range of poorly-paid and low-skilled jobs; and
- contract work increases management control over the work process and the workers.

Failure to demonstrate that contractual employment is in response to employee demand as well as a managerial preference will exacerbate these concerns.

Public service organisations require a staff profile which balances continuity and new blood. Personnel policies that involve too frequent transfer of senior and other key staff can lead to loss of institutional memory and a lessening of institutional loyalty.

Achieving change

In moving towards greater flexibility in employment arrangements, safeguards must be in place to ensure continuity in the workplace and to protect the reasonable career aspirations of employees. Commonwealth experience points to four key questions:

- More flexible and more diverse working arrangements will make supervisory control more complex. – *Has an appropriate performance management system been developed?*
- If staff needs for alternative working patterns are to be balanced against the need for continuity in the workplace, a planning framework for identifying numbers and types of staff needed in the future must be in place. – *Has an appropriate human resource information system been installed?*
- Where the numbers of part-time workers are to be increased, this could have the effect of marginalising those staff. – *Are mechanisms in place for protecting the career aspirations of employees who are not full-time and permanent?*
- To balance employees' and managers' needs. – *Has a distinction been made between position-based and person-specific arrangements for non-full-time and permanent working?*

Negotiations with trade unions and staff associations will precede amendments to public service legislation and orders, and must build on these four strategic areas.

Examples of change

In the *Australian* Public Service, the main area of improved flexibility in working arrangements over the past ten years has been in permanent part-time work.

The *Canadian* Government has recently issued a booklet entitled Flexibility in the Workplace to all departments, encouraging managers to approve employee requests for varied employment arrangements.

The *Malaysian* Public Services Department is emphasising flexibility in new appointments.

In the *UK*, the Mueller Report in the late 1980s recommended more flexibility in the Civil Service following the example of the private sector. By 1993, over 30,000 Civil Servants were working part-time, and flexible arrangements varied from working for part of the year to fixed-term appointments, and working from home.

Other useful material (current as of 1996)

The Australian Public Service Reformed. Government of Australia, Canberra, 1992 (AUS)

Flexibility in the Workplace. Treasury Board of Canada, Ottawa, 1993 (CAN)

Treasury Board Manual. Human Resources volume, Chapters 1 & 2. Ottawa (CAN)

New Zealand Public Sector Reform. State Services Commission. Wellington. 1993 (NZ)

Changing the Public Service Culture: A Radical Approach. State Services Commission, Wellington, 1991 (NZ)

Made to Measure: Patterns of Work in the Civil Service. HM Treasury, London (UK)

1.4.2 Managing redundancy exercises

Redundancy implies that an area of activity is no longer necessary or affordable within the public service. Where dismissal presupposes that the activity is required but the individual is not, redundancy emphasises that it is the particular activity which is no longer required within the public service.

Typically, redundancies arise when cost reductions are required or when efficiency improvements have been achieved.

Managing redundancy exercises requires a twin strategy: first, a targeting strategy for identifying those activities which should be ceased; and second, a strategy for retrenching an equivalent number of employees.

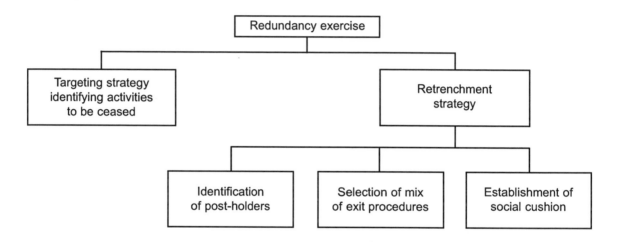

The context for change

The scale of public service employment in many Commonwealth countries expanded massively throughout the 1980s. A lack of comprehensive human resource planning and limited commitment to retrenchment policies have seen the effectiveness and role of traditional government bureaucracies come under scrutiny. Several pressures have had a significant impact on the size, structure and cost-effectiveness of operations:

- deregulation and transformation of statutory authorities to corporate or agency status;

- improvements by outside contractors with innovative methods of service delivery and raised performance standards;

- a culture of realism in a period of national economic difficulties, resulting in zero growth strategies, financial capping and public sector salary cuts;

- high public sector deficits, economic reforms and crises triggered by falling commodity prices and national disasters; and

- conditional funding from donor countries, the World Bank and the International Monetary Fund necessitating public service restructuring.

Management of public service redundancies has become a pressing issue across the Commonwealth.

Reasons for caution

Four principal risks can be identified in redundancy programmes.

First, and most self-evidently, the political risks are significant. Ironically, these risks are highest in situations where the public service is largest, as it is in these situations that public service pay, however inadequate, supports the living standards of the largest proportion of the electorate.

Second, at a technical level, the varied experience of redundancy programmes across the Commonwealth suggests that severance arrangements are likely to be most attractive to the most employable public servants as they have better prospects for alternative employment. Redundancy programmes can result in a loss of the best talent.

Third, the cost of redundancy programmes can outweigh the savings within a given budget period. In a situation where donor funds or credit may be unavailable for retrenchment, the short-term costs may make it impossible to achieve the long-term benefits.

For example, in one Commonwealth country, initial cost projections for a three-year programme came to more than six times the savings over the same three-year period. The total payback period would be about ten years. Statutory benefits amounted to 45 per cent of the costs, whilst 55 per cent of the costs related to ex-gratia payments.

Finally, there are the risks associated with sustainability. Unless payroll and human resource information systems are tightly and consistently limited to the redundancy policy, experience has indicated that major redundancy programmes can be followed by significant re-employment of retrenchees.

Achieving change

Ultimately, any redundancy programme requires two inter-related strategies as described above. Typically, targeting strategies entails:

- a review of the goals, objectives, functions, and structures of existing Ministries, departments, and units with a view to rationalising public service structures in the light of budget realities and plausible efficiency gains;

- the identification of areas of overlap and duplication of functions;

- an assessment of public service activities which could more efficiently be performed by private and NGO sector organisations;

- a review of personnel management procedures and regulations with a view to reducing the numbers of public servants employed in managing the systems and regulatory framework; and

- staff audits to ascertain whether the numbers and levels of staff employed correspond to the authorised establishment.

The related retrenchment strategies have three components: the identification of post-holders for retrenchment; the selection of the mix of exit procedures; and the establishment of social cushions for retrenchees.

The identification of post-holders for retrenchment requires a tactical and political assessment of the feasibility of introducing competence-testing, an approach much discussed but with relatively little track record of success.

In selecting exit procedures, redundancy management programmes are in essence drawing from five approaches:

- voluntary retirement, with a financial package which may be tax-free and pensionable;

- early retirement, on enhanced terms for public servants who are within a few years of retiring;

- mandatory retirement, although noting that attempts to change previously agreed retirement dates have been successfully challenged in many Commonwealth countries;

- involuntary retrenchment, noting the risk of partiality in the identification of target employees; and

- natural wastage resulting from a recruitment freeze.

Redeployment programmes must accompany any mix of exit procedures selected. Retrenchment will not be even across the service and procedures for encouraging the lateral movement of employees must be in place.

In establishing social cushions for retrenchees, again there are relatively few examples of successful government intervention. The options include:

- resettlement assistance through the distribution of land;

- cash payments;

- access to credit at below market rates; and

- entrepreneurship training and re-skilling.

It is the twin strategies of targeting and retrenchment which together must avoid the four principal risks described earlier. However, these strategies must be underpinned by a clear and sustained determination to avoid the need for further major redundancy programmes in the future. The pace of change in the public service is such that stability cannot be expected, and the possibility of future flexibility must be structured into all personnel management developments. Delegation in recruitment responsibilities, the changing role of service commissions, and the increasing emphasis on contractual employment must all be harnessed to ensure that staffing costs can be adjusted at the same accelerating pace as changing public service responsibilities.

Examples of change

Cutback management and retrenchment has become a feature of public service life in most Commonwealth countries.

In *Australia*, commercialisation policies, transfer of functions from within the Department of Defence to Australian defence industries, modernisation of the Civil Aviation Authority, and office automation programmes in administrative departments and taxation offices, have led to a lower requirement for labour. Australian public sector employment fell by 6 per cent from 1986 to 1991, with a reduction of 14,562 staff.

The *UK* reduced the number of Civil Service staff by 22 per cent from 1979 to 1989, revising its code of practice in September 1991 by devolving more responsibility and freedom of action to departments, which negotiate their own redundancy agreements and implementations under the guidance of central policy from HM Treasury. The share of public spending taken up by organisational running costs was expected to fall from 8.9 per cent in 1992/93 to 8.0 per cent in 1995/6.

The *Zimbabwe* Civil Service reduced employment by 26,OOO in 1994/95 as part of a phased 25 per cent reduction. A study is being undertaken to assist the formulation and design of the redundancy strategy.

Similar programmes and review processes have been introduced in *Tanzania* (15 per cent reduction), and *Zambia* (where the World Bank and IMF have linked structural funds to a 25 per cent reduction in head count over five years). Compulsory redundancies are being minimised. For example, phased reductions of 16,000 a year for three years in Kenya are expected to be achieved through 6,000 voluntary leavers and 10,000 volunteers taking early retirement.

Other useful material (current as of 1996)

Administrative and Managerial Reform in Government: A Commonwealth Portfolio of Current Good Practice. Proceedings of a Pan-Commonwealth Working Group Meeting held in Kuala Lumpur, Malaysia, 19-22 April 1993. Commonwealth Secretariat, 1993 (ComSec)

From Problem to Solution: Commonwealth Strategies for Reform. Managing the Public Service. Strategies for Improvement Series: No. 1. Commonwealth Secretariat, 1995 (ComSec)

1.5 Capacity Building and Management Development Institutes in the Context of Public Sector Reforms

Public sector reforms have been carried out in most Commonwealth countries. While the nature and type of reforms have varied from one country to another, they have been determined by both external and internal factors. Some reforms have been radical and fundamental while others have been largely incremental, resulting in changes in the structure and functions of the state. The reform process appears to have been facilitated and accelerated by Management Development Institutions or national public administration training institutes. These organisations have themselves undergone reforms based on a series of evaluative questions including:

- Who do they seek to influence (politicians or public servants) and are they effective in reaching intended audiences?

- Do these institutes have potential competitors when seeking to influence public managers and the public?

- What capacity do these institutes have in providing the required services?

- Do they need to reform themselves before participating in the public service reform process? What skills do they require?

- Have training needs been identified and if so, has the curriculum changed to suit the changing environment? and;

- How can management development institutes be strengthened in their role of facilitating the public administration reform process?

These questions and more, are based on the assumptions that:

- People can be made more effective as managers in the reform process if they develop knowledge, skills and attitudes;

- Knowledge and skills can be developed through training programmes;

- Attitudes including the value of other people, the value of providing service to clients of the highest possible standard, motivation, commitment, integrity, cultural and gender sensitivity are important in developing good managers;

- The training institutes must also go through a change process with a very strong client orientation ensuring that provision is demand driven rather than dominated by the interests of the training staff; and;

- Given the appropriate human and financial resources and the right environment, management institutes can deliver their services effectively and efficiently.

Background

Management Development Institutes were established in most of the Commonwealth countries soon after independence. Their role was to provide training, consultancy and research services to governments. The main target group and recipients of their services were top level, senior and middle managers within the bureaucracy. In addition to building capacity for the public sector, they were also expected to serve as think tanks through their research into public policy formulation and policy reforms.

In the developed Commonwealth countries, public administration was centred on the University. Traditionally, universities have been active in the pre-career training of public managers, primarily at the graduate level. Undergraduate training in public administration has usually been offered as part of an undergraduate political science programme. The set of undergraduate courses in public administration is rarely thorough enough to be complete preparation for a career in public management. In addition private sector and non-government organisation institutions have provided executive development programmes which public managers have attended.

The mandates for establishing management training institutions and for training top and senior managers in the public sector (Civil Service, local government and public enterprises) were fairly similar in essence. They were formulated on the same basis and as a result, the structures and objectives of these institutes bore the same characteristics. Some of these organisations were funded directly by governments and others were supposed to be autonomous and self-financing. Public sector reform in many Commonwealth countries, however, introduced pressures for these organisations to become increasingly self-sustainable. These pressures were reinforced by some of the following weaknesses of management institutes identified after they were formally established:

- Training tended to be treated as a discrete event rather than an ongoing, integral part of human resource management and development;

- The training function was seldom regarded by managers as a matter for their concern;

- Training policies were non-existent, but where they did exist, they often bore little relation to wider development policies or tended not to be implemented;

- Training needs were seldom assessed accurately or tended not to be acted on; and

- The design of training programmes and curricula too often ignored both policy and public sector needs and relied heavily on borrowed models, which were not adapted to the local conditions and environment.

The context for change

Because of bureaucratic procedures and practices, hierarchical reporting structures, the deterioration of infrastructure facilities, underfunding, understaffing and being underrated, the original image and importance of the Institute declined tremendously. Consequently, institutes were unable to provide the required services or to function adequately. The pressures for change were in the governance, objectives, methods of training and more importantly on customised delivery of services.

An evaluation of the role of the institutes revealed that, if their performance was to improve, they had to extricate themselves from bureaucratic procedures and re-examine their structures, the coordinating relationship and, above all, the control by parent or responsible Ministry of public service, personnel or human resources. Civil Service structures inherited from the colonial administration had many attributes that rendered the institutes unsuitable for the challenges of modern management. For instance, Civil Service posts were filled by administrators without adequate professional qualifications, promotions were excessively dependent on seniority rather than merit with negative implications for morale and the efficiency of the staff.

Review of the performance of Management Development Institutes

The critical review of most institutes, particularly in developing countries, bore the following criticisms and shortcomings:

- They were not focusing their curriculum and its delivery on the real needs of the client or consumer. Such needs were changing in line with the global and environmental changes taking place in society;

- Human resource management techniques were not moving away from mechanistic structures since human resource policies had become aligned with organisational strategy. Their approach was therefore, not client-centred;

- They remained hierarchical in structure, even in situations which required lean and flat organisations capable of delivering services to clients efficiently and effectively;

- Their organizational culture was pyramidal with the chief executive at the apex and staff along the base;

- While the clients had changed, the institutes had not changed fundamentally; and

- Consequently, the needs of the clients were not adequately served and criticisms were publicly expressed by the clientele.

The need for change in the status, structure and direction of the institutes was facilitated by the nature and type of Civil Service reform. In response to the challenges facing the public sector needs, the institute had to change their practices and focus.

The degeneration of Management Development Institutes

The institutes in developing countries were gradually pushed from the centre of advice and expertise to the periphery of the administration. They were no longer consulted before governments made policy decisions and were consequently accorded low status, inadequate funding and insufficiently skilled personnel to provide the required services. As a result, the institutes were no longer capable of offering the technical advice and services expected of them and were effectively marginalised by the system. Their training and research functions were referred to outside agencies to which governments paid heavily for the services that could have been provided by the institutes.

The following are some of the contradictory factors which lead to the decline of Management Development Institutes being involved in the policy reform process:

- Limited budgetary allocation by governments making it impossible to conduct research, offer best training services, attract qualified, competent personnel and provide facilities and infrastructure for executive training;

- Lack of a systematic approach to human resources development and an absence of a well co-ordinated and defined training policy for senior managers in policy development and management;

- Absence of institutional linkages for co-ordination and co-operation with the institutes became evidence of a poor management development policy and a lack of necessary leadership and guidance which sometimes resulted in the design of inappropriate curricula;

- Lack of appreciation of the value of training and development and its contribution to improved performance and policy management. This has resulted in the emergence of misplaced and negative attitudes towards management training, especially among the professional and technical personnel who often regard themselves as above training;

- Management development was, in the main, offered by the donor agencies often abroad or in the region by institutions, which often had little knowledge of local needs and social environment;

- Poor remuneration and conditions of service of staff made it difficult to attract and retain suitably qualified personnel, while the institutes' close links with the government denied them the necessary autonomy and flexibility needed for independent decision making in the recruitment, appointment and promotion of staff;

- Because of limited funding, lack of attraction of qualified and competent staff, whatever little training offered by the institutes became ineffective and insignificant. The impact of training on personnel was not effective, noticeable, or formally recognised as an important tool in improving the performance of human resources, particularly in the changing environment in which the public service was being reformed; and

- The low morale, poor remuneration, lack of incentives, absenteeism, poor promotion opportunities and fear of becoming redundant, which prevailed in the public service, also existed in the Management Development Institutes which were still part of the Civil Service. The institutes were therefore, bedeviled by the very same negative factors prevailing in the public service.

The paradox of marginalisation

The privatisation of certain public enterprises and the related commercialisation of agencies of government resulted not only in an increase in competition to provide services to government but also made it possible for Ministries to select training services from outside government institutions. Because of the deteriorating competitiveness in the institutes, they could not compete favourably with the already established institutions in the private sector. Government could now purchase services anywhere and, in most cases, preferred the more modernised, customer friendly, private sector training institutions which tended to design their training to suit the needs of the customer.

In some instances, when the government needed training services urgently but did not have adequate funds, it would expect the institutes to provide such services since they were government owned institutions. In equally worse situations, governments delayed making payments for services rendered by the institutes. Some of the institutes complained of non-payment by governments because Ministries exhausted their budgets before the end of the financial year.

Delay in payment or non-payment for services already rendered by the institutes affects their survival and incapacitates the delivery of services. They cannot compete favourably with other training institutions if financial resources are not available. One of the indirect and unintended consequences of these situations is that an institute is forced to provide services to clients who can pay promptly. In such instances, the institutes would be more than likely to offer training services to the private sector or non-government organisations who can pay on service delivered.

Attempts to transform the institutes in order to suit the changing environment and client needs is, therefore, paradoxical. The paradox lies in deciding whether to offer training services to government knowing full well that the government may or may not pay for the services rendered. Such decisions are made in the circumstances in which the grant from the government is no longer made available since the institute is supposed to be autonomous and self financing. The other side of the paradox is whether the institute should concentrate on those clients who can pay for services rendered even if they are in the private sector which had not been covered in the original intention of establishing the management institute. This transitional process is paradoxical.

The public service, as a learning organization, will require a culture characterised by:

- Commitment to continuous learning and turning individual learning into organisational expertise;

- Co-ordinating the results of studies, giving insights into best practice and disseminating results;

- Rewarding the process of learning; and

- Adding to and keeping up to date the intellectual capital available through research and study.

This is the environment and vision of the new public administration, which must inform training and development initiatives. One approach to translating this environment and vision into a training framework is through the development of competency-based human resource management.

Using competency-based human resource development approaches

Many public services have begun to use competency-based human resource management approaches. This competency approach facilitates the introduction of more effective, valid and useful criteria for recruitment, succession management and personnel and career planning for managers. It, therefore, provides a basis on which training and development programmes can be developed and instituted. The competency approach focuses on the content of training.

The following competencies seem critical given the environmental challenges outlined above:

- Building and sustaining relationships;
- Commitment to achievement;
- Effective communication;
- Honesty and integrity;
- Intellectual capability;
- Management transformation;
- Managing in the political cultural context; and
- Strategic leadership.

Towards curriculum and programme development

Curricula and programmes must facilitate the development of managers, capable of leading public service organisations which:

- focus on outcomes with an emphasis on people's needs and their convenience rather than administrative processes and structures, giving effective service to the public;
- move beyond efficiency in silos to high quality, outcome-focused strategic thinking. This must involve anticipating problems, networking and partnership;
- focus on service delivery partnerships with other parts of the Civil Service, using the power of information technology (IT). The training and development agenda would therefore, need to include the following elements:
    - the management of effective service delivery to the public;
    - the development of quality policy advice;
    - high quality, outcome-oriented strategic thinking;
    - effectiveness in communication, even with the media;
    - the effective handling of global dimensions to policy making;
    - management skills;
    - financial management and assessment of value for money;
    - leadership skills;
    - mentoring and coaching skills;
    - diversity management; and
    - ethics, values and principles of the public sector.

Examples

- The *Canadian* Public Service has developed a Management Trainee's Programme targeted at new managers;

- In *India*, there is a particular focus on the Indian Administrative Service, which is a group of 6,000 career officers who hold the most senior appointed positions in district, state and national government;

- Much of *Singapore* training for the senior public service focuses on preparing for the future. This concentrates on three themes: welcoming change, anticipating change and implementing change; and

- *Nigeria*, *Botswana*, and *Zambia* have developed programmes for senior and top executives.

- The *Canadian* Centre for Management Development (CCMD), the *UK* Civil Service College, *Eastern and Southern African* Institute (ESAMI), *Malaysian* National Institute of Public Administration (INTAN) have introduced corporate leadership programmes which have the following modules: leadership renewal, coaching, service quality, coordinated policy development and continuous learning.

Training and development methodologies

Public services are now utilising a range of approaches to ensure the effective delivery of training and development. Some of the methodologies used in the public service are: job assignments, mentoring and coaching. Some countries are also using distance learning innovations and technologies.

Training policy

The Management Development Institute's work can be programmed more effectively if a training policy exists. Training policies that are officially recognised, carry authority, are understood and implemented are rare. A well-formulated training policy can be invaluable to both managers and trainers concerned with the development and training of personnel. A training policy may cover the nation as a whole or the public service. National training policies are government's declared objectives and commitment to human resource development involving training. In broad terms it covers such issues as the nature of government's commitment to human resource development and training; how it is to be organised and managed; priorities in terms of content areas, levels or approaches; and how the organisation designated to deliver training will be structured and function.

The training that is offered by management institutes is generally based on a training needs analysis. Training needs analysis is a process encompassing the three stages of:

1. Identifying the range and extent of the training needs of the public sector;

2. Specifying those training needs very precisely; and

3. Analyzing how best the training needs might be met.

The third stage can be further subdivided into two parts:

1. Identifying the need for improvement in performance or addition to the competencies of the organisation's staff; and

2. Identifying which of these needs require a training intervention.

The needs that require training can be identified through the use of five main tools or windows that help to look into the business needs of the organisation and these are:

1. Human resource planning;

2. Succession planning;

3. Critical incidents;

4. Management information systems; and

5. Performance appraisal systems.

Training needs analysis can be looked at three different levels at which training needs are assessed. The levels can either be used to indicate the extent of the training or as ways to classify methods for identifying training needs. The most common structure of levels is as follows:

1. The organisational level – identifying training needs which affect the whole organisation e.g. orientation/induction training or training aimed at introducing cultural change across the organisation,;

2. The occupational group level – identifying training needs which affect particular occupations or groups e.g. training in new accounting procedures for finance staff or training for new managers; and

3. The individual level – identifying the training needs of individuals e.g. a particular member of staff requiring time management, or the skills to operate a new piece of machinery.

A distinction is sometimes used in finding out whether training is for present or for future needs. For example:

• Present needs are seen to relate to current objectives, for example training in competencies required for a current job; and

• Future needs relate to long term objectives e.g. training for some future jobs to deal with some future planned change of direction for the business or longer term change in the environment.

This distinction has its relevance in helping to plan the timing of training.

Reasons for caution

In some countries, Management Development Institutes have been able to cope with radical changes in society without going through a crisis of transformation. This is particularly prevalent in countries in which changes have been largely determined by internal factors. However, where external factors such as donor driven reforms have contributed to structural bureaucratic changes, the pace of response has been slow and in some cases has been met with resistance.

What is discussed here is a general observation of the changes with the institutes and does not necessarily apply to all Commonwealth countries.

The autonomy sought by Management Development Institutes has varied from one country to another. Some institutes were commercialised, such as the Civil Service College in the UK, while others have been privatised, such as the Royal Institute of Public Administration (RIPA) in the UK. This variation in autonomy is closely associated with the political, economic and social environment with in which it operates. The autonomous institutes can now offer services not only to government but also to the private sector and non-government organizations as long as they can pay for the services rendered. Privatisation of management institutes may not necessarily lead to an improvement in the provision of training services as the goal is likely to be affected by the profit motive. Fees may be too high for some Ministries to afford sending managers for training. Equally making the management institutes autonomous may not on its own enable them to improve their delivery of service to the public sector.

Training needs analysis should be treated with caution as not all training needs are identified through rigorous research. Methodologies used in needs analysis also vary with the nature and type of reforms and the availability of funds to conduct the needs analysis. The pace of expected change by society also contributes to lack of training needs analysis or to inadequate investigation of the required needs. In addition, not all training needs analysis stages of investigation are followed. They vary with time, availability of resources, skills etc.

Achieving change

The changes in the Management Development Institutes were achieved through the following processes or approaches:

- Commercialisation: autonomy was granted in the collection and expenditure of revenue. Economic rates are charged to customers with little interference from the parent Ministry. The recruitment, appointment, promotion and transfer of staff from one department to another became the responsibility of the Chief Executive. He or she had the right to hire and fire. The salaries of staff were competitive and not based on the public service scale. Autonomous status bestows upon the management institute the right to offer training services to any client who can pay for the services whether in government or in the private sector. The hierarchical structure also changes to suit the business needs of the institute.

  Objectives for training were clearly defined and appropriate resources and methodology put in place in accordance with the needs of the client. The delivery of service was client focused and varied with the ability to pay commercial rates. Following the commercialisation process, Ministries were free to seek appropriate training from any source whether private or public or based abroad. They were not bound to stick to the services of the institute. Autonomous status implied that the institute was still owned by government and still accountable to it. The board of governors might be appointed by the state but might come from various backgrounds. They were not necessarily Civil Servants.

- Privatisation: the Management Development Institute was completely owned by private individuals or organisations. It offers services to any including the public sector and charges market rates. The conditions of service for staff are in line with private sector organisations.

- Within the public service and the institute, there was a progressive shift from the mostly bureaucratic management model of the past to a learning organisation management model. A learning organisation is characterized by its ability to continually improve performance through new ideas, knowledge and insights. It is continually changing its behaviour to reflect new ideas. The institute, as a think tank, continues to search for and provide new ideas on management and interact with the public service as it delivers the service based on identified needs. The challenge for the institute is to determine how best to assist and guide the transformation without compromising core values of democracy e.g. rule of law, impartiality, integrity, competence, etc. In their new roles the institutes promote learning, learn from experience, value people, integrate learning into management practices, learn from serving people and evaluate process and outcome.

- Structural changes both within the public service and the institute were implemented. Organisations were downsized, had objectives and clearly defined performance targets set and appraisal systems put in place in order to ensure efficient and effective service delivery.

Examples of change

Civil Service College, *UK*, has become a learning organisation in that it has changed its structures, system and focus while continuing with its traditional values of objectivity, equity, impartiality, accountability and selection based on merit.

The Royal Institute of Public Administration (RIPA) in the *UK* has become a for-profit organisation.

The *Canadian* Centre for Management and Development (CCMD) is an autonomous institution while retaining its status and linkages with the Federal government. It has developed quality programmes suitable for top level, senior and middle managers in the Civil Service and directs a related research agenda.

The Management Development Institutes of *Zambia, Zimbabwe, Nigeria, Malawi* etc have been commercialised and become more autonomous.

The National Institute of Public Administration (INTAN) in *Malaysia* is also an autonomous Management Training Institute.

The Center for Management in *Barbados*, which is an autonomous body within the University of West Indies, delivers graduate and executive programmes. It recently launched an MBA for public service managers.

The Institute of Public Administration of *Australia* has advocated for an extension of its interests beyond the public service to encompass all the institutions of public administration, For example, changes should cover accountability, ethical values, probity, policy processes.

Other useful material (2nd edition)

Frances and Roland Bee, Training Needs Analysis and Evaluation. Institute of Personnel and Development, London, 1999

Agere, S., Promoting Good Governance: Principles, Practices and Perspectives. Commonwealth Secretariat, London, 2000

Government of Canada: A public service learning organisation: From Coast to Coast, June 2000

Hickey, S., Continuous Learning. Paper presented at CAPAM Biennial Conference in Malta, April 1996

Agere, S., Strengthening Management Development Institutes in the Public Service Reform. Managing the Public Service: Strategies for Improvement Services No 9, Commonwealth Secretariat, 1999

Draper, G., Teaching, Training and Management Development for Public Services in Agere, S. (ed) Promoting Good Governance: Principles, Practices and Perspectives.
Commonwealth Secretariat, London, 2000

Borins, S., The Role of Universities in Public Administration Education: Innovations and Trends in Management Development. 22nd National Seminar IPAC (ed) Donald Savoie, Autumn 1996 Vol. 3 No 3

Commonwealth Secretariat, Report on Public Service of Barbados: Training Needs Assessment, London 2000

A. Zinyemba and P.Ramaswamy, Report on the Transformation of the National Institute of Public Administration into a semi-autonomous Institution. 1998

Kirkpatrick, C and Mann, P., Knowledge, Training and Development: An Overview in Public Administration and Development. The International Journal of Management Research and Practice (ed) Paul Collins Vol. 19 No 1 Feb 1999

Borins, S Trends in Training Public Managers. A report on a Commonwealth Seminar. International Public Management Journal 2(2) (A) 2000

Ross, M Tanner, The changing role of government in New Zealand. Implications for training and development of public servants. International Review of Administrative Sciences Vol. 64 (1998)

Citizens First 2000. Report on "Have Your Say" A survey of improving government services in Canada. Institute of Public Administration of Canada, 2001

1.6 Top Executive Management Development Programmes

The changes that are taking place within the public service have an impact on the way services are delivered, the method of delivery, style of management and use of resources and technology. Some of the changes are so radical and structural that change agents and change sponsors require new knowledge, techniques, skills, information and resources in order to cope with the level and pace of change. The changes also impose upon public sector managers, bureaucracy and consumers the need for changes in the traditional behaviour patterns of those who deliver the services and those who manage. Consumers also expect a change in top management style as society responds to the internal and external pressures of change.

In response to these pressures and in an attempt to improve the delivery of service, a need has been identified to develop those who manage the service. Over the years within the Commonwealth, public administration institutes or schools of management have developed, organised and conducted several top executive programmes for public service and corporate sector managers. Participants in such programmes have included Ministers, Heads of Civil Services, Permanent Secretaries, Public Service Commissioners, Chief and top executives of public enterprises, Directors and Board Chairmen. The programmes have covered a wide range of topical areas and management issues. Within each area, specific issues of policy and management have been identified for the thorough examination and development of appropriate intervention strategies.

Two important features of the top executive programmes have been, first, the need to consolidate the comprehensive approach to managing organisations through strengthening the linkages between policy, strategy and operations; second, the need to broaden the perspectives of top executives and stimulate their thinking on how best management performance can be improved in their organisations within the framework of a changing environment. Underlying the two features is the continuous need to enhance management skills, build knowledge and to develop requisite attitudes in order to be effective leaders.

The programmes may take several forms such as policy oriented seminars, workshops focusing on specific issues requiring solutions, symposia, conferences and issue-based roundtables. In general the seminars, provide Chief Executives in the pubic sector with the strategic perspectives and functional skills necessary to lead their organisations into the future. The new millennium, for example, brings increasingly complex challenges for organisations, placing greater pressures for performance on CEO's and their organisations. The seminars can introduce participants to many recent innovations in management thinking and practice, and to management tools and frameworks that will enable them to deal with these challenges.

Recent events in Asia, Africa and the Caribbean, ongoing changes in international trading arrangements arising from the World Trade Organisation (WTO) and the ending of the LOME IV Conventions, serve to stay on top of current and potential geopolitical, social and economic changes. In a globally connected world, changes in far-flung countries and in other industries can have a sharp and significant impact on organisations in dispersed Commonwealth countries. The potential for sudden and dramatic changes in the environment prompts a close look at two other themes of reform programmes: the need for senior executives to develop skills in managing change, and the need for knowledge and skills to deal with the political and social aspects of public service management. Both are essential parts of leadership development.

Challenges for leadership

The issue of leadership is a major item on the agendas of both public and private sector organisations in the developing as well as the developed countries of the world. This is being driven in large part by the challenges facing organisations in all sectors in environments that are constantly changing. Some of the forces impacting organisations and creating challenges for leadership are:

- the pace of technological change, specifically information and communication technology;

- globalisation;

- the rising expectations of citizens and consumers in terms of the quality of service and demands for participation in decision making;

- the increasing diversity of society and the growing acceptance of the need for organisations to be more inclusive in their approaches to people;

- more performance focused organisations;

- managing networked organisations under the importance of alliances and partnerships; and

- the need to lead significant transformations in organisations.

One of the major strategic issues facing Commonwealth counties and their leaders is the need to alleviate poverty, which challenges both policy work and the service delivery activities of the public service. There is a growing need for more comprehensive approaches to development. Leaders must move away from the one-dimensional economic approach and this presents new challenges for public service leadership.

The context for change

In the last decade much emphasis, in the change process, has been placed on the need to improve productivity and meet citizens rising expectations of delivery of public services. This means that public sector organisations must innovate in order to deliver services more effectively and efficiently. In response to these changes a number of strategic questions are being asked, such as the following:

- How can public sector bodies further improve productivity while meeting expectations for better services? Are partnerships and contracting good alternatives?

- How can public sector managers and executives respond to the challenge of shifting boundaries and manage the increasingly complex multiple relationships which result from these shifts?

- How can public sector leaders and organisations respond in a holistic way to issues such as social exclusion, the environment and preventing crime?

- How should central government and local governments work with other public and private sector bodies to improve their public services and promote regional economic development?

- How do individuals, pressure groups, communities and others ensure that we become a representative democracy in which new policy developments command general public support?

- How to foster a public service ethos which the public and public service employees can share, in order to achieve social goals and objectives and improve accountability to taxpayers and users of public services?

- How to identify and develop the skills and competencies required by future public service leaders? and

- How to develop effective leadership in the public sector which is sensitive to the environment, focuses on the future, turns vision into action, learns from mistakes and builds support teams?

The pursuit of excellence requires a management style throughout the organisation, which encourages initiative and personal fulfillment. This can be achieved through a high level of training and development for staff and management. Work is changing more rapidly than ever. This is probably most obvious in the public sector, but demands on managers everywhere are changing. Organisations need to constantly develop their people and just keep pace with change. Consequently, human resource development is now a planned and structured process interwoven with an organisation's business strategy because that is seen as essential to its survival. Human resource development also includes self-development, which has two shades of meaning:

- Taking responsibility on oneself to develop one's career.

- Developing the whole self and not just the part of the person that fills the job role.

Some of the principles involved in self-development are as follows:

- Responsibility for learning and development is taken by the learners and not by the trainer or the line managers;

- The focus is on an individual's unique development needs, not the general needs of a work group to which an individual happens to belong;

- The individual is involved in the diagnosis of needs; and

- Involvement generates commitments to personal action.

Training and development programmes are designed to enable individuals, teams, and organisations to become more effective. They are aimed at overcoming deficiencies and maximising performance.

Training and Development Strategy

- Subset of human resource strategy;
- Human resource strategy designed to support corporate strategy;
- Reflects values of the organisation;
- Success dependent upon commitment;
- Needs to be forward-looking/proactive;
- Clear objectives and deliverables;
- Strong plans with tactical flexibility;
- Requires clear analysis, diagnosis and specification;
- Effective measurement processes; and
- Developing leaders for public service.

Methods of development

- Education programmes and training courses;
- Action learning projects;
- Coaching, mentoring, peer relationships, natural learning, self-development and learning contracts; and
- The use of informal management development methods:
  - Job rotation, job-sharing - "sitting by Joe", learning on the job, mentoring, coaching.

Four levels of evaluation

- Reaction: to course/training event;
- Learning: able to transfer extra skills/knowledge to job;
- Behaviour: changes as a result of training impact, seen effectiveness, relation with others; and
- Results: impact on performance of team, department, business, etc.– bottom line.

The learning organisation:

- Encourage people at all levels of the organisation to learn regularly and rigorously from their work;
- Have systems for capturing learning and moving it where is needed; and
- Value learning and continuously able to transform themselves.

Culture as a conscious strategy driven by the organisation

- It provides a sense of identity for employees, increasing commitment, making their work more intrinsically rewarding and making them identify more closely with fellow workers;
- It allows workers to "make sense" of what goes on around them, enabling them to interpret the meaning of different organisational events;
- It helps to reinforce the values of the organisation that is senior management;
- It serves as a control device for management with which to shape employee behaviour;
- It serves to co-ordinate the results of studies, giving insights into best practices and disseminating the results; and
- The process of learning should be rewarded, adding to and keeping up to date the intellectual capital available through research and study.

Achieving change

Significant changes have been observed among the participants of management courses organised by the Civil Service Colleges, Management Development Institutes, etc. In some countries, the performance of Permanent Secretaries on policy development and management has been noticeable while in other countries the impact of training has been negligible. Some Permanent Secretaries and Chief Executives who have been placed on contracts have produced good results in that their objectives were achieved efficiently and were appropriately rewarded. Training and development has also become part of executive contracts in some Commonwealth countries such as Singapore.

The competencies of Permanent Secretaries and Chief Executives have equally shown some improvement as exemplified by the results achieved. These improvements have come about as a result of properly planned curriculum and programme development.

Curriculum and programme development

Curricula and programmes must facilitate managers capable of leading public service organisations which:

- Focus on outcomes with an emphasis on people's needs and their convenience rather than administrative processes and structures, giving effective service to the public;
- Move beyond efficiency "in silos" to high quality, outcome-focused strategic thinking. This must involve anticipating problems, networking and partnership building; and

- Focus on service delivery partnerships with other parts of the Civil Service; using the power of IT and the management of risk.

The training and development agenda for public sector executives would, therefore, need to include the following elements:

- Management of effective service delivery to the public;
- The development of quality policy advice;
- High quality, outcome-oriented strategic thinking;
- Effectiveness in communication;
- Effective handling of global dimensions to policy making; and
- Management skills.

Curriculum and programme development must be firmly embedded in sound strategic human resource management and development frameworks. This framework must include appropriate recruitment and selection, sound performance management and appraisal systems, and career counselling and planning. The framework acknowledges the desirability of identifying "high flyers" and providing fast track mechanisms for their movement to the top of the public service organisations.

Curriculum and programme development must also be results focused and performance oriented. It is also clear that a training methodology is critical. Much adult learning happens on the job. For training to be successful it must be linked closely to work. Ideally, modules should be short but the learning programmes should be continuous. Experimental methodology is critical; coaching and mentoring are important components.

The training which brings about change generally refers to the acquisition of skills, knowledge and information by those who occupy decision-making positions in government. It aims to equip practitioners with the skills to enable them to improve their performance and ultimately, to deliver services to society. Training in these circumstances must be continuous, relevant and responsive to emerging trends and issues. Training is, therefore, regarded as an enabling instrument with which to develop a capacity to grapple with emerging trends, principles and perspectives of management, often drawn from practical experience.

Management development is used here to refer to the upgrading, advancing and improving of the skills and knowledge base of those practitioners who manage human, financial and material resources. Change in management practices and performance is achieved through training and development. To the extent that they enable managers to be efficient and effective, they are critical instruments in strategic planning, management and, more important, in the improvement and delivery of service to the public. The capacity to manage successfully is based on the extent to which knowledge and skill have been acquired and utilised positively and meaningfully.

The focus on top executive programmes is based on the following assumptions related to leadership:

- Good leadership is essential in all organisations if they are to produce high quality goods and services. This feature of management cuts across cultural boundaries;
- Leadership should be transformational. This means that leaders should be able to provide vision and direction for the organisation and that they should be able to energise and inspire other members of the organisation in the pursuit of organisational objectives;
- Leaders should encourage development and change, as opposed to control and maintenance of the status quo; and
- Leadership is necessary and sufficient for promoting effective organisational performance.

96

Examples of change

Top executive programmes have been planned and managed by various organisations throughout the Commonwealth countries. For example:

- *New Zealand* has, through its reforms, substantially altered the nature of public service leadership. Chief Executive Officers are now employed under limited-term performance based on contracts, as are all other senior managers. The focus is now very sharply on performance.

- In the *UK*, the Centre for Management and Policy Studies (CAMPS) was established in June 1999 as an integral part of modernising government agenda. The CAMPS is sited at the heart of government within the Cabinet Office and incorporates the Civil Service College. The CAMPS provides support to government through:

  - policy studies which will be a centre of excellence in research and development;

  - a range of programmes and seminars to support Ministerial and senior Civil Service corporate and professional development;

  - the Civil Service College with its range of programmes on modernisation, managing change and formal skills training; and

  - a programme of peer reviews to support departments in the implementation of the modernisation agenda.

- In the *Caribbean* the Centre for Management Development (CMD) is at the forefront of executive training. Its role is to prepare holistic managers to effectively face and manage the challenges of the business environment in the new millennium. It also offers diploma and advanced degrees for executive managers. The centre has also made significant achievements and continues to contribute to the enhancement of executive and organisational development throughout the Caribbean.

- The Commonwealth Association for Public Administration and Management (CAPAM) is a membership organisation of individuals and organisations interested in the study and practice of public management, and offers short-term courses and seminars for senior public sector executives. These programmes are sometimes held in partnership with the Commonwealth Secretariat and other centres of excellence in Commonwealth countries. The courses generally cover:

  - Overview of public sector reform;

  - Human resource management and development;

  - Organisational change and partnerships;

  - Information systems and standards of service;

  - Financial management and control; and

  - Policy development

  In addition, CAPAM holds national, regional and biennial conferences on current issues in public sector management.

- The *Eastern and Southern African* Management Institute (ESAMI), a premier management development on the African continent, offers short courses for senior and top public sector managers. ESAMI provides executives and managers the opportunities to widen their horizons, improved executive skills and to understand management as a process of balanced judgment;

- The *Canadian* Centre for Management and Development (CCMD) introduced a corporate leadership programme. The programme has five modules namely: leadership renewal; leadership and learning with an emphasis on coaching; service quality; co-ordinated policy development; and continuous learning.

- The National Institute of Public Administration (INTAN) in *Malaysia* offers management courses for top executives. Some of the programmes are held in partnership with the Commonwealth Secretariat, etc.

Other useful material (2nd edition)

Korac-Kakabadze, A, and Korac-Kakabadze, N., Leadership in Government: Study of the Australian Public Service. Ashgate, Aldershot 1998

Agere, S., Promoting Good Governance: Principles, Practices and Perspectives Commonwealth Secretariat, London 2000

Report of Commonwealth Advanced Seminar: Leadership Reform in the Public Service. 4-5 March 1996 Commonwealth Secretariat and State Service Commission of New Zealand, 1996

Brochure: The Centre for Management Development. University of West Indies, Caribbean, 1999

CAPAM in Partnership with the Centre of Public Policy of the University of Birmingham: The New Executive Programme. August 19-26, 2000

Cabinet Office (UK) Centre for Management and Policy Studies. (CAMPS) March 2000

Henley Management College: MBA Programme, Managing People Leadership
ESAMI 1990: Training Programme, Brochure.

The Bi-monthly magazine of the Strategic Planning Society June 1998
Report of a Seminar: Singapore-Commonwealth Advanced Seminar for Chief Executives 29 May- 9 June 2000

Borins, S., Trends I Training Public Managers: International Public Management Journal 2(2A) 2000.

Civil Service College, Brochure (UK) 2000-2001: A Directorate of the Centre for Management and Policy Studies

UK Stationery Office, Modernizing Government, March 1999.

Draper, G. "Developing Leaders for Commonwealth Public Service", Revised February 2002.

2.0 Making Government More Efficient

2.1 Matching the Structure to the Task

2.1.1 Selecting appropriate organisational structures

Organisational structure is the link between the organisation's mission and its actual practices. Organisational structure is the overall shape of the entity – its layers, its spans of control, and its relationships with its funders and customers. Unlike changes to management and work practices, changing organisational structure is not adjusting an existing pattern for a better fit, it is a change of the pattern itself.

Traditionally, the organisational structures of the public service have resembled the steep pyramids considered typical of a large bureaucracy. Established principles concerning the spans of managerial control, the need for vertical reporting lines, and centrally-determined grading structures, have ensured that the number of management levels and the number of managers at those levels, effectively follow a common formula across most of the public service.

Recent developments within public service management have shown that these structures are less immutable than had seemed the case. The public service, it transpires, can be organised within diverse groupings and structures which match the nature of the organisation more closely to the tasks for which it has responsibility.

Delegation of financial and personnel management, contracting out of services, the creation of agencies, privatisation, corporatisation and other moves have demonstrated that there is now a menu of organisational structures from which appropriate forms can be drawn.

The context for change

Reforming the organisational structure of the public service is a key strategy in improving efficiency within government. Restructuring seeks to address three concerns:

- *A concern that policy makers and service providers have become distanced from the public*

  The hierarchical and process-driven nature of government departments can result in lengthy communication channels denying management timely information and inhibiting the implementation of remedial measures.

- *A concern that the public service has become inflexible*

  Traditional public service organisational structures are designed for stability rather than change. The rapid development in public sector working practices and in technological support require equally rapid changes in organisational structure.

- *A concern that the public service has become inefficient*

  Activities once seen as fundamental are sometimes no longer necessary but continue to be undertaken using resources which might be better applied elsewhere.

Reasons for caution

Organisational restructuring has, broadly, been driven by two observations:

- that increased managerial autonomy frees up managers to develop imaginative solutions for business problems; and
- that establishing some degree of private ownership provides the basis for incentives for performance improvements – particularly when it is associated with strong market competition.

The results of applying these concepts to the public service have been remarkable. Previously uniform structures have evolved and diversified into a complex patchwork of organisational forms. Boards, trading enterprises, NGO contractors and one-stop multi-function services have added increasing variety to the public service scene.

A major challenge in that new and more diverse scene is that the boundaries are no longer clear as once they appeared. With the arrival of increasing varieties of operating or executive agencies within government, the traditional lines between the public service and the broader public sector is now harder to trace. More generally, with increasing corporatisation and greater contracting out, the line between the public sector and the private and NGO sectors is similarly more elusive.

The most challenging aspect of this shift concerns accountability. To its critics, the public service is characterised as process-driven, over-concerned with regulatory compliance and insufficiently attentive to results. That preoccupation with process has certainly not rendered it immune to impropriety – but, successful or otherwise, it did represent a coherent attempt to emphasise consistency and to remove any distractions from the ultimate accountability of politicians for the policies they select.

In that increasingly uncertain territory between the public service and the private sector, where the regulatory and process controls have been reduced, it is not yet clear what the new accountability approach should be. It is not always clear that coherent distinctions can be made between public and private interests or between managerial drive towards organisational survival and achieving public policy outcomes. In terms of systems for accountability, it is more clear what the public service is moving away from than where it is headed.

A second and related challenge concerns the attraction of the one-off "big fix" solution to public service shortcomings. Changing organisational structures can, at some considerable human and financial cost, address structural problems. If the problems are more directly related to managerial practices and support systems, or to weak or uncertain ethical frameworks, structural solutions are an expensive method for answering the wrong question.

The key lesson, highlighted in the Commonwealth Initiative for Public Service Reform, Towards a New Public Administration, is that the precise form and structure of the public sector cannot be deduced directly from experiences in other countries. The principles of change are, however, consistent across the Commonwealth. Successful reforms address the principles without accepting unquestioningly the forms and structures developed elsewhere. These principles of change in the public service are considered in Section 3 of this Portfolio.

Achieving change

The six components of reorganisation generally employed within the public service are set out below. They are not mutually exclusive.

(i) *Consolidation*

associated changes:

downsizing – reducing the size of the workforce;

reducing – reducing the size and scope of the organisation;

de-layering – reducing the size of the workforce by increased delegation, increased spans of control, and the removal of management layers;

centralisation – pulling back from decentralised or devolved organisational forms; and

abolition – closing of superfluous functions.

(ii) *Decentralisation*

associated changes:

deconcentration – the geographical relocation of parts of the organisation; and

horizontal restructuring – the creation of locally-based organisational units, each capable of providing a broad range of services.

(iii) *Devolution*

associated changes:

delegation of financial management and/or of personnel management – providing greater autonomy to managers at lower levels, within overall guidelines;

establishment of agencies – general delegation of authorities to cost and profit centres, with flexibility to achieve agreed goals within an agreed framework of accountability; and

establishment of internal markets - designation of cost centres with sufficient overlap of functions to enable budget holders to exercise some choices in "purchasing" from these internal suppliers.

(iv) *Corporatisation*

associated changes:

transparent funding – financial "ring-fencing" to identify all funding inputs, including government subsidies, allowing subsidised and unsubsidised prices to be established for all outputs;

change of legal entity – establishment of an organisation capable of addressing commercial objectives; and

vertical restructuring – the separation of interdependent activities previously undertaken within the organisation.

(v) *Contracting out*

associated changes:

contracting services out – pass responsibility for the provision of a specified level and quality of services to a private or NGO sector organisation;

contracting management out – retain ownership in the public sector for a specified period for a fixed fee or on a profit-sharing basis; and

leasing assets – the leasing of facilities or a brand name owned by the government to a private or NGO sector organisation for a specified period for a fixed fee.

(vi) *Privatisation*

associated changes:

selling unchanged – change of ownership only;

selling as a single entity;

disaggregating and selling – privatise constituent parts; and

selling the core – sell the profitable core following its separation from the less profitable or less strategic activities.

Across the Commonwealth, it is clear that organisational structures for the public service are selected for complex and frequently political reasons. Acknowledging this reality, there is, however, a rational model to which public sector policy makers aspire and which may be followed to a greater or lesser degree:

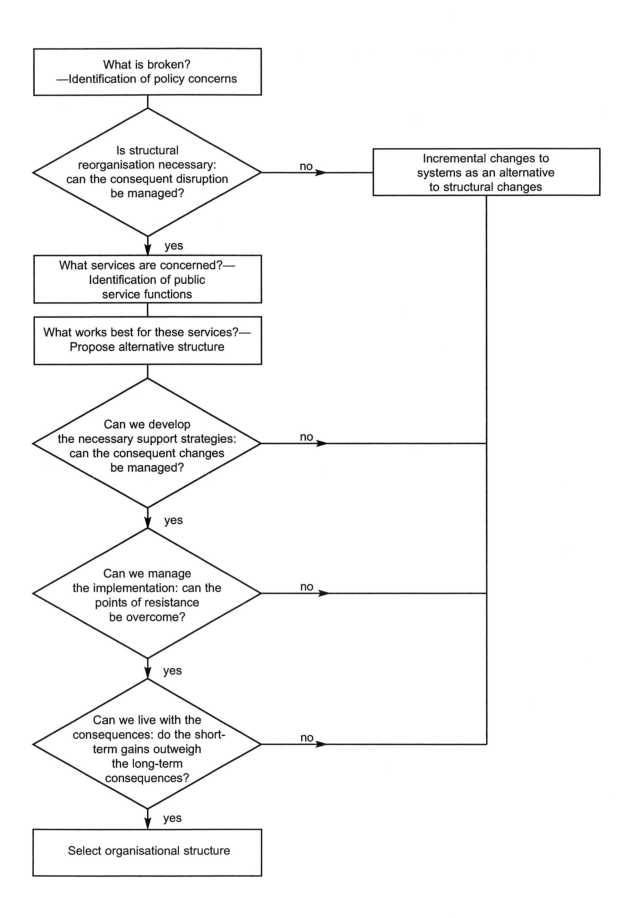

Subsequent entries in the Portfolio consider these questions in more detail in relation to the principal structural choices available to the public service.

Examples of change

In *Kenya*, in the process of structural adjustment programme implementation, the Government is involved mainly in the following areas:

- privatisation of a number of State corporations in order to make them more efficient;
- liberalisation of the economy through price decontrols and food marketing reform;
- law reforms to establish a more democratic society; and
- Civil Service administrative reforms.

In the *UK*, the structure of Government matters are handled by the Office of Public Service and Science and the organisational pattern of Government departments is ultimately the responsibility of the Prime Minister.

Recent examples of structural changes resulting from changes in policy include the creation of the Office of Public Service and Science itself and the Department of Heritage; the absorption of the Department of Energy into the Department of Trade and Industry, and the Department of Employment into the Department for Education. All cases reflect changes in the Government's political priorities.

The Next Steps Initiative, announced in 1988, aims at improving efficiency through the devolution of a number of executive functions of Government onto independent agencies whose Chief Executives are directly responsible to Ministers for their performance.

By February 1994, a total of 91 agencies had been established, together with 31 executive units of HM Customs and Excise, and 33 Executive Offices of the Inland Revenue.

It was expected that by 1996, approximately 75 per cent of the Civil Service would be working along Next Steps lines.

One major structural reform has been the reorganisation of major parts of the National Health Service into independent National Health Trusts responsible for the provision of services.

In *Canada*, the Special Operating Agencies (SOAs) are an important element in the ongoing restructuring and re-engineering of Government, and are intended to promote cost-effective and client-centred services. The SOA concept applies private sector norms in the planning and delivery of services either to the public or to other government departments. In particular, SOAs give greater authority to individual managers and employees.

The first group of SOAs were announced in 1989 and the concept was embraced and extended in the Government White Paper on Civil Service Reform in December 1990.

SOA candidates share five common characteristics. They are:

- discrete units of sufficient size justify special consideration;
- concerned with service delivery (rather than policy formulation);
- amenable to the development of clear performance standards;
- operate under a stable policy framework with a clear ongoing mandate; and
- staffed by managers and employees committed to the SOA approach.

Agencies are established via a Treasury Board decision, after submissions, which are accompanied by a business plan, which includes a performance contract and a framework document containing a mission statement and a definition of the operating relationships.

The improvement in services resulting from SOA status result from:

- clearly-defined operations;
- clear performance goals and strategies for attaining them;
- application of best public and private sector management techniques; and
- continuous monitoring of performance.

Each agency remains accountable to Ministers and Deputy Ministers. However, these assign the full range of authority for the running to a head who has to meet agreed performance targets.

Other useful material (current as of 1996)

What is a Special Operating Agency. Performance. Treasury Board of Canada, 1990 (CAN)

Becoming a Special Operating Agency. Treasury Board of Canada, July 1991 (CAN)

Next Steps Review, 1993. HMSO, London, 1993 (UK)

2.1.2 Determining appropriate size

Discussion of the *appropriate size* of the public service disguises two related questions:

- The scope of government responsibilities undertaken by the public service — how many tasks is the public service attempting to perform?

- The scale of the public service in terms of its staffing levels – how many public servants are employed to undertake those tasks?

The first question gives rise to considerations of what government does well, what it must do even if does not do it well, and where the political risks might lie in attempting to abolish poorly-performed public service functions.

The second question points more directly at productivity and, potentially, at downsizing.

The context for change

The last decade has seen an unparalleled debate concerning the size and role of the public sector. This debate has been powered, in varying measure, by the public disillusionment with the competence of government, changing views on the relationship between the citizen and government, and growing budget pressures.

Globalisation – the growing inability of national borders to restrict the flow of ideas or of capital – underpins every aspect of this debate. Public disillusionment with government has its roots in the over-optimistic assumptions of the 1960's and 1970's concerning the ability of the public sector to drive development by large-scale projects and large-scale spending. But that disillusionment can also be traced to ready comparisons which an increasingly global media offers between standards of living in different regions. The performance of the public sector, previously agreed somewhat fatalistically, has become more open for debate.

Within increasingly global markets, national economic policies are now tested against international yardsticks of competitiveness. The capacity of the public sector to establish the right regulatory frameworks for development, to enforce them, to develop national productivity capacity, to attract capital, and to act itself as a producer, are all "in" questions. Again, globalisation has played its part in challenging the form and function of the public sector.

The debate concerning the role of government has also been strengthened by a remarkably consistent stream of managerial and political ideas which emerged during the 1980's. In sum, these ideas, emerging from different settings, but globally reinforcing each other, emphasised the significance of distinguishing between those who decide what should be done, and those who should do it— between policy makers and implementors, or between purchasers and providers. Combined with a renewed conviction that market competition will improve efficiency, the managerial and organisational consequences for the public sector of these ideas have been vast.

In the 1990's, ideological rigour gave way to more considered evaluation of the newer organisational forms and distribution of functions, but the intensity of the international debate concerning the preferred shape and size of the public sector is undiminished. Tentatively, there is, however, some emerging consensus concerning one particular role of the public sector – that of aligning the need for personal freedoms and democratic accountability with the need to achieve a globally competitive position for the nation.

It is the ability of the public service to deliver the policy-making and regulatory basics that determines the overall capacity of the public sector. If not a *sufficient* condition, a competent public service is certainly a *necessary* condition for a competent public sector. The size of the public service is a fundamental concern in improving its competence.

Reasons for caution

Political neutrality is a key value in the public services of Commonwealth countries. However, that neutral public service operates within a highly-charged political environment and decisions concerning its size are made within that environment. Ultimately, therefore, although guided by rational organisational concerns for efficiency, the determination of an appropriate size for the public service will have a significant political content. Efforts to remove this consideration will prove to be time-consuming and ineffective.

In consequence of this delicate, and occasionally tense, compromise between organisational and political perspectives, the public service has shown itself to be a creature of extremes. With considerable justification, it has been frequently described as bloated, having absorbed excessive labour as a method of reducing unemployment or increasing political influence.

Conversely, however, there is a debate concerning the minimum size and capacity of the service in a few settings where managerial determination to drive down costs has produced what has been described as organisational anorexia.

This represents a concern that by reducing its size and scope unreasonably, the public service is driven by short-term goals at the expense of long-term national development objectives.

Achieving change

Commonwealth experiences indicate that in managing reviews of the public service, Ministry level or sectoral concerns must be balanced against opportunities in the public service for efficiency savings.

The identification of specific opportunities for the abolition or more effective organisation of public service responsibilities is best undertaken at Ministry level. The interrelationship between different activities within the same sector and the practical opportunities for efficiency savings are more readily understood by those who have daily responsibility for ensuring that services are delivered.

However, such operational reviews at Ministry level are likely to stop short of more radical proposals for restructuring or abolition. The proximity to the task, which enables Ministry-level officials to understand the implications of withdrawing service, also contributes to a loyalty to existing systems. External stimuli are necessary and these can be produced in two ways: First, operational reviews can be directed as part of a broader, frequently Cabinet-level, strategic review of services and responsibilities. Second, operational reviews can be stimulated by thematic efficiency programmes, which examine possibilities for cost reductions and service improvements in areas which cut across the public service.

The outcome of operational reviews informs the continuing development of business plans at Ministry level, in which remaining tasks are consolidated and the distinctive strengths of particular Ministries and departments are encouraged.

In sum, the reviews of the size of the public service are focused at Ministry level, but are driven by strategic concerns identified centrally, and by thematic concerns identified by a continuing efficiency programme:

Examples of change

In *Zimbabwe*, the Civil Service Reform Programme was based on the Public Service Review Commission of 1987. At that time the Civil Service had the following characteristics:

* a large and cumbersome service of about 192,000 people;

* a substantially inexperienced cadre operating in a highly centralised environment;

* serious overlap and duplication of functions;

* a lack of transparency, accountability and responsiveness; and

* a high degree of regulation inimical to initiative and innovation.

A major component of the Civil Service Reform Programme is the reduction of the size of Zimbabwe's Civil Service. Since 1992, the Zimbabwe Government, through the Public Service Commission, has adopted various strategies to reduce the size of the Civil Service:

* posts which remained vacant for 12 months were abolished;

* an obligatory reduction was effected by requiring Ministries to reduce posts by a given percentage; and

* a programme of early voluntary retirement was instituted.

By 1994, 12,700 out of a projected 23,000 posts had been abolished. Other concomitant measures which contributed to this development included:

* The reduction in the number of administrative levels in the service to ten grades. This rationalisation not only reduced the number of posts but also contributed to improved efficiency.

* The introduction of a policy of contracting out certain functions which could be better and more profitably performed by the private sector.

* A policy of decentralisation where certain functions and activities were transferred to local authorities with a view to bringing goods and services closer to the consumer. In most cases the functions were transferred without all the staff engaged in them.

In *Malaysia*, a Steering Committee on the Reduction in Size of the Civil Service has been established. Various measures introduced to control the size of the Civil Service include:

* control on the creation of posts with priority given to those which will make a positive contribution to economic development;

* review of vacant posts with abolition of those no longer considered necessary;

- reorganisation of organisational structures to create a flatter, less bureaucratic organisation with fewer administrative levels;
- review of the roles of statutory bodies with a view to reducing duplication and overlap of functions and activities;
- enhancement of the privatisation programme transferring activities away from the public sector to the private sector which can manage them more efficiently; and
- the introduction of new technology, particularly labour saving information technology and management information systems.

In *Kenya*, reforms of managerial practices within the Civil Service focus on five main areas: Civil Service organisation, pay and benefits, staffing levels, personnel management and training.

Other useful material (current as of 1996)

Choices in the Design of Decentralisation. An Overview and Curriculum for central government officials responsible for the reorganisation of administration at the local level, B. C. Smith. Commonwealth Secretariat, 1993 (ComSec)

The Manager's Deskbook. Treasury Board of Canada. Third Edition (CAN)

Improvements and Development in the Public Service, Malaysia. 1990, 1991 and 1992 (MAL)

Operation reviews; PSR Committee Report. Malta (MLT), The Civil Service: Continuity and Change. HMSO (UK), Zimbabwe Public Service Commission Review (ZIM)

2.1.3 Initiating market-testing

Market-testing is a process by which Ministries and departments assess whether the services for which they are responsible can best be delivered in the public or private sectors. Market-testing entails putting an activity out to competitive tender with internal and external bids assessed against the same criteria.

The context for change

There are a number of benefits which can arise from the market-testing process. First, when considering whether to accept an in-house bid or give the work to an outside contractor, the evaluation will look at improvements in the quality of service available from innovative methods of service delivery.

Second, there may be cash savings. It is axiomatic that where an activity is market-tested, and an external bid is successful, it will be because that bid offers a greater overall long-term value for money than the current method of provision. Where an in-house bid succeeds, the process of opening up that sector of public sector activity to competition in itself often creates opportunities for greater effectiveness.

Third, experience suggests that market-testing can lead to raised standards by making greater expectations explicit within contractual arrangements. Greater clarity about standards of service and better monitoring of performance against those standards, regardless of whether the work is retained in-house, is a vital feature of public sector reforms.

Reasons for caution

Market-testing is a demanding exercise placing considerable strain on existing personnel, on relations between management and public service unions, on technical skills and on political sensitivities.

The short-term risks arise under three headings:

- *Communication risks*: inadequate briefing of staff, managers, trade unions and suppliers and insufficiently considered contracts and specifications.

- *Management risks*: unclear objectives and uncertain review systems will undermine the management of a highly-charged process in which staff are being told, in effect, that a private sector organisation might better undertake their tasks.

- *Contract negotiation risks*: existing procurement procedures are unlikely to be sufficiently robust to manage major market-testing initiatives.

The more strategic risks concern underpricing by private sector bidders, with the possibility of cartel formations after the abolition of in-house providers.

Achieving change

A market-testing programme requires an adequately resourced and managed change team or unit, at Ministry level or centrally, with unambiguous authority to require detailed costing information.

In examining a particular activity, the following questions must be addressed prior to market-testing:

- Is the activity necessary? What are the implications if it is cancelled, reduced or combined with another?

- What is the full cost of the activity as currently undertaken within the public sector?

- Is the function or activity organisationally discrete? What will the consequential changes be of separating it?

- Are there any overriding policy reasons for deciding to abolish, contract out or privatise the activity?

- In the event of a decision being taken to contract out the activity, what use of existing staff and assets is proposed?

In general terms, activities which have been found to be particularly suitable for market-testing are:

- resource, especially human resource, intensive;

- relatively discrete;

- specialist or support services;

- subject to rapidly changing markets; and,

- subject to rapidly changing technology.

The process of market-testing will normally include the following activities for which appropriate time scales should be allowed:

- The activities to be tested must be examined to determine the precise scope of services, to define the requirements and determine the full cost. Using this information, a specification detailing the standards and performance targets is drawn up.

- The specification will then be used in the invitation to tender. Drawing up the invitation to tender will require appropriate legal advice. Normally, unless there are specific reasons, the existing providers will be asked to submit an in-house bid. They may be provided with access to consulting organisations to assist in the bid preparation.

- Tenders should be evaluated on the basis of quality, price, reliability and any other relevant factors to determine which offers the best overall long-term value for money.

- If the service is retained in-house, a service-level agreement is made with the in-house team. If it is contracted out, then a contract with the chosen supplier is established. In both cases appropriate standards of output and measurable performance indicators will be defined.

The time scale to be allowed for market-testing will vary according to the activity, its scale and degree of complexity. Any schedule must allow for the following activities:

- preparation of the specification of the work;

- preparation of the work standards and drafting of legal requirements;

- any necessary management reviews;

- invitation to tender and receipt of tenders;

- completion of the bid analysis process; and

- award of contract.

At all stages, the process of market-testing can promote adverse reactions from staff who will feel threatened with job insecurity and loss of status. Openness and frank communication is the only strategy for minimising resistance. When the decision to market test an activity is taken, staff involved must be fully informed both of the objectives of the exercise and of the criteria by which successful bidders will be judged.

Examples of change

In the *UK*, the Government White Paper, Competing for Quality, was issued in 1991. It set out the Government's plans to achieve better value for money by, in particular, opening up more of the public services to competition from the private sector.

Competing for Quality required Government departments to assess the scope for extending market-testing in their operations, and set targets for activities to be tested by September 1993. By that date, 1449 activities involving 44,000 activities had been scheduled for market-testing.

In 1992, the Efficiency Unit acquired responsibility from the Treasury for the overall policy on market-testing. While departments retained responsibility for their market-testing programmes, the Efficiency Unit acts in an advisory capacity, encouraging departments to examine opportunities, and acting as a clearing for best practices so that all departments can be made equally aware of prospects and opportunities and of practical considerations which need to be addressed.

In *Trinidad and Tobago*, Ministries and departments have been asked to determine whether a service might be more effectively provided by external agencies. Services already contracted out include:

* maintenance services for new police stations;

* security services at Inland Revenue Divisions, the VAT Administration Office and the District Revenue Office; and

* security services at post offices and mail delivery between the Airport and the General Post Office.

Other useful material (current as of 1996)

Administrative and Managerial Reforms in Government. A Commonwealth Portfolio of Current Good Practice. Proceedings of a Pan Commonwealth Working Group Meeting held in Kuala Lumpur, Malaysia, 19-22 April 1993. Commonwealth Secretariat, 1993 (ComSec)

"Competing for Quality". Government White Paper, HM Treasury. HMSO, 1991 (UK)

The Government's Guide to Market-Testing, HM Treasury. HMSO, 1993 (UK)

Realising the Benefits of Competition, The Audit Commission. HMSO, 1993 (UK)

2.2 Examining Structural Options

2.2.1 Introducing corporatisation

Commercialisation is a set of strategies which allows, and sometimes requires, services to compete within a market of similar services required by other suppliers. Commercialisation strategies do not require the ending of state ownership. They change the organisation from within by focusing on organisational and managerial restructuring, and can be supported by parallel initiatives aimed at changing the nature of the market itself, forcing the change on the organisation from without by exposing it to stronger competition.

Commercialisation strategies have two key dimensions: to provide a degree of managerial authority to pursue clear organisational objectives unobtainable within the mainstream public service; and to move towards competitive neutrality. Managerial authority provides the means with which to pursue an unambiguous set of organisational objectives. Competitive neutrality is, in essence, one aspect of the much discussed "level playing-field" on which goods and services produced by government-owned organisations do not benefit from direct or indirect subsidies, unless these are formally identified in the budget process. Service contestability is a significant step in this direction. This means that all inputs and associated costs are clearly identified and could, at least in principle, be tested against the costs of providing the service outside government.

The strongest form of commercialisation is *corporatisation*, a structural shift towards a more autonomous business unit, coupled with competitive neutrality.

The context for change

Corporatisation seeks to reduce costs and increase efficiency through the discipline of market competition, and by more flexible forms of human resource management. Where commercialisation has allowed competitive pricing and user charges for services, revenue may be generated, although this must be set alongside the capital and other investment necessary if the organisation is to compete successfully with comparable private sector services.

A reduction in the direct government involvement in service or manufacturing industries may be seen to bring political benefits where public sector inefficiencies are seen as linked to political interference.

Corporatisation may curb the power of producer interest groups, such as public sector unions, which might be regarded as having a restricting influence on the introduction of more flexible and efficient working practices.

The quality of services may be enhanced by allowing managers the freedom to manage within a clearly prescribed framework. In clarifying the political/administrative boundary, a clearer distinction can be made between strategic and operational issues, between policy formulation and implementation, freeing administration from political interference, and politics from administrative detail. One component of this separation of politics from service production results from the pressure within commercialised entities to expose costs of social commitments. The cost of, for example, subsidising transport for older people results from political concerns for equity, rather than managerial concerns for efficiency. Corporatisation encourages these costs to be exposed and subjected to more open debate.

Reasons for caution

As with all major changes in organisational structure, the conditions for successful corporatisation concern the ability and willingness of government to prepare the policy ground, to manage the change process, and to live with the political and administrative consequences.

Traditional public sector organisations can suffer from poor accounting systems, conservative management cultures, inadequate management or employee incentives and unclear performance conditions. Changing the organisational form, without changing the competitive environment or the management culture, will prove ineffective.

Preparing the policy ground begins with a consideration of deregulation. Tackling monopoly control by allowing privately-owned organisations to compete in markets which were previously the exclusive preserve of public service organisations places pressure on those organisations to commercialise, and provides subsequent incentives for efficiency.

The right to a degree of commercial freedom is balanced by the duty to report results back to key stakeholders, set against agreed targets. Sustainable structures for monitoring must be developed prior to corporatisation.

An emphasis on accountability provides an incentive to a corporatised entity to manage risk, but the necessary degree of autonomy given to the enterprise creates risks previously unfamiliar to the public service. Government may manage these risks through auditors' reports of the enterprises' financial position, and through monitoring of commercialised entities, capital expenditure programmes and debt positions. The risk of unanticipated financial or service problems is without doubt increased in commercial organisations.

Other consequences may include a degree of short-termism entering an area of production which is of fundamental importance to national development. The employment needs of particular communities, and broader social and environmental responsibilities may be traded for immediate efficiency gains. Without careful subsidy strategies, deregulation may encourage a reduction in service to those least able to pay but most in need, resulting in disparities in the perceived quality of services.

Finally, governments actively pursuing corporatisation strategies must undoubtedly live with some remarkable changes to the remuneration frameworks of senior managers. Autonomy in performance management for commercialised organisations has consistently led to the introduction of incentive payments and salary levels deemed to be comparable to the private sector. The relatively compressed salary structures of the public sector are decompressed with some vigour by newly-commercialised organisations. The results may provide some political difficulties.

Achieving change

Corporatising a public service function entails both restructuring and moves towards competitive neutrality.

Restructuring for corporatisation requires changes to organisational structures which are sufficient to allow the focused pursuit of explicitly commercial objectives, very particularly by ensuring adequate managerial autonomy in the areas of resource purchasing, marketing, employee performance management and pricing policy.

Driving an organisation towards commercial objectives implies a heightened degree of managerial accountability. All stakeholders, government, staff and customers, must be able to appraise the organisation's achievements in relation to commercial goals. This accountability implies some increased autonomy if the management is to be judged in terms of its commercial effectiveness. It must have real control of its resources, human and material, and must be sure of its environment.

Ensuring this increased autonomy requires an organisational framework which limits the involvement of government in decision making. This is generally, but not necessarily, achieved by establishing the organisation as a company or corporation, wholly owned by government. Such an entity is provided with some protection from shifting government policies, and subjected to clear performance targets through a performance contract. This specifies the assistance to be provided by government, and the commercial, service and other targets which the organisation has to meet. The legal employment framework provided by the organisation's incorporation as a company provides the opportunity for installing a more flexible management regime.

Service contestability is a necessary accompaniment to managerial autonomy. The identification of all inputs and associated costs prepares goods and services for entry into a competitive market. Of equal significance, however, service contestability acts as an indicator of the effectiveness of management in achieving value for money.

To assist the transition to a more commercial environment, it is probable that the organisation will be rationalised to some degree. Experience suggests that few areas of the public service can simply be converted into a commercialised entity, able to compete to any degree with other private sector providers, without some rationalisation of tasks and consequent downsizing as non-profitable areas of activity are closed down.

Rationalisation can clearly bring about considerable efficiency gains, but there may be high attendant costs depending on the scope of redundancy schemes for employees laid off as a consequence. Moreover, lay-offs may be concentrated within particular communities and there may be considerable pressure to divert public resources into these areas to prevent social and economic collapse. The budgetary burden for government may also be considerable for those countries providing unemployment and other public benefits.

Corporatisation requires that the setting of explicit commercial objectives and increased managerial autonomy are coupled with moves towards competitive neutrality. This means that in both resource input, and in product output, the organisation should not be subject to any special advantages by virtue of being owned by the government.

On the input side, achieving competitive neutrality requires that debt funding is not subsidised. Debt charges can be structured to eliminate the interest rate advantage traditionally associated with government ownership. In addition, the target return on government equity in the organisation can be set at a comparable level to that applicable in the private sector for an enterprise with a similar commercial profile.

Similarly, corporatised entities should not be restricted in their remuneration policies for staff, and should face charges on their commercial operations equivalent to the tax burdens faced by their private sector counterparts.

Competitive neutrality in output markets requires the removal of any barriers to competition, to ensure that prices and quality are fully subject to market disciplines. Competitive neutrality is not an obstacle to the government's use of corporatised entities to meet social obligations. Such obligations arise when government seeks to provide services at below cost prices. Within mainstream government operations, such subsidies are concealed within opaque reporting arrangements. Within some public enterprises, profitable activities may be used to cross-subsidise non-commercial activities. In a fully corporatised organisation, operating within a framework of neutrality, such subsidies are not opaque internal transfers; they become transparent external subsidies from government, fully costed within the government budgetary process.

Corporatisation requires the setting up of the appropriate legal instruments. In some cases a single enabling act will be sufficient. However, more often, each individual organisation will require special legislation.

The two principle routes which are followed are:

- State-owned limited liability companies in which the government owns all of the shares – formed according to the appropriate sections of company law with Articles and Memoranda of Association, or their equivalents, which define the objectives and constitution.

  The principle advantages of this method are relative simplicity and the additional ease of future part or total privatisation. Shares are simply sold on the stock market in the same way as in any other public flotation.

- The formation of public corporations, which generally requires specific legislation, which will define the objectives and constitution, and proposed methods of financing the new institution.

  Public corporations do not represent new developments, and are generally associated with institutions which are service oriented. The vigour with which commercial discipline has been applied to more recently established public corporations does, however, mark a significant departure from previous practice.

Example of change

Since 1984, *New Zealand* has experienced widespread deregulation and financial reform designed to remedy decades of poor economic growth. In that year, Government spending amounted to over 40 per cent of GDP and 31 per cent of employment. Government trading enterprises accounted for 12 per cent of GDP and 20 per cent of the gross annual investment.

A substantial part of the reforms consisted of the corporatisation and subsequent privatisation of state-owned trading enterprises, known as State Owned Enterprises (SOEs).

The important policy change can be described as follows: previously, Government had intervened in conditions of apparent market failure, acquiring trading activities in a wide range of sectors for a variety of reasons. This was replaced by the concept of Government failure which was concerned with poor productivity and consequent high costs, associated with Government-owned commercial enterprises.

The process was preceded by a reorganisation of SOEs on the basis of five key principles:

- Non-commercial functions would be separated from major SOEs.
- Managers would be required to run them as business enterprises.
- Managers would be responsible for the use of inputs, pricing and marketing within objectives set by Ministers.
- SOEs would be required to operate without competitive advantages and disadvantages so that commercial criteria could provide an assessment of managerial performance.
- SOEs would be set up on an individual basis according to commercial purposes and would be guided by boards modelled on the private sector.

The principal mechanism used to facilitate the divestiture of these enterprises was the State Owned Enterprise Act of 1986. Before corporatisation, many organisations or SOEs had a combined mixture of commercial and social objectives. A major aim of this Act was to give SOEs a clear commercial mandate, and Section 4 required that they should operate as successful commercial businesses.

The State-Owned Enterprises Act provided for the appointment of Boards of Directors accountable to the Ministry of Finance. From 1987, government-owned trading enterprises were required to fund spending from unsubsidised private sector capital sources and were expected to pay taxes and dividends.

By 1989, fifteen SOEs had been created. The process was then taken over by the subsequent privatisation programme in which SOEs were transferred to the private sector, a separate idea which emerged subsequently.

Other useful material (current as of 1996)

Bollard, A. and Mayes, D. Corporatisation and Privatisation in New Zealand, New Zealand Institute of Economic Research, Wellington, 1991 (NZ)

2.3 Contracting Out of Services

Contracting out of services is the process of transferring to the private sector activities, such as the provision of goods and services, normally or traditionally performed by the public service.

When services are contracted out, the government ceases to be a provider and instead becomes a purchaser of services on behalf of the public.

The context for change

Contracting out of services can deliver three objectives. First, through the clear identification of costs and specification of volume and quality, contracting out can act as a stimulus to cost reduction.

Second, by enabling the public service as purchaser to make choices in its preferred supplier, quality can be increased.

Third, contracting out curbs the power of producer interests where service delivery goals have been subverted by the desire of the producers to improve the interests of their staff at the expense of their customers or service recipients.

Reasons for caution

The ability of contracting out strategies to improve efficiency and quality depends on three factors: market structure, the information available to purchasers and the administrative costs of undertaking the transactions.

- Market structure

  The central motive underlying the contractual approach is to increase competition. However, competitive markets for particular services may not exist. There may be few outside firms willing or able to compete to provide the kind of service a government agency or department is looking for. This is particularly the case where the service is highly specialised in nature, such as some scientific services. Furthermore, there is evidence that on occasion originally competitive conditions may be undermined over time as provider organisations merge or form cartels.

- Information

  Services vary in complexity – providing refuse collection is far simpler than running a service for the mentally ill. Generally speaking, the better the quality of information available to the purchaser, the greater their ability to make informed choices regarding the service they require and judgements about the quality of the service they have received. Services vary in terms of the ease with which the outputs and outcomes desired can be specified, and in the human services this is particularly difficult to accomplish.

- Transaction costs

  The costs of managing the transaction between the purchaser and provider result from the process of drawing up a specification, putting it out to tender and awarding a contract, and then monitoring and enforcing that contract. Generally speaking, the less the information a purchaser has about a provider and the service being provided, and the lower the degree of trust that exists between the two parties, the higher the transaction costs.

Moreover, transaction costs will be greater with some kinds of contracts than others – lump-sum contracts may involve low specification costs, but, if trust between purchaser and provider is low, monitoring costs may be potentially high; price-per-unit contracts, however, may incur extremely high specification costs. As transaction costs escalate, so the advantages of contracting out strategies decline.

Achieving change

Contracting out is usually preceded by a market-testing programme. Such a programme will identify activities which may be carried out more effectively and efficiently in the private sector.

In general terms, activities which have been found to be particularly suitable for contracting out are:

* resource intensive,

* relatively discrete, producing specialist goods and services,

* subject to rapidly changing markets, and

* subject to rapidly changing technology.

Where the decision to put a service out to tender is made, the tendering process does not have to be competitive. The purchaser may already have extensive experience of a particular provider, albeit a commercial or not-for-profit organisation. In this case, the purchaser may use the established basis of trust to contract directly with this single organisation, indeed the purchaser may seek to sustain and develop this relationship over time. This model of "relational" contracting stands in contrast to the competitive tendering model which gives emphasis to a plurality of anonymous providers competing on a regular basis for a single contract.

Contracts themselves can vary according to the nature of the service being specified. The three basic forms of contract are as follows:

* *Cost-and-volume contracts*, in which the amount of work to be done and its total cost is specified, such as pay-roll services for x thousand staff.

* *Price-per-unit contracts*, in which the units of work are laid down and their price stated. In these contracts there may be little knowledge of the amount of work to be done, such as a standard recruitment service package.

* *Lump-sum contracts*, in which the contractor agrees to undertake a given quantity of work for a specified price, such as the management of a leisure centre.

In practice, contracts also vary in terms of whether they give priority to cost or quality, whether they include contract compliance clauses to ensure providers adopt good employment and equal opportunities practices, whether they focus upon the specification of inputs, outputs or outcomes, and so on. Where tendering is compulsory, the legislative framework will determine many aspects of the tendering process, in this sense defining the "rules of the game" within which purchaser and provider can operate.

Tenders should be evaluated on the basis of quality, price, and reliability to determine which offers the best overall long-term value for money.

If the service is retained in-house, a service-level agreement is made with the in-house team. If it is contracted out, then a contract with the chosen supplier is established.

The time scale for contracting out should be sufficient to allow for:

- preparation of the specification of the work;
- preparation of the work standards and drafting of legal requirements;
- any necessary management reviews;
- invitation to tender and receipt of tenders;
- completion of the bid analysis process; and
- award of contract.

Examples of change

In the *UK*, under a legislative programme beginning in 1980, local authorities have been required to subject an increasing number of services to competitive tendering. This formed part of central Government's programme of reforms of local government with a view to reducing the size and cost of local government expenditure, and to achieve greater value for money.

Reforms in the National Health Service have included the formation of provider agencies known as National Health Trusts and have been accompanied by active encouragement, through cash limits, of market-testing and the contracting out of numerous ancillary services, such as cleaning, security, laundry and catering.

The Government White Paper, Competing for Quality, was issued in 1991. It set out the Government's plans to achieve better value for money by, in particular, opening up more of the public services to competition from the private sector.

Competing for Quality required Government departments to assess the scope for extending market-testing in their operations and set targets for activities to be tested by September 1993.

By that date, 1,449 activities involving 44,000 activities had been scheduled for market-testing.

In 1992, the Efficiency Unit acquired responsibility from the Treasury for the overall policy on market-testing. While Departments retained responsibility for their market-testing programmes, the Efficiency Unit acts in an advisory capacity, encouraging departments to examine opportunities and acting as a clearing for best practices so that all departments can be made equally aware of prospects and opportunities and of practical considerations which need to be addressed.

In *Trinidad and Tobago*, Ministries and departments have been asked to determine whether a service might be more effectively provided by external agencies. Services that have already contracted out include:

- maintenance services for new police stations;
- security services at Inland Revenue Divisions, the VAT Administration Office and the District Revenue Office; and
- security services at post-offices, and mail delivery between the Airport and the General Post Office.

Other useful material (current as of 1996)

Competitive Tendering and Contracting out in UK Local Government, M. Paddon. Commonwealth Secretariat, 1992 (ComSec)

"Competing for Quality", Government White Paper, HM Treasury. HMSO, 1991 (UK)

The Governments Guide to Market-Testing, HM Treasury. HMSO, 1993 (UK)

Realising the Benefits of Competition, The Audit Commission. HMSO, 1993 (UK)

2.3.1 Promoting devolution

Corporatisation, divestiture and contracting-out strategies give primary emphasis to competition as a means of improving performance. *Devolution* seeks to create simplicity within complex organisations and combine this with more flexible results-oriented and customer-driven forms of management. Devolution entails the establishment of smaller business units within the public service, with funding and other inputs, and responsibilities and outputs, clearly delineated. There are different forms of devolution, the most well-known of which, executive agencies, are built upon the value of separating the policy formulation function of the public service from its operational side.

Devolution focuses on the delegation of managerial decision making within the public service and should not therefore be confused with deconcentration, where existing hierarchical and bureaucratic forms of control are often maintained despite the spatial dispersal of existing government activities. Nor should devolution be confused with decentralisation, in which political and managerial powers are delegated and spatially dispersed within a country.

The context for change

The primary objectives of devolution are:

- to reduce political involvement in administrative matters – by separating policy formulation from implementation, and strategy from operations, elected representatives are freed from immersion in administrative detail, allowing them to concentrate on policy matters;

- to increase efficiency – by giving managers freedom to use resources in a flexible and responsive manner, inputs can be combined more creatively to produce desired results, particularly where managers have an incentive to make savings as these are not automatically clawed back by the centre;

- to enhance quality – by delegating decision-making powers to those closer "to the end user", services can be delivered which are more sensitive to the user's needs;

- to enhance managerial accountability/reduce corruption – the development of the cost and performance centre model makes the activities of managers and staff more visible, both in terms of accounting for the use of budgetary resources and in terms of accounting for performance.

Reasons for caution

Devolution to business units within the public service requires a series of delicate balances:

- *Balancing diversity and uniformity within the public service*

  Devolution strategies seek to simplify the public service and improve management by freeing up business units and their managers to manage for results. However, the corollary of devolution is diversity, with the possible emergence of different charging practices, employment practices and financial accounting practices. Devolution ultimately points towards differential grading structures, performance incentive systems, and career structures. If managers are to be allowed to run business units as if they were divisions of a large commercial company, then they would expect this kind of freedom.

- *Balancing autonomy and co-ordination*

  Managerial autonomy necessitates more systematic co-ordination. Experience indicates that devolution can encourage segmentalism, with units seeking to follow their own agenda and priorities with the overarching Ministry reduced to a "holding company". Competition may begin to emerge between devolved units undermining co-operation and leading to opportunistic practices, such as the poaching of staff.

- *Balancing entrepreneurship and accountability*

  If devolution is to lead to improved management, then it must provide scope for public entrepreneurship, that is, leadership, vision, innovation and even a certain degree of risk-taking. However, management leadership must be balanced with political accountability and risk-taking balanced with probity.

The primary concern is that as an "arms-length" relationship develops between a Minister and the devolved business units within the Ministry for which he/she is responsible, then there may be a loosening of the accountability of the Minister to Parliament and the general public for issues concerning those units. Arguably, Ministers may feel less personally responsible as chief executives become called upon increasingly to answer direct to the legislature for perceived problems or failings within their agency.

Attempts to resolve accountability problems for devolved units within the public service have generally focused on the split between policy formulation and implementation. In this model, the Minister is accountable for setting the policy, with assistance from central advisers in the Ministry, and devolved business units for the manner in which that policy was implemented.

This division assists in identifying accountabilities to a point. However, in the public service, policy is not just a matter of what is handed down from Cabinet. Policy is also embedded in the everyday routines and practices of counter clerks, telephonists, street-level professionals, and the many others within the public service who seek to interpret policies and objectives and juggle with competing priorities as they ration scarce resources.

The balance between entrepreneurship and accountability is most delicate in relation to the question of probity. On the one hand, it is argued, tight controls encourage the development of managerial short-cuts, which in turn open the door to misuse of public funds. On the other hand, looser controls provide fertile ground for those who are seeking to achieve personal rather then organisational goals.

The enterprising manager of a devolved business unit must have flexibility to work with this reality, but the public and the legislature must be in a position to allocate responsibility for shortcomings without entering a complex debate as to whether the problem is policy or operational.

Achieving change

Devolution strategies are aimed at breaking down complex departmental structures into systems of accountable management units, in which unit managers have much greater financial, personnel and other freedoms which they exercise within a set of clearly specified boundaries – freedom within a framework. The devolved units are therefore both cost centres (identifiable units to which direct and indirect costs can be clearly attributed) and performance centres (units at which expedited performance standards can be clearly specified and monitored).

The degree of devolution can vary:

NOMINAL DEVOLUTION

Monitoring of "shadow budgets"
Control over small budgets concerning special items

Control over revenue budgets but restrictive financial regulations

Control over capital budgets

Flexible virement rules for revenue budgets and regarding over/underspend

Freedom to contract out

Control over own establishment levels and over some re-grading

Freedom to raise additional revenue through service charges

Freedom to raise additional capital

RADICAL DEVOLUTION

Devolution strategies have been applied primarily to those areas of government engaged in monetary transfers, regulation, some services to internal clients, and the delivery of material services and programmes. In a recent review of the Next Steps agencies in the UK, the Fraser Report noted that agencies differ also in terms of the key role they play within the sponsoring department. The Fraser Report suggests that agencies may be grouped in the following fashion:

- Agencies which are fundamental to the mainstream policy and operation of the department.

- Agencies which execute, in a highly delegated way, statutory (usually regulatory) functions within a stable policy framework which changes relatively infrequently.

- Agencies which provide internal services using particular specialist skills.

- Agencies which are not linked to any of the main aims of a department but which nonetheless report to its Minister.

The character of the agency will therefore affect its relationship to the parent department and how this relationship should be managed. It also has implications for the degree of devolution seen as appropriate, the sharpness of the policy/operations split, and the extent to which it may become an autonomous internal trading unit or is regarded as a potential candidate for privatisation.

In some settings, internal markets have been created. Internal markets may also assume a number of forms. At the simplest level, internal support services such as personnel, training, library, secretarial and other services may be reorganised on a trading account basis. Quasi-contractual agreements are then constructed between these internal business units and other parts of the organisation which are purchasers of their services. These agreements are sometimes referred to as service-level agreements. Usually, they are not legally binding contracts though purchasers may be given certain sanctions should providers fail to deliver what was specified in the agreement. The ultimate sanction is the right of the purchaser to "go outside" for a service, should the internally provided one fail to satisfy; here the internal market models are combined with elements of external contracting.

Internal markets may also be established for the provision of direct services. In the UK, the outstanding current example of this approach concerns the reorganisation of the National Health Service. In this instance, provider organisations are constructed (Hospital Trusts) which compete for contracts from district health authorities or general practitioners. Health care is still publicly funded but the purchase of service has been separated from its provision.

Examples of change

In the Commonwealth developing countries in particular, many governments are decentralising responsibilities to regional levels. *South Africa* is working on a new constitution which favours the provinces. *Zimbabwe* is decentralising in the areas of health, education and social welfare to local government.

Devolution of powers to eight provincial councils has been envisaged as a major historical landmark in the evolution of political and social institutions in *Sri Lanka*. It has also provided a unique opportunity to restructure the administration in a manner that would strengthen and enhance democratic policy by the people.

Other useful material (current as of 1996)

Choices in the Design of Decentralisation. An Overview and Curriculum for central government officials responsible for the reorganisation of administration at the local level. Smith, B. C. Commonwealth Secretariat, 1993 (ComSec)

From Problem to Solution. Commonwealth Strategies for Reform. Managing the Public Service. Strategies for Improvement Series: No. 1. pp31-32. Commonwealth Secretariat, 1995 (ComSec)

2.3.2 Introducing privatisation

Privatisation is the transfer of control of ownership from the public to the private sector. Such a transfer is necessarily associated with extensive market liberalisation and deregulation, changing the macro-economic context, the competitive environment and the labour market. Equally, however, such moves must be accompanied by re-regulation, ensuring that monopoly or powerful enterprises do not use their newly-unleashed market position to pursue unfair pricing policies or to prevent other competitors gaining access to key markets.

The context for change

The most frequently cited objectives of privatisation strategies are:

- to improve the government's budgetary position by generating additional revenue from the sale of the enterprise, an increase in receipts from taxes on the sales revenue of the enterprise, and from a reduction in the size of the subsidy paid to the enterprise by government;

- to increase efficiency and improve quality and productivity through increased competition;

- to reduce the size and influence of the public sector in general, and the extent of government involvement in industry in particular;

- to promote wider public participation and control through the diffusion of share ownership or the creation of management or employee buy-outs;

- to encourage private investment and to develop local capital markets; and

- to signal strong support for the private sector as an engine for development.

These objectives are not necessarily achieved simultaneously. For example, if the enterprise performance improves following privatisation, then tax revenues may increase leading to an improvement in the government budgetary position. However, the private sector capital which may have contributed to this improvement is not now available for other investment opportunities.

Reasons for caution

Governments' abilities to seize the opportunities which privatisation can represent are restrained by both the national capacity to develop and sustain a privatisation programme and the availability of acceptable purchasers.

Preparing the policy ground will require the government to:

- prepare and publish a privatisation policy statement;

- develop an institutional infrastructure with the capacity to identify appropriate enterprises for privatisation, undertaking analyses of financial performance and competitive position for each enterprise;

- review the legal and policy framework, codifying company law and liberalising the tax regime if necessary;

- prepare rehabilitation and restructuring plans, as necessary, to prepare enterprises for privatisation; and

- ensure the capacity to identify potential appropriate purchasers.

Successful privatisation also rests on the government's ability to manage the process of change. This will generally entail the establishment of an institutional framework for driving privatisation programmes forward. There are more successful examples of this being undertaken by central bodies, often within the Ministry of Finance, than under a decentralised system in which the parent Ministries or bodies are responsible for divestiture of some of their own holdings.

The unit charged with responsibility for undertaking the privatisation will be faced with change management tasks involved in:

- amending the legal form of the enterprise;

- restructuring the enterprise's finances, including revaluation and debt management, if necessary;

- physical rehabilitation of plant, equipment and other assets;

- reorienting the performance management systems towards the achievement of commercial goals, this may include significant changes in terms and conditions of employment, and will very probably include some downsizing of the enterprise workforce; and

- steering the sale, whether this is private, through a full or partial share flotation, or as the result of a management or employee buy out.

Successful privatisation programmes also require that the government can live comfortably with the consequences. Experiences to date with privatisation suggests that the consequences can be very diverse. There is no difficulty for government in living with success: improved services, growing economy, satisfied shareholders and workforce.

The difficulties arise in living with:

- large scale unemployment;

- under-priced property transfers, cronyism, and outright corruption;

- aggravated differences in personal incomes;

- over-reliance on foreign capital;

- excessive short-termism and an inability of government to control the market to meet national priorities, including environmental concerns;

- regional disparities;

- abuses of monopoly positions; and

- costs of preparing for privatisation disproportionate to the economic gains.

There is certainly no evidence that such consequences are inevitable. However, some combination of these concerns can be found, to varying degrees in some settings.

Achieving change

In its narrowest sense privatisation is a shift of ownership, removing organisations from the public sector. This goal may be achieved through a variety of strategies, the key elements of which are:

- **Stock market flotation**: consists of the sale of the enterprise to the general public with equity offered on a fixed price or through a tendering process. Shares can be marketed internationally or domestically, and all the equity may be sold or government may retain a proportion.

- **Sale to a third party**: consists of the sale of all or part of the shareholding to a single purchaser or group of purchasers. The enterprise may be sold as a going concern, or the assets of a defunct operation sold. The sale may be by private placement with investors, or a trade sale to the private sector companies. The price may be determined by competitive bidding, or by negotiation with potential buyers.

- **Management or employee buyout**: managers and/or employees acquire a controlling shareholding in the enterprise. It is likely to require that a high proportion of the purchase price is funded by borrowing and strong cash flow is necessary to meet interest and capital repayments.

- **Leasing/Franchising**: in certain circumstances, only the operations of the industry are privatised and the necessary assets are leased, generally for a predetermined period, after which they return to government control. In some cases the process is mixed, in that the infrastructure is sold to one organisation which then leases the facilities to the operating company.

- **Sale of assets**: another form of privatisation is the public sale of state-owned assets such as land, building and housing stock.

Privatisation may result in the transfer to the private sector of natural monopolies, in which case consumer protection has to be ensured by appropriate regulation. Essentially, regulation is based on the following principle forms:

- **The control of profits**: profits can be controlled through regulations which set the appropriate ratios: margins, returns on investment or capital employed or on dividends paid. The weakness of this method is that it removes one of the forces promoting efficiency, and even investment.

- **The control of prices**: the control of prices, particularly if linked to a formula which provides for a progressive reduction, in real terms, has been adopted in many cases. While this method will promote efficiency it can, nevertheless, lead to situations where investment suffers and profits are deemed to be excessive.

- **Performance indicators**: in industries concerned with providing a public service, and in which output is difficult to measure in financial terms, regulation may also include the setting of clear performance standards as far as levels and quality of service are concerned.

Other prerequisites for privatisation include the creation of appropriate legal instruments, the existence of appropriate financial mechanisms and the existence of a capital market.

Examples of change

In *Zimbabwe*, a Regional Consultation Workshop on Capacity Building for Management of Privatisation was held in March 1994. This workshop, attended by senior representatives of the privatisation system in *Ghana, Sierra Leone, Tanzania, Zambia* and *Zimbabwe*, was organised by the Commonwealth Secretariat and the Foundation for International Training (FIT) in collaboration with the Zimbabwe Institute for Public Administration.

The meeting recognised the urgent need to address the problem of developing national capabilities to manage the process of privatisation currently taking place. It was recommended that steps be taken to carry this initiative forward through future activities that promote human resource development for privatisation. It was therefore resolved that an Advisory Steering Committee be established, comprising senior representatives from the participating countries to assist the Commonwealth Secretariat and the FIT to formulate a plan of action for capacity-building for the management of privatisation

In the *UK*, the privatisation programme began in 1979 when the Government disposed of part of its holding in British Petroleum. During the following decade, sales of government holdings in seven private sector companies amounted to £8,389 million. During the same period, 21 further state-owned companies or public corporations were sold through private treaty for £1,250 million.

Sales of government-owned assets include the sale of motorway service areas and other property to lease or franchise holders, and, most significant, the sale of over one million state-owned houses to tenants which brought in £15 billion between 1979 and 1988.

The privatisation programme received added impetus when, in 1984, 51 per cent of British Telecom was floated for £3.9 billion, proving the fact that public flotations of this size were practical; 2.25 million applicants received shares. Institutions were excluded from this flotation and the premium on the part-paid shares rose to 90 per cent.

During the remainder of the decade, many utilities including the gas, water and electricity industries and a large part of the transport infrastructure were sold or prepared for sale.

While British Gas was sold as a single entity and the water companies were based on the previous regional authorities, the electricity industry was broken up between distributors, the supply network and the generators. (Subsequently British Gas has been required to separate the distribution network and make it available to competitors).

Preparation for privatisation of the rail network included breaking up the existing organisation into owners of the track and associated infrastructure, the rolling stock, and a number of operating companies which franchise the services.

Privatisation of utilities and monopolies gave rise to a number of concerns summarised into the following issues:

- the development of competition;
- protection of the public interest; and
- prevention of monopolistic pricing.

The main instrument of regulatory policy was either an operating licence which required certain activities or standards and, in the case of utilities, the development of industry-specific regulatory bodies charged with regulation in the light of the issues. Consequently, the regulator is charged with ensuring both satisfactory delivery and consumer protection.

In *Malaysia*, a "Privatisation Master Plan" was developed in 1993 with the aim of promoting the transfer to the private sector of as many as possible public sector activities.

The thrust of the policy includes the sale of equity, sale or lease of assets, management or private sector contracting out and "build operate" transfers or "build own operate" for infrastructure projects.

The plan assumes two main methods: a Government initiative where candidates are identified and bids for the organisation are solicited; and a private sector initiative where the private sector is encouraged to produce plans on the basis of its special strengths, including know-how, patents and capital.

Other useful material (current as of 1996)

Capacity Building for Management of Privatisation. Report of the Regional Consultation Workshop held at ZIPAM Centre, 1994. Commonwealth Secretariat, 1994 (ComSec)

Management of the Privatisation Process. A Guide to Policy-Making and Implementation. Commonwealth Secretariat, 1994 (ComSec)

Improvements and Development in the Public Service, 1990,1991 &1992, Malaysia (MAL)

2.4 Identifying Obstacles to Efficiency

2.4.1 Establishing an efficiency programme

Efficiency is the relationship between outputs, the goods and services produced, and inputs, the cost of the resources used to produce them. In short, efficiency is spending well.

Efficiency programmes are a series of inter-related examinations of current systems to identify opportunities for cost reduction (without lower standards) and performance enhancement (at no higher cost or, preferably, at lower cost).

The context for change

The point of entry for programmes to improve efficiency is commonly a requirement to reduce operating costs as part of budgetary restraint. The goal is to create a management ambition for cost reduction and performance improvement in all areas.

The rationale for efficiency programmes is that resources available to government are always under pressure: demand exceeds supply and expectations exceed what can be afforded. There is an ongoing requirement to review all activities to ensure that resources are used to best effect and that the public service can demonstrate sound stewardship.

Reasons for caution

Commonwealth experiences have highlighted some key pre-conditions for the introduction of successful efficiency programmes. First, they require a determination to develop implementation strategies – most frequently these entail:

- improved micro-accounting information systems, including the provision of expenditure and output information for cost centres and the development of activity-based costings;

- internal and external audit;

- management development training which produces managers who can be given the authority and incentive to manage efficiently, with freedom to maximise outputs from the resources they command;

- procedures for competitive tendering by existing suppliers of goods and services to government; and

- consideration of organisational changes to achieve greater efficiency, including corporatisation, contracting out, devolution and privatisation.

Second, Ministerial backing for change, and participation from those affected, with incentives to accept and support change and consultation with trade unions and representatives, are indispensable.

In general, efficiency programmes involve some expansion of the private sector's role in the provision of services. Purchasing and supply skills need to be further developed, which require:

- more and better training of managers in the skills of purchasing supply;

- mobilising the expertise of others, including the private sector, for example by seeking secondments and exchanges to improve these skills, or by buying in services; and

- sharing experience of contracting out between departments and agencies.

Finally, there is a key distinction to be made between static efficiency savings, such as the depression of wages, and dynamic efficiency savings in which organisational improvements lead to ongoing and systemic productivity improvements.

Achieving change

The introduction of efficiency programmes requires Ministerial backing and will be most successful when the reforms are overseen by a small unit with the authority to ensure compliance and with the resources to offer the necessary advice and assistance.

When examining individual tasks, three fundamental questions have to be addressed:

- Whether the task in question is necessary. If the task is judged to be unnecessary, or that its objectives can be achieved by other means at less cost, it can then be abolished with consequent savings to the public purse.

- Whether or not the task needs to completed in-house. In many cases, tasks may be completed more economically by other departments or by the private sector.

- Whether or not the task can be completed more economically, either through better organisation and more effective management or as the result of better training, development or the recruitment of appropriate skills.

A typical effficiency programme includes the following steps:

- The setting up of a very small team at the highest level, perhaps directly accountable to the Head of Government.

- A requirement placed on individual Ministries and departments to make specific and quantified proposals for efficiency savings (cost improvements) in general administrative expenditure for a determined period of time.

- The team vets and, in discussion with the originating Ministries, approves the proposals.

- The team provides regular progress reports to the Head of Government.

- A requirement placed on Ministries and departments to subject a particular area of work to detailed critical review.

- The team approves or challenges the proposals for action, before requiring implementation within a fixed period.

- Wide publicity given to the establishment of the team, the first reports, and the savings and other benefits, to create a competitive climate of achievement.

Examples of change

In *Singapore*, the Government is always seeking ways of improving efficiency in the public service. As a major part of this programme, the Service Improvement Unit examines thematic areas of possible efficiency savings in the Civil Service.

In the *UK*, an Efficiency Unit, created in 1979, reports directly to the Prime Minister's Adviser on Efficiency and Effectiveness. Its role is to advise on the improvement of efficiency and effectiveness of central Government. The context of change included concern for three main items:

- securing value for money;
- improving the quality of service; and
- improving managerial and organisational effectiveness.

The Efficiency Unit is also responsible for assisting in the development of the Government's range of public service reforms and, since 1992, is responsible for co-ordinating market-testing policy and activity.

The main instrument used is the Efficiency Scrutiny Programme. Government Departments were required to develop an Efficiency Scrutiny Programme on the basis of the stated aims and objectives and to provide a scrutiny team drawn from other areas than that being reviewed.

The Efficiency Unit is involved at every stage, providing advice and assistance, and a nominated officer who works closely with the team. The Efficiency Unit does not replace Ministers and managers who retain responsibility for the scrutiny, preparation of the report and recommendations, and of a subsequent action plan, and ensuring implementation and compliance. However, the Efficiency Adviser will monitor the process and comment on the outcomes.

On average each scrutiny takes 90 working days, from commencement of drafting a plan to compilation of the final report, and is estimated to cost £100,000.

By 1995, approximately 350 scrutinies had been undertaken, at a rate of approximately 2025 per year. Accumulated savings are estimated to be £1.5 billion and are currently generating savings of £100-200 million a year.

Other useful material (current as of 1996)

Administrative and Managerial Reform in Government: A Commonwealth Portfolio of Current Good Practice. Proceedings of a Pan-Commonwealth Working Group Meeting held in Kuala Lumpur, Malaysia, 1993 (ComSec)

Bollard, A. and Mayes, D. 1991, Corporatisation and Privatisation in New Zealand, New Zealand Institute of Economic Research, Wellington (NZ)

Executive Agencies – A Guide to Setting Targets and Measuring Performance. HMSO, June 1992 (UK)

2.4.2 Focusing on productivity

As a ratio between outputs and inputs, productivity can be measured with some precision when product sales in a competitive market allow the value added per unit of input to be calculated. Such objective measures allow comparisons across a sector or internationally. Without a bottom line, the public sector must look to relative productivity – the possibility that improved systems might allow fewer people to provide the same level of service as before or which allows service quality to be raised with the same level of staff – as sector-wide measures which refer back to value added by staff do not readily apply.

Focusing on productivity, even in the absence of measures which could be used for comparisons with other organisations, provides a powerful method for drawing attention to the need for constant improvement in personal performance and in management systems. Focusing on productivity in the public service encourages a mindset of continual search for opportunities to improve efficiency and quality.

In effect, this entire Portfolio is concerned with productivity improvement. Improving service quality and reducing public service costs is a priority for all governments. All sections in the Portfolio look at Commonwealth experiences in a particular area of improvement.

This section considers the motivation that drives implementation.

The context for change

Productivity and quality have proved themselves to be powerful concepts in the manufacturing and service sectors. As globalisation has exposed service providers to more intense competition, distinctions in the cost and level of service offered have become of increasing significance.

The application of these concepts to the public sector, in general, and to the public service, in particular, has also had considerable impact. There is scope for some debate about the suitability of particular approaches, and the risk that the mechanical application of formulae developed for the manufacturing sector might cost more in additional process than is gained in output. However, the overall effect of focusing on productivity in the public service has been to change the mindset of public servants from that of holding a position to that of serving a customer.

Reasons for caution

Productivity in the public service is a mindset, an orientation in which public servants are searching for opportunities to improve the systems within which they work in order to serve their customers, however defined, better. This orientation has two elements:

- a determination to find creative baseline measures of resources used and outputs achieved in the complex public service environment; and

- the motivation to identify opportunities to improve systems and procedures.

The determination to find meaningful baseline measures, and the motivation to look continually for incremental improvement, find expression in mechanisms such as quality control circles or work improvement teams. The key issue is that the determination and motivation find an opportunity for expression in such mechanisms – the mechanisms do not create determination and motivation.

The risk in focusing on productivity is that of replicating the mechanisms which are seen to be successful in some settings without replicating the orientation that drives them. Hollow systems provide form without content and make meaningful discussion of productivity more difficult.

Achieving change

Focusing on productivity requires:

- measures of resources used and outputs achieved; and
- the identification of incremental opportunities for systemic improvements.

In the complex and frequently process-driven environment of the public service, these two steps require some considerable energy and enthusiasm. The challenge is to generate such motivation.

Commonwealth experiences suggest that this requires the introduction of three innovations which are best described by taking some examples at Ministry level:

Innovation 1 – A champion of change

In successful productivity initiatives at Ministry level, a senior manager within the Ministry, with the support of the administrative head, has identified personally with the need to improve productivity, has personally modelled productive work practices, has established through all opportunities within the Ministry that productivity is a valid issue for discussion, and has assisted in the establishment of new systems and structures in the Ministry.

Innovation 2 – Establishing awareness of resource usage

Apart from those staff directly involved in developing budget estimates, few other staff have an overall picture of the resource requirements of the Ministry. Even those staff involved in managing the recurrent budgets may have little appreciation of the additional cost of staffing, buildings and equipment. Traditional public service financial management systems have many limitations and such data on inputs is difficult to ascertain. However, successful productivity initiatives at Ministry level have fostered an understanding of the scale of Ministry resource requirements, even if the indicators employed have been approximate. Examples of actions include outline information on staff numbers and budgets in Ministry newsletters and briefing notes provided to section heads.

Innovation 3 – Establishing a mechanism which stimulated practical proposals for incremental improvement

Work improvement teams and quality control circles at Ministry level provide an opportunity for a small group of staff, drawn from all levels of the Ministry, to step outside their usual managerial positions and to contribute to collective problem solving. The challenge for the groups is to focus on the defined areas of service or of organisation where they consider that a small change may produce a large result. The group will need to identify some indicators of the outputs of the Ministry and their suggestions will indicate how these might be increased with the same, or reduced, resource usage.

Cautious and incremental development of these innovations has allowed systems to be introduced at the same time as staff motivation to use them. It is this balance which is the key to achieving change.

Examples of change

In *Botswana*, Work Improvement Teams (WITS) have been established across the Public Service. WITS co-ordinators are trained, and encourage the teams to propose efficiency and quality improvement proposals to departmental senior management through the WITS co-ordinating structure. A newsletter describes progress across the service.

In *Singapore*, Work Improvement Teams have been established for many years. WITS represent a complete network of mutually inter-linking action groups constantly examining opportunities for service quality improvement.

Other useful material (current as of 1996)

Stretching the Tax Dollar: Making Operations More Efficient. Treasury Board of Canada (CAN)

Development Administration Circular No. 6 entitled Guidelines on Productivity Improvement in the Public Service, Malaysia, 1991 (MAL)

Development Administration Circular No. 7 entitled Guidelines on Quality Control Circles in the Public Service, Malaysia, 1991 (MAL)

Development Administration Circular No. 8 entitled Guidelines on the Manual of Work Procedures and Desk File, Malaysia, 1991 (MAL)

2.5 Removing Obstacles to Efficiency

2.5.1 Using efficiency audits

Efficiency audits are also known as value-for-money audits, and have much in common with efficiency scrutinies. All three activities are driven by staff within the Ministry or department, are guided by a framework laid down across the public service, and are supported by a small central unit which is able to offer advice and technical support.

Efficiency audits or value-for-money audits are undertaken to complement traditional auditing of financial statements and compliance auditing. Efficiency audits assess whether departmental outputs are being delivered economically and efficiently, and whether they are effectively contributing to the achievement of outcomes.

Efficiency scrutinies are broader activities, intended to solve problems rather than specifically to reduce costs.

The context for change

Internal audit approaches are not new, but their traditional role has been to ensure that departments comply with administrative and financial regulations. Efficiency audits broaden the base of internal audits, providing a value-for-money focus to complement:

- *financial statement auditing* – which assumes that assertions made in financial records are accurate; and
- *compliance auditing* – which assumes the probity and legality of departmental activity.

Reasons for caution

Commonwealth experiences suggest that there are some important preconditions to the successful introduction of efficiency audits:

- managers must be convinced that efficiency savings might be used, in part, to ease pressures in other service areas at a time of reducing resources;
- the efficiency audit team must have the confidence of the department head, and in exchange the department head must be prepared to support any resulting recommendations;
- the Ministry or department must be aware of the work of the audit team, and must be advised of the authority which they carry;
- the audit team must be credible, and willing to guarantee confidentiality (other than to the head of department) where sensitive information is required;
- the audit team must be fully independent of all aspects of operation and management of the functions which it is to review.

Achieving change

The introduction of efficiency audits can take place under three guises:

- as part of the internal auditing procedure;
- as part of the external auditing procedure; and
- as part of a general programme of reform, often in association with a small central unit co-ordinating responsibility for an efficiency programme.

Effective efficiency audits have:

- *a team that is committed to improved performance* – better value for money through reduced cost/higher quality of services;
- *an authoritative process* – authority provided by the head of department or Minister;
- *complete independence* – although the auditors may come from the department, their independence should be assured, and they should report direct to the head of department or Minister;
- *clear terms of reference* – nothing should be taken for granted and the audit should examine activities at all levels, including the justification for the public service being involved in this function;
- *precise time schedules* – schedules should be fixed and short, broken into five parts: setting up; investigation; action plan; implementation; implementation report;
- *well-documented implementation* – the audit or specification might identify an action manager responsible for the implementation of recommendations and, in due course, the implementation report.

Areas for efficiency audits should be of sufficient size, with sufficient potential for savings to justify the cost of an audit. However, this does not preclude smaller programmes which may offer generalisable lessons.

Each audit will be based on an agreed specification which will include:

- background of the audit;
- terms of reference;
- names of auditors and action manager; and
- timetable.

A typical timetable for an efficiency audit is:

- development of detailed audit plan and work schedule: approximately 15 working days;
- preparation of first draft findings: after approximately 60 working days;
- of the final report: after 90 working days.

The report should, wherever possible, be published. Alternatively, it should be circulated widely at all levels to ensure both understanding and support, and implementation.

The action manager should produce an action plan, within a few months of the date of the report. The implementation of the recommendations is the keystone for achieving efficiency. The action manager should be responsible for the success of the implementation, the monitoring progress, and for taking appropriate remedial action, and should report directly to the head of department or Minister.

A subsequent implementation report, which completes the efficiency audit process, should be final and factual, produced by the action manager within an agreed period, and published or circulated in the same way as the original.

Examples of change

In *Trinidad and Tobago,* traditional cash-based audits were seen to be insufficient as other information, concerned with value for money issues, was sought. Consequently, the Auditor General's Department introduced a limited form of efficiency auditing in 1972. This new audit was called Performance or Comprehensive Auditing. In 1986, a Comprehensive Auditing Division was formed and full comprehensive auditing procedures and an auditing programme were established.

The 1993-97 Strategic Plan of the Auditor General's Department identified increased conduct of comprehensive audits as one of its strategic objectives. A training programme was established and, in 1993, 70 persons were trained in the conduct of management audits and 8 were trained as trainers.

In the *UK*, an Efficiency Unit was created in 1979. The Unit reported direct to the Prime Minister's Adviser on Efficiency and Effectiveness. Its role is to advise on the improvement of efficiency and effectiveness of central Government. The context of change included concern for three main items:

- securing value for money;
- improving the quality of service; and
- improving managerial and organisation effectiveness.

The Efficiency Unit is also responsible for assisting in the development of the Government's range of public service reforms and, since 1992, is responsible for co-ordinating market-testing policy and activity.

The main instrument used is the Efficiency Scrutiny Programme. Government departments were required to develop an Efficiency Scrutiny Programme on the basis of the stated aims and objectives; and to provide a scrutiny team drawn from within the department, but not from the area to be reviewed.

The Efficiency Unit is involved at every stage, providing advice and assistance, and a nominated officer who works closely with the team. The Efficiency Unit does not replace Ministers and managers who retain responsibility for the scrutiny, preparation of the report and recommendations, and of a subsequent action plan, and ensuring implementation and compliance. The Efficiency Adviser will monitor the process and comment on the outcomes.

On average, each scrutiny takes 90 working days, from the start of drafting a plan to compilation of the final report, and is estimated to cost, on average, £100,000.

By 1995, approximately 350 scrutinies had been undertaken, at a rate of approximately 20–25 per year. Accumulated savings are estimated to be £1.5 billion and are currently generating savings of £100-200 million a year.

Other useful material

Efficiency Scrutinies – Managing Scrutinies A Guide for Ministers and Managers, The Efficiency Unit, Whitehall (UK)

2.5.2 Improving records management

A record consists of any information, captured in a reproducible form, which is necessary for the proper conduct of the public service. Records management is the function concerned with the capture of complete, accurate and reliable documentation of organisational activity to meet functional, legal, evidential and accountability requirements. *Records management* does not simply consist of the management of information or of data processing or of the application of information technology.

The context for change

Effective records management is a cornerstone of a responsible public service. In the absence of reliable information and records, available when required, public servants will not be able to maintain continuity in decision making. This is likely to result in the following:

- the rights of citizens to register property, to seek redress of laws, and to obtain services for which public funds have been allocated, are compromised or arbitrarily withdrawn;

- the integrity of public assets becomes inadequately protected; and

- as a result, the public service, and consequently the government, may be brought into disrepute.

Reasons for caution

Administrators in many Commonwealth and other countries are finding it increasingly difficult to cope with the growing mass of often incoherently managed paper records, and consequently find it difficult to retrieve the information necessary for the proper fulfilment of their tasks.

In most countries, a common, immediate reaction to the increasing challenge of records management is an over-reliance on new technology and computerisation.

Although modern information technology systems can make information handling easier, more efficient and less costly, the new systems can never become a panacea. Commonwealth experiences point to three weaknesses of many computerised records management approaches:

- **Technological weaknesses**: Information technology promises impressive results, but the new systems and equipment must be sustainable in the local conditions.

- **Economic problems**: Information technology requires significant capital investment in equipment and training. It is important to be certain that the new systems are affordable, including the ongoing cost of maintenance.

- **Operational barriers**: The culture of the organisation, the management and staff may not be consistent with the use of the new systems.

The introduction of computerised systems will not obviate the need for paper and other records. In most countries, computerised records do not represent legal records. For some time, paper records may also be essential as verification of the data held in the system and as a back-up in the event of systems failure.

Achieving change

Planning a new or improved records management system must begin with an in-depth analysis of the existing systems. This analysis will begin with a detailed records inventory which will define the following:

- **volume**: the amount defined in cubic feet, number of records or files, space or capacity used with an estimate of future needs;

- **media used**: paper/files/books; microfiche/film; magnetic tape/disk, optical disks/CD ROM, etc.;

- **creation**: when, how, why, by whom, in what form, are key questions;

- **distribution paths**: who, why, how, how often, and in what order do staff require the records;

- **life cycle**: the length of time that information is current and should be retained, and when and how it can be destroyed;

- **format**: any standard classification system or special form on which the information is gathered and stored;

- **organisation**: the filing systems, codes and indexes currently in use;

- **legal requirements**: certain documents may require special formats, be in a particular media, such as paper, and be subject to particular retention periods; and

- **vital records**: identification of vital records, defined as those the loss of which would seriously prejudice or inhibit the ability of the public service to fulfil its key objectives.

Each of the above will be examined in the light of an in-depth analysis of the organisation's functions, activities and transactions. Taken together with the records inventory, this analysis will provide a basis for the creation of a new records management structure focusing on:

- **Systems and technology**: The choice of an appropriate medium and system for record creation, storage and retrieval will be based on established information flow charts. This will include the design of appropriate forms and security systems necessary to protect the confidentiality and integrity of the information. The use of the information, together with any legal or potential legal requirements should be the primary factors in determining the choice of media technology.

- **Vital records policy**: Vital records must be defined, analysed and categorised. Some major categories of records may require different treatment. In particular, records of information required during catastrophes must be both secure and accessible, and information necessary for later reconstruction must be protected. Records necessary to protect rights and other legal requirements may require special treatment to protect originals.

  In each case, possible protection methods, such as duplication or dispersal, and potential storage facilities, appropriate operating procedures and accountabilities will be determined in the records management structure. The vital records policy should be consistent with disaster planning strategies.

- **Disposition**: The analysis of the information life cycle will indicate the period during which the information held will be active, useful or necessary. Legal requirements will play a central part in the process of determining a record preservation policy. The maintenance of records which do not fall into any of these categories is expensive and an unnecessary use of resources.

  A disposition policy will include procedures for the regular review and appraisal of records with a view to deciding whether they need to be retained or whether they have other values, of a cultural or historical nature, which will determine whether or not they should be transferred to national or other archives.

Examples of change

In *Trinidad and Tobago*, an existing, manual system based on paper records allowed for the following:

- registration and indexing of all records,
- cross-referencing of records,
- tracking of the physical movement of records; and
- retention and disposal scheduling.

Given the importance of proper management and control of information and the timeliness of information flow and retrieval, a move from a manual to an automated record management system, informed on an appropriate business strategy, was deemed desirable.

The National Information Systems Centre developed a software application, the Registry Information System, which can perform some of the functions outlined above. This system, though limited in that it is designed for single-user use, has been installed in 26 Ministries or departments.

Divisions within the Office of the Prime Minister have been selected to participate in a pilot Electronic Mail and Records Management System, which, in addition to the above functions, will provide increased search and retrieval capabilities and will allow for the electronic transfer of records.

Further planned improvements will:

- integrate the management of records with the management of data processing and MIS systems;
- streamline information flows within government departments; and
- encourage and empower staff to upgrade skill in handling recorded information.

In *Malaysia*, in 1981, a change of administrative style emphasising efficiency and productivity in the public sector took place. Improving information and records management is part of the reforms associated with this.

A number of initiatives began the implementation of these reforms including a study by a Cabinet Committee which found various limitations in the information systems for managing developments, such as incomplete, absent, inaccurate or late reporting of information and records and the existence of a number of unintegrated separate databases.

In 1985, the National Committee on Data Processing was set up to oversee the development of an information technology and data processing policy. In 1988 the Malaysian Administrative Modernisation and Management Planning Unit distributed the manual on Guidelines for Computerisation for Public Sector Management which provides guidelines for all aspects of implementing new management information systems.

In the same year the need to co-ordinate IT development led to the formation of the National Consultative Committee on IT with the remit to set standards and to promote co-operation between the public and the private sectors.

Other useful material (current as of 1996)

Government Information Technology Policies and Systems, Success strategies in Developed and Developing Countries, Han, C. K. H. & Walsham, G. Commonwealth Secretariat, 1993 (ComSec)

Information Technology Policies and Applications in the Commonwealth Developing Countries, Odera, M. & Madon, S. Commonwealth Secretariat, 1993 (ComSec)

Records and Record-Keeping: Introducing New Concepts, Records Management Office, Sydney, Australia (AUS)

2.6 Eliminating Corruption

Corruption can manifest itself as individual, organisational or institutional and can be found in both the public and private sectors. In the context of the state, corruption most often refers to criminal or otherwise unlawful conduct by government agencies, or by officials of these organisations acting in the course of their employment.

Combating corruption is a key indicator of commitment to good governance. Poor governance and corruption are major constraints to the pursuit of economic development. For example:

- Bribery increases the costs of government development programmes and spawns projects of little economic merit;

- Corruption undermines revenue collection capacity, contributing to fiscal weaknesses and macro-economic difficulties;

- Diversion of resources from their intended purposes distorts the formulation of public policy;

- The use of bribes to gain access to public services undermines stated allocation priorities, benefiting the few at the expense of the many; and

- Widespread corruption brings government into disrepute and encourages cynicism about politics and public policy.

In public management, weaknesses in public administration result in a decline in the probity of public servants and an inadequate legislative oversight of government. Further, corruption erodes the authority and effectiveness of public institutions. Improvements, therefore, in the effectiveness and transparency of economic policies and administrative reform can contribute significantly to the fight against corruption as well as enhance good governance.

A variety of anti-corruption strategies and measures have been initiated in both developed and developing countries. Anti-corruption agencies have been established in some countries and some have also adopted codes of ethics (conduct), with emphasis on curbing corruption. However, it is not yet clear whether the leadership in these countries has the political will to ensure the effective functioning of these anti-corruption instruments: provision of adequate funding, qualified and independent staff and enforcement of exemplary sanctions. A significant development is the fact that several countries are receiving the assistance of Transparency International (an international NGO leading anti-corruption crusades focused largely on international trade) in fighting some aspects of corruption. There is strong evidence that corruption undermines development efforts. One illustration is the linkage between aid effectiveness and corruption, which has become a regular discussion topic in meetings on development assistance (Consultative Group meetings and Round Tables), since 1997. Since a significant proportion of public spending in some developing countries is derived from development assistance, the linkage is part of the explanation for the increased attention paid to the fight against corruption.

Where corruption is endemic, it is the means to winning and maintaining the benefits of power. Corruption can infiltrate every aspect of government. An understanding of corrupted power systems may be necessary to re-assess democratic integrity. Answers will not be found in political will or anti-corruption commissions alone. Action needs to be pursued in all development activities, as well as in specific anti-corruption measures.

Key outputs could include:

- Transparent mechanisms for political funding;

- Appropriate levels of regulation;

- Performance management and pay policy in pubic services;

- Transparency in government policy and use of resources;

- Independent audit functions;

- Parliamentary oversight of standards and conduct;

- Systems to respond to citizens' complaints;

- Detection and punishment of corruption at all levels; and

- Systems of national and international commercial and criminal law to deter corruption and encourage investment.

Finally, the growing tolerance of diversity in the mass media in most countries with the emergence of independent newspapers and magazines would help the fight against corruption and enhance the use of the other methods of enforcing accountability. The publicity provided in the Press is a check on the abuse of power and this is having some impact in some countries. Equally significant is the fact that the Press in some countries is undertaking investigative journalism and using it to comment on both the conduct of public officials and the quality (or lack thereof) of public services in a manner that was unthinkable in the 1980's. However, the mass media remains underdeveloped in some countries and there is evidence of restrictions on freedom of the Press in others.

Towards an anti-corruption strategy

Although such action was not conceived in the first instance as an element in an anti-corruption strategy, the intervention of the World Bank, Commonwealth Secretariat, United Nations, etc in a number of areas helps countries to control corruption. Four types of action are seen to reduce opportunities for rent-taking by simplifying rules and by replacing administrative rules with market mechanisms:

1. Trade regime reforms, which limit the scope for discretionary treatment by customs officials and replace administrative action with price mechanisms in the allocation of import licences and foreign exchange;

2. Tax reform based on lower, uniform rates and simpler rules and the strengthening of tax administration and record keeping;

3. Regulatory reform, such as the abolition of price controls, the simplification of licence requirements, and similar measures; and

4. Privatisation, to reduce the size of the state enterprise sector under bureaucratic control.

The next three actions are examples of institutional strengthening to improve controls and reduce incentives for corrupt behaviour.

1. Civil Service reform, to restore a professional, accountable, realistically paid, and well-motivated bureaucracy;

2. Strengthening public procurement systems through the reform of laws, more transparent procedures, adoption of improved bidding documentation, competitive bidding and staff training; and

3. Modernisation of public sector accounting, upgrading internal auditing capacity, and strengthening the supreme audit institution.

The agenda could be broadened to include a research programme aimed at a better understanding of:

- The framework of economic incentives for corrupt behaviour;
- Whether some kinds of corruption are more dysfunctional than others;
- The relationship between corruption and political systems;
- Best practices in countries that have succeeded in curbing corruption; and
- Measures that industrialised countries could take to discourage corrupt practices by exporters. In addition, the World Bank should maintain a dialogue with watchdog organisations established to fight corruption and with governments seeking practical ways to reduce the moral and economic costs of corruption.

Other useful material (2nd edition)

Agere, S., (ed) Promoting Good Governance: Principles, Practices and Perspectives. Commonwealth Secretariat, London, 2000

Eigen, P. "Transparency International - The Coalition against Corruption in International Business Transactions", Development and Co-operation, 2,1. 1998

Victor Ayeni, Linda Reif and Hayden Thomas "Strengthening Ombudsman and Human Rights, Institutions in Commonwealth Small and Island States: The Caribbean Experience", 2000.

Victor Ayeni and Keshaw C. Sharma "Public Protector: Ombudsman in Botswana", Commonwealth Consultancy, 2000.

2.6.1 Strengthening anti-corruption measures

Corruption is the misuse of public funds for private profit. No public service is immune from corrupt practices.

Examples include bribery, nepotism, misappropriation of public funds or stores, irregularities in granting import/export licences, under-assessment of income tax and estate duty, irregularity in assessment of tenders and allocation of contracts, remission or reduction of fines and other dues.

The challenge for the public service is to make corruption a high risk, low reward activity.

The context for change

Corruption is an enemy of democracy. It reduces respect for government and the public service and has a detrimental effect on the national economy. The immediate consequences of corrupt practices in the public service are as follows:

- the companies which receive contracts as the result of bribes may not be the best for the job;

- the cost of the bribe is usually added on to the price or financed by reductions in quality;

- the cost of bribes is generally an inflationary factor, and in many cases represents a considerable outflow of capital offshore; and

- systematic corruption has a lasting damaging impact on the morale and reputation of the public service.

There are a number of government activities which are particularly susceptible to corruption. These are:

- public procurement;
- taxation;
- customs and excise;
- police (especially traffic police);
- licences and permits;
- provision of services where there is a state-owned monopoly;
- public service infrastructure contracts;
- construction permits and land-zoning; and
- government appointments.

The scope for corruption is increased by a number of factors:

- low levels of Civil Service pay, requiring additional sources of income;
- lax enforcement or absence of adequate auditing systems within the public sector;
- absence of systems for the regular monitoring of assets and liabilities of public servants;
- absence of widely-shared professional values and ethical standards for the public service;

- under-resourced independent judicial systems providing redress to the public; and
- weak governance institutions which can prevent the deterioration of standards, (including the Civil Service Commissioners), and which can detect failure (including the Office of the Auditor General).

Reasons for caution

Corruption cannot be legislated away. Legislation aimed at deterring corruption is unlikely to be effective unless it is accompanied by a raft of measures designed to ensure implementation, and maximise accountability and transparency. Such measures should minimise temptation, and demonstrate that ethical conduct is both practised and preached at all levels of the public service.

Achieving change

Strategies to reduce corruption fall into six broad categories

1. Strengthening and implementation of legislation

This focuses on improving government integrity through the strengthening and enforcement of existing law, designing effective penalties for bribers and recipients and the development of international support mechanisms.

This strategy must include the development of corruption-free, independent law enforcement agencies and the provision of an effective complaints mechanism which has public trust. This may include the setting up of a specific independent anti-corruption agency.

2. Tightening of systems and audit procedures

This consists of reforms of government procedures to increase transparency which will also discourage corruption. This involves the reform of all bureaucratic, especially procurement practices; the reform of political campaign financing, and, perhaps, of the electoral laws. These reforms should be accompanied by a strengthening of internal and external audits and of the independent judiciary.

3. Improvement of public service performance

Poor service quality encourages corruption as service users seek to bypass official bottlenecks and outdated regulations. Implementation of many of the interrelated reforms designed to improve public service performance outlined in this Portfolio will also discourage corruption. This may include addressing government programmes themselves, some of which may be susceptible to corruption due to poor design or, even, as the result of being unnecessary.

4. Development of a culture of "outrage"

This strategy concerns changing public attitudes through well-planned, long-term education programmes, and "hearts and minds" campaigns, aimed at both the public in general and the public service. The objective should be that corruption should no longer be viewed with cynicism, resignation and acceptance.

5. Positive encouragement to public service integrity

All measures to combat corruption must be reinforced by general reform of and improvements in public service terms and conditions of employment. Improved employment practices, regular and transparent reward systems, and payment, together with appropriate opportunities for career development and promotion, will reduce the pressure for corruption.

6. Strengthening the institutions of governance

As one of the contributing factors to increased corruption is weak governance, anti-corruption strategies must include strengthening the institutions of governance. For example, the Service Commissions are responsible for preventing failure, while government auditing bodies have responsibility for detecting malpractice. The effectiveness of such institutions might be reviewed.

Examples of change

In *Tanzania*, the recent process of trade and economic liberalisation has increased concerns about integrity in the national economy and in the public service. Consequently, in August 1995, a workshop on the National Integrity Systems was held in Arusha, which drew up a detailed proposal for a National Integrity Plan covering all aspects of public life, the public service and the business community. The workshop culminated in the signing of the Arusha Integrity Pledge whereby all participants affirmed their opposition to all forms of corrupt practices and publicly requested actions to be taken against such practices.

When the National Resistance Movement in *Uganda* took power, it recognised the dangers of widespread corruption and, as an initial step, established the Office of Inspector General of the Government to receive complaints and generally investigate practices.

In 1994, a high-level mission representing the EDIDM of the World Bank and Transparency International visited the country. Its report outlines the Government's fight against corruption and makes comprehensive recommendations as to further measures which might be taken to strengthen those measures.

In 1995, the Constituent Assembly increased the authority of the Inspector General of the Government by giving him executive authority in certain areas.

In *Malaysia*, the Anti-Corruption Agency (ACA) is the Government institution directly responsible for enforcing the laws against corruption.

The laws applicable to corruption include:

*   relevant Sections of the Penal Code;

*   the Prevention of Corruption Act 1961; and

*   the Emergency Ordinance No. 22, 1970.

Under these laws it is an offence for public servants to;

*   accept or give any gratification as an inducement or reward for action;

*   give any receipt or account which contains erroneous or defective information with intention to mislead; and

*   use an official position for pecuniary or other advantages.

The ACA has been given a variety of powers including authority:

*   to carry out positive vetting on public servants. Vetting is carried out from time to time, especially before or on promotion;

- to prepare the anti-corruption reports which are passed to the relevant Head of Department. As part of the streamlined procedure, Heads of Departments are required to take immediate action on any reports by the Anti-Corruption Agency;

- to investigate, arrest and prosecute those involved in corrupt activities, irrespective of position or post;

- to conduct surprise inspections or official visits to government departments in order to ensure the absence of corruption; and

- to initiate and conduct joint operations with other law enforcement agencies.

Other measures include requiring departmental managers to develop effective audit and control systems and ensure close supervision of Civil Servants' work; and ensure the application of the Clients Charter.

In *Trinidad and Tobago,* the conduct of public service employees is guided by Service Regulations and Codes of Conduct which, among other matters, prohibit gainful activities outside the service and the acceptance of gifts and rewards.

In addition, there is the Integrity in Public Life Act No. 8 of 1987 which requires persons in the public service to declare their financial affairs. Members of the House of Representatives, Ministers of Government, Parliamentary Secretaries and Chief Technical Officers are required to file declarations of incomes, assets and liabilities annually with the Integrity Commission.

Other useful material (current as of 1996)

The Civil Service of Malaysia – A Paradigm Shift (Chapter 7) (MAL)

Improvements and Development in the Public Service, 1992 (Chapter 7) (MAL)

Current Good Practices and New Developments in Public Service Management. A Profile of the Public Service of Trinidad and Tobago. The Public Service Country Profile Series: No. 4. p. 41. Commonwealth Secretariat, 1994 (ComSec)

2.7 Creating a Framework for Change

2.7.1 Introducing business planning

The public service, to be effective, must be concerned with the quality of the services that it provides. Government, therefore, needs to regularly review its operations in order to ensure that services are provided in the most efficient and cost-effective manner.

In the public service, a key tool in this process is the budget, which is the financial plan for the period in question. However, financial plans require organisations within the public service to think strategically about their programmes.

Business planning provides the opportunity for this strategic thinking. A successful business plan describes:

- the mission of the organisation – its identity and direction;
- the objectives of the organisation, and specific performance targets;
- the strategy by which those objectives will be achieved;
- the support mechanisms necessary; and
- the mechanisms for reviewing objectives and for reporting progress.

The context for change

The primary objective of business planning in the public service is to provide the government with accurate information regarding recurrent resource allocations and proposed capital expenditures. However, another important benefit is improved decision-making abilities at all levels, which result from the business planning process.

Business planning is applicable whether the service provided is internal to the government, such as policy advice, or external and mainly concerned with providing goods and services to the public.

This process ensures that Ministries are fully aware of the resource costs of their respective portfolios, and the value-added through long and short-term initiatives. Business planning is also important at the divisional and department level. In order to manage a programme effectively, a manager must be fully aware of the operating constraints, such as social, economic and policy considerations; financial and human resource concerns; impacts on other departments; trade issues and the external environment.

Benefits arising from business planning include subtle long-term advantages, such as changing and broadening managerial attitudes towards programme responsibility, and tangible, visible benefits, such as improved data collection for decision-making.

Reasons for caution

Business planning will fail unless the five main components of the process: mission, objectives, strategy, implementation and evaluation, are addressed in detail:

- The mission statement answers the questions: who are we? what is the business that the organisation is in? and where is it heading? The statement gives identity and direction. It states what the organisation aims to become, not what it is now.

- The objectives answer the "what" question. These are high-level objectives that an organisation wishes to fulfil and that translates the mission statement into specific performance targets. Long-term objectives, anything from three to five years, guide managers as to what to do now to have the organisation ready to produce desired results later. Short-term goals – or milestone accomplishments along the way – need to be established in order to ensure that the organisation stays on target and is in a position to evaluate progress. Objectives and goals must be measurable, they should be quantifiable, realistic and achievable.

- The strategy is the "how" of business planning. It determines the moves required in order to attain objectives. It addresses the questions: what must be done? when? how should we do it?

  To plan the correct strategy the Ministry or department needs to analyse current operations as well as identifying strengths and weaknesses, opportunities and threats. This analysis is carried out within the context of the stated mission and objectives.

- For a Ministry or department to "implement" its business plan successfully, it must provide the relevant mechanisms and infrastructure. The process must be institutionalised through the development of supportive policies and procedures, reporting systems, reward programmes, training programmes and technology. Implementation requires an "action agenda" which involves listing all relevant steps, stating who is responsible and by when, and then regularly monitoring progress.

- Strategy and objectives need to be periodically reviewed and evaluated to assess whether actions occur according to plans, and to adjust for priority changes caused by changed circumstances. Evaluation is necessary to assess performance. If goals are not reached, either the performance target or mechanisms used to achieve that target need to be reviewed. Performance measures establish a clear link between results and resources. They foster a results-oriented culture. Performance measures also aid the performance management review process, making it more objective and motivating.

Achieving change

Piloting business planning in the public service and then subsequently gearing up to full business and financial planning allows for measurement of the capacity of the public service to undertake the process. Success is more likely to ensue by phasing in coverage of the complete business planning approach rather than attempting full implementation across the board.

Ministries may undertake planning at the departmental level and then aggregate it at Ministry level. This means ranking priorities, and looking for efficiency and shared resources across the portfolio.

To introduce the new approach, managers may be required to attend seminars on business planning and could receive "hands on" assistance from external consultants to develop their initial business plans following approved guidelines. A sample Ministry business plan can provide managers with additional information on the level of detail required to substantiate their programme resource requirements.

The success of business planning depends on the following factors:

- *Active, visible support from Permanent Secretaries and heads of departments.* This means communicating the business planning philosophy to all levels in all programmes, to all support units, and to finance officers, human resources officers, operational managers and major inter-ministerial committees. Senior managers must be prepared to help junior managers conduct planning meetings and develop plans. They must also evaluate their subordinate managers on their performance in attaining the stated targets.

- *Permanent Secretaries and heads of departments accountable for implementing business planning.* This accountability, however, has to be pushed down the line to the lowest appropriate level by ensuring that an individual is responsible for achieving each goal stated by the organisation. Accountability is secured by placing a high emphasis on business planning in performance agreements and performance review processes.

- *Internal mechanisms for business planning established.* Focus groups with employees; surveys – internal and external; task forces, and project teams can assist in developing achievable but demanding objectives and in securing wide ownership of the mechanisms for reviewing goals and reporting progress.

- *Assistance to Ministries in completing their planning submissions.* At each stage in the planning process, staff from the Ministry of Finance, or other central agency, could help Ministries and departments and parastatal organisations to develop a coherent framework, relevant to the specific situation of the Ministry.

- *Feedback.* Business planning is iterative and can only improve through trial, evaluation and feedback.

Examples of change

In *Trinidad and Tobago,* in 1993, all Ministries and departments were asked to develop five year strategic plans to include:

- a vision or mission statement defining core purposes, strategic objectives and strategies for attaining them;

- an estimate of the physical, human and financial resources required; and

- yearly action plans on which to base annual budgeting estimates and to monitor and evaluate progress.

Responsibility for the execution of these instructions was given to the Permanent Secretary of each Ministry and implementation was as follows:

- appointment of a change team or steering group representing all levels of the organisation;

- setting up of series of workshops, think-tanks, and "brainstorming" groups on the following issues:
  - defining organisations, either Ministry or departments, mission or vision statement;
  - assessing the impact of environmental factors and forces;
  - assessing and analysing current and future realities;
  - identifying stake holders; and
  - developing strategies for planning.

This was followed by the appointment of a "planning team" which might or might not be the "change team", which then proceeded with the planning exercise.

During the exercise the following principles were followed:

- the relevant Ministers were kept informed of, and where possible, included in the process;
- efforts and results were communicated as widely as possible;
- responsibility for implementation was suggested and assigned; and
- plans included provision for evaluation of progress and compliance.

In *Malta*, business planning was introduced in pilot Ministries and geared up to full business and financial planning. The Ministry of Social Security and the Department of Health were first selected as pilots. The Ministry of Social Security being one of the largest spenders, while the Department of Health was in the process of reviewing its programme.

By 1993, all Ministries had submitted three-year business plans for the period 1994-1996. Plans were initially prepared at department level and were then aggregated to Ministry level.

Programme Managers were required to examine their activities over the period in question and had to concentrate on outputs resulting in:

- improved decision-making at all levels;
- smoother and more accurate budgeting and estimating;
- quicker identification of opportunities; and
- increased effectiveness, consistency and improved services.

Managers were provided with internal training through a series of seminars and received assistance from external consultants.

Other useful material (2nd edition)

Business and Financial Planning, Ministry of Finance, Government of Malta 1992 (MLT) Mission Statement of the Cabinet Secretariat, Trinidad and Tobago (TT)

Mission Statement of the Ministry of Health on a prototype for the proposed Regional Health Authority, Trinidad and Tobago (TT)

Institute of Public Administration of Canada, Business Planning in Canadian Public Administration, 2001

2.7.2 Managing change

In the public service, the key question is not whether change will happen, it is how it will take place.

Approaches for *managing change* are based on the following premises:

- change is always disruptive;
- change can be managed successfully;
- tried and tested approaches exist for successful change management; and
- when change is not managed, the results are often poor.

The context for change

The major dimensions of change in current public service reforms can be summarised as follows:

- changes in management culture and style following the move from administration, concerned with process, to managerial concerns to maximise efficiency;
- re-examination of work methods and changes in working practices consequent on the introduction of new technology;
- restructuring and reorganisation necessary to focus on outputs;
- changed performance management frameworks, emphasising output targets and accepting strict accountability through performance appraisal, with limited-term contracts and monetary incentives; and
- changes in financial management regimes to ensure transparency in the allocation of costs.

Reasons for caution

Change management presupposes that change drivers are able to influence key aspects of the process.

- **The establishment of measurable objectives**: effective change management requires that clearly defined, articulated and measurable goals, translated from organisational mission statements, form the basis of the action plans governing the change process.

- **The development of teamwork**: effective change management requires that team members identify with the department, Ministry or other unit, its objectives, as well as with their job; they participate in discussions relating to the effectiveness of the organisation; and respect their dependency on each other.

- **The strengthening of communication**: effective communication underpins effective leadership for change. Change management is a participatory process involving all levels of staff to ensure that all members of the organisation feel that they are making a contribution.

- **The recognition of mistakes**: change management requires that mistakes are recognised as opportunities to diagnose problems, and that dealing with them is part of the communication process.

If change drivers are unable to influence these four aspects of the change process, effective change management is weakened considerably.

Achieving change

Commonwealth experiences in managing change in the public service at the macro-level and in relation to incremental improvements indicate that:

- **Change requires a sufficient catalyst**: for successful and sustained change there must exist in the organisation a sufficient catalyst or tension, created either by a compelling vision of the future or a compelling threat in the present. In the real world, change is often driven by both, and the challenge for management is to harness them and achieve a balance.

- **People adapt to change more easily when they are involved**: successful organisations involve all staff in the change process, not just in providing feedback after the fact, but in the planning and implementation stages.

- **Managers must use power judiciously to build and maintain momentum**: successful leadership achieves far-reaching influence by delegating power and authority; giving staff responsibility for analysing critical issues; discretion and autonomy over tasks and resources, and recognition for their efforts.

Implementation of the change process involves four main steps, often described as the change journey:

Step 1: Preparation for change

Through continuous communication, this step includes securing the support and commitment of staff; ensuring that the reform goals are understood; identification of specific aspects of change and the contribution to be made by staff; and the establishment of a vision for the future.

Step 2: Analysis for change

The object is the identification of the gaps between the existing reality and the desired future, and the strengths and weaknesses of the organisation. This will include identification of both the forces and the "champions", supporters of change, and the resistances, those who stand to lose from, or who might otherwise oppose, change.

Step 3: Design for change

This consists of the preparation of a detailed implementation plan for the changes and reforms identified in Steps 1 and 2. The plan will include engagement tactics through which people will be involved and committed to reform. These include communication; authority and accountability; training and coaching staff to accept change; demonstrations of concern for staff, including potential losers; the creation of monitoring and reporting mechanisms; the approach to the risks associated with change; and the learning and development process.

Step 4: Implementation of change

Implementation will include the establishment and training of project teams; the development of strategies to overcome resistance and of the appropriate communication channels. It should provide opportunities for regular monitoring and evaluation at key stages; and, for ensuring that successful changes are institutionalised.

Examples of change

The Government of *Malta* is committed to a more efficient Public Service following the report of the Public Service Report Commission. A large number of changes have already been put into place, including:

- amendments to the legal framework of the public administration function;
- the establishment of "central change agencies" to lead and support administrative reform; and
- the restructuring of senior levels of Ministries and departments.

Change management approaches have been developed by the Management Systems Unit to assist change drivers at all points in the public service.

Experience in the *UK* Civil Service indicates that successful radical change depends on committed senior management winning the co-operation of staff. In recent years, a number of such changes have been implemented, of which two examples stand out: The first example involves changes in the structure of government, particularly in the creation of Executive Agencies as outlined in the Next Steps Initiative. While the principal objective of such changes is always greater efficiency, value for money, and accountability, it has always been recognised that the co-operation of staff is essential.

Usually staff involved moved with their functions to ensure continuity, although they were always offered the opportunity of returning to their original departments if they wished. This recognised the existence of a considerable loyalty to the parent departments, which, if lightly discarded, might result in a loss of efficiency.

A second example of radical change was the introduction of the practice of work measurement. In planning work measurement, the approach is always influenced by both the views of senior management and of the trade unions involved. The support and co-operation of, in particular, the latter can ensure the absence of resentment and can contribute to successful implementation of any changes.

In *Canada*, the introduction of Special Operating Agencies represented a similar radical change. In the establishment of the Canada Communication Group, the employees were, from the beginning, seen as the key to the success of the agency. In order to ensure co-operation and commitment the management adopted a policy of open management, whereby employees were kept fully informed of and were invited to participate in the problem-solving process.

During the planning stage the Chief Executive made a point of meeting staff at all levels, making presentations, answering questions and listening to views.

In the transition period, the objects of change – output orientation and customer satisfaction – were continuously reinforced and employees were further encouraged to suggest methods by which performance could be improved.

Improvements in levels of service and efficiency were rewarded with token gifts as at that time other, private sector, incentives, such as profit-sharing, were not available.

Two comparative surveys of employee views and perceptions were carried out. These were used to monitor attitudes to change, general job satisfaction and confidence in management.

In retrospect, the key to success in adapting to change was considered to be the practice of total communication and consultation with staff in order to secure trust in, and co-operation with, management.

Other useful material (current as of 1996)

Becoming a Special Operating Agency, Treasury Board of Canada, 1991 (CAN)

Managing Change in the Public Service – A Guide for The Perplexed. The Task Force on Workforce Adaptiveness. Public Service 2000, 1991 (CAN)

Career Management and Succession Planning Study, The Efficiency Unit. HMSO, 1993 (UK)

2.8 Promoting Good Governance

Good governance can be defined as the exercise of political, economic and administrative authority to manage a nation's affairs. This includes the complex array of mechanisms, relationships and institutions through which citizens manage affairs involving public life.

While there are many challenges for public administration emanating from these declarations, there are a few critical ones, which deserve serious attention by public administrators and policy makers alike. The first challenge is to define what good governance is. The second is to formulate and apply principles, such as ethics and values, as the foundation of a strong public sector. This includes an understanding of the evolution of values, specifically the tensions between old and new values, and the ethical challenges brought about by the new public management. The third challenge is how to design codes of conduct that can ensure that organisations set standards that are applicable across the board, that are clearly understood and enforceable and upon which training may be based. The last challenge is how to institutionalise such values into bureaucracy and how elected officials can promote good governance with a public service whose ethos and values are changing.

The context for change

The concept of good governance has come into regular use in political science, public administration, and development management. It appears alongside such concepts and terms as democracy, civil society, popular participation, and human rights, social and sustainable development. Within the public management discipline it has been regarded as an aspect of the new paradigm on public administration which emphasises: the role of public managers in providing high quality services that citizens value; increasing managerial autonomy, particularly by reducing central agency controls; demands for measures and rewards for both organisational and individual performance; the importance of providing the human and technological resources that managers require to meet their performance targets; and is open-minded about which public purposes should be performed by public servants as opposed to private sector providers.

A number of important perspectives emerge from this new paradigm which has been the subject of debate since the beginning of the public sector reform in many countries of the world. As a result of these reforms and the emphasis on good governance, various bodies e.g. the Non-Government Organisations (NGO's) also claim to have a role in the promotion of good governance. The emerging perspectives regarding good governance structures are: relationships between governments and markets; governments and citizens; governments and the private sector, elected and appointed officials; local government institutions and urban and rural dwellers; legislature and executive and relationships between nation states and international institutions.

These relationships have led many public management practitioners to formulate various procedures, rules and processes through which genuine good governance can be achieved, and have further identified the principles and assumptions that underpin good governance. The practitioners have also drawn on examples of best practice for use in putting the concept into practice. Different perspectives, principles and best practices have been the subject of debate at many national and international conferences, attempting to define good governance.

Attempts have been made to develop some characteristics of good governance. Some practitioners have argued that good governance can be attained by identifying the following characteristics and practices of poor governance:

- Failure to make a clear distinction between what is public and what is private, hence a tendency to divert public resources for private gain;
- Failure to establish a predictable framework of law, government behaviour and rule of law;
- Excessive rules and regulations which impede the functioning of markets;
- Priorities inconsistent with development, resulting in misallocation of resources;
- Non-transparent decision-making processes; and
- Lack of a code of conduct in managing the affairs of the state.

Good governance is, therefore, a wide subject area that includes:

- Economic liberalism which constitutes private ownership, investment and greater equality;
- Political pluralism, which refers to the democratic participation of people in the development process and decentralisation of authority from the centre;
- Social development which includes human rights, rule of law, an independent judiciary and a free press;
- Administrative accountability which refers to transparency, less corruption, economy, efficiency and effectiveness; and
- Public sector reforms, strategic planning and management of change.

Reason for caution

Different states, civil society, non-government organisations and private sector organisations who are the key players in the process of good governance tend to place emphasis on aspects in which they have interest or in which they dominate in terms of their available resources or their mandate. Within the struggle for supremacy of good governance are:

- The fear of domination by powerful groups and interests;
- The threats by those not likely to benefit from good governance or those who are likely to lose when good governance is legitimised, e.g. the military, dictators;
- Many self-appointed bodies now claim a right to have a role in the governance of the country. Some NGO's might even represent not internal but external interested parties; and
- Tension between and among stakeholder's e.g. politicians and Civil Servants; state and citizens etc.

Concerns have been raised about some governance issues. These concerns centre on such issues as: accountability for an activity which has been contracted out, maintenance of ethical standards in privatised industries, etc. Other tensions exist such as tension between decentralising service delivery and accountability to citizens; between the desire for flexibility and the risk of political mistake; between democratic participation and the capture of interest groups.

Achieving change

While there may be no best way of achieving good governance, the following stand out as the most common elements through which changes could be assessed and maintained.

Accountability

Accountability is a cornerstone of public governance and management because it constitutes the principle that informs the processes whereby those who hold and exercise public authority are held to account. Accountability encompasses processes whereby citizens hold their governors to account for their behaviour and performance directly through elections and via representatives of citizens in legislative assemblies.

Political executives and public servants are accountable through mechanisms of public scrutiny and audit. Political executives hold their subordinate officials accountable through hierarchical structures of authority and responsibility. In addition, various administrative tribunals and commissions hold legislatures, executives or administrative officers accountable to law.

The purposes that accountability are meant to serve are essentially threefold:

1. To control for the abuse and misuse of public authority;

2. To provide assurance in respect to the use of public resources and adherence to the law and public service rules; and

3. To encourage and promote learning in pursuit of continuous improvement in governance and public management.

Central to the processes of accountability is the fact that various pressures on governments have led to changes in both governance and public management as governments have sought to respond to these several imperatives and demands. At least three broad sets of changes or reform are critical in this respect:

1. The first initiative is to introduce a greater degree of devolution in managing public affairs;

2. The second initiative is to introduce a greater degree of shared governance and collaborative management in the conduct of public business; and

3. Thirdly, the efforts of governments to address demands both for results and for demonstrated performance with respect to results have led to changes in the way that governments are managed and report to citizens.

Transparency

Transparency is broadly defined as public knowledge of the policies of government and confidence in its intentions. This requires making public accounts verifiable, providing for public participation in government policy making and implementation, and allowing contestations over choices impacting on the lives of citizens. It also includes making available for public scrutiny accurate and timely information on economic and market conditions.

Combating corruption

Combating corruption is a key indicator of a commitment to good governance. Corruption can manifest itself as individual, organisational and or institutional. Poor governance and corruption are major constraints to the pursuit of economic development. For example:

• Bribery increases the costs of government developmental programmes and projects of little economic merit;

• Corruption undermines revenue collection capacity, contributing to fiscal weaknesses and macro-economic difficulties;

- Diversion of resources from their intended purposes distorts the formulation of public policy;
- The use of bribes to gain access to public services undermines stated allocation priorities, benefiting the few at the expense of the many; and
- Widespread corruption brings government into disrepute and encourages cynicism about politics and public policy.

Stakeholder participation

Participation can be defined as a process whereby stakeholders exercise influence over public policy decisions, and share control over resources and institutions that affect their lives, thereby providing a check on the power of government. In the context of governance, participation is focused on the empowerment of citizens and addressing the interplay between the broad range of civil societies, actors and actions. It occurs at various levels: at the grassroots, through local and civic institutions; at the regional and national levels, through flexible and decentralised forms of government; and also in the private sector.

Legal and judicial framework

A pro-governance and pro-development legal and judicial system is one in which laws are clear and are uniformly applied through an objective and independent judiciary. It is also one in which the legal system provides the necessary sanctions to deter or penalise breach. It promotes the rule of law, human rights and private capital flows. Enforcement involves firm action against corrupt behaviour at all levels.

Activities for popularizing governance issues

The promotion of good governance is the responsibility of all sectors, civil society participants and international organisations. There are a variety of activities and programmes that can promote good governance:

- Identify emerging issues on the role of the state, private sector and civil society in service delivery;
- Promote programmes that encourage forms of partnership between the public and private sector and civil society organisations in the delivery of public services;
- Develop new guidelines and principles for new approaches to good governance and demonstrate some success. Improve efficiency and the scope and quality of public service provision;
- Assist governments with public sector reforms that facilitate the promotion of good governance and eradicate corruption;
- Persuade governments, through dialogue, of the need for institutional and public sector management assessments, respect for human rights and the rule of law; and
- Help deal with especially complex issues of poverty alleviation and environment for which the quality of government performance is important.
- Conduct seminars, debates and conferences in which the best practices are shared between and among government officials at both policy and programme levels;

Achieving change

In order to facilitate and accelerate the promotion of good governance, to share principles of best practices with governments and to find appropriate solutions, some Commonwealth countries have mounted programmes on policy and management development. The focus of these programmes has been in the following areas:

- Governance structures and the democratic process

  The focus of this programme has been on the role of Parliament and its relationship with the Executive. The rationale for this focus was based on three factors: first, practically all Commonwealth countries have now embraced liberal democratic values. Their determination to guard these jealously has brought into greater focus the role of institutions such as Parliament and overseeing bodies in the consolidation of democratic reforms.

  Secondly, is the impact of ongoing reforms in other sectors, notably the economy and public administration. A significant feature of these is the far-reaching change towards more open, market-based economic arrangements and public sector reforms.

  Thirdly, the Commonwealth Secretariat, the Commonwealth Parliamentary Association (CPA) and other affiliate bodies such as the Local Government Forum, Commonwealth Association for Public Administration and Management (CAPAM) have striven to educate and support their members in dealing with the different dimensions of these developments.

- Strengthening Cabinet decision making

  A few programmes have been mounted which focus on strengthening Cabinet as the executive leadership machinery of the state. To assist systematic thinking about improving Cabinet performance, the focus of programmes has been on the basic functions of Cabinet, some typical deficiencies in the outputs of Cabinet activity and some of the institutional and process devices that have been employed in different countries to remedy those deficiencies.

- The political and administrative interface

  The programmes to support the formal relationship between the Minister (elected official) and the Permanent Secretary (appointed official) are based on the assumption that successful policy development and management depends upon a meaningful relationship between the two sets of officials and leadership. The interface or the working relationship between the politician and the Civil Servant becomes critical to the success of administrative reforms and good governance.

  The purposes of these programmes have been to redefine the roles and responsibilities of the Minister and Permanent Secretary in the implementation of the administrative reforms, identify policy and administrative boundaries between elected and appointed officials, and to share best practices, processes and procedures of enhancing the functional relationship through the exchange of ideas and experiences.

- Civil Service reform

  The reform of the state institutions so that they become more efficient, accountable and transparent, is a cornerstone of good governance. Effective reforms require political and administrative will and commitment, which should include the private sector and civil society.

- Local governance and institutional development

  Several management programmes have been organised to support and strengthen local government institutions and to build capacity to respond appropriately to the needs of local people. The programmes have assisted governments in making choices when confronted with the need to reorganise administrative and political structures and procedures designed to decentralise government and administration. Administrative reform for decentralisation is intended to achieve both good management and good governance more generally. Such programmes have emphasised the participation of people in decision making and development at local level.

- **Support of overseeing institutions**

  A lot of support has been provided to overseeing institutions, such as the Ombudsman. The support has been mainly in the training of staff and upgrading of skills and knowledge in the operation of their duties. Similar support has also been offered to electoral commissions, the judiciary, the comptroller and auditor general's office and anti-corruption commissions.

- **Anti-corruption measures**

  Commonwealth Finance Ministers at one of their fora proposed a number of solutions and strategies to fight against corruption. The following suggestions were made:

  – Popular mobilisation against corruption;

  – Involvement of the private sector and civil society in fighting corruption; and

  – The need for an international response: there is a strong case on a number of grounds for international co-operation in fighting corruption.

- **Leadership, policy development and managing change**

  Support for leadership development and managing change cuts across governance efforts. Effective leadership, essential for a good governance programme, is particularly important when countries are undergoing complex or systematic change involving civil society and the private sector. Effective leadership entails developing the capacities of everyone who can increase political and administrative commitment to sustainable human development. The seminars organised by the Commonwealth Fund for Technical Co-operation for Permanent Secretaries are a clear outcome of good governance as they focus on leadership and change management.

  Effective public sector leaders:

  – must be aware of both their internal and external environments and the implications of change;

  – must be prepared to question prevailing assumptions and facilitate dialogue;

  – must develop and articulate visions for the future;

  – need to allow people to explore new possibilities and to develop their potential;

  – need to build coalitions and collaborative relationships;

  – must ensure an alignment of performance with vision;

  – must be able to integrate different cultures, styles, sectors and disciplines;

  – must be receptive to information and be open to feedback;

  – must build support teams; and

  – must be willing to experiment and take risks in the areas of transformation and change.

Principles of good governance

Examples of building and implementing these components of a good governance programme are evident across the Commonwealth and include:

- The Commonwealth Secretariat has held many top-level seminars to formulate the strengthening of Cabinet offices in Barbados, Malawi, Zambia, etc.;

- Joint workshops for Ministers and Permanent Secretaries were conducted in Grenada, St.Kitts & Nevis, Sierra Leone, Mauritius, Swaziland, etc;

- Periodic workshops have been held to improve the leadership role of the Permanent Secretary and senior officials. Such workshops have been held in Canada, New Zealand;

- Anti-Corruption Commissions were set up in Zambia, Zimbabwe, etc. Ombudsman's offices have long been established in the UK, Canada, Namibia, Trinidad and Tobago, and Botswana. Vanuatu now has an Ombudsman's office staffed by qualified personnel;

- Governance Policy Units were established in the UK, Zambia, and Zimbabwe;

- CAPAM, the Local Government Forum have all addressed issues of good governance in the workshops that they have conducted; and

- The survey on how Canadians perceive governance and public service have resulted in the finding that five drivers determining service quality.

Other useful material (2nd edition)

Agere, S. Promoting Good Governance: Principles, Practices and Perspectives. Commonwealth Secretariat, London, 2000.

Draper, G., "Developing Leaders for Commonwealth Public Services". Revised February, 2002.

State of Governance: Mahathir Mohamed, Prime Minister of Malaysia. Public Administration and Development. The International Journal of Management Research and Practice Vol 18 No 5 December 1998.

Unpublished paper, Commonwealth Expert Group on Good Governance and the Elimination of Corruption in Economic Management 1999.

Commonwealth Secretariat: Strengthening Cabinet Decision-Making in Commonwealth Countries, 1999.

Aucoin, Peter and Heinzmen, Ralph. The dialectics of Accountability for performance in public management. International Review of Administrative Sciences Vol. 66 (2000)

M.M. Khan, Good Governance: The case for Bangladesh. Asia Journal of Public Management Vol. X No 2 Dec 1998.

Lord Nolan, CAPAM Biennial Conference, Report by S. Borins, 1998.

Kaul, M. An Outsider's Inside View: Managing Reforms in Government CAPAM, 2000.

The United Nations Development Paper (UNDP Report 1998)

Institute of Public Administration of Canada (IPAC), Citizen's First 2000. Summary Report: A survey on improving government services:

People-Centered Development: The Challenge of Globalisation, October 1999.

UK, Cabinet Office, Civil Service Reform: Report to the Prime Minister from Sir Richard Wilson, Head of Home Civil Service, 1999.

Citizens and Governance: Civil Society in New Millennium: Commonwealth Foundation in Partnership with Civicuz, September 1999.

2.9 Strengthening Cabinet Decision Making

The constitution provides the fundamental governance framework within which a society allocates and constrains the powers to govern in the public interest. It is a necessary, but insufficient condition of good government. Sufficiency comes from the Executive having the effective means of ensuring that good decisions are taken and executed. Major policy decisions are formulated by Cabinet, which also oversees the implementation of the same policies and programmes. In the Commonwealth, the apex of the policy process is the Cabinet.

Contextual issues

The questions which arise about Cabinets and their supporting systems are typically of very different kinds. For example:

- How does Cabinet stay in charge? How is Cabinet held to account to the legislature and ultimately the public?

- What kinds of decisions should go to Cabinet?

- How can national vision be linked with the budget and with the direction of the public sector?

- Where does Cabinet get advice and support on cross-sectoral and whole-of-government issues?

- What is the appropriate division of labour between Ministers and Permanent Secretaries?

- What information should Cabinet require from the public service on a regular basis?

- How can Cabinet Ministers and central agencies keep spending within agreed budget policy limits? and

- How does Cabinet control its own policy making when development resources are from foreign sources?

Role and functions

The role of the Cabinet is to shape and oversee the whole of government policy. It is through the Cabinet that the major interests relevant to whole-of-government policy are integrated and, where necessary, reconciled. For example, between Ministers collectively and Ministers individually; public interest and partisan politics; and commerce and social welfare.

In playing this role the Cabinet has three main functions which it and only it can perform effectively. These are:

- Giving strategic direction to the government as a whole;

- Ensuring effective decision-making arrangements for the government as a whole; and

- Maintaining the effectiveness and integrity of government systems.

Beyond its specific functions, the Cabinet, as the top decision-making body for the Executive sets the standard for policy making at subordinate levels of the system.

Common Cabinet failings

The successful performance of these functions is inhibited by a variety of failings. The most important ones include the following:

- Decisions made by the Cabinet are inconsistent with its own strategic framework and agreed priorities, whether because of pressure of events, crises, sectional (including donor) interests, unexpected developments, inadequate information, defective policy analysis or any combination of these;

- Decisions or actions taken by individual Ministers are inconsistent with agreed Cabinet strategy;

- The Head of Government dominates decision making to the point that important national interests are given inadequate attention;

- Important collective decisions are not taken, or taken badly, because of the hold-out power of individual portfolio Ministers;

- Departmental Ministers and officials pursue sectional interests to the detriment of "whole-of-government" objectives;

- There is inadequate co-ordination between departments either in introducing new policies or in implementing existing policies;

- Cabinet decisions are ignored by operating units or are implemented in ways not intended;

- Decisions taken by the political leadership are ignored by the Civil Service;

- The achievement of objectives which, in political or administrative terms, should be given high priority, is frustrated by the inflexible application of financial policies;

- Conversely, the achievement of agreed financial objectives is frustrated by inappropriate activities on the part of individual Ministers and departments; total expenditure frequently exceeds agreed budget limits;

- Cabinet decisions take inadequate account of other parties' (the legislature, public, international – including donors) opinion;

- Different parts of the government speak with different voices in public; and

- The government does not command the confidence of the public.

Some contributory causes

The essential first step in correcting these failings is to identify the contributory causes. The causes will often be multiple. The most common include the following:

- The Cabinet has no agreed strategy or clear order of priorities to provide a framework for individual decisions (including decisions on donor proposals);

- The Cabinet is over-burdened with business; the supporting structure of sub-committees is absent, inadequate, under-used or lacks authority;

- The Cabinet agenda is not systematically managed; too many minor issues come to Cabinet while major decisions of concern to government as a whole are taken in other forums or at lower levels;

- The Cabinet pays insufficient attention to long-term issues and to anticipating undesired developments;

- Portfolios are organised in a way which makes good decision making difficult, either by excessively concentrating power in some individuals, or by dissipating authority so that there is no coherence on important national interests;

- Issues are not fully discussed in the Cabinet; consensus in Cabinet discussions tends to develop prematurely; Cabinet members have no incentives to express dissent;

- The Chief Executive/Head of Government tends to by-pass Cabinet;

- Cabinet decisions are not effectively communicated to or understood by operating units;

- Cabinet size and composition are inappropriate; Cabinet members are chosen for the wrong reasons; Cabinet members have too few incentives to collaborate;

- There are neither adequate rules for the conduct of Cabinet business nor any authority capable of enforcing such rules;

- The Finance Ministry has excessive authority in relation to the rest of government;

- There is no public servant with the authority to manage from a whole-of-government perspective;

- There is inadequate differentiation between the roles of Ministers and Civil Servants;

- The competence, skills and values of the Civil Service, and the systems and structures of government, are inadequate or inappropriate for the tasks to be performed; Civil Service career patterns reinforce sectionalism;

- There are no agreed standards or systems for measuring the performance of government, nor institutional resources available to Cabinet for improving performance;

- There are no systems for managing external communications;

- External mechanisms for accountability and scrutiny are inadequate and/or are ignored; and

- There are no internal mechanisms for correcting these defects.

Remedies

To a large extent the remedies to these and other failings must rest on clarifying the responsibilities and relationships between and among the principal actors. Other remedies include:

- Establishing and maintaining the right balance between groups of activities and objectives as Cabinet's major task. Especially important are the relationships between the public interest and the interests of the party; between politics and administration; between policy and finance; between long-term and short-term objectives and policies;

- Heads of Government must also consider the appropriate checks and balances on power in the allocation of Cabinet responsibilities; and

- Institutions, processes and rules should be put in place to correct some of the above deficiencies.

Ensuring effective decision-making arrangements for government as a whole

- Cabinet must make some decisions for the government as a whole and this collective role must be able to override individual Ministerial interests;

- Arrangements are also needed to ensure that decisions, once made, are actually acted upon; and

- There must be a unit with authority to enforce rules in the interests of orderly decision making.

Maintaining the effectiveness and integrity of government systems

- Cabinet must ensure that the systems and structures of government, through which it receives advice and which implement the policies which it has approved, are fully effective for their tasks;

- Capability of the public service must be ensured through good human resources management practices;

- The operation of the processes around statutory appointments, and the governance arrangements for, and accountability of, Boards of Directors exercising state powers and/or resources should be ethical, transparent and accountable; and

- Cabinet must know, for a start, how well the government is doing. It needs both internal and external means of monitoring, evaluating and, wherever feasible, improving the performance of government.

Other useful material (2nd edition)

David Walker, " Tigress Surrounded by Hamsters" article in the Guardian, March 1999
Comment by Participants in Commonwealth In-country workshop on Improving Cabinet Decision-making 1999.

United Kingdom Cabinet Office, "Cabinet Committee Business: A guide for Departments", 1997.

Budget Speech for the 1998 Budget for the Republic of South Africa

United Kingdom White Paper " The Civil Service: Taking Forward Continuity and Change" January 1995.

Lipson, "The Politics of Equality", CAPAM, Practice Knowledge Centre.

Arthur Kroeger, Commonwealth Seminar on Developing Public Policy Capacity for the 21st Century, Ottawa, 1997.

Alex Matheson and William Plowden. Excerpts form Governance for the XX1st Century Series: Occasional Paper No2 Strengthening Cabinet Decision-making in Commonwealth Countries. Commonwealth Secretariat 1999.

Nick Manning, "Institutional Arrangements for Supporting Cabinet", Economic Development Institute, World Bank 1998.

2.10 Management of Transitional Government: Change, Choice, Continuity

The Commonwealth Heads of Government committed themselves, amongst other issues, to the promotion of just and honest government. Following this declaration there have been numerous workshops, conferences and seminars held by CAPAM and the Commonwealth Secretariat to translate what just and honest government means, the form it should take, the values and ethics that underpin it. These fora have also included discussions of best practices developed by the public administration as an instrument of the state, the relationship between agents of the state e.g. elected and appointed officials, executive and judiciary, etc.

In essence, all these conferences and seminars have addressed the best ways and means of promoting and adjusting to change and crisis, making choices in management and the delivery of service, and simultaneously maintaining some elements of continuity within the political and administrative system. Change, choice and continuity, while sounding contradictory, can be managed effectively by both the political and administrative machinery of the state in the right environment. It is the critical balance of advocating changes and making choices and at the same time continuing with tradition that can constitute crisis and uncertainty about the outcome.

Transition is defined as a movement, development or passage from one stage or form to another. It connotes an element of foresight, planning and purpose. Transitions require a particular management style. It is in the movement from one type of management to another that transition problems can be experienced which would require a new type of management different from the traditional approach.

The crisis in transition has come about as a result of experiences that many Commonwealth countries are facing. The transformation is unprecedented and is characterised by the need for greater freedom for self-expression in the political sphere and improved material well-being and better delivery of services.

Many Commonwealth conferences and workshops have shown that, despite the diversity of Commonwealth countries, there has been a common pattern in their responses. So strong was the common pattern that it could be labeled a new paradigm in public administration. The new paradigm which has emerged in a little more than a decade emphasises the role of public managers in providing high quality services that citizens value; advocates increasing managerial autonomy, particularly by reducing central agency controls; demands measures and rewards of both organisational and individual performance; recognises the importance of providing the human and technological resources that managers need to meet their performance targets; and is receptive to contestation and open-minded about which public purposes should be performed by public servants as opposed to the private sector.

It is the response to these inevitable changes that can result in management crisis, choices in service delivery, and at the same time continuity with the past practices or improving upon them.

The context for change

The new paradigm in public administration has been variously known in different countries by different names. The names, while different, have a similar meaning. Such names as re-engineering, revitalising, renewal, restructuring, rejuvenation, modernising etc., have been used by different countries in an attempt to address the issues of change, choice and continuity. The change process is driven by a number of pressures such as:

- The emergence of a post-industrial, knowledge-based, global economy;

- The need to reduce the cost of government;

- Improved quality of services to citizens;

- Increased accountability through delegation, decentralisation, devolution or empowerment whatever the peculiar circumstances dictate;

- The increasing trend towards the separation of the policy and delivery aspects of government;

- Increased managerial autonomy and setting clear performance targets;

- Re-evaluating the role of the state, which led initially to an extensive privatisation programme and then to the involvement of the private sector in financing public sector infrastructure; and

- Introducing competition into the public sector through market-testing initiatives.

Both public administrators and policy makers face these challenges, for while government policies may come and go, the Civil Service represents the corporate memory to provide the continuity to a nation's administration and sustain its well-being. They both require skills, knowledge and information on how to adjust to the changing environmental and political agenda.

Typology of political, economic and administrative transitions

While transitions vary in quality and quantity, the common characteristic is that there is a change in the political control and management of the state. The following are different types of transitions:

- Transitions following systemic and political collapse;

- Transition brought about by armed conflict in which the former opposition assumes power or from military to civilian rule;

- Transition through popular revolt;

- Transition through negotiation between the powers that be and democratic leaders;

- Aborted transition by the rulers of the day refusing to hand over power to elected representatives;

- Transition from a colonial government to a national government;

- Transition from a multi-party system of government to a one-party system committed to socialism;

- Transition from a one-party system to a multi-party system that is based on the principles of a free-market system; and

- Transition from a democratic state dominated by one political party for many years to one in which the political party that has been in opposition for years assumes power following democratically held general elections.

Some of the consequences of these transitions on public management are:

- The Civil Service can be highly centralised and politicised;
- The Civil Servant can be partisan through active participation in implementing political programmes of the ruling party and its government;
- Restructuring, downsizing, decentralisation, devolution, deregulation, debureaucratisation, privatisation;
- Focus on customer orientation;
- Use of performance standards for service delivery;
- Empowerment of employees; and
- More transparency and improved accountability mechanisms.

Implications for Civil Servants

The challenges to bureaucracies include the ability to:

- work with the new government's framework;
- contribute to holistic programmes that cut across other departments;
- manage consultation with diverse policy communities that contribute to the policy development of a Ministry;
- manage partnerships with Non-Government Organisations, private sector, contractors, and donors;
- respond to demanding and sophisticated clients who may be knowledgeable in the use of the Internet to diagnose a problem;
- work effectively in a diverse, multicultural and multilingual society;
- use information technology; and
- lead complex and diverse management teams.

From the top Civil Servants, i.e. the Permanent Secretary, Cabinet Secretary, etc., the challenges focus on leadership style in that he or she is expected to develop:

- Stronger leadership with a clear sense of purpose, trust, vision, values, and leadership qualities;
- Better business planning from top to bottom;
- Sharper performance management;
- A dramatic improvement in diversity;
- A public service more open to people and ideas and which hires relevant talent and expertise; and
- A better deal for staff.

For the political and administrative interface, the choice between change and continuity often manifests itself in the intricate and sensitive relationship between the public service and a new government during a transition. There are two dimensions in this relationship:

1. Administering politicians

If a transition is to be smooth and a new government is to take charge with the minimum of problems, it becomes incumbent upon senior public servants to prepare for the prospect of a change of government. For public servants, transitions are tense and uncertain times based on speculation about election outcomes, new Ministers and even new policies.

During the period of uncertainty associated with transition, public servants will implicitly tend to seek to ensure survival of the department, to stress policy continuity and to meld overall organisational purpose in terms of a prospective new government's expressed policy preferences. The basic thesis is that public servants want transition to proceed with as little disruption of their normal managerial environment as is feasible.

New governments invariably assume that public servants not only control policy but also even control those who front for their chosen policies, the Ministers. The process of socialising new Ministers into their positions by public servants, so that government functions, can be misinterpreted as administering the politician.

2. Politicising the Administration

When new Ministers and their governments assume their new positions, they are likely to be simultaneously uncertain, nervous and eager. The combination can lead to tension between public servants and their new masters as each tries to sense the respective boundaries of their interactive relationship. Crisis in the relationship generally surfaces when enthusiastic new Ministers encounter their senior officials in formal hierarchical relationships for the first time.

As Permanent Secretaries are the fulcrums from which a new government's policy launch will be made, it is probably wise to treat them with care. Permanent Secretaries will expect to be heard by Ministers. Abusing a Permanent Secretary will not serve government well in the long run. The process of ensuring that public servants take the political perspective of the Minister can be misinterpreted as politicising the administration.

Reasons for caution

The transformation and consequential transitions in the political and administrative machinery of the state have their origins in global and domestic developments in politics, trade, technology and public management that are outside the jurisdiction of any one state or group of states but that impact powerfully on domestic aspirations, policies and institutions.

The national responses to global challenges differ from one country or region to another. Success in one country may be a failure in another because of the prevailing socio-economic and political conditions. The solution, therefore, of a problem in one country may not necessarily have the same result when adopted and implemented in a different country. However, public sector reform and the new public administration paradigm have emerged in response to a number of pressures including: globalisation which has become a reality at all levels (political, economic and social); the rapid pace of change, as demonstrated by the information revolution; rising citizens' expectations of governments, for quality and service; the ongoing pressures of the debt crisis; the overall international promotion of reform ideas, particularly in developing countries and via the reform initiatives of international organisations.

A consensus emerged out of the CAPAM Inaugural Conference, in 1994, and was reconfirmed at the CAPAM Biennial conference in 1996, that New Public Administration provides high-quality services that citizens value. It advocates increased managerial autonomy, particularly from central control, it measures and rewards organisations and individuals on the basis of whether or not they meet demanding performance targets, and it provides the human and technological resources that managers need to meet their performance targets.

In transitional governments, it should be noted that in general, political parties, particularly those with a strong ideological bent, are impatient to put their own stamp on numerous areas of public policy. Many politicians in new governments fear the prospect of being captured by permanent officials whose experience is vastly greater than their own. The incoming politicians are likely to share the general suspicion of the growing influence of permanent officials over public policy and government decision making.

It should be noted that there are no courses one can take on how to be a Prime Minister, Premier or a Cabinet Minister. However, for politicians, transition planning in many ways thus becomes a crash course in what to do and how to do it the day they take power. It is worth noting that a transition signals the arrival of a new government with maximum energy but minimum knowledge replacing one with minimum energy but maximum knowledge. A new government without a clear policy agenda will often arrive with firmly held prejudices about bureaucrats, with an appetite for quick fixes and a strong desire to do things differently from the outgoing government.

Public servants should equally be aware of the general criticisms laid on them by politicians upon assuming power. New governments now speak openly about the need to bring bureaucratic organisations under political control. Many have accused the public service of being uncreative, lethargic, overstaffed, incapable of challenging the status quo or of being self-critical.

The lesson that can be learnt is that a transition brings together two groups with markedly different values and perspectives and no assurance that the relationship will work. We have also learnt that no two transitions are alike, that careful planning is vitally important and that the ideological bent of an incoming government is important as is its previous experience in government, the political mood and economic circumstances. Further we have learnt that there are no two political leaders that are alike. Each has his or her own distinctive set of prejudices, values and priorities.

Achieving change

Commonwealth experiences suggest that there are lessons to be learnt from managing transitions:

- Leadership plays an important role in managing transitions. Every leader has a combination of strengths and weaknesses and a wise leader will take steps to reinforce the weak areas. The newly elected Prime Minister or President should take an objective look at themselves and then take steps to strengthen their weak points. On assuming power, the new Prime Minister should carefully review the existing machinery of government;

- Political leaders should also refrain from bureaucrat-bashing;

- Political leaders who wish to re-orient government policy on what they perceive as an entrenched bureaucracy should arrive in government with a game plan which sets out clearly its objectives and directions. The game plan must be sufficiently detailed for Cabinet Ministers and senior officials to understand its implications for their departments;

- Upon being elected into office, most governments set up transition teams composed of party officials, public servants, academics, etc, to manage succession. The transition teams are temporary organisations whose role is to provide advice on logistical, personnel, organisation and policy considerations that influence how the leader chooses to establish the government.

- The leader should form a strong transition team and put a transition plan in place when being sworn into office. It should be recognized that relations between the public service and incoming governments, especially during the transition period, are greatly influenced by the decision-making process of the outgoing and incoming Cabinets;

- In some countries the opposition parties and public service share information on transition planning and the requirements of government before the elections. This gives the opposition party an appreciation of how the public service works and in turn gives senior public servants an appreciation of the general direction the party would like to give to government. However, the sharing of information between public service and opposition parties before assuming power should be carefully planned;

- Political parties are advised to strengthen their research and policy capacity. In some countries party affiliated policy research centres or institutes are developed. These institutes could well push political parties to be more forthcoming in presenting detailed policy prescriptions and in educating politicians on the requirements of policy making and in understanding the challenges of governance; and

- Most governments appoint political advisers to the Minister. The advisers are not necessarily Civil Servants but are a link between the party, Civil Service, constituency and other public bodies related to the Minister's functions. Equally some Ministers do not necessarily rely on the advice of public servants but widen their area of consultation to even include university think tanks.

In all these transitions, the key players are the Minister, Cabinet Secretary, Permanent Secretary and the political adviser if he or she is available.

Examples of change

In *Canada*, both in the Federal and Provincial governments, transitional teams were formed to manage succession and firmly assume power in the political and administrative machinery. Transitional teams were temporary;

In the *UK* (2001), each Minister is allowed to appoint two political advisers to assist in the assumption of power and management of a Ministry. Political or special advisers can handle relations with the party, write briefs on departmental policies for government backbenchers and deal with constituency parties;

In the Caribbean, special advisers are increasingly playing an important role in the political and administrative interface. While it is a new phenomenon, it is now being practised in *Trinidad and Tobago, Barbados*, and *Grenada* (2001);

In Africa, *Nigeria* (2000) seems to have instituted a system of appointing special or political advisers to assist the Minister in his management of a government department; and

Australia and *New Zealand* have long established the traditions of appointing special advisers who are not necessarily public servants to assist with transitions.

Other useful material (2nd edition)

Ahmad Sarj , Public Administration in Transition: Global Challenges and local perspectives: Paper presented to CAPAM, July 28, 1997.

Sandford Borins, A Report on the Second Biennial Conference of CAPAM: The New Public Administration: Global Challenges, Local Solutions, June 1996.

Government in Transition: Report on the inaugural conference of CAPAM, Charlottetown, Prince Edward Island, Canada 28-31 August 1994.

Borins, Sandford. The Shifting Boundaries of Government. A United Kingdom International Conference. March 1998.

Civil Service Reform: Report to the Prime Minster from Sir Richard Wilson, Head of the Civil Service, published by Cabinet Office (UK), 2000.

Konig. P., Policy Planning and management dialogue with countries in transition. Public Administration and Development (ed) Paul Collins Vol. 16 No. 5 Dec 1996.

The New Public Administration: A re-examination of the Political Administrative interface. Paper presented by Senator Wade Mark, Minister of Public Administration in Trinidad and Tobago, July 1998, Bangi, Malaysia

Agere, S., Redefining Management Roles: Improving the Functional Relationship between Ministers and Permanent Secretaries: Managing the Public Service Strategies for Improvement Series No.10, 1999.

Thomas, P. Beyond the buzzwords: coping with change in public sector. International Review of Administrative Sciences (SAGE) London, Vol.62, 1996.

3.0 Improving the Quality of Services

3.1 Open Government

3.1.1 Improving public reporting

Public reporting is the practical expression of open government. It encompasses three related categories of information to be provided to the public:

- information about government as a holder of information – what records are maintained, and how is accuracy ensured?

- information about government as a business – how much does it spend, on what, with what intention, and with what result?

- information about government as a service provider – what services are available, at what price, and at what quality?

Improving public reporting is both a point of principle, consistent with the emphasis in the Commonwealth Heads of Government Harare Declaration on just and honest government, and a pragmatic step towards improving the performance of the public service.

The context for change

Improvements in management systems and organisational structures are a necessary, but not sufficient, condition for sustainable improvement in public service performance. Pressure for change *within* the public service must be matched by continuous pressure for change from *outside* the service. This requires a public that is confident in its dealings with the public service, a public that has adequate information by which to judge the performance of the public service, and a public that knows the standards of performance that the service has set for itself.

In sum, public expectations of quality performance from the public service are a key component of performance improvements. Realistic but demanding public expectations are sustained by improvements in three dimensions:

- confidence in the accuracy of the information used by the public service;

- access to information on the cost and purpose of services; and

- clear statements of the quality standards which the public service aspires to.

Reasons for caution

Improvements in all three dimensions of public reporting require sound records management within the public service, appropriate publicity, and a culture of openness. There are material, systems development and training costs associated; and any strategy for improving public reporting will be undermined by announced improvements which cannot be sustained.

Achieving change

Commonwealth experiences suggest a three-fold strategy:

- Build confidence in the accuracy of information which government holds through legislative or administrative action, providing the public with:
  - the right of access to all non-personal information held by government which does not endanger national security, law enforcement or free trade; and
  - the right of access to personal information for the person concerned, so that facts may be verified and the information amended if it is inaccurate.
- Improve transparency in government as a business by:
  - providing details of government expenditure in a manner which an interested member of the public can understand; and
  - publishing costs and savings estimates with all policy proposals.
- Emphasise the role of government as a provider of services by:
  - providing information to the public on the range and standards of service which they should realistically expect; and
  - developing complaints procedures.

Further details on *Establishing a customer orientation* are provided in Section 3.2 in this Portfolio.

Examples of change

In *Canada*, the Access to Information Act gives citizens and corporations access to Federal Government records that are not of a personal nature. The Act complements other procedures for obtaining Government information. It aims to make the widest possible use of information within the Government by ensuring that it is organised to facilitate access by those who require it. A particular initiative in improving public reporting is the Privacy Act, which gives Canadian citizens and people present in Canada the right to have access to information that is held about them by the Federal Government. The Act also protects against the unauthorised disclosure of personal information. In addition, it strictly controls how the Government will collect, use, store, disclose, and dispose of any personal information.

In the *UK*, a Code of Practice on the release of Government information with improved access to information, subject to certain exemptions, came into effect in April 1994. Codes of Practice for Local Government and the National Health Service followed. The new statutory right of access to health and safety information and statutory right of access, by the subject, to personal records held by Government will require legislation.

The Government of *Trinidad and Tobago* has adopted a Communication Strategy to communicate with the public. The main objectives are:

- to bring co-ordination and focus to the Government's communication activities;
- to provide a standard against which achievements may be measured; and
- to ensure that all the public is reached.

All forms of communication media are used, including newspapers, TV and radio, advertisements, and exhibitions.

In 1993, the Government of *Zimbabwe* introduced a system of White Papers for proposed changes in the law. As a recent example, the White Paper proposing changes to the law on Marriage and Inheritance aims to stimulate public debate on issues of law which affect the lives of most Zimbabweans.

Other useful material (current as of 1996)

Management of Government Information Holdings. Treasury Board of Canada, 1989 (CAN)

Info Source, Privacy. Treasury Board of Canada, 1992-3 (CAN) Info Source, Access to Information Act. Treasury Board of Canada, 1992-3 (CAN)

Improvements and Development in the Public Service. Government of Malaysia, 1990, 1991, 1992 (MAL)

The Civil Service of Malaysia – A Paradigm Shift (MAL)

Annual Report of the Public Complaints Bureau, 1992 (MAL)

White Paper on "Open Government", Cm. 2290. HMSO, London, 1993 (UK)

3.2 Quality Systems

3.2.1 Introducing a quality management approach

Quality management approaches regard the public service as a series of related units and processes, each of which ensures that their output exactly matches the requirements of the next unit or process – their customer. So customers are not only the public, they are also the next department or unit in the organisational chain which produces quality service for the public.

Quality outputs which match the requirements of the customer are not necessarily expensive, elaborate or luxurious. They are fit for the customer's purpose, reliable, and provide value for money.

The context for change

Quality management originated in the private sector, particularly in the field of manufacturing, where lapses in quality mean customer complaints, waste of materials and products, increased costs in putting them right, and, most fundamentally, loss of consumer confidence. It is more difficult in the public sector to define a product, particularly in policy areas, and the emphasis within government has been on those areas where a service is provided to the public. However, policy development has not been excluded from the growing pressure on government to focus on quality.

Strengthening the concern of the public service to achieve quality services – services that meet the public's expectations, reliably and at reasonable cost – has become a priority for government. Rising consumer expectations, continuing fiscal pressures and a growing conviction that the public service should continually justify its outputs in terms of their price and effectiveness, have provided a strong motivation to identify techniques and approaches which have proved to be of value in other settings.

All organisations need to identify customers and what they value – however, this presents particular difficulties in the public service. The fact that the public service is, ostensibly, a hard environment in which to apply quality management makes it even more important to try. When it is difficult to identify customers and their expectations, the classic conditions exist for an organisation to become self-contained and inward-looking.

Reasons for caution

Formal quality management approaches have shown themselves to be of immense value in a wide range of public sector and private organisations. There is however a substantial history of expensively abandoned attempts to introduce over-elaborately specified systems within the public service. Critics have alleged that on occasion the quality movement has failed to follow its own instructions, and that in focusing on the development of a quality process, it has lost sight of the practical need to improve service quality at a reasonable cost and within a reasonable time scale.

Achieving change

Quality management approaches successfully introduced within the public service of Commonwealth countries demonstrate five key components:

First, whether following formal benchmarking approaches or the ISO 9000 route to quality improvement or otherwise, quality management approaches rest on systems which for each department:

- identify the internal and external customers;
- establish the *features* which they value in the services they receive – such as timeliness, speed, accuracy and reliability;
- establish *standards* for each feature of the services valued by customers; and
- *monitor* service delivery against those standards.

Second, quality management requires a high level of staff commitment to improve service standards engaged by:

- coherent *performance management* systems based on open appraisal and specific personnel targets;
- *training* to ensure a common understanding of quality across the department;
- *recognition* of work well done by individuals and by the department as a whole;
- a clear and unambiguous *example* of diligent work and concern for standards set by senior officials.

The third component of a quality management approach underpins the previous two. Systems will only be sustainable and commitment can only be inspired within a climate of trust. This is not a simplistic implication that little can be achieved without workplace harmony and sound dialogue with staff associations and public sector unions. These may be aspired to but cannot be taken for granted, particularly at a time of rapid change and probable downsizing. The issue of trust concerns predictability and consistency of approach. When short-term pressures overwhelm long-term developmental goals to the degree that an impression is created of arbitrary management or inexplicable policy reversals, both organisational systems and individual commitment to quality will fail.

The fourth component consistently found in successful quality management is a *problem-solving* mechanism, such as the quality improvement teams, work improvement teams or quality circles, increasingly found within public service organisations. Systems and committed staff detect areas of concern, trust enables them to solve problems imaginatively and to propose cost-effective improvements.

The fifth and final component is the *quality management structure* which:

- guides the development of the quality systems, develops strategies for inspiring commitment, alerts management to a deterioration in trust, and co-ordinates problem solving activities; and
- maintains quality firmly on the agenda at all levels of the department.

Typically, such a structure entails a steering committee, chaired by the head of department with senior managers as members, planning for quality initiatives, developing a strategic direction for the department, and monitoring quality improvement. Other committees would report to the steering committee with responsibilities for training initiatives, support to the problem-solving teams, and for studying areas of emerging concern.

Examples of change

Quality management approaches were embodied in the *Canadian* Government's Public Service 2000 (PS2000) initiative to renew the Public Service of Canada. PS2000 espoused client satisfaction, employee involvement and continuous improvement.

Through an Inter-departmental Quality Network chaired by the Treasury Board Secretariat (TBS), over 40 departments and agencies meet and exchange experiences on quality practices. To support further the work of departments, TBS has published a "Guide to Quality Management" and in order to keep abreast of initiatives in other levels of government, TBS chairs a National Quality Network that currently represents the Federal Government (including its regional offices), 10 provinces and six major cities.

In *Malaysia*, the special focus on Quality Management began with the launching of the Excellent Work Culture Movement in November 1989. The main objective of the Movement was to enhance public awareness of the importance of providing quality products and services, thereby institutionalising a culture where quality becomes a way of life. Action programmes include:

- A manual on Quality Implementation which outlines the critical stages involved in implementing quality management at organisational level.

- Twenty Development Administrative Circulars serve as guidelines on quality.

- A comprehensive quality training programme has been formulated by the National Institute of Public Administration.

- Inspections are conducted by the Chief Secretary to the Government and heads of departments to monitor the implementation of the quality improvement programmes.

- Many recognition incentives have been introduced to reinforce positive attitudes.

In *New Zealand,* the public sector organisations that have adopted quality management, for example, the Department of Survey and Land Information and the Ministry of Commerce, have tended to be service delivery rather than policy advice agencies.

In *Singapore*, each Ministry takes responsibility and is accountable for its quality of service. Accordingly, Ministries and statutory boards appoint senior officers as Quality Service Managers who monitor and upgrade the quality and service provided by their organisations. In April 1991, the Service Improvement Unit was set up, under the Prime Minister's Office to review and assess the current quality of service provided by departments; make recommendations or suggestions on how service levels can be upgraded and improved; and to serve as a channel for the public to suggest improvements. A comprehensive system of Work Improvement Teams is in place across the Public Service; a similar approach has recently been adapted in *Botswana*.

In the *UK*, the Citizen's Charter initiative has played a part in emphasising the citizen's right to expect a reasonable level of service from all public service employees. The Charter Mark is an award for excellence in delivering public service. It was first announced in the Citizen's Charter White Paper in July 1991. The first 36 awards were presented by the Prime Minister in 1992 and the aim is to promote high standards of information and openness, choice and consultation, courtesy and helpfulness.

Other useful material (current as of 1996)

Administrative and Managerial Reform in Government: A Commonwealth Portfolio of Current Good Practice. Proceedings of a Pan-Commonwealth Working Group Meeting held in Kuala Lumpur, Malaysia, 19-22 April 1993. Commonwealth Secretariat, 1993 (ComSec)

Quah, J. S. T. Sustaining Quality in the Singapore Civil Service. In: Government in Transition. The Inaugural Conference of the Commonwealth Association for Public Administration and Management, Charlottetown, Canada, 28-31 August 1994. Commonwealth Secretariat, 1995 (ComSec)

Pearson, V. L. Increasing quality in government services: a modern imperative (Canada). In: Government in Transition. The Inaugural Conference of the Commonwealth Association for Public Administration and Management, Charlottetown, Canada, 28-31 August 1994. Commonwealth Secretariat, 1995 (ComSec)

Guide to Quality Management. Interdepartmental Quality Network, Human Resources Development Branch, Treasury Board of Canada, October 1992 (CAN)

Quality Practices. A String of Pearls. Interdepartmental Quality Network, Human Resources Development Branch, Treasury Board of Canada (CAN)

Guide to Quality Management. Government Review and Quality Service Division, Administrative Policy Branch, Treasury Board Secretariat, Ottawa, Canada (CAN)

Development Administration Circulars Nos. 1, 3, 4. Guidelines on Strategies for Quality Improvement in the Public Sector, 1993 (MAL)

Doing it Better, Doing it Right. Public Sector Task Force on Productivity. State Services Commission, Wellington, 1992 (NZ)

Creating a Quality Service – An Information Note. Cabinet Office, Office of Public Service and Science, Development Division, 1994 (UK)

With HMSO into TQM - Her Majesty's Stationery Office, from HMSO Publicity (PU23), St Crispins, Duke Street, Norwich NR3 1PD (UK)

3.2.2 Ensuring a right of redress

A *right of redress* is of particular importance in the public service. In the absence of a choice of supplier, individuals need mechanisms to settle their grievances quickly, simply, and fairly. Redress mechanisms, sometimes known as service recovery mechanisms, also bring wider benefits, acting as a check on the actions of service providers and providing quality controls that force management systems to identify and correct underlying problems in policies and practices.

A right of redress is an assurance that what was wrong will be put right, through explanation, apology, compensation or other remedy. It begins with a complaints mechanism which is:

- *readily accessible* to users of services;
- *simple to operate*, with clearly set-out procedures and responsibilities;
- *speedy*, with time limits for dealing with complaints;
- *objective*, with provision for an independent means to investigate complaints, if necessary;
- *confidential*, protecting the privacy of complainants; and
- *integrated* with the organisation's management information systems.

The office of the Ombudsman, where this exists, provides a baseline protection against maladministration, that is, the failure of the service to follow due process. A right of redress is complementary to the protection offered by the Ombudsman.

The context for change

The establishment of a right of redress is a fundamental component of a customer orientation for the public service. As such, the users of public services, their customers, are increasingly requiring that services are provided in a way which are clearly responsive to their changing needs. Equally, governments are increasingly encouraging customers to be reasonably but assertively demanding through mechanisms such as the right of redress, in order to place pressure on public services to continue with improvements.

Reasons for caution

The mechanism for providing redress, and the complaints procedure which underpins it, must be reliable and productive if it is not to undermine its own purpose. It is widely held that the costs of establishing complaints systems are more than offset by the systematic reduction in the number of errors made by the service. There is, as yet, little concrete evidence to support this assertion, and some realistic assessment of costs must be factored into the overall development strategy.

Achieving change

Recent experience within the Commonwealth suggests that the overall framework for customer-service improvements, including the establishment of *principles* for redress, is set at a strategic level for the whole public service. The establishment of *specific complaints mechanisms* is generally undertaken at Ministry or department level. Whether such mechanisms are to be established across the service or, within an overall framework, Ministry by Ministry, the steps required are:

- identify the procedures by which complaints are to be investigated, defining the roles and responsibilities of staff and imposing time limits at each stage;

- establish the procedures for appeal or review if the complainant remains unsatisfied;

- review existing legislation and agency responsibilities, including those of the office of the Ombudsman, to ensure consistency;

- consult with members of the legislature and other elected officials to ensure that a reasonable working agreement can be maintained between officials responsible for responding to complaints, and elected officials who may have been approached by a constituent in relation to the same issue;

- determine the policy for public reporting of the complaints system, in particular, highlighting areas of particular dissatisfaction;

- review training implications; and

- publicise the complaints system widely.

Examples of Change

The Government of *Canada* is strongly promoting integrity in procurement within the public service. It has been concerned to provide the right of redress when procurement decisions have been found to be unfair. The relevant departments ensure that any supplier, whether from within or without Canada, is encouraged to lodge formal or informal complaints if they have reason to believe that they have been dealt with unfairly.

In *Malaysia*, the Public Complaints Bureau of the Prime Minister's Department, established in 1971, is an independent organisation which looks into the nature of various complaints concerning all public agencies. Its restructuring in 1992 strengthened its administrative machinery to manage public complaints more effectively. The Bureau functions as the main channel for the public to forward their complaints or grievances on:

- dissatisfaction with services rendered by public servants, e.g. lack of courtesy, delay in providing services;

- administrative actions and decisions which are alleged to be unfair, against existing laws and regulations inclusive of misconduct, misappropriation, abuse of power and maladministration.

The Service Improvement Unit of the Government of *Singapore* encourages all members of the public to complain if they feel that they have received poor treatment from any part of the public service. The Government of *Mauritius* has just established a Public Complaints Board with a similar remit.

The *UK* Government introduced the Citizen's Charter in 1991, with a view to improving all aspects of public service to individuals, in particular, improving the mechanism under which customers could register complaints and obtain redress. The Government is establishing a Complaints Task Force to advise on setting-up and improving complaints systems.

Other useful material (current as of 1996)

Current Good Practices and New Developments in Public Service Management: A Profile of the Public Service of the United Kingdom. The Public Service Country Profile Series: No. 2. pp 1O4–106. Commonwealth Secretariat, 1995 (ComSec)

Development Administration Circular No. 4, 1992, Managing Public Complaints (MAL)

The Civil Service of Malaysia – A Paradigm Shift, Chapters 3 and 8 (MAL)

3.2.3 Establishing a customer orientation

A *customer orientation* for the public service is a priority in many Commonwealth countries. The principles of customer orientation have been well defined in the UK Citizen's Charter and similar initiatives can be set out as:

- setting and publicising *standards* for the service that individual users, and private sector firms and other organisations that use public services, can reasonably expect;

- providing full, accurate *inforrnation* about how services are run, what they cost, how well they perform and who is in charge;

- the public sector should offer *choice* wherever practicable and systematic consultation with users of services to determine priorities for service improvements;

- front-line staff should offer a *courteous and helpful service* wearing name badges and providing convenient opening hours;

- service users should have access to an easy-to-use complaints procedure; and if the service has been defective, they should receive an apology, a full explanation and swift and effective *redress*.

The context for change

There are two forces operating to make the establishment of a customer orientation a priority for the public service.

On the one hand, service users – individual citizens, private sector firms and others who use public services – are increasingly defining themselves as active customers rather than passive recipients of public services. Across the Commonwealth, users of public services have growing exposure to improving customer practices in private sector firms and, through the media, are increasingly able to make international comparisons about standards in the public service. In sum, users of public services are placing pressure on the public service to reorient its priorities towards its customers.

On the other hand, many governments have recognised that it is by encouraging service users to be reasonably, but assertively, demanding that momentum for service improvements will be maintained. Governments are recognising that developments and improvements to systems and structures will only go so far in improving services. These internal pressures for improvements must be matched by rising external pressures from customers if the public service is to continue to improve.

Many Commonwealth governments are seeking to create a virtuous circle in which rising standards in the public service send a signal to customers that improvement is possible and that they should expect more; and increasingly demanding customers send a signal to the public service that it must focus on the needs and expectations of its service users.

Reasons for caution

A customer orientation is fundamental to a modern public service, but it must be seen within the context of the full range of responsibilities of the public service. In particular, the customer orientation must reflect the need to improve services and the manner of their delivery, within the resources that can reasonably be allocated, bearing in mind the overall government responsibility to avoid burdening its taxpayers with excessive demands, or future generations with excessive debt. Equally, the customer orientation must recognise that improvements in service quality may not always be evident in the short term to the customer. Hospital patients have every right not to be kept waiting unduly and to be treated courteously – but they have a more profound right to expect treatment which will offer them the best long-term health prospects. They will readily be able to judge the former but might have difficulties in assessing the latter.

Achieving change

Commonwealth experience suggests that there are three levels of change necessary for the establishment of a customer orientation.

At a *strategic level,* to set the context for change across the public service, a clear message must be sent from senior levels to indicate:

- that customer service is to be improved;

- the framework for those improvements, indicating the immediate priorities and the mechanism for monitoring progress; and

- that improvements will be broadly resource-neutral, with developments made within existing budgets.

At *Ministry or department level,* steps are necessary to:

- introduce customer service training for front-line staff, those who interact daily with the public, to provide them with the awareness and skills necessary for a responsive customer service;

- broader training for all staff highlighting the importance of customer service and disseminating the messages sent from senior levels; and

- establish complaints procedures and consider the identification of customer contact officers, with a particular responsibility for monitoring developments and proposing practical steps for improvement to department management.

At the *level of specific services provided,* it is necessary to:

- identify the customers and the features of those services which the customers consider important;

- specify standards for each feature of the service valued by customers;

- publicise those standards; and

- monitor service standards and encourage customer suggestions and complaints.

Examples of change

The success of *Canada's* Government Telecommunications Agency (GTA) is based on customer orientation. GTA has introduced a number of mechanisms to ensure that it understands customers' needs. These include: two senior-level interdepartmental committees, the Government Telecommunications Council and the Telecommunications Advisory Panel, which include customers among their members; and Product Focus Groups, which provide information that allows GTA to improve its services.

In *Malaysia,* customer orientation has been introduced with the implementation of quality management in public sector agencies and the launch of Client's Charters by the Prime Minister in June 1993. As at December 1994, a total of 318 agencies had formulated their Client's Charter, which is either exhibited, posted at strategic places or produced in booklet form for distribution. An award for the best formulated Client's Charter was introduced in 1993.

Statistics NZ is *New Zealand's* national statistical office. It provides a wide range of commercially-marketed and supplied information services, as well as meeting its obligations under the Statistics Act to provide most of the official statistics in New Zealand. In recent years, Statistics NZ has faced the challenge of converting a department with a traditional public service culture into a customer-orientation agency. It has done this very successfully and now has an Information Marketing Group, which develops customer services, disseminates information, and informs the media, commercial and community users of the Department's products.

The *UK* Government is introducing a customer orientation in the public service through the Citizen's Charter, launched by the Prime Minister in July 1991. The Charter is a ten-year programme to raise the standards of public service and make them more responsive to their users. Significant developments include the publication of 38 individual charters, covering some of the main public services providing the public with, often for the first time, published standards of service, information on performance, complaints procedures and ways to obtain redress. The charters are reviewed and improved annually. Among the charters are the Patient's Charter, Parent's Charter; British Rail Passenger's Charter; Jobseeker's Charter; Taxpayer's Charter; London Underground's Customer Charter; and the Child Support Agency Charter. In some cases, new laws have been passed, for example, to make sure that Citizen's Charter principles are applied to the privatised utilities, that comparative information about local authority performance is published, and to strengthen inspection arrangements in schools.

Other useful material (current as of 1996)

Bruce Rawson et al. PS2000. Report of the Task Force on Service to the Public, 9 August 1990. Government of Canada, Ottawa (CAN)

Public Service 2000, Service to the Public. Task Force Report, October 12, 1990 (CAN)

Development Administration Circular No. 3, Guidelines on Client's Charter (MAL)

The Civil Service of Malaysia – A Paradigm Shift 1993, Chapter 3 (MAL)

The Citizen's Charter. Raising the Standard. Information Pack. HMSO, London, 1991 (UK)

The Citizen's Charter. Second Report. HMSO, London, 1994 (UK)

3.3 Measuring Success

3.3.1 Improving standard-setting

Sustained improvements in the overall performance of the public service require the introduction of measurable standards of performance for services, made widely available to service users. Standards place a direct responsibility on both the individual public servant and the organisation to perform. They help in the identification of strengths as well as weaknesses.

By setting standards for their final outputs, departments provide guidance on the level of service that can be reasonably expected by service users and the public. Publishing service standards complements the development of performance indicators which act as a management tool for monitoring a particular programme or activity, or the performance of an organisational unit, such as a Ministry or department.

The context for change

Standard-setting, providing information for service users and the public concerning the level of quality which can reasonably be expected from the public service, meets two needs. First, it provides the public with sufficient information to assess the performance of the public service, providing some assurance that the service is sensitive to the views of its users. Second, it provides a continuing source of pressure for service improvements.

Reasons for caution

Setting and publicising standards is, intentionally, the start of a one-way movement. Published standards represent a baseline from which service quality should only improve. Sustaining the service at or above those standards, presents a particular focus for the credibility of the public service. Subsequent deterioration in the service, however unavoidable, will reflect starkly on the overall service.

Achieving change

Standards must refer to things that matter to the public. They must indicate the anticipated quality of particular services, and particular features of those services, that are valued by the public.

The key test is that standards must be:

* specific;
* measurable and stated in terms of cost, time and quality;
* achievable and realistic;
* regularly reviewed; and
* publicised in plain language.

194

Examples of change

In *Canada*, the establishment of service standards was part of the reform of the Public Service associated with the Public Service 2000 initiative. In its February 1994 Budget, the Canadian Government announced that standards for service would be established and published for each department and that a declaration of quality service delivery would be issued.

In *Malaysia*, the internal processing standards and output standards are documented in the Department's Quality Handbook and in the Client's Charters which record the quality standards applicable to service users.

In *Trinidad and Tobago*, setting standards is a voluntary activity of individual Ministries and departments. One particular initiative in improving standard-setting is the annual service contracts between the Ministry of Health and the Regional Health Authorities which provide operational aspects of health services. The performance of these Authorities will be evaluated in terms of outcomes, such as the number of patients seen, and eventually in terms of the health status of the population, for example, disease-specific mortality and morbidity rates.

In the *UK*, the Citizen's Charter provides quality standards which can reasonably be expected by the users of an increasing number of public services.

Other useful material (current as of 1996)

Abdul Rahman, A. Productivity and Quality Management in the Public Sector in Malaysia. In: Administrative and Managerial Reform in Government: A Commonwealth Portfolio of Current Good Practice. Proceedings of a Pan-Commonwealth Working Group Meeting held in Kuala Lumpur, Malaysia, 19-22 April 1993. Commonwealth Secretariat, 1993 (ComSec)

Development Administration Circular No. 3, Guidelines on Client's Charter (MAL)

Raising the Standard: Britain's Citizen's Charter and Public Service Reforms. Foreign and Commonwealth Office, 1992 (UK)

Development Administration Circular No. 3,1993, Guidelines on Client's Charter (UK)

3.3.2 Introducing performance indicators

Performance indicators are statistics, used as a management tool, which reflect the activities of the public service, and give insight into how well it is functioning. Performance indicators are used to monitor a particular programme or activity, or the performance of an organisational unit, such as a Ministry or department.

Performance indicators reflect all aspects of the public service, some of which hold little interest for the general public. Accordingly, they are first and foremost a management tool. They are accompanied by published service standards which are of more immediate relevance for service users and the public.

A good performance indicator is:

- relevant in determining the performance of the programme or activity, service or unit being evaluated;

- quantitative, as far as possible, to enable measurement and analysis;

- based on information which can be readily obtained at minimal cost;

- based on data which is accurate; and

- credible within the public service.

A distinction is often made between the terms performance measure and performance indicator. The term performance measure is often used when economy, efficiency and effectiveness can be measured precisely and unambiguously. However, when it is not possible to obtain a precise measure, it is usual to refer to performance indicators – provocative and suggestive signals which alert managers to the need to examine an issue further.

The context for change

In much of the public service, the bottom line of profit does not exist. The outputs of the public service are multiple, complex, and often immeasurable. It is, therefore, difficult to assess the final impact of the resources allocated to public services. Without profit or rate of return measures, public service organisations have turned their attention to various proxies and surrogates of performance, referred to as performance measures or indicators.

For public service agencies, performance measurement is a major aspect of accountability. Financial reporting alone is insufficient to meet this requirement as, although it covers the collection and distribution of funds and the allocation of resources, it does not show the service provided nor the quality of these services. A set of performance measures is needed to provide a balanced and accurate picture of an organisation's performance.

Reasons for caution

Unless performance indicators are sufficiently robust, then those who supply the raw data for their compilation may be tempted to distort information in order to present themselves, their services, or their organisations, in the best light. This is particularly true if the emphasis is placed upon performance review for control purposes rather than for organisational learning.

There may also be a tendency to overemphasise quantification. This can drive out qualitative performance indicators which capture a more holistic view of particular activities or services. Similarly, too many indicators are unproductive, leading to managers suffering from information overload. Paralysis through analysis, and important performance messages getting lost in the plethora of unnecessary detail, will follow.

Some performance measures overemphasise the short-term dimensions of performance and ignore the longer-term, more enduring, aspects of performance. This problem can be minimised by using a mix of long-term and short-term indicators.

Achieving change

As a management tool for achieving an improved service, performance indicators depend on a management team's conviction that they offer a useful guide to decision making. Performance indicators which do not inspire conviction will not influence decision making.

In introducing performance indicators, the following elements of Commonwealth experience should be taken into account:

- base the indicators on issues that seriously matter to management about the activity or organisation – reviews of low-cost, marginal operations can be undertaken on an ad hoc basis;

- ensure that the indicators do not squeeze out qualitative concerns in the hunt for hard data;

- ensure that the people who provide the basic data for the indicator believe in them – they will be tempted to provide low-quality information if it is to be factored into what they regard as low-quality indicators;

- never collect new data unless the collection costs can be fully justified, and always consider the possibility of ceasing some existing data collection; and

- bear in mind that for a given activity or organisation, the performance indicators should provide the equivalent of a readily assimilated, broad-based score card, providing staff and managers with an early warning of concerns or achievements at a glance.

Examples of change

In *Malaysia*, the New Performance Appraisal System has been accompanied by the development of performance indicators and annual work targets.

In *New Zealand,* traditionally, Public Service reporting has been heavily oriented towards financial measures. However, the Public Finance Act 1989 provided the legislative reporting framework for Government departments and requires output-based reporting. The Act stipulates that a statement of service performance should accompany the reporting on each class of outputs produced. The statement of performance represents a consolidation of a department's performance measures at the end of the year.

In the *UK*, a particular initiative in introducing performance indicators has been to compare the performance of local authorities in England, Wales and Scotland under the Citizen's Charter framework. The Local Government Act 1992 empowered the Audit Commission to require local authorities to publish information on standards of performance achieved over a range of indicators. In 1994/95, there were a total of 77 indicators. Early evidence suggests that local government, in general, is reacting favourably to the discipline of the Citizen's Charter and the Commission's performance indicators.

In *Zimbabwe*, the new performance appraisal system which is being developed focuses on objective-setting, measurable outcomes, training needs, and continuous dialogue between managers and staff. This is assisting in the development of meaningful performance indicators.

Other useful material (current as of 1996)

Performance Information and the Management Cycle, A joint publication of the Management Advisory Board and its Management Improvement Advisory Committee, No. 10, February 1993. Australian Government Publishing Service, Canberra (AUS)

Guidelines for Establishing Performance Indicators in Government Agencies. Malaysian Administrative Modernisation and Management Planning Unit, Prime Minister's Department, 1993 (MAL)

Citizen's Charter Indicators, Charting a Course. Audit Commission. HMSO, London, 1992 (UK)

Executive Agencies: A Guide to Setting Targets and Measuring Performance. HM Treasury. HMSO, London, 1992 (UK)

4.0 Improving Partnerships with Organisations/Agencies Outside Government

4.1 Setting the Framework

4.1.1 Contestable policy advice

The strength of the public service can be judged by its ability to ensure the provision of achievable, realistic and timely policy advice to government. A government needs, although might not always welcome, sound guidance on how and to what extent its desired objectives might be best met. The public service is the primary provider of such policy advice. However, it is argued with increasing force that if the public service is the only source of such advice, then it will inevitably show some degree of bias in order to minimise disruption for itself in the future.

The context for change

Across the Commonwealth, clear moves can be seen towards the separation of policy advice from the operational or service delivery functions of the public service. There are two pressures for change. First, in combining policy and operational functions, it is argued that neither task is performed well. The daily pressures of service delivery militate against the long-term planning and programme evaluation implicit in the provision of policy advice. Equally, it is argued, the intellectual attractions of policy making draw scarce public servant time away from the more pragmatic and pressurised responsibilities of maintaining a service.

Second, and more profoundly, separating policy advice from operational responsibilities removes the temptation for the public service to bias its advice in favour of its own continued existence, even if alternative and more efficient service providers are available. The separation of these functions is intended to reduce this "capture" of policy advice by a particular, in-house, service provider.

In many situations, a complete split between policy advice and service delivery is both impractical and unhelpful. Policy making must be grounded in the reality of what is achievable and a relationship with the service-providing function helps to keep that pragmatic perspective. The degree of separation is a question of judgement in any functional area. Where policy advice can be separated from other responsibilities, to a greater or lesser extent, it opens up the possibility that, like service delivery, it need not necessarily be performed by the public service itself.

It is improbable that policy advice will ever become a fully purchasable product, outsourced completely to a range of competing suppliers. Defining the provision of policy advice as a specific and separate task does, however, both emphasise the centrality of this work for the public service, and open up the possibility of including organisations outside the public service in its provision.

The trend towards more contestable policy advice can be seen as consistent with a move away from a reliance on a centralised bureaucracy in which the public service plays the predominant role in many sectors, towards a series of partnerships in which the public service plays a leading regulatory role, but is only one provider amongst many.

Reasons for caution

There are several cautions to be considered in increasing the degree of contestability in the provision of policy advice.

First, where there are several players involved in policy discussion, the consultative process is more complex than it would be if the policy making was undertaken only in a particular Ministry or department. This is in principle a positive step towards open government, but, if not well managed, it can be an opportunity for political intrigue.

Second, there is little advantage in rescuing policy advice from the capture of a section of the public sector only to have it recaptured by an external interest group. Contestability implies that the merits of a particular policy-making body are considered objectively, not that the public service is regarded as intrinsically less competent.

Additionally, in defining policy advice as a key product to be provided to government, some attention must be given to the availability of appropriately skilled staff. In many situations, the expectation of a ready supply of competent and high-calibre policy analysts to staff policy units developed in the public service has proved overoptimistic.

Achieving change

Structural changes have been used to great effect across the Commonwealth in separating policy advice and service delivery functions within the public service. Most particularly, out-of-service delivery following market-testing has allowed the public service to focus on policy. Equally, the development of service delivery agencies within the public service has established businesslike units within the public service, with enhanced managerial flexibility and defined service responsibilities, providing a clear demarcation between the service providers and the policy makers.

These moves have led to significant improvements in the quality of services and of policy advice, but they raise complicated issues of accountability. It is far from clear whether it is the service provider or the policy maker who is at fault when major problems emerge.

The lesson for change which emerges most strongly from Commonwealth experience is that such structural changes are useful devices but are not ends in themselves, and may prove to be short-lived if accountability concerns dictate further changes.

Less dramatic organisational changes have included the strengthening of central policy-making units, and a reorientation of the central co-ordinating agencies in the public service. In many settings, financial and human resource management responsibilities have been delegated from the Ministries of Finance. the public service, and the service commissions to the line Ministries and departments. This is partly in order to empower local managers, but it is equally undertaken to free up capacity in the central agencies so that they can assume a stronger role in providing strategic policy advice.

Ultimately, achieving change requires that one question is repeatedly asked – will this development result in an improvement in the quality of policy advice provided to the government?

The quality features of good policy advice are that it is achievable, realistic and timely; and it is a pragmatic willingness to change structures and systems, conscious that further changes will be necessary, sooner rather than later, which will drive improvements.

Examples of change

In *New Zealand,* a key feature of State sector reform has been the desire to increase the contestability of advice. To achieve this, in some departmental restructuring, there has been an explicit separation of the policy advice function from the service and operations functions. As a result, there are many Ministries whose prime output is policy advice, e.g. the Ministries of Health, Education and Transport. As an illustration of this principle, the former Ministry of Defence was restructured in 1989 into two distinct organisations: the New Zealand Defence Force, responsible for providing the country's military forces, and a new, much smaller, Ministry of Defence responsible, primarily, for policy advice on strategic and military capability issues.

In the *UK*, there have been suggestions that the provision of policy advice should be put on the same customer/contractor basis that now applies to service delivery through Next Steps Agencies. The Treasury and Civil Service Committee of the House of Commons recently examined this topic and heard suggestions from some quarters that senior officials should be employed on fixed-term contracts, with a clear remit related to producing answers on policy issues. Under the present system, most policy proposals originate from Ministers and/or those Civil Servants who are specially designated to produce policy advice. Political advisers play a part in this process and the Prime Minister's Office has its own advisers in the form of the No. 10 Policy Unit.

Other useful material (current as of 1996)

Efficient and Effective Policy, Keith, K. J. 1993, Law Commission, Wellington (NZ)

New Zealand: Changing the Public Service Culture; A Radical Approach, 1990, State Services Commission, Wellington (NZ)

Government Management, Volume 1, Treasury, 1987, Government Printer, Wellington (NZ)

4.1.2 Deregulation

A useful working definition for the term regulation is: government instructions on how human, financial and other resources can be allocated and used. Regulation is intended to maintain order.

The term *deregulation* conveys the sense that the rules by which order is maintained in the private and NGO sectors have become too complex and too onerous and must be reduced. An alternative term, re-regulation, might convey more accurately that the regulatory load must be lightened but cannot be removed altogether.

The context for change

The task of the public service is to harness the energy and the enterprise of the public, private and NGO sectors towards national development, not to stifle them.

Regulations accumulate on a case-by-case basis in response to specific concerns. The difficulty is that while, individually, each regulatory requirement may service a valid purpose, collectively the impact can be to undermine enterprise and voluntary activity.

Most Commonwealth governments are now concerned to undertake periodic or continuing reviews of the combined impact of all regulations on the private and NGO sectors to consider whether the regulatory framework:

- represents the most appropriate form of government intervention;
- inhibits the effective allocation of resources; and
- serves sectional interests at the expense of broader national development.

Reasons for caution

In many Commonwealth settings, concerns are being expressed about the regulatory load in many sectors of the economy and national life, for example:

- public and private sector labour markets and employment bargaining;
- telecommunications, transport and the financial services sector;
- agricultural marketing; and
- wages and consumer prices.

Addressing concerns in such diverse areas makes two particular demands of the public service. First, it must have the policy analysis capacity to recomrnend a coherent deregulation/re-regulation strategy in any particular sector, learning from international experiences.

Second, and most fundamentally, the public service must be oriented towards national development goals and not merely fixed to specific technical approaches. Deregulation is not a goal in itself, it is a means towards an end – national development. Without such an orientation, public service strategies and policy recommendations risk trading one form of rigidity for another.

Achieving change

Deregulation programmes across the Commonwealth are focusing on:

- existing legislation, requiring a rejustification of all regulatory requirements;
- forthcoming legislation, ensuring that no additional burden is created without a compelling reason; and
- regulatory enforcement, examining procedures from the user's perspective and reorienting public servants towards assisting businesses and NGOs to comply with essential requirements.

Before implementing change to existing regulatory programmes or developing substantive new regulatory requirements, departments and agencies need to demonstrate that:

- a problem or risk exists, government intervention is justified, and regulation is the best alternative;
- the public has been consulted and has had an opportunity to participate in developing or modifying regulations and regulatory programmes;
- the benefits of the regulatory activity outweigh the costs;
- the regulatory activity impedes, as little as possible, national competitiveness; and
- the overall regulatory burden has been minimised by abolishing outdated requirements.

The key to successful regulatory review is to examine the current requirements from the user's point of view. The involvement of national and local government, the interests of Ministries, and overlapping responsibilities between agencies can create more difficulties than the regulations themselves. The challenge to the public service is to determine how it might best assist individuals and businesses in meeting essential requirements, rather than simply finding opportunities to prevent activities which fall below required standards.

Examples of change

In 1983, *Ghana* embarked on a Reform Programme against the background of a decade of unprecedented economic decline and crisis. Deregulation was done as part of the Reform Programme through a shift from direct controls to greater reliance on markets in order to enhance efficiency in the economy generally and, in particular, the efficiency of resource use. The Reform Programme entailed extensive deregulation in the macro-economic and the structural and institutional environment. This meant a redirection of the State's role away from direct intervention to monitoring and supervision in the framework of clearly defined rules and market-based policies. The implications of this shift for the Civil and Public Service and for management generally have been far-reaching. It has meant a fundamental reorientation of attitudes in the Civil Service through a well-designed programme of retraining and improved incentives.

In *Canada*, in the 1992 Budget, the Minister of Finance set the stage for regulatory review. The Government began a department-by-department review of existing regulations to ensure that they resulted in the greatest prosperity for Canadians. Part of this review required a public "rejustification" of existing regulations to ensure that those which stifled the creativity and efficiency of Canadian business or which served no public good, were removed. The Treasury Board Secretariat monitors departmental performance and the effectiveness of this policy.

Deregulation in *India* has been used to strengthen market forces to ensure greater competition, thus reducing the role of the State as a regulator, welfare provider and producer. It has resulted in the liberalisation of different regulations, such as industrial licensing, to encourage competition in the economy. As an element of broader economic policy, it has resulted in structural adjustment programmes for the Indian Economy as a whole.

In *Malaysia*, the deregulation process started as a Government directive. A central agency, the Malaysian Administrative and Management Planning Unit of the Prime Minister's Department, responsible for introducing administrative improvements in the public sector, undertook a major study on deregulating the licences and permits pertaining to the business sector. This study identified areas in which a national deregulation exercise could assist the initiatives of individual departments.

The close collaboration between the Government and the private sector under the Malaysia Incorporated Policy greatly assisted the deregulation initiative. Feedback and the identification of rules, regulations and administrative procedures which are cumbersome and dilatory in nature are done through the Consultative Panels established at federal, state and district levels.

Deregulation was a key feature of the general programme of economic liberalisation that occurred in *New Zealand* in the decade since the election of the Labour Government in 1984. As a result, New Zealand has now eliminated most forms of restriction on entry to markets, removed the price controls that were formerly applied to a large list of items, and abolished regulatory monopolies and licensing that applied to many professions and trades. The last major step of deregulation was the Employment Contracts Act which was passed in 1991.

Other useful material (current as of 1996)

Government in Transition. The Inaugural Conference of the Commonwealth Association for Public Administration and Management, Charlottetown, Prince Edward Island, Canada, 28–31 August 1994. Commonwealth Secretariat, 1995 (ComSec)

Regulatory Affairs Guide, Treasury Board of Canada Secretariat, October 1992 (CAN)
1994 Federal Regulatory Plan (CAN)

Competition Policy and Government Regulatory Intervention, Haarmeyer, D. Economic Development Commission, Wellington, 1988 (NZ)

Briefing Papers, The Treasury 1984 & 1987, Wellington (NZ)

4.2 Reorienting the Public Service

4.2.1 Intergovernmental restructuring

Intergovernmental restructuring is the re-balancing of the powers and responsibilities of national and local, federal and provincial, governments.

The goal of intergovernmental restructuring is an improved partnership between the levels of government, with each undertaking those tasks which it performs best.

The context for change

For many Commonwealth countries, the rationalisation of responsibilities at central and local levels has been driven by an urgent need to improve accountability and performance. In addition, there have been concerns with the extent of public access and involvement in local government processes and a desire to foster greater public participation.

Restructuring of federal/provincial or national/local intergovernmental boundaries has improved efficiency within government, where it has resulted in a stronger sense of ownership of development goals. Additionally, the clarification of mutual roles and responsibilities and, in particular, the rationalisation of mechanisms for financial transfer between levels of government has enhanced fiscal transparency.

Reasons for caution

Restructuring and changing responsibilities brings its own risks. Time and energy spent on reorganisation is taken away from policy analysis and service delivery. Institutions at national and local levels that face abolition will devote considerable ingenuity to protecting the interests of their stakeholders after reorganisation, which is not always consistent with the interests of their taxpayers or service users. Changes in local tax burdens consequent on reorganisation are unpopular and provide a destabilising influence on the new structures.

Achieving change

Intergovernmental relationships can be restructured or realigned through four primary means:

- formal constitutional change, to redefine the roles and responsibilities of the federal or national government and provincial or local government;
- non-statutory intergovernmental agreements which set out obligations and commitments for governments in specific policy areas, such as the environment;
- statutory agreements which establish specific obligations and objectives for each level of government, such as intergovernmental fiscal transfers; and
- informal agreements or commitment among political leaders to undertake a certain course of action.

Commonwealth experiences suggest that in any of these approaches:

*   an intergovernmental affairs issue will only be treated as a high priority if there is a clear and durable consensus among federal/national and provincial/local government leaders to do so;

*   effective working relationships between political leaders and public servants are required;

*   progress is more likely when governments address a small number of related issues rather than a broad range of unconnected items;

*   framework agreements and credible time frames are key instruments in the successful management of intergovernmental affairs;

*   open, continuous communication with the stakeholders and clients affected by possible public policy changes is necessary;

*   non-government experts can often be used as neutral intermediaries to manage differences between levels of government;

*   working groups of officials can be used to prepare the necessary policy advice and follow-up; and

*   incremental change is facilitated by the acceptance of "asymmetric relationships" between levels of government in which it is recognised that the exact balance of responsibilities between federal/national and provincial/local government need not be identical for all provinces/local governments.

Examples of change

In *Sri Lanka*, it is hoped that devolution of powers to eight provincial councils will be seen as a major landmark in the evolution of political and social institutions by providing an opportunity to restructure the administration to strengthen and enhance democratic policy making.

In *Australia*, at both the Special Premiers' Conferences in Brisbane in October 1990 and in Sydney in July 1991, the Premiers and Chief Ministers agreed to a significant correction of the Federation's vertical fiscal imbalance, as well as complementary reallocation of functional responsibilities and a significant reduction in tied grants. Furthermore, they considered that this must be followed by the establishment of more effective mechanisms for co-operation among the various levels of government within the Federation.

At the subsequent Premiers' and Chief Ministers' Meeting, major decisions were taken in the areas of regulatory reform, the establishment of the Financial Institutions Scheme for Australia, agreement on the uniform road rules and to an Intergovernmental Agreement on the Environment.

In *New Zealand*, in 1989, the structure of local government was reorganised and reformed. A pattern of small territorial councils was revised to create units of sufficient size to implement a programme of managerial reform. Those reforms applied the principles of accountability, transparency and contestability to generate an agenda of change. Significant in it were changes in the role of the Chief Executive to become the sole employee of the council and the employee of all other staff; an obligation to publish and consult over an annual plan with newly-established community boards; a requirement to separate the operational side of councils into trading enterprises, which win work competitively; and a requirement for councils to publish locally-selected performance indicators.

Other useful material (2nd edition)

The European Community: A Political Model for Canada? by Peter Leslie (Minister of Supply and Services, Canada, 1991) (CAN)

Distribution of Powers and Functions in Federal Systems by Dwight Herpenger (Minister of Supply and Services, Canada, 1991) (CAN)

Paintu, Martin "After Managerialism: Rediscoveries and Redirections: The Case of Intergovernmental Relations", Australian Journal of Public Administration, December 1998

4.2.2 Local empowerment

Local empowerment is the orientation of the public service towards providing local communities with the capacity to influence, organise and shape their own destiny.

This emphasis on capacity building reflects the importance of public service actions which leave behind a legacy of competent organisations, able to continue with the provision of training, enterprise development and other services, in the longer term. While the development of key organisations, and as a step towards that, key individuals, is important – the eventual objective is that of enhancing collective community confidence.

Local empowerment is, most fundamentally, a partnership between the public service and local communities.

The context for change

The pressures for efficiency and effectiveness in the public service reflect concerns that the public sector is over-charging and under-performing. Very particularly, it reflects a concern that the traditional structures and systems of the public service are remote from the concerns of many citizens and, consequently, without broad support and encouragement from the community, require a high and growing level of resources to sustain them.

Local empowerment, through partnerships between the public service and local communities, is an orientation within the public service which seeks to address these concerns and to build initiatives which, because of their local support, are both sustainable and cost-effective.

Local empowerment initiatives recognise that:

- communities have more commitment to their members than service delivery systems have to their clients;
- communities understand their problems better than external professionals;
- professionals and bureaucracies deliver services – communities solve problems;
- institutions and professionals offer "service" – communities offer "care";
- communities are more flexible and creative than large bureaucracies;
- communities are cheaper than service professionals;
- communities enforce standards of behaviour more effectively than bureaucracies or service professionals; and
- communities focus on capacities to get things done – public service systems focus on deficiencies.

Reasons for caution

Partnerships between the public service and local communities run the risk of romanticisation. The public service in Commonwealth countries has been established to ensure that public funds are spent equitably and transparently towards the achievement of democratically-determined national objectives. In considering innovative approaches for circumventing any public service shortcomings in delivering sustainable and cost-effective services, the underlying concerns for equity and transparency should not be overwhelmed by enthusiasm and expediency.

The difficulty for the public service is that in some sections of the community, its legitimacy has been so challenged that almost any alternative to traditional public service bureaucracies can appear attractive to policy makers. Where inner city poverty and alienation has rendered formal job training ineffective, where systematic discrimination has removed the rationale for paying taxes and licence fees, radical alternatives which build on the community structures existing within such hard-pressed communities must be found. However, while the public service has every reason to doubt its traditional approaches, many examples of ineffective financial management systems and ill-defined accountabilities point to the need for the public service to retain confidence and certainty in its underlying principles.

Achieving change

Public service organisations can create a spectrum of opportunities, which different communities can seize as they are ready. Governments can remove barriers to community control; encourage organised communities to take control of services; provide seed money, training, technical assistance; and move the resources necessary to deal with problems into the control of community organisations.

When governments put ownership and control into the community, their responsibilities do not end. They may no longer produce services, but they are still responsible for making sure needs are met.

The range of development issues which community-based organisations or projects are likely to confront, and consequently the skills they will need to acquire or have access to, are given below:

- Project development

  A key task for the public service is to assist community-based organisations in formulating viable proposals.

- Financial planning

  Community organisations invariably complain of underfunding, generating both concern and cynicism within government. As well as ensuring that bids represent value for money, funding agencies should also ensure that funds are sufficient to allow the organisation to achieve its objectives realistically.

  Adequate planning and the ability to recruit and retain competent staff require some financial stability which is severely compromised by the annual funding round. Commonwealth experiences suggest that approvals of up to three years be recommended – subject to rigorous annual review.

  Lead Ministries in the public service may propose that staff development costs are reflected in approvals. Funders can suggest, or on occasions insist, that direct overhead items, like training, be added to the bid for funds.

  If they wish to develop local groups, lead Ministries need to make available resources for institutional development (training, consultancy, etc.) which are not necessarily linked directly to project delivery.

- Staffing and recruitment

  To minimise the recruitment and staffing issues frequently found in community organisations, including high staff turnover, problems of burnout, and poor internal industrial relations in many settings, lead Ministries can:

  - encourage groups to adopt more realistic salary levels;
  - insist that organisations draw up proper job descriptions;

- sit on interview panels; and

- ensure that employment issues are included in training provision.

• Building local networks

Lead Ministries can attempt to design jointly with local groups a strategic framework for development and support. A few of the key steps include:

- **mapping the landscape**: a comprehensive picture is required of the group population and the availability and quality of support provision;

- **promoting coalitions and networks**: area-based coalitions of organisations can be encouraged covering similar constituencies, thematically or geographically;

- **shared services**: small centres capable of managing the routine administrative affairs of a number of organisations on the basis of incomes can be established;

- **shared facilities**: coalitions of groups for the joint purchase or development of premises, thereby promoting closer co-operation and dispersing overhead costs, can be encouraged; and

- **community consultancy resources**: pump-priming funds to establish a "community consultancy team", a pool of expertise to provide training, consultancy or hands-on support, can be provided.

Community groups receiving public funding are accountable for their use of those funds. Refer to the Portfolio section on Improving the Accountability of Funded Bodies.

Examples of change

In *Bangladesh*, the Grameen Bank was set up in 1976 as an alternative credit delivery system catering to very poor people. By mid-1994, it had disbursed more than a billion US dollars in credit amongst two million borrowers, 94 per cent of whom were women. A recent World Bank study showed that Grameen is a financially sound institution. It has a strong institutional identity because the Grameen members have bought the shares, and their elected representatives make up the majority of the Board of Directors that determines its policies. This initiative has shown that once access to credit is assured, the poor can quickly break through the vicious poverty cycle and meet their basic needs. They can accomplish much when they are organised properly and allowed to participate in taking investment and consumption decisions together in small groups of like-minded persons. There is a lot of peer support as well as peer pressure that helps to ensure the maintenance of credit discipline. However, such micro-level, non-government initiatives require substantive and well co-ordinated macro-level policy support from government to succeed.

In *Canada*, one particular initiative has been the Comprehensive Land Claim Agreements to guarantee Aboriginal people a role in the decision making that affects the management and conservation of resources. These Agreements have provided for the establishment of resource management boards referred to as Public Government Institutions. These institutions are typically comprised of equal numbers of Aboriginal and Government nominees and are empowered, usually through separate Acts of Parliament, to perform a variety of resource management functions in geographical regions which include both Crown lands and settlement lands. Although Government retains ultimate jurisdiction over the resources in question, the Boards are granted significant autonomy in their operations and direct their own administrative, technical and research staff. The Boards are expected to play a key role in tapping traditional knowledge within individual communities by holding public hearings and engaging in consultation at the local level.

A particular initiative in the *UK* in local empowerment is the Inner City Task Force Programme set up in 1988. This Programme aims to promote improved co-ordination at the local level between the activities of central Government departments, local authorities and other organisations. This activity is equivalent to the building of local partnerships. The Inner City Task Forces are small teams which operate in 16 of the most deprived urban areas. They come from a wide variety of backgrounds – central and local government, the private and voluntary sectors – and have a wide range of experience. They concentrate on the economic regeneration of designated inner city areas by improving local people's employment prospects, stimulating enterprise development and strengthening the capacity of communities to meet local needs. The Programme which has been in existence since 1988 has had time to develop a successful track record.

Other useful material (current as of 1996)

Government in Transition. The Inaugural Conference of the Commonwealth Association for Public Administration and Management, Charlottetown, Prince Edward Island, Canada, 28-31 August 1994. Commonwealth Secretariat, 1995 (ComSec)

Gwich'in Comprehensive Land Claims Agreement (CAN)

Nunavut Land Claims Agreement (CAN)

Information pamphlets on Small Business Development Company Limited and YTEPP Partnership in Training (TT)

PA Cambridge Economic Consultants. An Evaluation of the Government's Inner Cities Task Force Initiative. Vol. 1. Main Report. Department of the Environment. November 1992 (UK)

4.2.3 Decentralisation

Decentralisation is a shift of responsibility and accountability towards the public service at regional, provincial or local levels.

The major objectives of decentralisation are:

- more balanced development;
- more realistic projects and programmes;
- more effective co-ordination of development activities at local level;
- strengthening of local political institutions and increasing popular participation in development; and
- greater mobilisation of local resources.

The context for change

Since the mid-1970's, governments have been increasingly concerned to adapt and develop the structures and values of the public service to achieve greater efficiency and more responsive services. Improved quality at less cost has been the imperative. These changes have largely been driven by continuing economic crises in developing and developed countries, which have in turn arisen from deteriorating terms of trade, over-extended borrowing and a somewhat abrupt change of policy by the lending institutions during the 1980's.

Against that background, decentralisation has been seen in many settings as the response to one or more of nine concerns:

- *Local needs*: decentralisation can be a more flexible and therefore more effective way of meeting local needs than central planning.
- *Eradication of poverty*: in some settings, decentralisation is seen as particularly relevant to meet the needs of the poor.
- *Access*: decentralisation is used to improve access to public services.
- *Acceptance of change*: decentralisation and participation can encourage ownership of the profound social changes which development entails.
- *Decongestion*: decentralisation is often perceived by government as an opportunity to reduce congestion at the centre.
- *Unity and stability*: locally based institutions can meet distinctive local needs, particularly those of minority ethnic groups.
- *Participation*: participation following decentralisation may enhance civic consciousness and encourage political maturity.
- *Mobilisation of resources*: decentralisation can facilitate the necessary harnessing of popular energies and local resources of skills, labour, materials and cash necessary for the maintenance of development projects.
- *Co-ordination*: decentralisation can improve the co-ordination of development activities.

Reasons for caution

Decentralisation in one form or another has been pursued in many Commonwealth settings but in view of the breadth of civil, political, economic and cultural factors involved, it has proved particularly challenging in its implementation. Decentralisation requires strong political commitment and administrative support.

Decentralisation requires a consideration of regional boundaries. Delimiting sub-national areas is never straightforward, and the most appropriate area for a particular government function may not be ideal for another. Compromises between conflicting principles are necessary. For example:

- boundary-setting must address conflicting physical, economic, social, and human geographical factors;

- efficiency criteria may vary and be at odds with other aims – large areas presumed to provide economies of scale may not fulfil the requirements of minority sub-groups; and

- social and political objectives may be at odds with administrative feasibility, and will be limited by the methods used to finance decentralised activities or functions and the availability of administrative and financial management skills.

Achieving change

Decentralisation is a two-way process. It requires clarity on national and strategic issues which must be addressed centrally, and on operational and local policy decisions appropriate for decentralisation.

The basic requirements for successful decentralisation are:

- *Political will* – specifically, consensus that decentralisation constitutes an effective means of increasing local participation and making government more representative.

- *Regular consultation* with all major interested parties, both local and central, on the principles, methods and rhythm of the process.

- *Administrative commitment* of concerned institutions and their personnel to the success of what, in most Commonwealth settings, has proved to be a gradual decentralisation programme. Co-operation is required so that new responsibilities are successfully assumed.

- Realism and prudence on the part of the *local government* in analysing its capacities and abilities to handle the various tasks to be decentralised.

- Acceptance of *incrementalism*, applying decentralisation features as and when the right conditions are created. Incrementalism can include an asymmetric approach in which reforms are adopted differently in different parts of the country, accepting the need to coexist with different organisational models according to specific conditions, and relaxing the principle of administrative uniformity.

- *Collaboration with local associations and organisations* in the implementation of the decentralisation process.

- Sufficient *capacity of the central government* to manage the process, create the conditions for success, and reinforce weak local organisations.

Decentralisation programmes in Commonwealth countries are addressing the following issues:

- *Choice of geographical areas*: with defined purposes and objectives in view, and with a concern for equity.

- *Choice of functions*: there is a very wide variation in the range of functions available for decentralisation. The particular functions identified are determined significantly by the strength of local institutions.

- *Management of intergovernmental relations*: redefining the legal status of the decentralised institutions requires a rebalancing of the comparative powers of the decentralised and central authorities.

- *The degree of financial autonomy*: the source of finance, whether from local taxation/raised revenue or from a central government grant, and the method of allocation of any grant affect the degree of dependency of the decentralised authority on the central authority. The degree of autonomy enjoyed by the decentralised authority to determine the precise application of resources shapes the decentralisation programme.

- *The form or method of participation*: the manner of securing local participation in the decentralised authority, whether through consultation, representation on management bodies, or full local representative government, is at the heart of the decentralisation process.

Examples of change

Malta has recently established a system of local government in which some services have been decentralised to local councils, which contract all work out to the private sector under the management of a small central administration.

Zimbabwe is decentralising responsibility in the areas of health, education and social service welfare to local government.

In *Sri Lanka*, devolution of powers to eight provincial councils has been envisaged as a major historical landmark in the evolution of political and social institutions. It also provides a unique opportunity to restructure the administration in a manner that would strengthen and enhance democratic policy by the people.

In *New Zealand*, the reforms in the education sector illustrate the principles of decentralisation. The intent of the reforms was to abolish the Department of Education which had previously dominated both policy making and the delivery of education services. The new system was based on the following features:

- Schools would be the basic building block of education administration, with control over their educational resources, to be used as they determined, within overall guidelines set by the State.

- The running of the school would be a partnership between the professionals and the particular community in which it was located. The mechanism for such a partnership would be a Board of Trustees.

- Each school would set its own objectives within overall national guidelines set by the Government. These objectives would reflect the particular needs of the community in which the school was located.

- Schools would be accountable, through a nationally-established agency, for the public funds spent on education and for meeting the objectives set out in their charters.

- Schools would be entitled to purchase services from a range of suppliers.

- A Ministry of Education would be established to provide policy advice.

In *South Africa*, a precondition for the success of the transformation process is the devolution and decentralisation of authority to departments and provinces. This enables them to act creatively and flexibly in translating the broad goals of transformation and national policy guidelines into specific strategies that are capable of responding effectively to local needs and circumstances. This is in line with the priority of the Reconstruction and Development Programme to bring governance closer to the people.

An example of decentralisation in the *UK* is the option of relocation. Government departments are expected regularly to consider relocation to sites offering best value for money, easier labour markets and increased operational efficiency.

Originally, there was a centrally-directed Dispersal Programme, under which a number of departments decided to move staff away from London. However, the current focus, introduced in 1987, is on a delegated, value-for-money approach. This places the responsibility for taking relocation decisions with departmental Ministers who are best placed to take into account all the various factors involved. There is, therefore, no longer a centrally-directed programme, though the Treasury acts as a central source of experience and expertise. Departments report each year to the Treasury on their progress with, and plans for, relocation.

Other useful material (current as of 1996)

From Problem to Solution. Commonwealth Strategies for Reform. Managing the Public Service. Strategies for Improvement Series: No. 1. Commonwealth Secretariat, 1995 (ComSec)

Government in Transition. The Inaugural Conference of the Commonwealth Association for Public Administration and Management, Charlottetown, Prince Edward Island, Canada, 28-31 August 1994. Commonwealth Secretariat, 1995 (ComSec)

Smith, B. C. Choices in the Design of Decentralisation. An Overview and Curriculum for central government officials responsible for the reorganisation of administration at the local level. Commonwealth Secretariat, 1993 (ComSec)

New Zealand Public Sector Reform, State Services Commission, Wellington, 1993 (NZ)

4.2.4 Improving the accountability of funded bodies

Many bodies external to the public service are funded by government. These range from parastatals or state-owned enterprises, through companies in which government holds a significant proportion of the shares, to the vast range of boards and other statutory bodies which are subvented by government.

These bodies share two features – they receive, directly or indirectly, public funds and they operate outside of the regulations which determine the structures and systems of the public service.

The context for change

There is growing concern across the Commonwealth about the accountability of funded bodies as:

* a significant and, in many situations, a growing proportion of public expenditure is routed through them;
* their actions have a substantial impact on the society of which they form part;
* the electorate views the Government as being ultimately responsible for shortcomings in the delivery of services by all funded bodies; and
* in addition to their subvention through recurrent expenditure, they are responsible for assets which were acquired with public funds.

The challenge for the public service is to adopt a managerial orientation which addresses four significant issues:

* consistent with moves to put some distance between policy making and service delivery, a growing range of services are provided by arms-length funded bodies;
* the responsibility of the public service is to achieve value for money in all government expenditure, not only that which it directly administers;
* in improving the performance of funded bodies, the public service must recognise that their public funding requires them to be responsive to popular concerns as well as to market or other economic signals; and
* the population of funded bodies is subject to increasingly rapid turnover as more rigorous evaluations are leading to some closures, and strong privatisation policies are moving functions out of the public service into arms-length bodies as an intermediate step.

Reasons for caution

Funded bodies include:

* bodies owned by the state but legally distinct from the public service and established under specific enabling legislation;
* companies in which the state owns a significant proportion of the equity;
* enterprises fully owned by the state; and
* statutory boards and councils providing regulatory services.

This diversity of funded bodies brings with it an equal diversity of governance and organisational structures, from boards of directors nominated by government to management committees with authority to select replacement members themselves.

It is widely recognised that this context can provide a dense concentration of more or less attractive appointments, subject to relatively little public scrutiny, responsible for providing services which are not measured against any clear criteria of success. Where this applies, there are three preconditions for any successful improvements to accountability:

- building a constituency for change – developing some consensus on the need for action either by public debate or through discussions with key board members and chairpersons;

- a shared perception of the current situation between the central agencies in the public service, particularly the Ministry of Finance, the Auditor General and the Attorney General; and

- political interest in improving accountability and a willingness to nominate amenable chairpersons, where appropriate, and to consider legislative changes.

Enhanced accountability of funded bodies brings its own longer-term challenges. For example, it provides the public and interested parties with the information necessary to fuel robust political and social debates concerning the balance between bottom-line commercial performance and social responsibilities, and concerning salaries and benefits outside the public service. Such developments represent, in principle, a welcome move towards openness, but in practice may require a new level of media relations skills within the public service.

Achieving change

The principles of improving the accountability of funded bodies can be simply stated. For each body or agency outside the public service receiving funding, other than through a commercial contract for services rendered to government, the parent Ministry and the central Ministries responsible for finance and economic planning should be able to state succinctly:

- *The resources made available to the body including those directly provided by government:*
    - direct grants or subventions;
    - payments made under contract with government;
    - free or subsidised use of capital, buildings, equipment or other assets owned by government;
    - free or subsidised use of public servants' time; and
    - fees, charges and income from other sources.
- *The outputs expected from and produced by the body:*
    - the regulatory, advisory, commercial or other services which the body has been established to provide; and
    - the actual outputs set against that mandate.
- *The organisational and procedural principles by which the body is governed:*
    - the degree, if any, to which it must adhere to public service procedures and regulations;
    - systems for ensuring that merit and equity are paramount in staffing; and
    - the statutory or other basis for financial and asset management.

- *Current accountabilities within the public service, and within the funded body for:*
  - determining the level of public funding to be provided;
  - reconciling actual outputs with those expected; and
  - adherence to required organisational and procedural principles.

Improving accountability invariably requires procedural changes within the public service, generally requires a change of senior personnel in the funded bodies, and frequently requires legislative amendments. Such developments are intended to monitor funded bodies by ensuring clarity under these four headings. However, experience suggests that it is only by clarifying the present position – by producing baseline data through an initial survey or audit – that sufficient concern can be generated for the process to begin.

Examples of change

In *Malta*, parastatal accountability is linked with the Financial Delegation and Accountability initiative which envisages the decentralisation of financial administration throughout Government. Recommendations on financial delegation are the subject of a policy document that has been approved in principle and now awaits implementation.

In *India*, an instrument of accountability of public enterprises is termed the Vigilance Machinery. There is a Central Vigilance Commissioner and the Central Bureau of Investigations which examines allegations of improper conduct, corruption, deviations from procedure for improper considerations, etc. In order to prevent this instrument of accountability becoming an inhibitor of actions, the Government decided to remove the employees of public enterprises below Board level from the purview of the Central Vigilance Commission and to entrust the vigilance responsibility up to this level to the Board itself, with an internal machinery to assist it. The actions and decisions of the members of the Board, however, continue to be within the purview of the Central Vigilance Commission.

Other useful material (current as of 1996)

Public Enterprise Management: Strategies for Success, Report of Commonwealth Roundtables (Cyprus, India and Malaysia), Commonwealth Secretariat, London, 1989 (ComSec)

Performance Contracts. A Handbook for Managers. Commonwealth Secretariat, 1995 (ComSec)

Report of the Auditor General, Minister of Supply and Services, Ottawa, Canada, 1976 (CAN)

Royal Commission on Financial Management and Accountability, Final Report. Minister of Supply and Services, Hull, Canada (CAN)

4.3 Forming Alliances

4.3.1 Developing partnerships with the private sector

The public service is the disciplined core of the larger public sector. It is the responsibility of the public service to manage the economic and regulatory frameworks within which the public and private sectors can thrive. The public service increasingly recognises that it is in a strategic *partnership with the private sector* in achieving social and economic development, and that operational partnerships with the private sector provide particular opportunities for cost-effective initiatives.

The context for change

Trade liberalisation and increasingly rapid international movements of expertise and capital have changed the ingredients of national economic success. Previously, growth could be derived from strong primary production and industrial capacity, with managed markets providing a safe environment for national trade, all supported by a public service designed to manage and maintain stability through regulation.

Today's more open international markets are redefining national economic development as international competitive success. Strategic value-added production, dynamic enterprises and a skilled workforce are the new ingredients. The role of the public service has changed from that of a passive administrator, concerned with stability, to that of an active player, managing rapid regulatory change and cautiously encouraging public expectations in order to facilitate private sector initiatives.

In sum, the public sector has entered the equation of economic success. It must now take its full share of praise or blame for the economic circumstances in which the country finds itself. The public service is unavoidably in partnership with the private sector – the challenge is to make it a productive partnership.

Reasons for caution

Partnerships between the public service and the private sector take place on both strategic and operational levels. Strategic partnerships concern the construction of a broad national consensus for economic and social development. Operational partnerships concern the approaches by which the public service facilitates the growth of the private sector, and harnesses private sector strengths to achieve specific development objectives.

At either level there are many reasons for distrust, and Commonwealth experiences are pointing towards a checklist for ensuring that the partnership is productive:

- Shared risks and benefits

  All partners must accept that there is sufficient overlap in their goals to allow a common approach to problem-solving.

- Shared power and responsibilities

  Each partner must be prepared to bring their distinctive strengths to the negotiations – whether it is access to capital, public confidence, political support or expertise – and to be prepared to share some of these strengths with the others, and accept some responsibility for the results that ensue.

- Effective communications

  Mutual understanding regarding expectations and assumptions, and concerning tactical difficulties and conflicts of interest, is a prerequisite.

- Adaptability and mutual respect

  Goals will evolve over time, and without a recognition, even if occasionally grudging, of the good intentions of the other party, partnerships will falter.

Achieving change

Productive public service/private sector partnerships are built at two levels – strategic and operational. Strategic partnerships are at the highest level of policy making and require that the public and private sectors see the nation as one corporate entity in which both are working together in pursuit of shared corporate goals. Partnerships at this level are supported by high-level consultative panels and fora, involving senior mangers and leaders from both sectors, and politicians. Strategic partnerships lead to highly visible collaborations offering common development goals for all sections of society.

Operational partnerships take place at sectoral, Ministry or project levels. In assessing Commonwealth experiences, two types of operational partnership can be identified: those that encourage collaboration, and those that encourage competition – both are necessary.

The public service can foster collaboration with and within the private sector by:

- supporting the development of trade associations and other fora which provide networks for sharing best practices and for mutual benchmarking;

- reshaping the delivery of its own regulatory services so that companies experience a public service that is concerned to ensure their competitive success; and

- developing criteria within which non-competitive alliances can be formed between the public service and private sector companies to solve particular business problems facing government.

The public service can foster fair competition by:

- a comprehensive review of the regulatory environment (see the Portfolio section on Deregulation); and

- improved policies and practices for procurement (see the Portfolio section on Improving the procurement process).

Examples of change

Developing strategic partnerships with industry in the *Malaysian* context is through the Malaysian Incorporated Policy introduced in February 1983. This Policy, which is one of the major strategies for national economic growth, requires that the public and private sectors see the nation as a corporate or business entity, jointly owned by both sectors and working in tandem in pursuit of shared corporate goals. Policy implementation can take the form of consultative panels, fora, seminars, workshops, training programmes and even funding. This Policy was given further emphasis and importance with the introduction of the guidelines on how to implement Malaysia Incorporated.

In the *UK*, the Department of Trade and Industry (DTI) set up the Managing in the 90's Programme. Its purpose is to help companies address the challenges of worldwide economic uncertainty, changing markets, demographic change, saturation of demand, environmental concerns, increased competition from newcomers to the marketplace and a more discerning end-user. Activities include the production of high-quality, informative publications and seminars. The aim is to inform and enthuse businesses so that they become more aware of best practice and in this way become better able to share it with others. One of the DTI's most successful schemes is called "Inside UK Enterprise". This scheme enables representatives of UK businesses to visit leading companies employing management practices in a wide range of product areas. Key personnel can see successful methods and ideas in practice and are able to speak directly to those able to pass on their knowledge and expertise. It is a concept which is now being adopted in several other countries.

At operational levels, in *Canada*, Public Works and Government Services Canada (PWGSC) undertakes several activities which foster and strengthen relationships between clients and industries that market and sell their products to the Canadian Government. Common Purpose Procurement is an area where the Government can initiate activity to encourage a partnership approach committed to solving business problems within Government. This type of procurement is used for procuring integrated information technology systems for the Canadian Public Service. Suppliers are selected to help clients define and solve business problems through a continuing alliance between the client and the supplier. The supplier and the Crown share the responsibilities, risks, investments and results of the specific business endeavour. Through sharing the roles and responsibilities, innovations in defining timely solutions to problems result. Alliances such as this can potentially be extended beyond procurement into system implementation, system operation, and maintenance for a one-time stabilisation period.

Other useful material (current as of 1996)

Common Purpose Procurement Framework. Public Works and Government Services Canada, November 1993 (CAN)

ISO 9000: Improving Quality is the Bottom Line, Let's Talk Business. Public Works and Government Services Canada, October 1993 (CAN)

Improvements and Development in the Public Service, 1990 and 1991 (MAL) The Civil Service of Malaysia – A Paradigm Shift, Chapter 17 (MAL)

4.3.2 Developing partnerships with NGOs

Governments enter *partnerships with non-governmental organisations* (NGOs) for many reasons:

- an increasing number of NGOs have contractual relationships to deliver services on behalf of government departments;

- some NGOs mobilise resources in support of government policies and programmes, in such diverse fields as literacy, unemployment, adult education, and community development;

- some NGOs undertake research or establish innovative programmes and inform governments of their results in order to advocate particular responses; and

- governments' attention may be drawn by NGOs to the impact of public or private sector policies or actions.

NGOs operate at the interface between government and the public service, on the one hand, and civil society more broadly, on the other. As with the private sector, NGOs are inevitably in a partnership with the public service. The challenge for the public service is to make it a productive partnership.

The context for change

NGO/public service relationships are complex. They are also dynamic, changing as the nature and purposes of NGOs have evolved, and as the overall context of the work of both has been transformed.

New approaches by both NGOs and governments have resulted in the growing responsibilities of NGOs to provide service delivery and resource mobilisation under contract to government, while continuing to hold some responsibilities for bringing about broader social and economic change.

A major issue arises in the area of contracted service delivery and resource mobilisation. In some countries, NGOs devote a considerable part of their efforts and derive a considerable part of their finance from such contracts. However, if this contractual relationship is to be a positive partnership, there must be a commonality of framework and vision, not only between the public service and NGO, but also, in the case of international development projects, between the donors and the final recipients of funds.

The major issues which arise in the area of broader change and development activities are:

- NGOs have often pioneered and promoted innovative programmes and policies subsequently supported or adopted by governments, for example in the area of gender and environmental issues. This has an impact on public service activities in these areas.

- NGOs which have pioneered new forms of provision or service feel that in taking them over, governments tend to remove the innovative components and swallow them into the public service. Their sense of achievement is thus sometimes tempered by one of failure.

- Conversely, governments feel that it is unreasonable and may be undesirable for public policy to be shaped by unrepresentative innovations driven by NGOs.

- Some NGOs feel that there are too few lines and means of communication available which enable them to share the results of their research and innovation with public servants, or to make representations about policy changes. Reciprocally, some public servants feel that NGOs are often too secretive about their work and do not wish to share their findings, views and ideas. Some also feel that NGOs are too ready to share these in the public arena before attempting to communicate and discuss them with government.

Reasons for caution

Dialogue towards improving collaboration with NGOs is undermined by:

- *Tensions resulting from poor accountability.* In theory, both governments and NGOs are accountable to the public. But the more this is not evident in practice, the more each tends to be suspicious of the other.

- *Tensions from blurred boundaries.* The boundaries between the concerns and interests of the public service and of NGOs have never been sharply drawn, but at a time of rapid social change and increasingly formal contractual relationships, the boundaries are particularly blurred. This is a poor basis for a positive partnership.

- *Tensions inherent in financial dependence.* A strong concern expressed by NGOs and the public service in many Commonwealth countries relates to the growing level of financial dependence that many have on government. Governments are torn: they are eager for NGOs to do more, but want them to raise more from a public or international donors that may be unable or unwilling to contribute further. At the same time, many NGOs feel that they risk losing their independence if they take government funds. Some hold the view that contracted work for government will undermine the sustainability of NGOs in the long term.

Achieving change

Typically, partnerships between the public service and NGOs have been improved by:

- undertaking a critical analysis of the services provided by NGOs – key areas to be addressed include client group, service capability, quality of service and level of training of personnel;

- determining the services that can more effectively be provided by NGOs and, distinctly, by the public service;

- clarifying the distinctive contributions of NGOs and the public service to policy making; and

- the development of a public service/NGO policy forum at national level.

The Livingstone Roundtable organised by the Commonwealth Foundation in 1988 recommended that each country should aim to have a written policy on NGO/Government relations which would include:

- criteria for defining and recognising NGOs, e.g. local or indigenous and foreign;

- a distinction between welfare and development NGOs;

- a statement on the sectors of the society, the economy and the environment in which NGOs should operate;

- an explanation of the system for institutionalising dialogue between NGOs and government; and

- an explanation of the system for involving NGOs in government policy formulation and development planning.

The Roundtable concluded that this should be an official government document but the main responsibility for its preparation should rest with the NGOs themselves.

Commonwealth Foundation guidelines for good policy and practice regarding NGOs on the part of governments cover:

* creating the right environment for NGOs through clear definition and proper recognition, reflected in appropriate laws and regulatory processes, developed in consultation with NGOs;

* having frameworks to facilitate consultation and communication with NGOs; providing appropriate support for NGOs; and

* distinguishing NGOs from organisations established by governments.

Good understanding and respectful relationships between the public service and NGOs emerge largely from good, clear information. Mystery breeds suspicion and misunderstanding. Open and accessible information between the public service and NGOs fosters productive partnerships.

Examples of change

India has had successful experiences with NGO's in implementing education, national planning and rural development programmes. In 1986, India established the Council for Advancement of People's Action and Rural Technology (CAPART) to channel government finance to the voluntary sector for specified rural development activities. CAPART is a semi-autonomous body, registered under the Societies Act, which is accountable to Parliament. One of the reasons for CAPART'S success is the strength of the voluntary movement in India and the many NGOs capable of taking advantage of its project assistance. Nevertheless, CAPART had not disbursed as many funds to NGOs as it intended, possibly due to the undue emphasis by Civil Servants working for CAPART on documentation and financial accountability requirements; and the inadequate accounts and technical appraisals provided by NGO staff. To rectify this, CAPART has been providing training for both NGO and government officials in performance measurement, and for NGOs in book-keeping accounting. It has also financed external personnel to conduct project appraisals for NGOs on its behalf.

The CAPART model in India is the only example of a parastatal organisation being involved in NGO relations. Other institutional mechanisms are located either in the government or the NGO sector. For instance, the Ministry of Culture and Social Services in *Kenya* and the Ministry of Plan Implementation in *Sri Lanka* are examples of the former, where government departments deal directly with NGOs (foreign NGOs in the case of Sri Lanka). GAPVOD in *Ghana* and TANGO in *Tanzania* are examples of "umbrella" NGOs which have been established to negotiate with government on behalf of NGOs. However, these alternatives have not been tested in the same way as CAPART because government project funding to the NGO sector has been more restricted, both in absolute terms and in relation to external funds.

In *Bangladesh*, an illustration of a successful government/NGO partnership has been the establishment of the Grameen Bank which has effectively developed programmes and direct benefits for poor sectors of society.

In *Trinidad and Tobago*, government forms partnerships with NGOs for the purpose of providing services to the public in critical areas. This is done mainly through the provision of annual grants to organisations as a contribution to their operations. These organisations, by and large, either provide a service for a sub-set of the population for whom no service exists, or they provide specialised services which are supportive of government efforts in respect of an issue deemed to be of national importance. Serious consideration is now being given to broadening this partnership, particularly in respect of social service delivery.

The *UK* Government has established the Voluntary Services Unit in the Home Office which co-ordinates and acts as a signpost between NGOs and all government Ministries. However, attention has been taken to ensure that such a unit should foster rather than hinder effective communication.

In *Zimbabwe*, co-operation between NGOs and government has been particularly effective in cases of emergency relief. For example, during the emergency relief programme for Mozambican refugees, the government called upon the expertise of local NGOs, such as the Association of Women's Clubs, to give their services in pre-school activities and skills training. The planning of the programme was carried out jointly by a committee consisting of government departments and local NGO representatives.

A long-term example in Zimbabwe is the literacy programme. Before independence, a local NGO, ALOZ, was responsible for the whole literacy programme. With independence and the government's recognition that literacy was the key to development, the government worked together with ALOZ to develop a new programme. In this was a division of responsibilities, taking account of the experience and expertise of ALOZ.

Other useful material (current as of 1996)

From Problem to Solution. Commonwealth Strategies for Reform. Managing the Public Service. Strategies for Improvement Series: No. 1. Commonwealth Secretariat, 1995 (ComSec)

Smith, B. Choices in the Design of Decentralisation. An overview and curriculum for central government officials for the reorganisation of administration at the local level. Commonwealth Secretariat, 1993 (ComSec)

Strategic Issues in Development Management: Learning from Successful Experiences.

Report of Workshop/Study Tour on Co-operation between Government and Non-Government Organisations, India, 12-23 February 1990. Commonwealth Secretariat, 1990 (ComSec)

Strategic Issues in Development Management: Learning from Successful Experiences, April 1989 Commonwealth Secretariat (ComSec)

Non-Governmental Organisations: Guidelines for Good Policy and Practice. Commonwealth Foundation, 1995 (CF)

4.3.3 Developing partnerships with academic institutions

Commonwealth experiences indicate that enhancing the capacity of government for policy making is the key to improving economic management and fostering development. This capacity can be greatly strengthened if the policy analysis and co-ordination units in the public service draw on the national and regional expertise available in universities and research institutions.

The context for change

There is mutual advantage from a partnership between academic institutions and Ministries and departments. Academic institutions are an important source of advice in the development of policy and management practice. At best, they can provide:

- alternative policy proposals for delivering government objectives;
- experts for advisory committees;
- a sounding-board for emerging policy proposals;
- a research capacity;
- consultants to examine detailed aspects of policy, administration and management; and
- training in public management and in public policy analysis.

Reasons for caution

In many instances, the relationship between government and the universities and research institutions has often been one of mistrust and lack of co-operation. At worst, academic institutions see the public service as short-sighted and ideologically-driven, and the public service sees academic institutions as uninterested in developing practical solutions to real public policy problems. Such a starting point provides a flimsy basis for partnerships.

Achieving change

The experience of many Commonwealth countries indicates that developing partnerships between the public service and academic institutions requires that five key issues be addressed:

- Balancing supply-driven research with demand-driven consultancy

  This issue revolves around how much time academics in universities and research institutions should devote to research in their discipline, on the one hand, and to consultancy assignments from government or other organisations, on the other.

- Improving the standing of local experts

  Governments are frequently under pressure to recruit foreign-nominated consultants, and dialogues towards partnership must consider approaches by which this can be resisted where appropriate local expertise exists.

- The loss of experts within universities and other institutions

  Secondments and exposure to the public service management culture can result in high level staff being lost to academic institutions as they move to the public service, the private sector, or overseas. In some Commonwealth settings, close working relationships between the public service and universities has resulted in a shortage of academic staff.

- The early involvement of academic experts in policy difficulties

  Crisis requests compound the perception of academics that public management is intrinsically short-term and encourage an overly-cautious approach.

- The regular involvement of public service managers in curriculum development and academic teaching

  Programmes at all levels are strengthened by the involvement of senior staff able to bring practical experience to bear on complex issues.

Examples of change

In *Ghana*, the Civil Service Law mandates the establishment of Ministerial Advisory Boards that bring together the top management of each Ministry and carefully selected outside experts, mostly academics from the universities and research institutes. This process has enabled many university staff to participate in the Government policy-making process.

Links have been established between the Government of *Trinidad and Tobago* and the University of the West Indies for the training of administrative officers in Public Administration. Both organisations have provided technical assistance to each other, particularly in relation to training and education programmes.

In *Canada*, one particular initiative took place in January 1993 when the Government joined forces with three major universities to create The Institute of Government Informatics Professionals. The overall objective of the Institute is to provide advanced professional training for IT professionals employed by the Canadian Government. The Institute offers a selection of about 40 university-accredited courses, each equivalent to a one-semester undergraduate course. Students can accumulate credits towards a Bachelor's degree. Training is carried out at Government facilities by professors from the participating universities. The Institute's curriculum is under the guidance of an Advisory Board. Both the Advisory Board and the Curriculum Councils represent a partnership of government, industry and the university communities. Since the programme was launched response to it has been extremely positive.

In the *UK*, one particular initiative in developing partnerships with academic institutions has been set up by the Department of Trade and Industry as part of the Managing in the 90's Programme. This Programme is intended to improve management practice in British businesses rather than within the Civil Service itself. It is an awareness programme designed to help managers in British companies respond to change, to adapt, to innovate and to plan for continuous improvements. The Programme provides seminars, workshops, literature, videos, etc., and signposts managers to further sources of help. Academic institutions have provided much of the input to the Programme and have helped to prepare the content of the printed materials which the DTI issues to industry, as well as organising seminars and events for businessmen.

Other useful material (current as of 1996)

From Problem to Solution. Commonwealth Strategies for Reform. Managing the Public Service. Strategies for Improvement Series: No. 1. Commonwealth Secretariat, 1995 (ComSec)

Current Good Practices and New Developments in Public Service Management: A Profile of the Public Service of Canada. The Public Service Profile Series No. 1, pp.119-122. Commonwealth Secretariat, 1994 (ComSec)

Current Good Practices and New Developments in Public Service Management: A Profile of the Public Service of Trinidad and Tobago. The Public Service Profile Series No. 4, p59. Commonwealth Secretariat, 1995 (ComSec)

Current Good Practices and New Developments in Public Service Management: A Profile of the Public Service of the United Kingdom. The Public Service Profile Series No. 2, pp.123-125. Commonwealth Secretariat, 1995 (ComSec)

4.4 Improving Partnerships

The concept of partnership can be defined as a framework of policies, practices, procedures, processes and certain assumptions that can provide guidance for managing the economy and for improving the process of development, which, in turn, can ultimately benefit consumers and the nation as a whole. It can also be defined as "people and organisations from some combinations of public, business and civil constituencies who engage in voluntary mutually beneficial, innovative relationships to address common societal aims through combining their resources and competencies." (The Copenhagen Centre, 2000).

Partnership for development can also be defined as an agreement negotiated by the state and social partners, namely private sector institutions and civil society organisations. The common denominator of different forms of partnerships is the pooling of resources (financial, human, technical and intangibles such as information and political support) from public and private sources to achieve a commonly agreed social, economic or environmental goal.

Partnership therefore, constitutes:

- a symbiosis of public and private sector/civil society organisations;
- a framework of policies, practices and procedures for managing the economy;
- a negotiated agreement between stakeholders; and
- the social construction of bridges between the public/private sectors and civil society.

The context of change

Experience in Commonwealth countries shows that the concept of partnership is not new, as it has always aimed at finding the best possible ways and means of managing the economy and ultimately improving the delivery of service to the public and consumers alike. It has, therefore, been used as an instrument either for change, continuity and/or innovation in dealing with the issues, concerns and problems of development. The rationale for its use as an instrument is based on the assumption that the symbiosis of the public/private sectors and civil society, in the appropriate and right proportions might improve the management of the economy and consequently development as a whole.

Assumptions of the historical development paradigm:

- The private sector alone is incapable of the allocation of resources alone in society;
- The nationalisation of certain enterprises and creation of new state owned enterprises is not feasible or successful;
- Because of the poor performance of economies, the private sector has been recognised as an engine for development; and
- The state is regarded as a facilitator of development – therefore need for partnership.

The objectives of partnership include:

- The continued development of an efficient economy capable of economic growth and operation;
- Empowering citizens with the necessary resources and opportunities to make meaningful decisions regarding the uplifting of their lives;

- To make society more inclusive, reduce poverty and long-term unemployment; and
- To ensure that the benefits of growth and development are more equitably distributed.

Critical sectors in partnership

Three critical sectors play a key role not only in promoting good governance but also in sustaining human, economic and political development:

1. The state creates a stable and conducive, political and legal environment;

2. The private sector acts as an engine for development, generating jobs and income; and

3. Civil society facilitates political and social interaction by mobilising groups to participate in economic, social and political activities. In addition, civil society connects individuals with the public realm and the state through various interest groups and organisations. It can also provide checks and balances to government power and monitor social abuses.

Forms of partnership

Partnerships can be formal and informal. They can exist at local, national and international levels. There are some forms of partnership that are formed, particularly in developing countries of the Commonwealth, under pressure from social unrest, as conditionalities from donors, after a dialogue with critical stakeholders, and as part of regional integration.

In development terms, partnership can be used synonymously with technical co-operation. In development projects, for example, partnership can include NGOs, both national and local, government bodies, donors, multilateral and bilateral agencies, church organisations and community-based organisations. Partnership can also be forged in different sectors of the economy, such as health, education, rural development and infrastructure development as well as providing basic social services for the poor sections of the community or other socially disadvantaged groups.

Partnership between public/private sector/civil society has more recently emerged and is increasingly being considered as a result of many economic, political and social trends in the transformation process. Such transformation is also the result of globalisation and attempts to improve the delivery of public services, and at the same time improve the management of the economy.

The trends towards decentralisation, democratisation, economic liberalisation, the protection of human rights and the rule of law, reduction of bureaucracies and the delegation of functions to lower levels of government have all contributed to the rationale for exploring how partnerships expand the quantity and quality of public services delivered at the local level.

As a result of these transformations there emerges a broad range of arrangements that involve a combination of state and non-state actors for the fulfilment of traditional state functions.

Rationale for the shift in assumptions in support of partnership:

- Direct result of globalisation and national competitiveness agendas;
- Economic co-operation at regional level;
- Evidence of mismanagement of public enterprises;
- Quest to find better methods and practices of development and management;
- Access to broader skills/expertise;
- Improved quality of public service delivery;
- Cost savings;

- Access to technology; and
- Better accountability

Types of reforms

- Public sector reforms have created opportunities for more productive links between the State, NGOs and the beneficiaries themselves – citizens. Decentralisation is a demonstration of these changes of attitudes, policies and practices;

- Economic changes, characterised by structural adjustment programmes, have accompanied the political processes that have had a direct impact on the functional relationships between the public sector, private sector and civil society;

- Liberalisation of the economy and privatisation policies have allowed the emergence of a new autonomous private sector that is becoming a key protagonist in national development;

- Multipartism, where it did not exist, has seen the emergence of political parties representing interests that support partnership reforms; and

- The emerging and growing role of civil society organisations with their focus on civic rights.

All these reforms have immensely contributed to the need to formulate better structures for working together toward the solution of problems, resolution of conflicts and delivery of goods and services to society in a more efficient manner.

Reasons for caution

Impediments to Partnership Formation and Management:

- Lack of an effective decentralised system of government which enables local levels to share the potential benefits of partnership;

- Unfriendly rules and outdated procedures that govern budget processes and can become a deterrent to partnership development;

- Inadequate and inefficient formal mechanisms that promote the participation of citizens;

- Parallel operations that create duplication, overlapping and hence waste of already scarce resources;

- Lack of political support, guidance and direction;

- An environment which does not foster a partnership management culture and partnership initiatives;

- Lack of partnership credibility: factors influencing credibility include the competence and credibility of staff in the partnership unit, mutual trust between the partnership staff and partners, consultation and involvement of stakeholders and the process of evaluating and communicating the findings and conclusions; and

- Lack of legal and regulatory mechanisms to ensure compliance, consistency and continuity.

Guiding principles for successful tripartite partnership

- Partnership must be home grown;
- Leadership commitment to partnership;
- Balance between vision and social reality;
- Address issues of disparity between the poor and rich;
- Need for involvement of all stakeholders;
- Right combination of skills, knowledge and attitudes;

- Available and retrievable information;
- Trust, openness; and
- Clarity of objectives.

Ethics in partnership

- Ethical standards must be clear;
- Standards should be reflected in the legal environment;
- Employees should know their rights;
- Decision-making processes must be transformed;
- Political leadership must lead by example;
- Clear guidance on the interaction between public/private sectors and civil society;
- Ethical conduct of managers;
- Policies and procedures should demonstrate commitment to partnership; and
- Accountability mechanisms should be in place.

Lessons from experience

Lessons are drawn from those countries that, first have already established formal partnerships and accountability frameworks, secondly from those that are operating informally and thirdly those countries that are in the process of establishing a social dialogue between the three stakeholders

- Public/private sector and civil society partnerships represent a powerful way of addressing development challenges and resolving conflicts, confusion and duplication;
- For partnership development and management to be effective, it is necessary to focus on key critical development issues and craft solutions;
- For partnership to be meaningful, there is need to identify key players such as:
  - key leaders who provide vision, direction and motivation;
  - change agents who inspire people to participate in projects;
  - co-ordinators who undertake concrete organising tasks.
- Partnership formation and management require sufficient time and resources to make the project work;
- Political will and state support is critical;
- Financial, technical and human resources are critical to success;
- Informal networks are essential for the operation of formal arrangements;
- The provision of a legal and regulatory framework which establishes the authority of the partnership is key;
- Formal structures with functions, roles and responsibilities clearly stated, clear guidelines, and agreed approaches for problem solving should be considered. For example, objectives achieved through negotiation, consultation, information sharing, researched-based decision making and conflict resolution;
- Effective social dialogue can be maintained through regular newsletters, annual reports, seminars, workshops, study tours which constitute a powerful means of communication; and
- Stakeholders must see the benefits derived from such a partnership or dialogue.

Achieving change

The following are some of the comments that can be made for the countries that intend to form a social dialogue in order to adjust to the changes taking place in society. The comments and steps to partnership are based on the experiences of other countries thereby constituting best practices.

- An awareness campaign should be launched to popularise the programme once a decision has been made to establish a social dialogue;

- Preventive measures should be taken to ensure that potential impediments to partnership formation are minimised, e.g. simplifying management procedures through the reduction of red tape;

- The setting up of a committee of representatives of public/private sector, civil society organisations to oversee the implementation process of the partnership programme;

- Institutional strengthening of relevant agencies such as the Cabinet, commercialisation and privatisation offices, and other organisations involved in managing tripartite relations between the stakeholders;

- The widest possible consultation and co-ordination between stakeholders should be conducted before, during and after social dialogue is created;

- Mutual trust between and among stakeholders should be established in order to facilitate the formation and management of the social dialogue; and

- Ensure links with decision-making processes by planning the partnership unit in the Prime Minister's Office to strengthen linkages between policy makers and administration.

Examples of partnerships

In *Malaysia*, for example, developing partnership with industry is seen through the operationalisation of the Malaysian Incorporation Policy, introduced in 1983, as one of the major strategies for national economic growth. The policy requires that the public and private sectors see the nation as a corporate or business entity, jointly owned by both sectors and working in tandem in the pursuit of shared goals. Policy implementation can take the form of consultative panels, seminars, workshops, training programmes and even funding. This Malaysian model has been generally referred to as Smart partnership;

Many countries in the South East Asian Region, e.g. *Taiwan, Singapore, Malaysia, Thailand* and *South Korea* have been influenced by the rise of the business sector in the UK and USA. Public/private partnership arrangements were becoming more common and successful. The growth of the private sector was accompanied by similar growth in the civil society sector;

In *Botswana*, former President Sir Ketumile Masire, advocated the support of Smart partnership to policy makers. Botswana now has an established mechanism of a social dialogue with stakeholders;

South Africa launched the National Economic Development and Labour Council (NEDLAC) in order to bring together government, business, labour and community interests, through negotiation, reaching consensus on all labour legislation and all significant social and economic legislation;

Most of the Commonwealth developed countries have established mechanisms of collaborating with the private sector, civil society organisations and community-based groups e.g. in *the UK, Canada, Australia* and *New Zealand*;

The African Development Bank (ADB) and the Asian Development Bank (ADB) have advocated the formation of such forms of partnership in order to promote development;

In the Caribbean, *Barbados* has taken the lead initiating such dialogue;

The Commonwealth Partnership for Technology Management (CPTM), The Southern African Initiative for Development (SAID); and other examples

In the *UK*, the Social Compact was formed as a basis for a partnership between government and the voluntary sector, underpinned by a set of principles.

Other useful material (2nd edition)

Collins, P.(ed) Applying Public Administration in Development. Guidepost to the Future. John Wiley & Sons Ltd, 2000.

Governments as Partners: The role of Central Government in Developing New Social Partnerships: The Copenhagen Centre, Ashridge (Brochure), 2000.

The Report of the Canada-Commonwealth Business Forum's 1998 Conference in Ottawa, Canada. Organised by the Commonwealth Business Council in association with Public Policy Forum.1998.

Tengku Mohd Azzman Shariffadeen, Managing Transformation through ICT and Smart Partnerships: Malaysian experience, 1998.

CAPAM Biennial Conference 1998: Seminar Session Paper: Public Sector Partnership with the Private Sector and with Civil Society by Florence Mugasha, Malaysia.1998.

CAPAM Biennial Conference 1998: Partnering with the Private Sector: Some more equal than other by Guy Callender and Judy Johnstone, University of Technology, Sydney, Australia, July 1998, Bangi, Malaysia.1998.

Partnership for Good Governance for a Globalised World: A Commonwealth Agenda for 21st Century by Gordon M Draper. Paper presented at the Institute of Public Administration, Australia National University in conjunction with CAPAM, Darwin, Australia 8-10 September 1999.

Agere, S, Promoting Good Governance: Principles Practices Perspectives: Commonwealth Secretariat, London, U.K. 2000

Asian Development Bank (1995). Governance Sound Development: An unpublished paper by Donberger, S and Ferndez, Public-Private Partnerships for Service delivery: Business Strategy Review, The Strategic Planning Society Vol 10 Issue 4, Winter 1999.

Aitken,J. Public Sector Partnerships with the Private Sector and Civil Society in New. Zealand, paper presented at CAPAM 1998 Conference in Malaysia. 1998.

Sir Kenneth Stowe, Professional Developments: Compact on relations between Government and the voluntary and community sector in England and Wales in Public Administration and Development Journal, 18, 519-522 (1998).

Rob Brown, What should Public/Private Partnership (PPP) mean? London, 1999.

Website. http://www.ncvo-vol.org.uk/main/gateway/compact/ntml

4.4.1 The New Partnership for Africa's Development (NEPAD)

A recent development in the area of global governance has been the establishment of the "New Partnership for Africa's Development" (NEPAD). Canada's Prime Minister on a tour of Africa in April, 2002 stated: "The 21st century will be a century when Africa will truly become part of the international community". What is required to put Africa back on the agenda of the world is: "Good Governance, respect of human rights, electoral discipline … peace and security, openness and elimination of corruption".

NEPAD is an African initiative for African development and it is the result of joining together the Millennium Partnership for African Recovery Programme (MAP) and the OMEGA Plan at the request of the Organisation of African Unity (OAU). The partnership is a commitment by African leaders to get rid of poverty and place the continent on a path of growth and development. It is based on the practice of good governance, democracy and human rights. NEPAD will deal with the following items for action:

- the requirements for development;
    - peace, security, democracy and political governance;
    - economic and corporate governance;
    - regional co-operation and integration;
- the priority sectors;
    - infrastructure;
    - information and communication technology (ICT);
    - human development i.e. health, skills development;
    - agriculture;
    - promotion of production and exports;
- the mobilisation of resources.
    - increasing savings and capital inflows through further debt relief;

NEPAD is a pledge by African leaders that they have a pressing duty to eradicate poverty and place their respective countries on the route to sustainable growth and development. Concurrently, they need to actively participate in the world economy. The programme is based on the determination of Africans to extricate themselves and the continent from the malaise of underdevelopment and their exclusion in a globalising world. The continuing marginalisation of Africa constitutes a serious threat to global stability.

The need for change, in terms of development, is based on the following statistics from Africa:

- 340 million people live on less than US $1 per day;
- the mortality rate of children under 5 years of age is 140 per 1000;
- life expectancy at birth is only 54 years;
- only 58 % of the population have access to safe water;
- the rate of illiteracy for those over 15 years is 41%; and
- while there are 567 mainline telephones per 1000 people for high-income countries, in Africa there are only 18 per 1000 people.

The New Partnership calls for a reversal of this situation. What is needed is a bold and imaginative leadership that is committed to sustained human resource development and poverty eradication. There is a call for a new partnership between Africa and the international community to overcome the gap after years of unequal relations.

A critical dimension in setting the continent's destiny is the negotiation of a new relationship with the developing countries. The requirements of negotiating and accounting to a variety of donor agencies supporting development programmes is cumbersome and inefficient. The new relationship should set out mutually agreed performance standards and targets for both parties. There are many cases where the failure of projects is caused not only by poor performance but also by bad advice.

The four primary objectives in the implementation process include the following:

1. Establishing a governing structure with the mechanism to strengthen Africa's capacity to lead her own development and to improve co-ordination with other partners;

2. Ensuring that there is capacity to lead negotiations;

3. Ensuring that there is the capacity to accelerate the implementation of major regional development agreements;

4. Strengthening Africa's capacity to mobilise additional external resources for development.

In order to implement the New Partnership for Africa's Development there is a need to recognise the need to sequence and prioritise. The initiating Presidents proposed that programmes be accelerated in collaboration with development partners to address and improve the following:

- communicable diseases – HIV/AIDS, malaria and tuberculosis;

- information and communication technology (ICT);

- debt reduction; and

- market access.

Work has started on all of these initiatives by a variety of partnerships. Africa's participation and leadership needs to be enhanced for better service delivery.

Many initiatives in the past have been developed including the Lagos Plan of Action and the Abuja Treaty. They have failed for three major reasons:

1. timing (Cold War paradigm);

2. lack of capacity for implementation; and

3. lack of genuine will.

African leaders are making a commitment to the African people and the world to work together in rebuilding the continent. It is a promise to promote peace and stability, democracy, sound economic management and people-centred development. It is also a pledge to hold each other accountable in terms of the agreements of the programme – Africa holds the key to its own development. This development can only be attained through a genuine partnership between the world and Africa based on mutual trust, shared commitments and binding agreements.

Other useful material (2nd edition)

NEPAD Website: www.dfa.gov.za/events/nepad.htm

The Toronto Star, April 13, 2002, p. A14 (Canadian newspaper)

5.0 Making Management More Effective

5.1 Developing Managerial Capability

5.1.1 Strategic approaches to management development

Management development is the means by which leadership in the public service is renewed and strengthened at a time of continuous change in the environment in which the service must operate. A strategic approach ensures that the need for management development is structured into all planning decisions.

The context for change

Managerial capacity and determined leadership are crucial elements in public service performance improvements.

The direction and thrust of public service reform efforts in Commonwealth countries demand a particular increase in managerial capability to:

- drive organisational change;
- manage moves away from an administrative culture towards a managerial culture;
- provide leadership skills;
- encourage a spirit of accountable entrepreneurism; and
- respond to the delegation of decision making from the centre to line Ministries and departments.

There is no one best way to develop managerial capacity. The use of centralised training programmes throughout the public service is increasingly giving way to locally planned activities for management training.

Reasons for caution

Where it exists, the tradition of sending individuals on centrally planned, formal courses, with limited concern for impact or relevance, has led to some cynicism. If management development is to be incorporated into all organisational change, and if the financial and opportunity costs are to be justified, it must be associated with a continual focus on results. Enabling managers to grow into their constantly expanding tasks is essential, and to attract the appropriate investment it must also be credible.

Achieving change

A strategy for all public service reform will include an assessment of the implications of change in terms of new demands for managerial capability. Whereas the overall reform strategy may be formulated centrally, the detailed management development implications will probably be determined at Ministry or department levels.

Commonwealth experiences suggest that strategic management development approaches are underpinned by seven foundations:

1. Management development must be acknowledged, both by words and actions, to be a priority. It is the human resource equivalent of a capital charge; and it is the cost of maintaining the human capital of the service.

2. There must be a recognition of the long-term and continuous nature of managerial learning coupled with a willingness to try new approaches, particularly on-the-job training.

3. The changing relationship between the central personnel management agencies, the service commissions and the Ministry of the public service or similar bodies, and the line Ministries and departments must be reflected in the responsibilities for management development. These central co-ordinating and control agencies will increasingly take responsibility for ensuring that there is a management development strategy, and for monitoring quality and effectiveness, complementing the role of the line departments where the detail must be developed.

4. Departmental managers must promote consultation and open communication about management development strategies and activities at all the levels for which they are responsible. The support of employees must be obtained by their understanding of the need to continually review and increase management capacity in line with organisational change.

5. Departments must be given sufficient autonomy, including financial autonomy, to develop their own management development plans, and the flexibility to use all appropriate methods.

6. The development of managerial capability requires that gaining skills and competencies must be rooted in the work situation. Work-based management development strategies emphasise the importance of self-development, systematic coaching of managers by their bosses, mentoring, project work, action-learning methods, team building, and other on-the-job developmental activities.

7. Management development also requires systematic off-the-job training and exposure. Strategies presuppose the existence of a market of management training resources available to the public service, and of negotiated opportunities for exchange and exposure to other public and private sector environments.

Examples of change

The *Malawi* Government has recently established the Malawi Institute of Management to upgrade managerial competence in both the public and private sectors through training and consultancy activities.

Although quality management is still in its infancy in *New Zealand*, the experience of the public service suggests that a number of preconditions are necessary for quality management to work:

- senior management commitment is fundamental to success;

- only when quality management becomes a core feature of government policy can a public service chief executive make the necessary commitment to it; and

- quality management should not be embarked upon if major restructuring or organisational change is likely.

In the *UK*, the radical changes in the structure and culture of the Civil Service has been supported by an increased investment in management development programmes. The responsibility for these has been firmly located at the level of the department or implementing agency; and strategies combine competence-based, on-the-job activities with formal courses for various managerial levels.

The *Zimbabwe* Public Service Reform Commission Report emphasised the urgent need for a comprehensive strategy on management development for the entire service.

Other useful material (current as of 1996)

Reilly W. and Clarke R. Training for Public Management. A Handbook for Management Development, Commonwealth Secretariat, 1990 (ComSec)

Parikh I. J. & Farrell P. Approaches to Women Managers Training, Commonwealth Secretariat, London, 1991 (ComSec)

Doing it Better, Doing it Right, Public Sector Task Force on Productivity 1992, State Services Commission, Wellington (NZ)

With HMSO into TQM – Her Majesty's Stationery Office, from HMSO Publicity (PU23), St Crispins, Duke Street, Norwich NR3 1PD (UK)

5.1.2 Operational approaches to management development

Management development is the means by which leadership in the public service is renewed and strengthened at a time of continuous change in the environment in which the service must operate. *Operational approaches* take advantage of challenges as they arise, and provide pragmatic, frequently on-the-job, responses to organisational change.

The context for change

All public service reform strategies have a management development component. However, the traditional method of using external, off-the job, programmes cannot provide an adequately tailored response to specific organisational changes. In parallel with their use of formal training programmes, Ministries and departments need to integrate the process of management development into their day-to-day work activities.

In employing operational approaches to management development, the public service will:

- support key elements of change as they are introduced;

- provide an impetus for leadership and direction in the implementation of change policies; and

- convey the perception of a flexible and responsive organisation, sensitive to management pressures.

Reasons for caution

Management development strategies prepare staff for the challenge of leading through continuous change. Not every change requires a formal management development response, and the risks of encouraging dependency and reducing initiative should be noted.

In encouraging a pragmatic operational approach to management development, it should be noted that centralised training systems obscure the costs of short-term training as Ministries often do not have their own training budgets and merely respond to invitations to send individuals on courses.

Achieving change

Commonwealth experiences suggest that operationally focused management development approaches require the following underpinning:

- Baseline data which identifies the actual and required competencies of individual managers or supervisors within the department so that management development activities can be directed towards real and practical needs for skills and knowledge.

- A pervasive management commitment to develop the skills and capacity of subordinates. Managers may be reluctant to take on the additional responsibility for developing their subordinates on the job, but it must be specified as part of their own scheme of service.

- Work-based methods for management development, including coaching, must be institutionalised in the department's day-to-day work practices.

- The evaluation of investments in management development activities, in terms of their effects on job performance, must be adopted as an integral part of the training process.

- The initial high costs of broadening the range of work-based management development practices must be acknowledged.

The effectiveness of operational approaches to management development may be assessed by the following indicators:

- fewer individuals sent on formal courses;

- more in-house seminars/workshops which develop management skills;

- managerial job descriptions which feature on-the-job coaching of subordinates as a priority responsibility;

- more mentoring, group work, action-learning, project work, job rotation and self development activities;

- a system for setting group work and individual targets and for measuring performance; and

- a system for evaluating management development activities.

Examples of change

In *Malaysia*, management development is viewed as a vital component of the Total Quality Management and Client's Charter Initiatives in the Civil Service, where training functions are being decentralised to operational units.

Other useful material (current as of 1996)

Dodge, R. B. Learning in an organizational setting: The public service context; Canadian Centre for Management Development, June 1991 (CAN)

Continuous Learning: A CCMD Report. CCMD Report No. 1; Canadian Centre for Management Development, May 1994 (CAN)

5.2 Effective Information Systems

5.2.1 Creating an information systems strategy

Information systems are the systems that store, transmit and process information. They may be based on any combination of human endeavours, paper-based methods and information technology.

An *information systems strategy* is a plan for developing information systems which maximise the ability of the organisation to achieve its agreed objectives. A strategy provides the framework for the organisation for ensuring compatibility between systems, prioritises development, and encourages the elimination of redundant systems.

The context for change

Underlying all management activities in the public service is information, made useful and available through information systems. Many organisations have invested in information technology to improve their information systems but have done so in an ad hoc manner, dealing with each new system on its own merits. The resulting systems are incompatible, duplicate effort, and fail to increase organisational effectiveness. An overarching information systems strategy is needed to guide and co-ordinate the use of information technology.

Information systems strategic planning consists of a series of steps from identifying organisational objectives, to auditing information systems resources, to prioritising future information systems developments, to detailing an implementation plan. As a strategic exercise affecting the whole organisation, it must involve senior management.

A successful strategy brings the following benefits:

- information systems opportunities and needs are identified and prioritised according to public service objectives rather than to technical criteria;

- top management develops commitment to a strategic vision for information systems;

- compatibility between information systems is ensured, thus avoiding wasted investments; and

- attention is focused on the need to eliminate or re-engineer redundant information systems, reducing the very significant risk that poor systems will be expensively computerised.

Reasons for caution

Information systems strategic planning may falter when:

- there is little demand for information and little experience of the problems caused by an ad hoc approach to information systems;

- there are insufficient in-house skills in strategic planning, information systems analysis, design and management, management services and project management;

- organisational sub-units resist this top-down approach;

- the required participation, openness and feedback are not present;

- departments are unwilling to share their information with others; and

- the external environment is too unstable to permit long-term planning.

Achieving change

Overall, the strategic planning exercise answers three questions:

- Where are we now?

- Where do we want to be?

- How do we get there?

In Commonwealth experience, a strategic decision-making body, involving departmental heads and IT managers with the "clout" to push through change, will manage the resourcing for strategic planning, make decisions on the options suggested, and ensure that plans are implemented. The steps required within the public service are, broadly:

1. Define objectives and opportunities

Information systems help the Ministry, department or unit achieve its objectives. If the objectives are not clear, use short-term plans, although this may make it difficult to prioritise and review the IT contribution to the organisation.

Undertake a survey to outline and prioritise information-related problems and opportunities presented by technological developments.

2. Establish the information requirements

Identify the information required to support the organisation's key activities. This information may be generic and shared across the organisation or may be specific to a particular unit.

3. Outline the generic systems required

Identify the general information systems required and the technologies on which to base them. For example, there might be overlap in the financial information needs of different Ministries and a shared financial information system could be proposed, based on a computer network.

Alternative solutions, with their costs and implications, should be explored with the goal of ensuring the future compatibility of all systems, even those which are currently unrelated.

4. Conduct an information systems audit

Survey the existing information-related resources of the public service. This audit covers:
- organisational structure and staffing;
- paper-based records;
- computer applications with their hardware, software and networks;
- information systems undergoing or awaiting development; and
- sources of training and support.

In this way, the gap between existing and required information systems is identified.

5. Determine major issues affecting information systems

These issues will probably include:

- finance and skill constraints;
- cultural constraints within the public service;
- the short-term need to improve paper-based records versus the long-term need to computerise them;
- the conflicting forces of centralisation, standardisation and decentralisation; if information and staff are to move freely within the organisation, then standards for data items, software, hardware and networking must be imposed. Current approaches are to centralise major information systems, but to allow units to build their own microcomputer-based systems; and
- access to and attitude of information systems vendors and developers.

6. Decide information systems priorities and strategies

A broad indication of system priorities and preferred types of technology must be distilled even if full costs and benefits are impossible to estimate with any real accuracy.

7. Outline a strategy for information systems development and implementation

Evaluate the alternatives and determine:

- implementation: by existing computer centre, or by delegation to individual units, or by creating a new information systems organisation, or by contracting out;
- system development: creating new systems in-house (providing a better fit to needs) or buying a package from outside (providing a quicker, cheaper solution);
- training: using in-house technical staff, or in-house users, or vendors, or external trainers;
- system operation: running and supporting computer systems with in-house staff or contracting to a facilities management firm;
- procedures for tendering and selecting externally-purchased services; and
- how compatibility between different but related information systems will be assured.

8. Assess financial and human resource implications

Provide specific details on:

- funding, its source and time-scale;
- any new organisational structures;
- management of new information systems and related organisational changes;
- new skills needed and old skills no longer needed; and
- implications for training and jobs.

9. Develop the action plan for strategy implementation

It is important that plans allow for the explicit abandonment of systems which are not providing valued information.

Experience suggests that information systems strategic planning takes six months to one year to complete, and frequently provides a strategic framework for a five-year period.

Examples of change

Malta's Government is achieving the benefits of a planned, integrated approach to information systems since its strategy was formulated in 1990. Its approach, led by the Head of the Civil Service, has been logical and structured, but also responsive to political realities rather than dogmatic.

Information systems strategy was first formulated for the *Singapore* Civil Service in 1981. The result has been massive computerisation within Government; a computer network linking Ministries and allowing common systems for personnel and finance; and a skilled, informed workforce. Critical success factors have been a central agency for planning, the co-ordination and promotion of information systems; the standardisation of software development methods allowing IT staff mobility; and a large investment in staff skills.

The *UK* Government's Central Computer and Telecommunications Agency encourages and provides best practice advice on strategic planning of information systems. As a result, an information systems strategy is an integral part of planning in most Government departments.

Other useful material (current as of 1996)

Report on the Information Technology Policy Workshop, 12-16 November 1990, London. Commonwealth Secretariat, 1990 (ComSec)

Han, C. K. & Walsham, G. Government Information Technology Policies and Systems. Commonwealth Secretariat, London, 1993 (ComSec)

Odera, M. & Madon, S. Information Technology Policies and Applications in the Commonwealth Developing Countries. Commonwealth Secretariat, 1993 (ComSec)

From Problem to Solution: Commonwealth Strategies for Reform. Managing the Public Service, Strategies for Improvement Series: No.1. Commonwealth Secretariat, 1995 (ComSec)

Presentation to the Implementation Board on the Activities of CIO to Support Government Restructuring. Office of Information Management Systems and Technology, Treasury Board Secretariat, 1993 (CAN)

Blueprint for Renewing Government Services Using Information Technology. Treasury Board of Canada, Ottawa, 1994 (CAN)

The Civil Service of Malaysia – A Paradigm Shift (Chapter 6, pp. 449-572 (MAL)

Information Systems Strategic Plan. Government of Malta, Valletta,1990 (MLT)

Getting the Bits Right – A Guide to Best Practice in the Provision of Information Systems in the State Sector. State Services Commission, 1992, Wellington (NZ)

Central Computer and Telecommunications Agency, Guidelines for Directing Information Systems Strategy. HMSO, London, 1988 (UK)

Open Systems in Manufacturing. Integrated information – A Strategy for Success? Department of Trade and Industry, London (UK)

5.2.2 Implementing computerised management information systems

Management information systems produce information that assists managerial decision making. They include databases, budgeting, accounting and financial systems, and personnel records.

The context for change

The successful computerisation of management information systems brings the following benefits:

- improved decision making through the provision of relevant, timely information;

- early warning of performance problems;

- more senior staff time free to focus on planning;

- quick and easy access to information; and

- fewer paper records clogging the office.

Computers often fail to deliver these benefits because computerisation is not approached systematically or because there is not a full appreciation of computers in the context of the department's operations.

A structured approach, involving a series of steps from problem analysis to design, to implementation, is required in order to avoid:

- systems which meet current but not future needs;

- systems which meet the needs of only one group;

- "technical fixes" which just introduce computers without seeing that management attitudes, processes and structures must also change to deal with new information flows; and

- equipment breakdown through failure to plan for maintenance or a suitable environment.

Reasons for caution

General prescriptions must be treated with caution. Computerisation of management information systems will run into difficulties when:

- there is little willingness to share information between Ministries or departments;

- there is a lack of in-house skills in numeracy, data presentation and interpretation;

- staff have unrealistic expectations and glamorise the technology;

- managers fear that computerisation will lead to a loss of control;

- a radical change is introduced without consultation; and

- funding for the long-term maintenance of the computers, and for continuing management development, has not been identified.

Achieving change

Computerisation must be preceded by planning an information systems strategy which sets compatible standards for systems and implementation methods, determines priorities and, above all, which ensures that computerisation is not locking poor systems or redundant practices into place. The possibility of ceasing activities must always be considered before the possibility of computerising them. Computerisation follows three main stages, on a time scale varying from a few days for a small database to several months for an organisation-wide application.

1. Problem definition

Study the implications of computerised management information systems by:

- identifying current shortcomings and defining the organisational territory: is the need local or organisation-wide?

- developing indicative 2-3 year estimates of benefits, and capital and operating costs;

- assessing the implications of not proceeding;

- identifying the major risks and assumptions entailed in computerising management information systems;

- locating possible sources for the information system; and

- developing a broad project timetable with resource and responsibility implications.

If outline approval is given, establish a project team of managers, technical staff, and users, including mainly internal staff, but also drawing on cross-government support staff, individual consultants; and/or external organisations, including equipment vendors, consultancies, and donors.

Assess sourcing options on the grounds of available in-house and external skills, cost, need for confidentiality, need for staffing, flexibility, need for fresh perspectives, legislation and expediency.

Expand the management system objectives and benefits into a comprehensive, prioritised list of requirements. This necessitates wide-ranging discussion about the management information outputs:

- Who will use the information?

- What information do they want and why?

- When do they need it?

- In what form do they need it?

- What will they use it for?

It is important to reconfirm that the management information in question is relevant to existing organisational concerns. Ceasing to produce information is always an alternative to computerising its production.

Develop the functional specifications, i.e. what exactly the computerised system must do.

Choose software sourcing, assessing the potential of available off-the-shelf software packages, customised packages altered to provide a better fit to organisational needs, custom-made software written specifically for the organisation, and re-engineered software which the organisation is already using.

2. Solution design

Unless the "package" option is chosen, create a detailed design of how the software will store and process information.

Specify needs for any new computing equipment, looking ahead to future needs, speed of operations, compatibility with existing systems, and options for maintenance and repair. Design the new roles, processes, and organisational structures which will support the computing facility and the management information output.

3. Implementation

Prototyping allows staff to use a working model of the management information system and highlight revisions to be incorporated before the final version is produced.

Train staff how to use the new system. In addition, undertake information, management and computer awareness training for managers who do not directly use the system but who will make use of the information that it produces.

Document all details of the software and guidelines for operation to prevent this information being lost if key staff leave.

Some months after its introduction, and at regular intervals thereafter, evaluate the system. Re-examine managers' requirements and change the system if problems are identified.

Examples of change

The *Canadian* Software Exchange Scheme shares Government-owned software between departments and encourages its implementation. By avoiding duplication of effort and external purchasing, it saved $30m in 1993.

The Sarawak Economic Development Corporation *(Malaysia)* developed a management information system that produces monthly performance indicators for all public sector companies. New review meetings and organisational structures were created to act on the system output. Early warning of below-target performance was provided and problems tackled early. Average company profits rose after the system's introduction.

Singapore's National Computer Board is the primary source of assistance for computerised management information system implementation across Government. It provides consultancy and training, purchases equipment, and develops and manages Government management information systems. Its scale economies, co-ordination and promotion functions have helped introduce over 300 systems into Government and created management information system departments in every Ministry.

The *UK* MINIS system provides information for Ministers on resource allocations, targets and performance of all departments. Poor performance has been identified earlier than previously, and resources can easily be re-allocated between different management units.

Other useful material (current as of 1996)

Odedra, M. Information Technology in Developing Countries – An Annotated Bibliography. Commonwealth Secretariat, London, 1990 (ComSec)

Information Technology in Government: The Caribbean Experience. Commonwealth Secretariat, London, 1990 (ComSec)

Han, C. K. & Walsham, G. Government Information Technology Policies and Systems. Success strategies in developed and developing countries. Commonwealth Secretariat, London, 1993 (ComSec)

Odedra, M. & Madon, S. Information Technology Policies and Applications in the Commonwealth Developing Countries. Commonwealth Secretariat, 1993 (ComSec)

Presentation to the Implementation Board on the Activities of CIO to Support Government Restructuring. Office of Information Management Systems and Technology, Treasury Board Secretariat, 1993 (CAN)

Blueprint for Renewing Government Services Using Information Technology. Treasury Board of Canada, 1994 (CAN)

The Civil Service of Malaysia – A Paradigm Shift (Chapter 6, pp 449-572 (MAL)

5.3 Advice and Consultancy

5.3.1 Developing internal management advisory capacity

Internal management advisory capacity is developed by an array of services provided through the central personnel management office or Ministry of the public service, line Ministries and departments, and through ad hoc task groups focusing on particular change management challenges.

The context for change

The evolution of internal advisory capacity has started, traditionally, with Organisation and Methods units within the Establishments Division, with responsibility for assessing the scope for efficiency improvements in response to requests for additional posts.

The growth of the public service and the increasing responsibilities of central personnel management agencies have led to the establishment of management services units, frequently free-standing, within the Ministry of the public service.

The development of devolved consultancy capacity within line Ministries and departments, the increasing management consultancy responsibilities of information technology units and the attractions of engaging external consultants, have left some management services units unsure of their role. In consequence, they can be locked into a downward spiral in which lack of confidence leads to their presenting over-cautious and inadequately defined recommendations which, in turn, fail to convince heads of departments that an internal consultancy resource can add value to managerial decisions.

Reasons for caution

Strengthening the internal management advisory capacity, whether in line Ministries and departments or centrally in the Ministry of the public service can, at worst, provide a larger haven for staff with no other logical career move in the public service. Strengthening capacity should entail a stronger focus on advisory outputs and not on establishment inputs.

Achieving change

Broadly, internal management advisory capacity can be located in the central personnel management office or Ministry of the public service, in line Ministries and departments, and in ad hoc task groups assembled at any point in the service to focus on specific issues of change.

In selecting the appropriate mix of approaches, Commonwealth public services are increasingly seeking to ensure that two distinct functions are available within the public service. First, managers should have access to a responsive advisory service which can assist them in selecting methods and approaches which will enable them to achieve organisational goals.

Second, a pro-active and more directive advisory service is necessary to propose and manage organisational change consistent with the larger goals of an agreed public service reform or development plan.

The first function highlights the need for managers to identify advisory services as a valued resource – an investment in future efficiency which justifies some initial outlay. Many advisory services operate on a cost-recovery basis, with requesting Ministries and departments being charged a realistic price for services, in order to establish this relationship.

This responsive advisory service presupposes a climate in which managers at all levels are motivated to seek improvements, and are aware of emerging possibilities for organisational development, in particular, the potential advantage of benchmarking and quality management approaches.

The second advisory function is directive, with the authority to intervene in all aspects of public service management without a request from the relevant departmental head. This function is the operational arm of any public service reform or improvement programme, and draws its authority from that programme.

The success of moves to strengthen the central management advisory capacity, the capacity within line Ministries and departments, and in developing a tradition of ad hoc task groups assembled from across the public service to focus on particular change management challenges, must be judged by the following three criteria:

First, a successful array of internal advisory services allows managers to choose to invest in advice.

Second, it provides a focus by which managers may be directed to receive advice as part of a larger programme of change.

Third, it ensures that the credibility of the advisory staff is high, and is maintained by an emphasis on practical experience and short-term secondments.

Examples of change

In the *Kenyan* Civil Service, management consultancy is carried out by the Management Consultancy Service Division of the Directorate of Personnel Management. Government policy directs that private consultants should only be engaged when human resources are not available internally. The client organisation is required to furnish the Directorate of Personnel Management with a full briefing of the project and clear terms of reference. This ensures selection of the most appropriately qualified team of consultants. The Management Consultancy Services Division is responsible for the introduction of modern management principles and practices to achieve optimal staff utilisation and productivity.

The *Malaysian* Administrative Modernisation & Management Planning Unit in the Prime Minister's Department provides management consultancy to Government agencies. It has two main methods of delivering service:

• recommendation of methods and solutions or action programmes; and

• as a facilitator to help the client identify, diagnose and solve problems.

Many projects combine these two methods. A preliminary survey is carried out prior to agreement of the terms of reference for the project.

The Management Services Unit in *Malta* was so successful in delivering benefits to clients that it has now become a wholly Government-owned company which competes for consultancy business in the open.

The Management Services Department (MSD) in *Singapore* is a newly-privatised company that arose from an internal Management Services Department. Departments now make their choice of external consultants, one of them being MSD.

In the *UK*, departments may adopt their own management advisory systems. They must be cost-effective and are frequently subject to market-testing. There is an emphasis towards assignments in quality improvement and customer service. The Treasury has a central role in encouraging the sharing of good practice.

Departments also have access to central specialist internal management advisory capacity, e.g. the Manpower Audit team, which specialises in the use of resources, especially staff. Training standards are set by the Treasury in consultation with departments. Staff are trained centrally for the application of consistent standards across the Civil Service.

Other useful material (current as of 1996)

Canadian Centre for Management Development, Research Publications: (1) Leadership for a Changing World: Developing Executive Capability; (2) Upward Feedback in the Public Service of Canada (CAN)

Improvement and Development in the Public Service, (Chapter 13, pp 261-284), Malaysia, 1990 (MAL)

Improvement and Development in the Public Service, Chapter 13, pp 603-623, Malaysia, 1992 (MAL)

Corporate booklet issued by the Malaysian Administrative Modernisation and Management Planning Unit (MAL)

Public Service and the Public Servant, Martin, J. 1991, State Services Commission, Wellington (NZ)

5.3.2 Improving the management of external consultants

The public service can often benefit from advice and assistance from external sources. Effective *management of external consultants* is crucial as the service may feel that it has gained little from an external consultant whose presence distracts from operational pressures, and whose reports will add to the many unread volumes on Ministry shelves.

The context for change

At a time of dramatic change in the public service, the value of external consultants increases as they offer a short-term solution to limited change management capacity in the public service, and can provide insights into the experiences of other institutions facing similar challenges.

Reasons for caution

There are three areas of difficulty in using external consultants: the management supervision required; their potentially limited understanding of local concerns; and the costs incurred.

Reasons for caution in relation to management supervision centre on the difficulties faced by the public service in monitoring and steering the work of high status consultants, particularly as it is the limited capacity of the public service which has made their assistance necessary.

The risks of consultants failing to recognise local concerns are increased if the perceived status of the consultants inhibit local staff from critically evaluating their work, or if the tensions generated by the apparent disparity of remuneration between external consultants and local staff leads to an over-critical response.

The costs of external consultancy are high. The peripheral costs of project management, provision of support staff, and negotiated follow-up can make the total out of proportion to the initial concern.

Achieving change

Extensive Commonwealth experience in using external consultants to work for the public service has provided some pointers towards best practice in the following four stages:

1. Pre-contract

In defining the problem and assessing the value of engaging external consultants, three key factors are consistently identified:

- the involvement of counterparts from an early stage to encourage ownership and commitment;
- the explicit identification of managerial time to supervise the contract negotiations, the actual project, and the subsequent follow-up; and
- clearly agreed procedures which establish the role of central agencies when formal tenders are required and when individual negotiations at departmental level are appropriate.

2. Contract negotiations

Selection meetings and other negotiations with potential consultants must focus on the practical deliverables which will result from the project. The terms of reference should cover:

- a clear identification of the problem to be addressed;

- information about the existing background and context, in particular, details of previous studies and related projects or consultancies, and a realistic appraisal of current and future budgetary constraints and other resource limitations;

- all factors likely to have an impact on implementation planning and sequencing including budget cycle details, national holidays, proposed starting date, periodic progress review and control dates, and completion date;

- reporting strategy (when? to whom? in what form? how many copies?);

- the final product expected of the consultants (reports, blueprints, adequately trained counterpart staff, etc.);

- input to be provided by the client agency (staff support, documentation, transport, accommodation, permits and introductions);

- input to be provided by the consultants (personnel, man-hours, back-up materials, specialist equipment and training);

- financial arrangements (interim payments, final fees, travel and per diem expenses, costs of support, charges for additional work and penalties);

- liaison arrangements between client agency and consultants;

- exclusions from the assignment and similar limitations (copyright, confidentiality, and security requirements); and

- details and addresses of all relevant contact persons.

3. Project implementation

The involvement of external consultants is primarily a mechanism for obtaining skills. Supervising a contract during implementation requires considerable managerial time and determination if frequently observed difficulties are to be avoided. These may include:

- inappropriate changes to the consulting team during the course of the project;

- delays in negotiating contract amendments; and

- excessive focus on written outputs and insufficient involvement of local staff and counterparts.

4. Follow-up

Evaluation must begin with the question, "Has the public service gained from the process?" rather than from the more frequently asked but narrower point, "Were the terms of reference covered?" Key points to consider are:

- Has the exercise been cost-effective? Did the consultants provide genuine added value?

- Have internal counterparts benefited satisfactorily from exposure to the consultant's experience and methodology?

- Have the results been unexpected, and if so, why?

- Has the management of the contract been successful? Did it develop strong but directed working relationships?
- Can the recommendations be implemented?

Examples of change

The *Kenyan* Government actively encourages the establishment of local professional societies and registration boards so that public agencies can then be required to give preference to locally-based consultants.

Before external consultants are appointed, *Malaysia* requires all Government agencies to obtain prior approval from the Committee on the Appointment of Private Management Consultants, serviced by the Malaysian Administrative Modernisation & Management Planning Unit.

In the *UK*, the Treasury, the National Audit Office, and the Local Government Management Board have all issued authoritative guidelines on the selection and use of management consultants.

Other useful material (current as of 1996)

General Circular Letter No. 5 of 1980, The Committee on the Appointment of Private Management Consultant in Administrative Modernisation (in the national language) (MAL)

Buyers and Sellers: Negotiating Contracts in the Public Sector, Proceedings of NZIPA Seminar, Research Papers Vol. VII, No. 2 1991. New Zealand Institute of Public Administration, Wellington, 1991 (NZ)

Selection and Use of Management Consultants. National Audit Office, London, 1989 (UK)

Seeking Help from Management Consultants. HM Treasury, HMSO, London, 1990 (UK)

5.4 E-government – What is it?

Occurring worldwide is an evolution of both information and communications technology. The Internet is basically changing our lives – affecting the way we work, the way we learn, the way we do business and personally interact. *E- government* is a way for governments to utilise new technologies to provide citizens with more convenient access to information and services; to improve the quality of services and to provide greater opportunities for public participation to ensure accountability.

E-government presents some unique opportunities to move forward in the 21st century with government services that are of higher quality, more cost effective and create partnerships between citizens and their governments. However, concerns have already been expressed about the gap between the groups that have access to technology and those who are without the proper technology. This is also known as "the digital divide". In order to ensure that countries do not become part of the digital divide and as the knowledge economy continues to grow, expanded dialogue, partnerships and co-operation between public, private and civil society is needed.

Government can improve in terms of quality and the citizenry's participation in it, through e-government in four important ways:

1. It will be easier for people to have their say in government;

2. People will get better services from government organisations;

3. People will receive more integrated services since different government organisations will be able to communicate more effectively with each other; and

4. People will be better informed because they can get current and comprehensive information about government laws, regulations, policies and services.

In an e-government situation there are four potential clients for ICT services:

1. the government itself – government to government;

2. employees;

3. the private sector or businesses; and

4. citizens.

One of the most promising aspects of e-government will be its ability to bring citizens closer to their government and its services. While the technology and connectivity is widely available, and even more so after the Y2K computer standardisation and upgrading, many governments have not taken full advantage of its benefits. This is particularly true of developing and Small and Island States of the Commonwealth.

As the 20th century drew to a close and we began talking of the post-industrial era, the significance of these widespread changes became increasingly evident. The impact of these changes could be seen at several different levels. While manufacturing was a key component of the industrial economy, the services sector had, by the end of the last century, become a major new source of wealth creation. Information and intelligence, displayed in terms of people or smart machines, became more important as mental labour gained precedence over physical labour. With this came globalised production as information technology allowed information to cross borders with ease while new modes of communication turned the world into a global village. All of these factors have had a profound effect on the way we live and work as well as how we contribute to our communities and our economies.

The final decades of the industrial era saw the world embracing a new age of digital information and knowledge. The growth of technology, the increasing utilisation of the Internet and the forces of globalisation have opened up the frontiers of opportunities and challenges of what has now been accepted as the "Knowledge Age". Governments cannot ignore the fundamental changes that are affecting the lives of the citizens they serve. Undoubtedly, these changes are bound to have an impact upon the policies, structures, mechanisms and processes of governments as well.

Benefits of government integration

In brief, some of the general benefits of the introduction and management of an e-government system include:

- lower costs as well as improved efficiency and quality of services;
- more effective linkages between citizens and government;
- improved efficiency of government workers; and
- facilitated transparency and accountability.

Achieving change

New technologies are changing the way public administration is being run due to the intertwining of information and communication technology (ICT) and public sector reform. Many governments have recognised that the application of ICT to all levels of government is an important part of public sector reform. There have been a multitude of changes in the public sector throughout the Commonwealth due to the transformation of government with new technologies.

There are predictions that e-government or e-governance will transform our political institutions, revitalise our democracies and fundamentally change the interface between citizens and frontline government. Some Commonwealth countries are using technologies to deliver services to the citizen and to get feedback on the issues of the day. In 1998, one of the Gold Award Winners of the CAPAM International Innovation Awards programme was "Ontario Delivers". This submission brings real-time technologies to citizens in common areas such as shopping malls to conduct government transactions (e.g. licence renewal).

The increasing growth and demand for interactivity between government and citizenry means that governments will need to become more and more innovative and creative in the way government organisations and personnel interface with citizens. This will result in new ways of organising government itself.

The growing interactive society is making huge demands on government. Public sector departments, which are mainly hierarchical and process-driven, are not generally able to respond to public demands. Meeting these demands will require the public sector to adopt more entrepreneurial and client-oriented models.

E-government is a tool and regardless of how powerful, it has limited value and relevance by itself. Value arises from its application to specific goals and objectives. In many Commonwealth countries citizens can inform departments of changes of address or request information online. This is an important tool for those who interact with government for services or benefits. The use of information and communication technology to encourage citizen participation can be a liberating and democratising force within government.

As new networking technologies create new means of information exchange, the traditional structure of government will undergo terrific pressures to evolve and adapt. Institutions will need to constantly adapt and change and be innovative. Both developed and developing Commonwealth countries will need to develop strategies and best practices for the use of new technologies within government. Government will need new attitudes, new ways of thinking, new strategies, realigned structures, innovations, creativity and entrepreneurship.

Commonwealth examples

E-government, involving the electronic delivery of integrated citizen-centred public services, is an initiative which can result in greater convenience and speed for the public. The Internet world is constantly changing and at an alarming speed. As the Internet changes, so do public expectations of government service and response time. With such speed, it is no longer possible to keep up by working faster or more efficiently using old and existing technologies and processes. Government workers need to adapt to this new context.

The key to e-government is to design a system that will be convenient to the public and provide what the public wants. E-government will bring citizens and the community closer to government. Civil society in turn must assess this relationship with the citizenry in terms of the desirable degree of transparency and the extent of confidentiality. Government needs to be innovative, enterprising and creative.

All over the world, governments are attempting to manage e-technology in different ways. Governments are captalising on e-technology to improve people's lives. Generally, governments are aiming to make e-technology the servant of society in order to improve the quality of communities, to make economies stronger and to bring people closer together. The Commonwealth is committed to making good progress in getting services online. For example, the goal was to have over 90% of agencies with appropriate services online by the end of 2001. Many countries have invested in and initiated e-government programmes.

Australia

Australia has become a known leader in e-government investment and initiatives. It was rated fifth in 2001 out of twenty-two countries in terms of e-government leadership in a study conducted by the Accenture Consulting Group.

Some of the major benefits of *australia.gov.au* are:

- making government online more user friendly;
- simplifying access to a comprehensive range of information and services online from all government agencies;
- ensuring Australia keeps pace internationally, particularly with countries such as the United Kingdom and Canada;
- assisting government online to help drive the uptake of e-transactions and the Internet more broadly in the economy; and
- setting the framework for cross agency linked transactions.

The Australian government continues to develop and invest in online ventures and partnerships. Some of the following are priorities for the future:

- the next phase of electronic service delivery needs to focus on the quality and effectiveness of the services;

- these services need to be driven by demand for services by key stakeholders not developed for their own sake;

- this means that agencies need to build extensive evaluation processes;

- they need to test the effectiveness of online service delivery;

- in the new era of e-government, citizens are at the very core of service delivery; and

- Commonwealth governments must aim to have higher quality online services available with additional transactional capability and be integrated with other services, agencies and tiers of government.

Singapore

In Singapore, they have introduced a mechanism called "The Enterprise Challenge" which funds experimentation trials which could bring about quantum improvements in the public service. "The Enterprise Challenge" was one of the entries from Singapore in the 2000 CAPAM International Innovations Awards Programme. Through this initiative, new ideas are encouraged through Work Improvement Teams and Staff Suggestion Schemes.

New Zealand

The New Zealand Government intends to be among the governments which actively manage e-technology to make life better for its people. Overall, that requires government to do two things:

- Create the environment where others – the private sector, communities and individuals – can make the most of e-technology; and

- Capitalise on e-technology to improve the way government serves New Zealanders.

Canada

The Canada Site, with gateways for Canadians, Canadian Business, and non-Canadians, focuses on citizens' needs for information services. Each gateway, and more than 30 clusters, is led by a department working with other levels of government and non-governmental organisations. This horizontal and vertical initiative places Canada in the forefront of e-government.

If you are a Canadian who needs a job, a parent concerned about an unsafe toy, or you want to visit a national park – you want information from your government. If you are a business that needs a contact to arrange financing for an export deal – you want information from your government. If you are a Canadian travelling abroad and have had your documents stolen – you need help to get them replaced quickly. What you do not want is a difficult search through the labyrinth of departments, agencies, and other organisations that make up government. You need answers which are available through one portal via the Internet.

When Canadians were asked what a government website should be they responded:

- accessible to all;

- simple to understand;

- easy to access anywhere at any time; and

- not too government focused.

Turning that thinking into a reality in a short time required innovations in management that successfully enabled people from 28 federal departments and agencies to work together. It took real cross-departmental collaboration and consultation to deliver the Canada Site. The resulting client-focused web portal resulted from innovative thinking about how to realise the government's goal of making information and services available online for all Canadians to access in a timely and convenient manner. The structures and processes developed are now considered best practices in developing government websites. This investment has moved Canada closer to its goal of being known around the world as the government most connected to its citizens.

The Canada Site and gateways have been using client feedback to gauge success and plan innovations that will continue to improve client services, satisfaction, and ease of use. The site is being analysed to make sure that authoritative information is presented and duplicate information eliminated, and to determine what gaps exist so they can be filled.

This will lead to more service integration within the Government of Canada, and across jurisdictions. An enhanced Canada Site, launched in 2001, includes innovative inter-jurisdictional partnerships so that all governments can work together to provide convenient, client-based information. Possibilities are also being explored to provide a foreign language capability for non-Canadians.

Critical success factors

A range of factors will determine the success of the e-government strategy. "Hitting the Target" – the three essential characteristics of e-government are

- Convenience and Satisfaction;
- Supporting Activities; and
- Integration and Efficiency.

The most critical of these are:

- Broad support and advocacy for the programme;
- Willingness to change the way agencies work together, share, manage information and services;
- The ability to change the culture, skills, governance and financial arrangements in agencies to support e-government;
- Starting small and growing quickly, but at a speed consistent with customer expectations, adoption rates and acceptability;
- Ensuring equality in access to information and services;
- Developing acceptable privacy and security safeguards, including authentication;
- Putting a facilitative, enabling legal environment in place;
- Investing in adequate knowledge infrastructure; and
- Some early successes to build on.

Other useful material (2nd edition)

Frost, Peter. "Streamlining Government". Management and Training Services Division, Commonwealth Secretariat, Commonwealth Yearbook, 2002.

Riley, Thomas, B. "Electronic Government and Public Sector Reform". Commonwealth Centre for Electronic Governance, Commonwealth Yearbook 2002.

Badger, Dr. Rod, "e-Government: beyond Bricks and Mortar". Keynote Address at the Annual International Conference of the Institute of Public Administration Australia, Sydney, Australia, November 2001.

Teo, Eddie, "Public Sector Leadership in the 21st Century". Presentation at CAPAM Conference, Cape Town, South Africa, 2000.

Salway,Peter, "Serving the Knowledge Age: Realigning the Public Services for the Knowledge Advantage".

Communications Canada, "Engaging Citizens Through a User-oriented Interface with Government". Submission for The CAPAM Third International Innovations Awards Programme, March 22, 2002.

"Why an e-government strategy?". www.e-government.govt.nz

Inter-American Development Bank, "e Government". www.iadb.org

5.4.1 E-governance

E-governance is a process which organisations, institutions, companies and governments use to guide themselves. It refers to the way these bodies interact with each other, with their clients and citizenry. Basically, it is how society organises itself for collective decision making and how it provides for a transparent mechanism for seeing these decisions through to implementation. Most institutions and government agencies are ill-prepared for the dramatic changes in information technology and human knowledge. Yet citizens increasingly expect the same level of service from governments as they do from the private sector. The traditional role of government has been to provide stability in times of change. Governments therefore need to change the theory and practice of decision making and policy formulation to meet the demands of a knowledgeable society.

E-governance is beyond the limits of e-government which is defined as the delivery of services and information to the public using electronic means. E-governance goes one step further and allows the direct participation of constituents in government activities. In India, for example, one State Council is proposing to hold its Council meetings in local venues for citizen participation.

E-governance is not just delivering information over the Internet but rather how citizens relate to government and each other. E-governance will truly allow citizens to participate in the decision-making process, reflect their needs and welfare by utilising e-government as a tool.

In a joint study by UNESCO and Comnet-IT, they define governance as the process by which society steers itself. The interactions between the state, private enterprise and civil society are being increasingly conditioned and modified through the influence of information and communications technology (ICT). Five examples of these shifts in dynamics are exemplified by:

1. the use of the Internet by the civil society, NGOs and professional associations;

2. the mobilisation of opinion and influence on decision-making processes that affect them;

3. the increasing electronic delivery of government and commercial services and information;

4. the electronic publication of draft legislation and statements of directions for public feedback; and

5. on the infrastructure side, the increased adoption of e-enabled community centres, the liberalisation of telecommunication markets and trends towards web-enabled mobile telephone and digital television are facilitating this evolution.

In addition, as the Internet becomes a primary access point for millions of citizens to link with government, researchers and educators will need to consider issues like:

- how will e-government influence the performance of public organisations?

- what are the organisational effects of e-government and information technology?

- what are successful implementation strategies for e-government initiatives?

- what skills do public employees need to maximise their performance in an information age?

Many claim that e-government, e-governance and information technology empower individuals within organisations to move beyond the automation of paper-based transactions, resulting in a decentralisation of organisational decision making. More research is needed to determine if e-government and e-governance facilitate decentralised decision making.

The goal of organisational transformation and collaboration must also be a primary concern for those organisations working to improve public organisations through e-government and e-government initiatives. As technologically wise citizens worldwide come to expect more of their governments, public agencies will be capable of providing the services and access required.

However, transformation in public sector governance and accountability is likely to be blocked by administrative culture, structure and processes that may be poorly suited for a digital world, as nearly everything about the digital state requires horizontal governance. The Canadian government for example, through the Canada Site, has relied upon a vertical architecture of power and decision making. The central task facing both policy makers, and political leaders, at least those interested in leading the transition to the digital age, lies in orchestrating and managing effective responses.

Governance is about effective co-ordination in a dynamic environment where both knowledge and power are distributed. Every organisation is built on governance, whether formal or informal, ineffective or successful. The rise of e-governance refers to the new patterns of decision making, power sharing and co-ordination – made possible, or even necessary by the advent of IT.

The public sector is not immune to such forces. Indeed, government finds itself under the dual strain of becoming both a partner and competitor with business in an online environment. As a result, digital government refers to an IT-led reconfiguration of public sector governance – and how knowledge, power and purpose are redistributed in the light of new technological realities.

Other useful material (2nd edition)

Following on earlier work, Comnet-IT in association with UNESCO has developed a number of country profiles detailing current status and developments in this area.

International Centre for E-governance, "Governance in the 21st Century". www.icegov.org

Inter-American Development Bank, "e-Government". www.iadb.org

UNESCO and Comnet-IT, "Joint UNESCO and Comnet-IT Study of e-government". www.comnet.mt/country

Melitski, Jim, "The World of E-Government and E- Governance". Solutions for Public Managers, ASPA, www.aspanet.org/solutions/egovworld

Allen, Barbara Ann; Juillet, Luc; Paquet, Gilles; Roy, Jefferey, "E-Governance and Government On-line in Canada: Partnerships, People and Prospects". To be published in Government Information Quarterly, 2001.

5.4.2 The cautions of public-private partnerships in e-government

Commonwealth countries around the world are spending vast amounts of money to develop, implement, and manage electronic government (e-government). The partnerships between the public sector and their private sector counterparts seems to be the best approach to implementing an e-government environment. This collaboration is not a static, one-time venture. It often takes numerous years with a variety of partners to build, operate and transfer electronic infrastructure into the public service.

The implementations of these infrastructures are often measured for success. The results show significant failures in terms of:

- missed deadlines;
- budget overruns; and
- standards that are lower than originally agreed upon.

It is widely understood that go-it-alone ICT/e-government strategies are costly to the public sector and have not achieved the desired levels of performance or transformation desired by governments. Governments are seen to lack IT competence, to have difficulty "keeping up" on their own with the changing new economy, and they lack the incentives to innovate. There is room for improvement in the implementation of e-government and partnerships with the private sector are viewed as one important way to address these shortcomings.

Government reports indicate that the most widely touted rationales for partnering with new-economy firms are the need to:

- be innovative;
- share the risk;
- reduce research and development costs; and
- increase the quality of government programs and services.

Partnerships should be used to conceive, develop, operate and evaluate e-government applications. Despite the fact that there is no conclusive theoretical or empirical support for the assumption that outsourcing will always lead to more focused organisation, higher flexibility, lower costs and staffing levels, economies of scale and to the solution of all problems with IS (Information System) departments, governments appear to be totally committed to collaborating with the private sector in the creation of e-government.

Outsourcing arrangements can take many forms. They can range from simple external operational relationships in areas like electronic banking and data processing, to more robust arrangements to create sophisticated interactive services. The former may be no more than a traditional arms-length performance contract between a principal and an agent in which the service or good is produced to standards set down in the contract. The latter arrangements involve multi-year, collaborative partnerships in the concurrent fulfilment of both public policy objectives and the goals of the private sector partners.

It can be argued that public-private partnership management is a complex and growing challenge to today's mangers, many of whom have not had the management training or the exposure to such agreements, let alone experience with the technology. Many believe that there is no "one size fits all" strategy to the management of partnerships within e-government.

Reasons for caution

Beyond the general challenges of partnership, there are some special features of e-government alliances that make them even more difficult for governments to work with. These challenges include:

- private sector partners being asked to create and, often, run and maintain systems central to the most important service functions that governments perform;
- many e-government technology partnerships are likely to be multi-party arrangements;
- the memberships of these networks may not be stable through the life of a partnership with government; and
- the goals of ICT partnerships may have to be more flexible and "renewable" than those of a traditional public service contract.

These challenges are further complicated by the following:

- How does one establish a management framework for partnering?
- How do you find the right partners?
- How to you make the right partnering arrangements?
- Who is managing the relationships with partners in a network setting?
- Who is measuring the performance of e-government partnerships? and
- How are governments enhancing their capacity to perform these tasks?

In order to respond to the failures of an ICT project, the following changes need to be addressed:

- a reframing of the overall approach;
- the need for better management at the project level;
- the need to manage the project in relation to government goals and objectives;
- a clearer definition of the higher business purpose;
- governments need to approve and plan projects not on a single basis but as part of a larger system (enterprise-wide);
- there is a requirement for an enterprise-wide leadership structure and decision-making process; and
- the Chief Information Officer (CIO) takes a lead role in the enterprise management.

At the same time there are potential problems with selecting and securing the right partners for the ICT project. Often the right partner(s) and agreements are hindered by the government's procurement policies and procedures.

Impediments in traditional government procurement systems include:

- the policy of going with the lowest bid;
- the use of standardised contracts;
- the inadequate penalties for non-performance;
- the tendency for risk avoidance;
- an inflexible, 'request-qualifications-proposal' process for awarding contracts; and

- an inability for most governments to come to a quick closure of the contract award process especially in today's environment where there are speedy alliances developing in the ICT industry – this can potentially result in the loss of contracts as the proponents have other assignments

There is a need to find a balance between the existing system and the open-ended, informal, networking, negotiating environment of the private sector. This balance will allow governments to enter into value-added partnerships with an emphasis on the product rather than the process and thus reduce the time required to finalise the agreement.

This raises both organisational, human resource and accountability questions. From an organisational perspective, the key issues are the capacity of individual agencies to partner on their own. Does the agency require a centralised body to back up the initiatives? Secondly, there are almost as many approaches to the organisation of e-government human resources as there are governments. Due to the potential implications and failures of the implementation of e-government for service delivery and the co-ordination across the entire system, it is becoming common to have central co-ordinating bodies involved in both government-wide and agency-level strategic planning. This central group should be involved in developing innovative accountability frameworks and also be part of the procurement process itself.

Regardless of how the outsourcing in this area is organised, government agencies have to have access to a wide range of experts capable of:

- building strategic plans that integrate e-government initiatives into the wider strategic objectives of the government as a whole;
- conducting market surveillance and analysis, particularly with a view to identifying appropriate technologies;
- selecting private sector partners that will have a good strategic and cultural fit with the agency; and
- negotiating significant partnering arrangements.

Many e-government initiatives potentially have significant implications for the restructuring of government services and it is essential, therefore, that governments have the internal capacity to advise on where these projects are taking them. Until very recently, it has been particularly difficult for governments to attract and retain ICT experts, especially in an environment in which salary expectations are high, the supply is limited, specialists are nomadic in nature and not dedicated to one company for a career and the experts are being courted daily by the private firms with which they are negotiating.

Studies have found that certain values tend to foster an effective partnership relationship. The values include:

- trust;
- flexibility;
- collaboration;
- information sharing;
- networking; and
- ethical negotiations.

Failure is due to a lack of organisational and human capacity to manage technological partnerships. Some governments are unable to successfully implement and adapt to an e-government environment because they cannot adequately manage technology projects. Too much has been emphasised on the management of the project rather than the management of the relationship with the service provider.

What is the degree to which governments are prepared to alter from the contract compliance model to a shared performance model? Unfortunately, this part of public administration research and government thinking has not been a priority in the past. Nonetheless, the best contract management practices should include service delivery standards; quality, quantity and timeliness schedules; fees related to performance and how the suppliers performance is to be tested against standards.

OECD governments, realising that IT performance measurement has been not that efficient, have begun to address the performance management of partnerships. Admitting that IT project performance measurement has been spotty in the past, OECD governments have begun to address the performance management challenges of enhanced partnerships. To ensure that departments and central agencies are capable of monitoring the progress of their initiatives, certain tools have been developed to assist with performance management. Examples of such tools include:

- the enhanced management framework;
- the business case;
- the project charter; and
- the traditional internal audit function.

Governments need to look at success stories from the areas of e-business and e-commerce and extract from these cases the elements of good strategic alliance management. The best practices can then be adapted to the public service to better manage public-private partnerships.

Other useful material (2nd edition)

NEPAD www.dfa.gov.za/events/nepad.htm

5.5 Knowledge Management

In the past, Commonwealth countries have dealt with the issues of records management, human resource management, financial management, information systems management and information systems strategy as independent entities and have thus controlled and managed them separately. As governments develop and deal more with Internet technologies there is a growing need for a holistic approach to the linkages between each of these systems. The rubric that links the former independent entities is "Knowledge Management".

This holistic approach to the creation, maintenance, use and disposal of records is increasingly important to all public sector organisations. Making information available to support the business of these agencies will lead to more efficient, effective and economic governments. These principles constitute the foundation of accountability which in turn supports the building of democracies. In fact, knowledge management is a serious governance issue. Through a knowledge management system, governments can work towards breaking down the barriers of productivity. These barriers include:

- underfunding of a Ministry;
- understaffing and overstaffing departments;
- misallocation of human and financial resources;
- absence of financial discipline and the monitoring of performance;
- corrupt practices, nepotism and favouritism;
- absence of a code of conduct and guidelines;
- lack of ownership and involvement in the design of performance agreements, goals and functions; and
- poor leadership and low morale of employees.

In terms of leadership, Singapore stresses that knowledge management systems assist their government. The systems provide input and emphasise the importance of strong leadership; talent attraction; talent management; talent development; and the importance of public sector values (meritocracy, impartiality, incorruptibility, service excellence).

The International Records Management Trust (IRMT) has noted that aid agencies are starting to recognise the need to strengthen records management in relation to institutional capacity building and policy reforms. The previous weaknesses are due to financial managers and others not having the systems designed and implemented to collect and manage the relevant information.

Items which are not included in government systems, which impeded departments/Ministries in their ability to manage government knowledge, included:

- parallel systems with no cross referencing;
- no tracking or projections;
- systems operated at the departmental or organisation level rather than across the government structure (siloed);
- individuals were not considered part of the corporation; and
- knowledge management was not considered as a strategic resource.

The European Centre for Development Policy Management in a policy brief on Knowledge Management outlined some challenges for capacity builders. Their thesis explored ways to improve capacity builders' activities. They called for capacity builders to invest more in knowledge sharing as a means to improving the importance of their work.

It has been found that in developing countries, a remarkable opening towards more democratic and transparent governance is in progress. Development is coming to be seen as a joint responsibility of governments, communities, civil society and the private sector. Participation, empowerment, public-private partnerships and joint action are new ways to win the fight against poverty. The capacity to build and manage knowledge is viewed as central to development.

For many people, new information and communications technologies (ICTs) are the right tools at the right time. If used wisely, investments in information, knowledge, and ICTs can help generate wealth and jobs, build bridges between governments and citizens, forge relations among organisations and communities, and improve the delivery of essential services to poor people.

In rich countries, information and communication technologies and especially the Internet are spreading throughout society, the workplace and the market. For those who have access to the new tools, the opportunities are immense. Countries investing in the Internet are likely to benefit from wider and cheaper access to informational, educational and medical resources and services. The Internet and related technologies can create value, jobs and help people to engage in trade. In Bangladesh for instance, the use of cellular phones in rural areas has helped increase the income of women. In 1998, at the CAPAM Biennial Conference, the Bangladesh entry into the International Innovations Awards Programme was honoured by winning the Bronze Award for "Village Pay Phone – Grameen Telecom".

Capacity development is the "process by which individuals, groups, organisations, institutions and societies develop abilities (individually and collectively) to perform functions, solve problems and set and achieve objectives." More specifically, it is a way for groups or organisations to increase their ability to contribute to poverty elimination.

While the purposes of capacity building apply in the information "sector", it is argued that capacity building approaches can be quite different in other sectors. The differences can be attributed to some characteristics of information and knowledge management that set them apart from other development activities.

Key Questions when considering Capacity Building in a Knowledge Management environment:

1. Whose capacities are being built?
   - decision makers
   - information custodians and producers
   - ultimate beneficiaries

2. What capacities are being built?
   - awareness and empowerment
   - skills
   - resources

3. How are capacities being built?
   - partnerships
   - collaboration
   - appropriate measures and an open approach that is replicable

While development agencies seek ways to make beneficial use of information and ICTs for development, relatively poor linkages seem to exist between the numerous international initiatives in this area. This results in a disconnection between rather ambitious agendas and the action on the ground, and many missed opportunities for joint action. While diversity can stimulate creativity and innovation, the various initiatives need 'gluing' together to form useful relationships.

A concerted approach by the various participants should include the following elements:

- Complementarity

    A complementary approach aims to build on the varied experience of many participants, to bring quality into capacity-building approaches, and to ensure that developing countries get the best and most appropriate advice, not just what's at hand. Avoiding duplication through task division and collaboration is important. Complementarity means accepting that many participants, including the private sector, have legitimate roles to play and that each has its own added value. It requires that each participant is clear about its aims and roles, is transparent on its strengths and weaknesses, and is committed to working together. Information sharing tools such as databases illustrate how such issues can be tackled.

- Incentives

    As was indicated above, complementarity flows from attitudes and cultures and the extent to which people and organisations are willing to cooperate. Co-operation and partnership do not always flow of their own accord. A key factor is incentives. Funding agencies can help stimulate "co-operativity" by the way they fund activities. To foster partnership, sponsors need to be more creative, perhaps becoming "partners" themselves, perhaps financing process and preparation as well as implementation, perhaps funding issues or problems rather than institutions.

- Multipliers

    One of the most important parts of capacity building is to share and pass on skills and knowledge. Training of people in partner organisations, both in developing countries and among donor organisations continues to be necessary. However, in the information "domain", it is rare for the ultimate users or beneficiaries to be directly reached by international efforts. It is crucial, therefore, that partner organisations in developing countries also learn to become capacity builders, to multiply and apply the skills they have learned. This is sometimes difficult for a development agency to implement, as every partner whose capacities are enhanced is potentially a future "competitor". It is nevertheless essential if sustainability is the objective.

- Invest in Knowledge

    All the partners in development can benefit from capacity building. This applies as much to the "developed" agency as to the recipient partner. As well as developing resources, tools, and skills to share, development agencies need to know about capacity building and the roles they can play.

    This means that capacity builders should critically assess their own capacities, ensuring that they are appropriate and that they help address real development problems. Learning to facilitate, catalyse and nurture, and support is essential. It also means looking critically at how aid is delivered and managed, and seeking to speed up and improve internal procedures that may erode the process of capacity building. It means investing in co-operation and partnership and learning to do these well.

Other useful materials (2nd edition)

International Records Management Trust, "Principles and Practices in Managing Financial Records: A Reference Model and Assessment Tool". London, U.K., March, 2001.

Ballantyne, Peter; Labelle, Richard; and Rudgard, Stephen, "Information and Knowledge Management: Challenges for Capacity Builders". European Centre for Development Policy Management- Policy Management Brief #11", July, 2000.

Salway, Peter, "Serving the Knowledge Age: Realigning the Public Services for the Knowledge Advantage".

Teo, Eddie, "Public Sector Leadership in the 21st Century". – Presentation by Mr. Eddie Teo, Permanent Secretary(Prime Minister's Office), Singapore, at Plenary #3 in CAPAM Conference, in Cape Town, South Africa, October, 2000.

Agere, Sam, "Promoting Good Governance: Principles, Practices and Perspectives". Commonwealth Secretariat, London, U.K., 2000.

6.0 Improving the Management of Finance

6.1 Setting the Framework

6.1.1 Reforming financial management

The principles of *financial management* are stewardship, purchase and accountability.

The public service is responsible for protecting the value of the physical and financial assets owned by the government. Failure to maintain buildings or property, allowing their value to fall, and failure to protect financial assets from misappropriation or from devaluation, represent failures of stewardship.

The public service purchases goods and services on behalf of the government. It can be argued that as a large proportion of these purchases are made internally – by funding departments and Ministries – the public service is purchasing from itself. Sound financial management requires the public service to obtain the best value for money through such internal purchases and through its contracts with private and NGO sector organisations.

The principles of accountability lie behind the concerns for good stewardship and effective purchasing. Public service managers are accountable for their stewardship and for their purchasing to their Ministers and, through them, to the public. Financial management reforms are concerned with holding managers accountable for improved stewardship and purchasing strategies.

Reforming financial management finds full expression in improvements to the budgetary process. The budget is the formal expression of expected or estimated financial activity for a particular period. A budget will normally detail expected revenues and expenditure, and can be separated into revenue and expenditure budgets.

In the public service, budgets are often part of the appropriation procedures, when departments outline expenditure plans on which appropriations are made.

The budget is also an instrument of control. Approval of a budget often determines and fixes the department's operations for the period. Traditionally, public sector organisations have not been allowed to divert expenditure from approved to other purposes and, at the end of the period, unspent funds are normally returned to the centre.

Reforming the financial management process includes a move towards output-based management, and the increased accountability of managers with an accompanying liberalisation of budgetary controls.

Improvement of the budgetary process is a key element of this procedure, especially as the budgetary process is a key tool in financial management and control. The budget must be seen as a flexible document adaptable to changes in circumstances and to different time scales, appropriate to both capital projects and to operating or running costs.

The context for change

Since the mid-1970s, governments have been increasingly concerned to adapt and develop the structures and values of the public service to achieve greater efficiency and more responsive services. Improved quality at less cost has been the imperative. These changes have largely been pushed by continuing economic crises in developing and developed countries, which have in turn arisen from deteriorating terms of trade, over-extended borrowing, and a somewhat abrupt change of policy by the lending institutions during the 1980s.

However, the changes have also arisen from a new set of managerial strategies for the public service which have opened up the possibility that greater results can be achieved from fewer resources by strengthening lines of accountability and defining intended outputs more sharply.

Financial management reforms have been at the centre of the response to these economic crises, and have been equally fundamental to the new managerial strategies adopted in the public service.

Reasons for caution

Financial management reform has failed when:

- *it has been seen as a technical problem with little attitudinal content* – the impact on existing status differentials, areas of influence and, in the worst case, opportunities for budget distortions, can be considerable;

- *it has been implied that new structures can be insulated from weak or undisciplined managerial systems* – few examples of successful enclaves can be found; delegated responsibilities, agency status, and other new structures, are only as effective as the underlying foundations of probity and diligence across the whole public service will allow;

- *it has not been driven* – the absence of a central organisation with the authority and determination to make changes, and the capacity to assist and lead by example, will undermine the reform; and

- *it has led to unacceptably high compliance costs* – to feel committed to the reforms, managers must be able to see the benefits in terms of efficiency or service quality.

Achieving change

The elements of financial management reform are described below. In summary, they fall within a broad value-for-money orientation as follows:

- Improving the management of inputs:
  - introducing capital charging;
  - improving state management;
  - improving physical asset management;
  - improving the procurement process; and
  - using activity-based costing.
- Focusing on outputs:
  - achieving an output orientation; and
  - delegation of financial management.
- Improving management information:
  - strengthening external audits:
  - strengthening internal auditing systems: and
  - introducing accrual-based accounting.

- Improving management systems:
  - restructuring and classification of accounts; and
  - introducing flexible budgeting.

The key mechanisms used in driving these changes are:

- *Application of rates of return*: where outputs, such as goods and services produced, can be measured in financial terms. The rate of return is the ratio between the financial value of the outputs and the value of the inputs or resources used.

- *Imposition of cash limits*: where outputs cannot be measured in financial terms, control and limitation of expenditures can be achieved by making financial resources limited, through strict budgetary controls.

- *Output or performance-based management*: where outcomes, outputs and efficiency targets, and performance indicators are an integral part of the budgetary process.

- *Delegation of authority*: to the delivering departments and agencies, including the right to decide on changes to expenditure plans.

- *Emphasis on accountability*: so that the effective use of delegated authority can be monitored.

- *Performance-based incentives*: all participants in a programme, purchasers, providers, and consumers, should feel the benefits of improved systems.

- *Use of market principles*: provision of services opened to competition, wherever possible. Alternatively, separation of purchaser, provider and regulator functions, wherever feasible and sensible, with maximum usage of market and price mechanisms even inside the public sector.

Examples of change

In *Ghana*, the National Institutional Renewal Programme (NIRP) has an agenda designed to promote a wide range of public service reform and capacity development. In 1995, the NIRP National Technical Group published a Methodology for Capacity Enhancement and Institution Training to provide guidance and assistance to departments.

In 1990, the Government of *Malaysia* introduced the Modified Budgeting System (MBS). The objective of the MBS is to improve the budgetary process, particularly in relation to accountability, allocation of resources and the implementation of programmes by government agencies.

MBS stresses the relationship between inputs, outputs and the impacts of a particular programme or activity. Under this system, government agencies are required to determine their achievement targets in terms of outputs and impacts of every programme or activity for which there are "programme agreements" between the agency and the Federal Treasury.

In providing a performance measurement of programmes/activities, the MBS is in line with the value-for-money concept which strives to achieve three objectives: economy, efficiency and effectiveness.

In *New Zealand*, the Fiscal Responsibility Act 1994 is the last in a series of measures designed to enhance the transparency with which the Government manages public funds. This Act emphasises:

- a requirement for regular and explicit fiscal reporting, including a change to accrual accounting;
- the provision of benchmarks against which fiscal performance can be measured where outputs and outcomes are agreed between management and the Minister;

- a more open and transparent budgetary process;

- review and legislative debate on, and eventual reform of, public sector financial reports; and

- a shift from controls over inputs to controls over outputs.

In the *UK*, the Financial Management Initiative, launched in 1982, marked the start of a general and co-ordinated drive to improve financial management in government departments. One of the key aims was to devolve responsibility for budgets and financial control to line management, units and individuals, giving them clear objectives and full information necessary for appropriate decision making.

The Multi-Department Review of Budgeting in 1986 focused on the need for top management to set priorities, manage resources and review the performance, and for achievements to be reviewed regularly.

The Government Purchasing Initiatives aimed to develop professionalism in government purchasing and to set up a unit to improve value for money through best practice.

The Next Steps Initiative aimed to improve efficiency through the devolution of a number of executive functions of government onto independent agencies whose Chief Executives are directly responsible to Ministers for their performance.

Other useful material (current as of 1996)

From Problem to Solution. Commonwealth Strategies for Reform. Managing the Public Service. Strategies for Improvement No. 1. Commonwealth Secretariat, 1995 (ComSec)

McCulloch, B. Accounting and Management Reforms in New Zealand Government. In Administrative and Managerial Reform in Government: A Commonwealth Portfolio of Current Good Practice. Proceedings of a Pan Commonwealth Working Group Meeting held in Kuala Lumpur, Malaysia, 19-22 April 1993. Commonwealth Secretariat, 1993 (ComSec)

Pallot, J. Accounting and Financial Management Reforms in New Zealand Central Government: Context and Critique in Administrative and Managerial Reform in Government: A Commonwealth Portfolio of Current Good Practice. Proceedings of a Pan Commonwealth Working Group Meeting held in Kuala Lumpur, Malaysia, 19-22 April 1993. Commonwealth Secretariat, 1993 (ComSec)

Scott, G. & Ball, I. Financial Management Reform in the New Zealand Government. The Treasury, Wellington (NZ)

Putting It Simply – An Explanatory Guide to Financial Management Reform. The Treasury, 1989, Wellington (NZ)

Efficiency and Effectiveness in the Civil Service. HMSO, London, 1982 (UK)

Financial Management in Government Departments. HMSO, London, 1983 (UK)

Civil Service Management Reform: The Next Steps – 8th Report of the House of Commons Treasury and Civil Service Committee (UK)

Improving Management in Government: The Next Steps. Report to the Prime Minister by the Efficiency Unit. HMSO, London, 1988 (UK)

6.1.2 Achieving value for money

In the complex, politically-led environment of the public service, value for money is just one measure of management success – to be set alongside other measures which emphasise probity, accountability, equity, and loyalty, both to the ideals of a neutral public service and to the priorities of the elected government.

Achieving value for money is, however, a key mindset in the search for management effectiveness in the public service.

All public service organisations produce outputs, which consist of goods and services; and outcomes, which are the consequences or impact which those outputs have on society or the community.

Value for money is the maximisation of three main elements, known traditionally as "the 3 E's":

- *Maximising economy* implies minimising the cost of resources or inputs used (spending less).
- *Maximising efficiency* entails increasing the amount of goods and services produced from a given level of human, financial or other input (spending well).
- *Maximising effectiveness* is increasing the impact of the goods and services produced for the community (spending wisely).

Value for money can be expressed as a series of ratios:

$$\text{VFM} = \underbrace{\frac{\text{Amount of input}}{\text{Cost of Input}}}_{Economy} + \underbrace{\frac{\text{Amount of output}}{\text{Amount of input}}}_{Efficiency} + \underbrace{\frac{\text{Degree of desired impact}}{\text{Amount of output}}}_{Effectiveness}$$

The context for change

Public demand for an increase in the range and quality of services, together with the extension of the role of government in all aspects of economic and social activity, has placed increasing demands on frequently diminishing public service resources.

One consequence of this pressure on resources and the growth in public expectations has been the introduction, in the public services of many Commonwealth countries, of a range of public management reforms emphasising the need to increase cost-effectiveness and improve the quality of output. Value for money, with its emphasis on economy, efficiency and effectiveness, is a key mindset in achieving these reforms.

Achieving value for money is an orientation in which performance and value-for-money audits or assessments assist managers to determine:

- the causes of inefficiencies and uneconomical practices;
- real customer requirements;
- the full costs of outputs which will assist in pricing or budgeting procedures;

- opportunities for rationalisation or possible economies in the use of capital equipment and capital expenditure programmes;

- opportunities for other economies, such as reduction in overheads and inventory reduction; and

- opportunities to develop other sources of income generation.

Value-for-money audits also determine whether performance indicators agreed under any output-based management systems are appropriate; and whether internal auditing procedures are adequate and effective.

Reasons for caution

Achieving value for public money through effective financial management in the public service is fundamental to performance improvements. It is a journey rather than a destination; an orientation and not a set of pre-defined systems and techniques.

Achieving value for money requires that managers be motivated and able to achieve improvements in economy, efficiency and effectiveness. This, in turn, requires that they be able to identify and, where feasible, determine the cost and quantity of the inputs to their operations and the quantity and impact of the outputs. A range of techniques are available to assist them in uncovering these variables and in assessing options for improving performance – from performance audits to market-testing. These are techniques to be selected from, in order to pursue the larger goal.

Commonwealth experiences suggest that in emphasising value for money, a risk arises that means are confused with ends – that techniques are seen as goals to be aspired to, rather than devices which assist in the change process but which might have a limited life. A value-for-money orientation requires that mangers be focused on the key elements of inputs and outputs, but flexible in their use of techniques for achieving change.

Achieving change

There are two components to the establishment of a value-for-money orientation in public service managers:

- Conveying the key concepts

  Traditionally, the public service has been seen as a series of inter-related and tightly prescribed positions, each with specific areas of responsibility and each contributing to an unchanging whole. The elements of value for money – economy, efficiency and effectiveness – and the key concepts of cost and volume of inputs, and volume and impact of outputs, require that tasks within the public service are seen as a process leading from human and financial inputs to community or national impacts or outcome.

- Providing a repertoire of techniques

  With the key concepts clear, options for improving value for money can be assessed at work unit, department or Ministry levels. The techniques to be employed must be selected pragmatically, according to the skills available and the potential cost of utilising an approach which is over-elaborate for its context.

The majority of techniques in which managers may need training, and where they may need access to centrally co-ordinated assistance, are covered in this Portfolio. Examples of these techniques which are particularly relevant to achieving value for money include:

- conducting performance or efficiency audits;

- introducing full or activity-based costing, in association with capital charging, if appropriate; and

- market-testing to be followed by contracting out of services.

Examples of change

In *Malaysia*, the main thrust of the reforms has been through improving the budgetary procedure and controls systems. The objective of the Modified Budgeting System (MBS) is to improve the budgetary process, particularly in relation to accountability, allocation of resources and the implementation of programmes. MBS stresses the relationship between inputs and outputs; and departments are required to determine their achievements in terms of outputs and outcomes. Thus, in providing for performance measurement, MBS also helps to secure value for money.

In *New Zealand*, the emphasis is on improving standards of reporting and accountability coupled with reforms to budgeting procedures which take account of changes towards output or performance-based management. Departments present budgetary estimates in terms of desired objectives and expected outputs. These are then translated into performance indicators against which management is evaluated.

Together with the introduction of accrual accounting and capital charging, the true cost of goods and services is known, enabling comparisons and thus promoting value for money.

In the *UK*, the concept of value for money is often seen as the driving force in reforming financial management in the public sector from which all other initiatives follow naturally.

Value for money frequently arises in an auditing context. Part of the remit of the Audit Office is to conduct value-for-money audits as part of the external audit procedure. However, it is common for value-for-money audits to receive priority within an organisation's normal management structure, often as part of the internal audit procedure. Value for money is also one of the criteria used in making purchasing decisions, in particular, whether to use internal or external sources.

Application of the value-for-money concept, with its emphasis on total costing, has also encouraged the application of capital charging and consideration of all assets and liabilities, and the introduction of accrual accounting.

Particular areas directly subject to value-for-money criteria include the following:

- internal appraisal of capital projects;

- post-contract reviews of projects; and

- special reviews of services, either whole units of government or expenditure programmes.

Compliance is assured through the external auditing arrangements, where the Auditing Offices are empowered to undertake regular value-for-money audits. As a result, internal auditing procedures take account of these requirements.

Other useful material (current as of 1996)

From Problem to Solution. Commonwealth Strategies for Reform. Managing the Public Service. Strategies for Improvement No. 1. Commonwealth Secretariat, 1995 (ComSec)

McCulloch, B. Accounting and Management Reforms in New Zealand Government. In Administrative and Managerial Reform in Government: A Commonwealth Portfolio of Current Good Practice. Proceedings of a Pan Commonwealth Working Group Meeting held in Kuala Lumpur, Malaysia, 19-22 April 1993. Commonwealth Secretariat (ComSec)

Scott, G. & Ball, I. Financial Management Reform in the New Zealand Government. The Treasury, Wellington (NZ)

Putting It Simply – An Explanatory Guide to Financial Management Reform. The Treasury, Wellington, 1989 (NZ)

Fiscal Responsibility Act: A Brief Overview. Treasury Briefing Note. New Zealand Treasury, Wellington, 1994 (NZ)

Effciency and Effectiveness in the Civil Service. HMSO, London, 1982 (UK)

Financial Management in Government Departments. HMSO, London, 1983 (UK)

Civil Service Management Reform: The Next Steps – 8th Report of the House of Commons Treasury and Civil Service Committee (UK)

Improving Management in Government: The Next Steps (Report to the Prime Minister by the Efficiency Unit). HMSO, London, 1988 (UK)

6.2 Improving the Management of Inputs

6.2.1 Introducing capital charging

Capital charging is the accounting for the full cost of capital assets used in the provision of goods and services. This allows a calculation of the true economic cost of goods and services, enabling comparison with other providers to be made.

The context for change

Accounting for the cost of capital through a policy of explicit capital charging is conducive to good financial management in the public service. Capital charging makes clear the full costs of goods and services produced by departments, so that Ministers can make more informed decisions about the costs and benefits of government policies. The specific objectives in doing this in a public sector entity are to provide the information and incentives needed for efficient management of the government's investment.

If departments or Ministries do not bear the cost of capital, they may be seen as the preferred provider, even when more efficient producers exist. Ignoring this cost is likely to result in poorly informed decision making and misallocation of resources. Having departments bear the cost of their capital allows Ministers to make more informed choices on the basis of the full costs of the goods and services needed to achieve policy objectives. The government is more likely to achieve value for money when capital is no longer treated as being free, because the bias in favour of capital-intensive production is addressed.

Many departments supply goods and services to third parties. If the price charged does not at least recover the total costs, including the cost of capital, then the government is effectively providing a subsidy. If the total cost exceeds the price that the government wants consumers to pay, then transparency could be achieved by making a specific budget appropriation to cover the expected shortfall.

The government should expect the benefit from its investment of taxpayers' funds in a department to at least match that available from competing investments in the private sector. In effect, capital should be used as efficiently by departments as by a private firm with comparable operations and risks.

The capital charge gives managers a signal as to the government's expectations from its investments in the business of the department. It allows asset management decisions to be made at the departmental level rather than continually referred to a control agency. A capital charge gives managers information to make clear trade-offs between tying up government resources in a given asset as opposed to using alternative means of production.

Reasons for caution

Above all, capital charging requires reliable information on departments' net assets which will, in turn, require a thorough inventory of the government estate. This multi-disciplinary operation will require appropriately qualified personnel, including lawyers, surveyors and engineers, to establish title, maintenance required and market value.

Where the inventory cannot be reliably undertaken, and where the conflicts that it generates between user departments and central agencies over title, value, and liabilities cannot be managed at reasonable cost and within a reasonable time frame, capital charging will not be feasible.

Capital charges are most effective when combined with a consistent financial management framework and, ideally, accrual accounting. Together, these changes provide departmental managers with the opportunity, incentive, and information, to produce desired outputs at the lowest cost.

Achieving change

Incentives for efficient performance are also enhanced by delegating control over inputs (for example, cash, fixed assets and human resources) to chief executives, and then linking this increased authority with accountability for the production of agreed outputs. The adoption of accrual accounting provides the opportunity for better decision making through the presentation of a clearer picture of assets and liabilities, while application of a capital charge to net assets and liabilities provides better information on their true cost.

In concept, the idea of a capital charge is quite straightforward. The underlying mechanics, including capital-asset pricing, however, are complex and open to debate. This suggests that although it is possible to implement a capital charge regime in a single budget cycle, it may take some years to bed down and for gains to be fully realised.

One way to make the cost of capital explicit is to formalise the government's investments as debt and equity capital. Interest would be paid to the government on debt and dividends (after tax) on equity. This corporate form is used in several jurisdictions for assessing required rates of return for government-owned commercial enterprises.

For non-commercial government departments, however, it may be more practical to levy a capital charge that emulates interest, dividends and taxes. Departments typically are debarred from incurring debt in their own right and are exempt from income tax.

Where practicable, charge rates should be negotiated with individual departments based on weighted averaged costs of debt and equity capital and expected future growth (holding gains) for private-sector counterparts. This will involve reviewing and agreeing these variables to ensure that a relevant charge rate is arrived at for each department. Where no appropriate private sector comparisons exist, standard rates would need to be set by the government.

The capital base represents the value of the government net investment in a department. The values used need to be capable of being ascertained reasonably and reliably. There should be little scope for "creative" manipulation of the numbers. Audited accrual-based financial statements are likely to provide the best usable estimates of net assets.

The capital charge is applied to each department as an entity, rather than to its various outputs (goods and services produced). In making decisions about existing new investments required to produce their outputs, departmental managers must take the capital charge into account. This does not mean that the charge rate should be applied as a hurdle rate for individual assets in which the department invests. This is because:

- individual assets do not contribute equally to the overall financial performance of the department;

- the risk associated with specific assets or projects may not be the same as that applying to the department as a whole; and

- the capital charge represents only a proportion of the total cost of capital because it excludes the present value of future expected growth.

Examples of change

In *New Zealand*, as from July 1991, all government departments have been subjected to a charge for the level of capital employed in their operations. This reflects the opportunity cost to taxpayers of the funds employed. At the end of each half year, a charge on capital employed is added to the department's costs. The charge is calculated by applying an agreed rate to the department or agency's capital base:

Capital charge = Charge rate x Capital base

Initially, all departments were charged at a standard rate of 13 per cent. However, with experience it became possible to set more individual rates taking account of each department's particular activities.

When the charge was introduced, departments were funded in such a way so that the effect was largely fiscally neutral, that is, departments received full compensation for the charge as it impacted on the output purchased by government. However, the costs of goods and services sold to external customers were also increased proportionately to the capital charge. Departments were then asked to recover these increases through higher prices or by lowering overall costs. It was recognised that this could not be achieved immediately but the overall effect was to promote a more efficient use of resources.

In the *UK*, capital charging operates at two levels:

- Departmental trading units and government agencies must include in their costs (on which their performance is partly based) interest on capital at a rate fixed by the Treasury. This is one aspect of working towards full economic cost.

- In agencies of central government, the National Health Service and latterly local government, interest is charged within the management (internal) accounts to impress upon local managers the real cost of assets held and thereby encourage the efficient use of them.

Other useful material (current as of 1996)

From Problem to Solution. Commonwealth Strategies for Reform. Managing the Public Service. Strategies for Improvement No. 1, pp. 58. Commonwealth Secretariat 1995 (ComSec)

McCulloch, B. Accounting and Management Reforms in New Zealand Government. In Administrative and Managerial Reform in Government: A Commonwealth Portfolio of Current Good Practice. Proceedings of a Pan Commonwealth Working Group Meeting held in Kuala Lumpur, Malaysia, 19-22 April 1993. Commonwealth Secretariat, 1993 (ComSec)

Pallot, J. Accounting and Financial Management Reforms in New Zealand Central Government: Context and Critique. In: Administrative and Managerial Reform in Government: A Commonwealth Portfolio of Current Good Practice. Proceedings of a PanCommonwealth Working Group Meeting held in Kuala Lumpur, Malaysia, 19-22 April 1993. Commonwealth Secretariat 1993 (ComSec)

Better Accounting for the Taxpayer's Money: Resource Accounting and Budgeting in Government. HMSO, London (UK)

6.2.2 Improving estate management

The *estate* is the land, buildings, equipment, and perhaps the infrastructure, owned by the government. This represents in all countries a massive accrued investment.

The context for change

The government estate represents a very significant resource and is commonly one of the most neglected. It is often not recorded or systematically valued, and sometimes is only partially used. Maintenance is often unsystematic, incomplete or belated requiring increased resources for repair and loss of value. Inappropriate, limited, or incomplete utilisation of the estate represents an under-use of scarce capital resources. Management of this estate is now being recognised as a key area for reform and development.

Unsystematic, incomplete or belated maintenance leads to deterioration and damage, requiring increased resources for repair and loss of value. The benefits from improved estate management are:

* cost reductions through better use of accommodation;

* better planning in the nature and timing of major capital transactions, to take place at the best time for the user;

* personnel benefits from more suitable accommodation;

* reduced overall maintenance costs through planned maintenance; and

* identification and release of surplus resources for alternative uses.

Improvements in estate management are associated with a wide-ranging, comprehensive and mutually-supporting range of public sector financial management reforms and relate closely to capital charging. The introduction of capital charging will include payments in respect of the value of accommodation, perhaps on the basis of an opportunity-cost rent. When it is apparent that the estate is not available free of charge, departments are encouraged to consider efficient usage of the estate and transfer surpluses which can then be used for alternative purposes.

Reasons for caution

It is likely that a complete record of the government estate does not exist, that records are out of date, and that there is no central record against which they can be checked. It is also likely that no up-to-date report as to the physical condition and maintenance requirements exists

Correction of these weaknesses will require the implementation of a thorough inventory of the government estate. This will necessarily be a multi-disciplinary operation requiring the use of qualified personnel, including lawyers, surveyors and engineers, to establish title, values and maintenance requirements.

It is possible that conflicts between user departments and central authorities may arise, particularly over title, value, and liabilities.

In any introduction of capital charging it is necessary to delegate part, at least, of the management of the estate to user departments, thus requiring appropriately qualified management expertise at a lower level.

The presence of central authority, both to ensure compliance and to provide assistance, advice and training, is also necessary. As estate management is recognised as a key aspect of management, it should feature as strongly as other topics in management training courses, and form part of the criteria on which a manager's performance is evaluated.

Increased awareness and understanding of the size, nature, value and condition of property should be coupled to increased responsibility and accountability for the estate, in effect introducing the best private sector practice to the public sector.

Achieving change

Managing the estate is part of mainstream activity and so it should feature strongly in mainstream management training courses. The objective is to train managers to take an active and informed view of their asset base. Managerial awareness will increase if managers' performance on their property assets is judged and valued with the same vigour as their people management or financial skills.

In general, the importance of the estate's finances should be made visible to management. They should be included in the "business" plan, as part of the capital budget, which should be available to managers at all appropriate levels.

If a central authority or property-holding and management agency does not already exist, then one should be created, or at least authorised, to set standards, arbitrate disputes, offer advice, assistance and necessary expertise, and should be empowered to ensure compliance.

All departments should be required to conduct a thorough inventory and an in-depth report on the quantity, quality, title, value, use and maintenance requirements, and the cost of the estate under their control.

Steps to introduce some form of capital charging in which departments pay the full costs for accommodation and other estate should be introduced. Direct costs associated with land, buildings and infrastructure should be itemised in a capital budget and should include:

- internal rent;
- depreciation;
- local taxes on property and occupation;
- planned maintenance; and
- utilities and service charges.

Departments should be encouraged to review their accommodation and other estate requirements and to return, or otherwise appropriately dispose of, that surplus to their requirements.

Managers should be encouraged and trained to become "intelligent customers" of their professional advisers, able to instruct them clearly and interpret their advice.

Responsibility for maintenance should be delegated, as far as possible, to user departments which should be encouraged to use planned maintenance techniques and appropriate advice, as well as the assistance and training made available.

Examples of change

In *Malaysia*, public property management is the responsibility of the Management of Government Buildings Division of the Prime Minister's Office. Maintenance of Federal properties is the responsibility of the Public Works Department.

Public property management policy is based on the following principles:

- construction and acquisition of appropriate buildings at minimum costs;
- optimum use without waste;
- appropriate maintenance;
- refurbishment or demolition and replacement of dilapidated properties; and
- transfer of surplus properties to alternative use.

Problems of poor maintenance in the past were attributed to financial allocation and to management and organisational problems. Financial allocation problems included:

- insufficient allocation;
- delays in transfer; and
- allocations used for other purposes.

Management and organisational problems were the result of the absence of central organisation over the allocation of maintenance funds. Each department applied for maintenance funds which were then transferred to the Public Works Department which was responsible for the implementation of maintenance work.

Reforms of the system were based on the following principles:

- Funds were allocated direct to the PWD on the basis of estimates based on departmental requests for maintenance.
- Heads of departments were permitted to manage maintenance and to undertake minor repairs, such as contracts to clean buildings and maintain surroundings, maintain and repair air conditioners, electrical fittings, water pumps, plumbing and toilets, etc.

Estate management has also been reinforced by an insurance fund for Government properties managed by the Contract and Supply Management Division of the Ministry of Finance; while the Valuation and Property Services Department in the same Ministry provides appropriate professional expertise in valuation and compulsory purchase, and property management.

In the *UK*, the government estate has been traditionally organised into distinct areas: the Civil Estate, the Defence Estate, and the Operational Estate. The reforms in estate management have been part of a series aimed at improving accountability and value for money, and have included reforms to costs and the introduction of capital charging.

Under the Property Repayment System, the broad cost of accommodation, later refined with increasing works delegation, was recouped from each department.

In 1990, the Civil Estate was effectively divided into the Consumer User Estate (CUE), managed by the Property Holdings Division, and specialised or dedicated-user estates, managed by occupying departments and agencies.

The CUE portfolio is managed as a common resource by Property Holdings (PH) so as to be able to offer departments accommodation at best value for money. PH's objectives are to meet accommodation requirements economically, efficiently and effectively; and to recover the full cost and collect opportunity-cost rents from all departments.

Under the Common User Estate, departments are responsible and accountable for the amount, location, quality of accommodation used, and for payments for them. Departments using the CUE are tied to the PH to enable it to carry out its role.

Under these reforms, accommodation is recognised as a key resource, and departments are encouraged to approach it from the point of view of stewardship, the application of planned maintenance techniques, periodic reviews of needs and use, and to release any surplus or excess.

Other useful material (current as of 1996)

From Problem to Solution. Commonwealth Strategies for Reform. Managing the Public Service. Strategies for Improvement No. 1. Commonwealth Secretariat, 1995 (ComSec)

McCulloch, B. Accounting and Management Reforms in New Zealand Government in Administrative and Managerial Reform in Government: A Commonwealth Portfolio of Current Good Practice. Proceedings of a Pan Commonwealth Working Group Meeting held in Kuala Lumpur, Malaysia, 19-22 April 1993, Commonwealth Secretariat, 1993 (ComSec)

Pallot, J. Accounting and Financial Management Reforms in New Zealand Central Government: Context and Critique in Administrative and Managerial Reform in Government: A Commonwealth Portfolio of Current Good Practice. Proceedings of a Pan Commonwealth Working Group Meeting held in Kuala Lumpur, Malaysia, 19-22 April 1993 (ComSec)

The Manager's Deskbook. Treasury Board of Canada. Third Edition, 1993 (CAN)

Treasury Board Manual. Real Property Management Volume. (CAN)

Scott, G. & Ball, I. Financial Management Reform in the New Zealand Government. The Treasury, Wellington (NZ)

Putting It Simply – An Explanatory Guide to Financial Management Reform. The Treasury, 1989, Wellington (NZ)

Fiscal Responsibility Act: A Brief Overview. Treasury Briefing Note. New Zealand The Treasury, Wellington, 1994 (NZ)

Efficiency and Effectiveness in the Civil Service. HMSO, London, 1982 (UK)

Financial Management in Government Departments. HMSO, London, 1983 (UK)

6.2.3 Improving physical asset management

The *physical assets* of governments are land, buildings and the variety of value objects procured or used by departments in the course of carrying out their activities. These include stationery, maintenance and other stores, office equipment, including computers, vehicles and machinery, and military equipment.

While individually perhaps of modest value, the total cost of these assets represents a considerable investment. Physical assets are vulnerable to:

- losses associated with spoilage, resulting from inappropriate storage arrangements;

- losses resulting from theft and pilferage, consequent on insecure storage and inadequate stock control and accounting systems;

- losses arising from weaknesses in logistics – the distribution, location and storage of goods;

- losses brought about by inadequate maintenance, which result in:

  - shortened life and the consequent need for early replacement of the equipment; and

  - stoppages and losses of production which follow unnecessary breakdown.

Physical asset management is a key aspect of the public service responsibility for the effective stewardship of national resources, and must cover:

- planning;

- acquisition or procurement;

- operation and maintenance; and

- disposal.

The context for change

The physical assets of the government represent a very significant resource and are commonly among the most neglected. They are often not recorded or systematically valued, and sometimes only partially used. Storage and security arrangements are frequently inadequate often leading to significant losses through spoilage or theft.

Unnecessary or inappropriate purchasing and disposal policies encourage a misuse of scarce resources. Unsystematic, absent, incomplete or belated maintenance leads to deterioration and damage requiring increased resources for repair and replacement.

Proper systematic physical asset management results in the efficient use of resources and, consequently, in increased value for money.

Physical asset management requires:

- a changed focus for managers, shifting concerns from spending for asset creation towards the management of assets to support the efficient provision of services;

- staff development to ensure improved asset management capabilities; and

- clear guidance to encourage the adoption of uniform management practices, systems, standards and forms of accounting.

The principal benefits resulting from improved physical asset management include:

- a reduction of spoilage resulting from inappropriate storage arrangements;
- a reduction of theft and pilferage consequent on insecure storage and inadequate stock control and accounting systems;
- adequate stock control systems and increased security permit identification and release of surplus resources for alternative uses;
- reduced overall maintenance costs through planned maintenance;
- savings resulting from better planning in the nature and timing of purchasing and procurement; and
- benefits associated with the availability of appropriate equipment at the proper time, including cost reductions through correct use of equipment.

Reasons for caution

In many situations, there is no complete or current inventory of government assets, nor a central record against which physical condition and maintenance records can be checked. Compiling this information base requires a thorough inventory of all government property. This is a multi-disciplinary operation requiring the use of appropriately qualified personnel to assess values and maintenance requirements.

It is possible that conflicts between user departments and central authorities may arise, particularly over title, value and condition of the goods, especially as many of the goods will have been purchased out of departmental appropriations.

Development of adequate storage and other facilities necessary to preserve the physical integrity of goods and equipment may require expensive new buildings and structures or the modification of existing buildings and structures.

Improving physical asset management also requires the examination and reform of government procurement processes and policies regarding disposal of surplus or obsolete assets.

Such a package of reforms must to be driven by a central body with the authority to ensure compliance and the resources to provide the necessary advice, assistance and training.

Achieving change

Stewardship of government property is a mainstream management task. Managers must take an active and informed view of their asset base and performance in relation to property assets, judged and valued with the same vigour as people management or financial management skills. Physical asset management must be part of all business plans, and reflected in the capital and operating budget.

The importance and value of all government physical assets should be made visible to all staff. The most common problem is the assumption that such goods are "free" or easily replaced. In this respect, all government assets should be the responsibility of individual managers who should be accountable for them.

Physical asset management covers three distinct areas: procurement, use and maintenance, and disposal.

1. Procurement

Poor procurement leads to unnecessary and uneconomic purchases. The first step in improving physical asset management is a thorough review or internal audit of the procurement systems.

2. Use and maintenance

As a means to improving the maintenance and use of existing assets, departments should be required to conduct a thorough inventory and prepare an in-depth report on the quantity, quality, title, value, use and maintenance requirements, and cost, of the government property under its control. In the case of goods susceptible to spoilage or damage, the report should cover the storage and security arrangements.

These inventories and reports should be backed up by a full report or internal audit of the stock control and accounting, and maintenance systems.

The cost of the often significant losses through spoilage, pilfering and theft should be underlined by requiring management to report on them as a separate line in the periodic accounts.

In order to avoid unnecessary breakdown and to secure full-life availability of vehicles and equipment, all departments should be required to adopt planned maintenance techniques, using appropriate and duly recorded schedules. Care should be taken to ensure the existence and adequate supply of essential spare parts.

Distribution systems should also be examined regularly. Over-centralisation can result in unacceptable delays in supplying goods to the user. Excessive dispersion will result in costly high stock levels, increased staff and buildings, and, perhaps, problems in monitoring and control.

3. Disposal

Disposal of surplus, obsolete or used assets should be governed by clearly laid down procedures, clearly accountable, and properly audited so as to secure maximum value for money.

Commonwealth experiences indicate that the key to successful physical asset management is the adoption and implementation of appropriate internal management systems designed to secure proper purchasing, use, security and maintenance, and eventual disposal; supported by strong and effective internal and external audit functions.

Good physical asset management practices are encouraged by well-managed programmes of devolution in which responsibility for asset management, and accountability for the results obtained through the use of the assets, are located within the service-providing units.

Examples of change

In *New Zealand*, the Ministry of Works has taken steps to corporatise the Works Consultancy which highlighted the need to have adequate benchmarks in terms of measuring in-house efficiencies in relation to the private sector.

In *Mauritius*, a one-week workshop was held in 1995, attended by overseas practitioners. The objective was to propose an appropriate Asset Management model to strengthen the capacity of the Government to manage all physical assets.

In the *UK*, the Next Steps Initiative, announced in 1988, aims to improve efficiency through the devolution of many executive functions of government to independent agencies whose Chief Executives are directly responsible to Ministers for their performance.

Other reforms in the health service and in education have included the formation of independent bodies with charitable trust status. This process was accompanied by the transfer of physical assets; the recipient bodies were required to produce complete inventories of all assets, develop appropriate procurement and disposal policies, develop internal audits and adopt planned maintenance systems.

6.2.4 Improving the procurement process

Procurement is the overall process of acquiring goods and services to meet customer needs. Procurement consists of a cycle which starts when the need is identified, and ends when the goods and services are paid for.

Purchasing is a component of procurement and requires particular skills in sourcing goods and services, and negotiating contracts and subsequent liaison with suppliers.

The context for change

Public pressure to increase the range and quality of services, together with the extension of the role of governments in all aspects of economic and social activity, has placed increasing demands on frequently diminishing resources.

One consequence of this pressure on resources and the growth in public expectations has been the introduction, in the public service of many Commonwealth countries, of a range of public management reforms emphasising the need for increasing cost-effectiveness and improving quality of output. Improvement of the procurement process, with its emphasis on economy, efficiency and effectiveness, is a key mindset in achieving these reforms.

The public service carries a dual responsibility for improving the procurement process. First, as a very significant purchaser of goods and services, it strongly influences domestic and, in some situations, overseas markets by its procurement activities. These activities can, at best, stimulate national productivity and, at worst, signal to domestic markets that considerations other than price, quality and ethical production policies influence sales.

Second, as the spender of public money, the public service carries the responsibility for ensuring that it obtains maximum value for money in all its procurement activities.

Reasons for caution

The key balance is the extent to which the purchasing function is centralised in a central, specialised service unit, or delegated to user/customer departments. The advantages of a centralised purchasing unit are based on the specialist purchasing skills and the "buyer" power, resulting from accumulated purchases, leading to lower prices.

Traditionally, the public sector has tended towards a centralised procurement unit. However, the weaknesses of this system in practice are:

- a tendency towards slow and unresponsive bureaucracy, undermining efficiency savings with hidden administration costs;

- an inability to react quickly to changes in market conditions; and

- an over-emphasis on bulk purchases leading to excessive inventories with associated storage costs and costs of lost or spoilt goods.

Where delegation has been introduced, weaknesses in the training, expertise and professionalism of departmental purchasing staff have to be corrected. The challenge is to find a pragmatic balance in which specialist procurement can be centrally managed with appropriate technical support, while more generic procurement is delegated.

The balance is largely determined by the degree of competition in the market in which purchases have to be made. A weak market with a few strong and relatively unchallenged suppliers suggests that a strong purchasing authority is required to negotiate favourable terms. In a highly competitive market, prices and quality are determined by market pressures, and delegated purchasing will produce value for money.

The risk is not recognising when the nature of the market has changed. The rapid development of a highly competitive market for personal computers left some central IT procurement agencies in a position of bulk-purchasing equipment, only to discover that Ministries and departments had purchased more suitable equipment at better prices.

Achieving change

Pre-requisites to improving procurement procedures are as follows:

- There should be a clear delegation of the authority to agree prices and to purchase generic supplies. This authority should be accompanied by appropriate performance indicators so that the effectiveness of purchasing can be evaluated.

- Specialist training should be made available to delegated purchasing staff.

- A clear purchasing strategy consistent with overall financial objectives should be developed for purchasing staff.

- Appropriate management information systems should be available to provide information on existing expenditure – how much? on what? and with whom? – together with the existence of appropriate accounting and record-keeping systems.

- Flexible organisational structures are required to cope with rapid changes in demand and market conditions.

Examples of change

In *Canada*, the Public Works and Government Services Canada (PWGSC) is a common services agency which provides both procurement and contracting activities for both material and real property, maintains the government infrastructure (buildings, roads and bridges, and museums), pays government bills, and collects government receivables.

Procurement of commercially-available, off-the-shelf goods and standard services was recognised as being expensive, with an excessive turnaround delivery time. Client departments had long felt the need for authority to purchase off-the-shelf goods quickly and with minimum red tape, especially where price and delivery were common denominators.

In response to this demand, PWGSC introduced a fast-track electronic purchasing gateway using readily available personal computer-based technology. PWGSC clients now have access to electronic catalogues for over 50,000 line items with price, quantity and delivery information. This forms the basis of a system whereby departments can issue their own electronic purchase orders to Canadian suppliers.

Moreover, the introduction of an open-bidding service permits publication of all requirements of goods and contracts for services over a determined value to potential suppliers through a subscription service.

These systems are being developed into a database providing contract histories and up-to-date information on prices, quantities, and usage, with a bid-matching service so that suppliers deemed particularly suitable can be sent appropriate information.

In *New Zealand*, as part of the financial management reform programme, authority for purchasing decisions has been delegated, as far as possible, to the managers concerned. It should be noted that part of those reforms included the lifting of import controls, which after a long period of strict regulation led some sector agencies to favour imported over locally-produced goods.

In 1994, the Ministry of Commerce issued two booklets on Government purchasing in New Zealand – Guidelines to Suppliers, and Guidelines for Purchasers.

For Government purchasers, the booklet contains a checklist on implementing Government policy, with the emphasis on using the New Zealand Industrial Supplies Office, multi-stage procurement processes, the need for alternative proposals and the importance of encouraging innovation, and the use of new products.

Guidelines to Suppliers is intended to assist suppliers and potential suppliers understand, and operate in, the government purchasing environment. It includes:

- an explanation of the role of the New Zealand Industrial Supplies Office established to support government purchasing policy by facilitating contact between public sector buyers and suppliers through an exchange of information on purchasing requirements and domestic industry capabilities;
- a background to State sector reforms;
- a list of purchasing contacts in government departments and agencies with an indication of likely needs; and
- how and where further assistance might be obtained.

Another aspect of New Zealand Government policy is active encouragement in the use of local and "domestic" products, i.e. products wholly or partly produced under the Australia-New Zealand Closer Economic Relations Agreement.

In the *UK*, the Efficiency Unit of the Cabinet Office in its 1984 report, Government Purchasing, concluded that the government was not getting best value for money and identified a number of causes for concern, including:

- lack of professionalism among staff concerned with purchasing;
- inadequate training and career development for staff specialising in purchasing;
- insufficient exposure to commercial experience;
- insufficient awareness of cost and time-saving techniques; and
- inadequate information systems.

In 1986, the Government Purchasing Initiative resulted in the creation of the Treasury's Central Unit on Purchasing (CUP). CUP's role was to offer help and advice to central government departments and agencies on best purchasing practice and achieving value for money. Another function consisted in monitoring compliance with recommendations made in the report, Government Purchasing.

CUP's role has been extended to provide advice and guidance to departments on the commercial aspects of market-testing activities and project management in the works/construction activities.

Other useful material (current as of 1996)

The Mangers' Deskbook. Treasury Board of Canada. Third Edition. 1993 (CAN)

Government Purchasing in New Zealand – Guidelines for Suppliers. Ministry of Commerce, Wellington, 1994 (NZ)

Government Purchasing in New Zealand – Guidelines for Purchasers. Ministry of Commerce, Wellington, 1994 (NZ)

Government Purchasing. Progress Report to the Prime Minister. HMSO, London, 1992 (UK)

6.2.5 Using activity-based costing

Costs are the total value of resources used in producing goods and services. Accurate costing is an essential part of sound financial management. With accurate costing, goods and services can be priced correctly, hidden subsidies or losses can be avoided, and comparisons with alternative providers made.

Costs are made up from two elements:

- *Direct or variable costs*. These relate directly to a product and will vary with variations in the output of the product. Examples of direct costs include raw materials, components and direct labour.

- *Indirect or fixed costs*, sometimes known as overheads. These cannot be related directly to a single product, but are shared with other products and do not necessarily vary with output. Examples of indirect costs include rents and land taxes, administrative or financial costs.

Traditionally, public sector organisations have concentrated on direct costs, and have tended to ignore indirect costs, such as cost of capital, investment in estate and capital equipment, and administrative and overhead costs.

Total costing or the total acquisition cost does include indirect costs, in particular, the cost of capital.

Where indirect costs are taken into account, they must be allocated to individual departments or products. However, often their allocation among departments and/or products is arbitrary or based on precedents which no longer reflect the current status.

Activity-based costing takes this concept a stage further and consists of tracing individual costs back to the primary activity which led to them being incurred. It is mainly concerned with the indirect or fixed cost elements. Under activity-based costing, these are no longer apportioned on a traditional or arbitrary basis. Instead such costs are allocated as closely as possible on use or volume. In other words, it is a method of changing indirect costs into direct costs.

Activity-based costing is a powerful technique within the repertoire available to public service managers. It is a means and not an end, and should be used where and when appropriate and realistic.

The context for change

The growth of public demand for the extension of the role of the government in all aspects of economic and social activity has resulted in a greater demands on limited and frequently diminishing economic and financial resources.

As the activities of government have widened and become increasingly complex, the importance of accountability for, and efficient management of, public resources is being recognised.

Efficient use of all resources can only be guaranteed if all costs are taken account of, including indirect costs, and, in particular, the cost of capital.

Activity-based costing:

- provides accurate service-cost information, facilitating management decision taking;

- provides a better understanding of the impact of indirect costs;

- recognises differences in input consumption;

- exposes examples of hidden cross-subsidisation;

- enables a more equitable allocation of costs by enabling departments to pay for resources consumed; and

- identifies opportunities for developing cost centres. These are different parts of the organisation, based on major groups of activities and products, which can be viewed as discrete entities and whose performance, in financial terms, can be analysed, monitored and controlled separately.

Reasons for caution

The allocation of costs is not an objective science. While direct costs do vary with output, the variation is not necessarily proportional. On the other hand, indirect costs may not be completely fixed and may vary with changes in output. A definite allocation of any cost is partly dependant on judgement and convention. In many cases, the allocation of costs can only be made on the basis of agreed ratios. For example, the use of the comparative financial value of outputs or on occasion inputs is common. However, there are many cases in which answers provided by these methods are only approximate.

In summary, activity-based costing entails some assumptions; and the accuracy and credibility of the information it generates is only as good as the accuracy and credibility of the assumptions on which it rests.

The technique is based on effective and comprehensive management information systems, which may be very labour intensive, and apart from being costly, may tie up scarce trained human resources which may be required elsewhere.

The successful introduction of any form of activity-based costing will also require the active co-operation of management and staff. The term "cost centre" can be highly emotional and it is likely that many individuals will feel threatened by the implications of highlighting the true costs of their departments or products. It is important that the positive aspects of the exercise are emphasised.

Activity-based costing systems need frequent revision as structure and systems change. The symptoms of outdated costing systems are:

- wide variations between actual and budgeted cost information;

- low level of usefulness of information for internal decision making;

- managers' lack of confidence in official systems;

- parallel, independent information systems are developed;

- operational managers denying ownership of costs; and

- the need for frequent and manual adjustments to results and reports.

Achieving change

The introduction of any reform of costing practices should be part of a broader series of financial reforms achieving improved value for money. Reforms particularly associated with activity-based costing are: introducing capital charging, improving procurement and improving estate management.

Such a comprehensive set of reforms requires a central authority in a position to co-ordinate reforms, ensure compliance, and provide the necessary support with advice, assistance and training.

Introducing activity-based costing requires:

- an analysis of the existing public service operations, service-wide or at the level of individual Ministries or departments, to identify the major activities, or major groups of activities, which comprise those operations;

- an analysis of the direct and indirect costs associated with each activity or group of activities;

- an assessment of the opportunities for continued monitoring of all costs and for the calculation of activity-based costs;

- an assessment of options for regular dissemination of comparative activity-based costs to managers which allows them to:

  - identify changes over time; and

  - identify cost increases or decreases resulting from their management decisions.

Examples of change

In *Malta*, as part of a series of financial reforms, the classification of accounts and organisations was restructured in 1992, and management financial accounting reports based on the Chart of Accounts were available from 1993. Previous classifications had evolved to a point when there was no longer an underlying structure which addressed the reporting needs of operating departments and Ministries.

The revised breakdown of accounts was based on two-fold analyses:

- The Chart of Accounts which identified the nature of the transactions. This provided a breakdown of each cost centre where basic operations could be identified, and where revenues, recurrent and capital expenditure, and below-line transactions, were recorded.

- The Organisational Classification which identified responsibility for transactions, from the highest level down to heads of cost centres.

This reorganisation allowed for the development of reliable and informative reports and facilitated rational decision making on the basis of known costs and benefits.

In *New Zealand*, output costing has been developed as an extension of activity-based costing. It was recognised at the outset that no one costing system would be appropriate for all situations, though all would focus on outputs and cost-incurring activities. Within wide parameters, the following factors were identified as fundamental to the design of a costing system:

- the level of information required by users;

- the complexity and diversity of cost objects;

- the frequency of cost allocation;

- the reporting structure of the department; and

- the cost of maintaining the system.

The *South African* Government has introduced the Medium-Term Expenditure Framework which requires departments to link expenditures systematically to strategic aims; and, as part of a move away from the incremental budgeting of the past, departments will be required to establish clear outputs and priorities, together with key performance indicators, clear monitoring procedures and business plans.

Also in South Africa, a key strategy designed to achieve optimal utilisation of human and other resources is the Medium-Term Personnel Framework. This will be used to determine policies and fiscal allocation in a five-year period. Personnel costs are tied to programmes being offered by the various departments and thus facilitate the costings.

In the *UK*, a number of initiatives aimed at improving value for money include improvements to procurement and accounting and costing procedures. In particular, the introduction of accrual-based accounting systems and of capital charging has facilitated the identification of the full cost of activities. This development was further encouraged by the introduction of a comprehensive market-testing programme which, per se, required the availability of accurate costs of individual activities.

Other useful material (current as of 1996)

McCulloch, B. Accounting and Management Reforms in New Zealand Government. In Administrative and Managerial Reform in Government: A Commonwealth Portfolio of Current Good Practice. Proceedings of a Pan Commonwealth Working Group Meeting held in Kuala Lumpur, Malaysia, 19-22 April 1993. Commonwealth Secretariat, 1993 (ComSec)

Pallot, J. Accounting and Financial Management Reforms in New Zealand Central Government: Context and Critique. In: Administrative and Managerial Reform in Government: A Commonwealth Portfolio of Current Good Practice. Proceedings of a Pan Commonwealth Working Group Meeting held in Kuala Lumpur, Malaysia, 19-22 April 1993. Commonwealth Secretariat, 1993 (ComSec)

From Problem to Solution. Commonwealth Strategies for Reform. Managing the Public Service. Strategies for Improvement No. 1. Commonwealth Secretariat, 1995 (ComSec)

Improving Output Costing – Guidelines and Examples, Parts I and II. Treasury, Wellington, 1994 (NZ)

Life-Cycle Costing. Guidance Sheet (No. 35). Public Competition and Purchasing Unit, HM Treasury (UK)

Efficiency and Effectiveness in the Civil Service. HMSO, London, 1982 (UK)

Financial Management in Government Departments. HMSO, London, 1983 (UK)

6.3 Improving Management Information

6.3.1 Strengthening external audits

External audit is a check, a process of verification or examination, of an organisation's accounts and records by an independent authority.

The purpose of an external audit in the public sector is to provide assurance to taxpayers as to the integrity of public finances (the financial audit), and also to ensure that value is being achieved in public spending (the value-for-money audit).

The context for change

Since the mid-1970s, governments have been increasingly concerned to adapt and develop the structures and values of the public service to achieve greater efficiency and more responsive services. Improved quality at less cost has been the imperative. These changes have largely been pushed by continuing economic crises in developing and developed countries, which have in turn arisen from deteriorating terms of trade, over-extended borrowing, and a somewhat abrupt change of policy by the lending institutions during the 1980s.

However, the changes have also arisen from a new set of managerial strategies for the public service, which have opened up the possibility that greater results can be achieved from fewer resources by strengthening lines of accountability and defining intended outputs more sharply.

Financial management reforms have been at the centre of the response to the economic crises, and have been equally fundamental to the new managerial strategies adopted in the public service.

These reforms have been accompanied by changes in budgeting procedures and a liberalisation of many financial controls, as managers are provided with the opportunity to manage flexibly to achieve specific objectives.

However, this process of liberalisation also increases the possibility of fraudulent or other misuse of public funds. Consequently, countries have strengthened, or are in the process of strengthening, their auditing procedures through legislative changes; changes in remit, for instance to include value-for-money auditing; and through increased resources, enabling more thorough audits to be undertaken.

Reasons for caution

Changes to, and the strengthening of, the external auditing procedures must be introduced with care, preferably as part of an ongoing comprehensive, mutually-supporting set of reforms, aimed at improving financial management in general.

The understanding and positive support of departmental managers must be secured through consultation and training. It is important that managers should convey a positive message about external auditing, emphasising its role in the identification of systemic weaknesses as a counterbalance to its role in finding fault.

A key precondition to strengthening external auditing is the availability of the necessary human resources. External auditing in the public sector is becoming closer to practices in the private sector. Auditing bodies must therefore be prepared to match private sector skills and training procedures, and must compete with the private sector in training, hiring and retaining skilled personnel.

Systems designed must include provision for ensuring compliance with any recommendations which may arise in reports on audits carried out. A common weakness is the absence of any such provision, which results in reports being shelved while malpractices continue.

Achieving change

Effective external public auditing must be based on certain key principles:

* clear boundaries between the government, which determines policy; the public service which implements policy; and parliament or the legislature, which oversee both policy and implementation on behalf of the public;
* independence of public auditors by statutory prescription of their status, including methods of appointment and removal from office, and of funding arrangements;
* resources should be allocated by the legislature, not the government or the public service;
* statutes should also prescribe the audit remit, and include freedom to determine the nature and scope of work;
* there should be unrestricted access to documentation and the right to seek explanations from those responsible for activities; and
* auditors should submit reports to the legislature, where there should be proper arrangements for their consideration.

Financial audits should be carried out at regular intervals by properly qualified staff, who are part of an independent organisation, with authority to require answers to questions, and with authority to ensure compliance.

The auditor is responsible for ascertaining if:

* all reasonable precautions are taken to safeguard the collection of public monies;
* whether issue and payment of monies have been made in accordance with proper authority and that payments have been properly charged and supported by sufficient vouchers or proof of payment;
* whether the use, control and write-offs of public assets have been made in the proper manner and according to regulations;
* whether all accounts and records are well and correctly maintained; and
* whether monies have been expended for purposes for which they were allocated and the activities for which money was spent have been carried out in the in the most efficient manner.

The independence of the Auditor General, or comparable position, is emphasised by the presentation of annual reports to a strong Public Accounts Committee or similar high profile Parliamentary Committee, able and willing to bring issues of concern to the attention of the full legislature.

Examples of change

In *Kenya*, the Office of the Controller and Auditor General is a Constitutional Office. The external audit function is further strengthened by a Public Accounts Committee which is a Select Committee of National Assembly.

The Exchequer and Audit Amendment Act of 1985 provided for the appointment of an Auditor General (Corporations) to be responsible for auditing the accounts of State corporations in view of their more commercial nature.

In *Malaysia*, the responsibilities and role of the Auditor General are provided for under the Federal Constitution and the Audit Act of 1957 (revised in 1972).

The Auditor General's Reports are tabled in Parliament/State Legislative Assemblies and referred to the Public Accounts Committee(s) which considers financial management on behalf of the legislature. The Committee(s) may take remedial action, compliance of which will be followed up by the Public Accounts Committee.

In the *UK*, although some agencies are audited by private sector firms, most audits are carried out by the National Audit Office (NAO); while local authorities and health authorities are supervised by either the Audit Commission, the Scotland Accounts Commission, or the Northern Ireland Audit Office.

The National Audit Office is headed by the Comptroller and Auditor General, who is appointed by the Queen, on the advice of the Prime Minister and the Public Accounts Committee. The independence of the NAO is assured since the Auditor General is not appointed for a fixed term, his salary is paid from the Consolidated Fund and does not require annual approval, and his removal from office is the prerogative of the Sovereign, following an address from both Houses of Parliament.

The Comptroller and Auditor General alone decides on the extent and conduct of audits and reports made to Parliament. He/she is empowered to appoint staff and determine their rates of pay.

The NAO publishes their value-for-money reports – for Parliament and the public, to provide assurance, information and advice on the use of resources in departments and other audited bodies.

The NAO reports are considered by the Public Accounts Committee, which then makes its own report to Parliament, including recommendations to Government. The Government's response is subsequently laid before Parliament in the form of Treasury Minutes. The NAO later follows up to ensure compliance.

Other useful material (current as of 1996)

The Treasury Board Manual. Canada (CAN)

The Civil Service in Malaysia – A Paradigm Shift (MAL)

Improvements and Developments in the Public Service, Malaysia (MAL)

Public Audit Manual, National Audit Office/Overseas Development Agency (UK)

Helping the Nation Spend Wisely – A Guide to the National Audit Office/National Audit Office (UK)

The Scope, Objectives and Methods of the NAO's Financial Audit. National Audit Office, 1993 (UK)

6.3.2 Strengthening internal audits

Internal audit is an independent assessment of the effectiveness of management systems to ensure that:

- departmental objectives are achieved;

- resources are used economically and effectively;

- established policies, plans, procedures, laws and regulations are complied with;

- assets and interests of the department are safeguarded from losses of all kinds; and

- the integrity and reliability of computer systems are maintained.

While internal audit aims to assist management by providing objective and timely information regarding the strengths and weaknesses of the organisation, it is not an extension or substitute for line management.

The context for change

Public demand for an increase in the range and quality of services, together with the extension of the role of governments in all aspects of economic and social activity, has placed increasing demands on frequently diminishing public service resources.

One consequence of this pressure on resources and growth in public expectations has been the introduction, in the public service of many Commonwealth countries, of a range of public management reforms emphasising the need for increasing cost-effectiveness and improving quality of output. Value for money, with its emphasis on economy, efficiency and effectiveness, is a key mindset in achieving these reforms.

Against this background, traditional systems for financial management do not provide a sufficiently strong emphasis on performance. External audits frequently focus on monetary control and in consequence there is little overall evaluation of departments' activities and outputs.

Internal audit provides management with an additional monitoring mechanism, providing objective reports on ongoing infrastructure changes and on the effectiveness of the management of allocated resources.

Reasons for caution

As in most areas of financial reform, the successful introduction of internal auditing is dependent on the co-operation of managers and employees. The principal danger when introducing internal auditing is negative management, where the audit is seen largely as a system of control, and not as a management aid or tool which will, in the long term, encourage best practice and success in improving quality and value for money.

Internal audit units must be properly staffed and have a clear remit including the necessary authority to examine all aspects of the organisation's operations. Absence of appropriate authority will limit the value and reliability of the audit.

Reports from internal audit units must be published and circulated partly to ensure individual awareness of weaknesses, and partly to allow for assurance that recommendations will be acted upon.

There is a temptation for internal audit units to become involved in a critical examination of policies. Examination of the appropriateness of outcomes and the effects of the policy should not be part of an internal audit.

Achieving change

Internal audits are systems-based audits, the prime responsibility of which is to ensure that various control systems are operating effectively. The following areas must be covered by internal audit:

- the reliability and integrity of information;

- compliance with policies, laws and regulations;

- safety of assets and resources;

- efficiency in the use of resources; and

- accomplishment of aims and objectives.

Commonwealth experience points to a four-stage strategy for improving internal audit:

- The introduction of standards for internal audits, disseminated by a manual or policy document;

- The creation of internal audit units at Ministry or department level, and the provision of a central monitoring point for the frequency, coverage, and standards of internal audits;

- The institution of comprehensive training programmes for internal auditors;

- A programme review by a central auditing monitoring unit to ensure that departmental internal audit teams are complying with the required standards, to identify areas for improvement, and to disseminate best practice.

Examples of change

In *Malaysia*, in 1979, the Treasury Circular No. 2, "Implementation of Internal Auditing in Federal Government Agencies", set the scene for the introduction of internal auditing in government departments. In 1993, a total of 17 Ministries and departments had set up Internal Auditing Units (IAUs).

IAUs are responsible for carrying out independent observations on the agency's activities and operations on a regular basis, reporting findings; and making recommendations with regard to corrective measures which may be required.

As far as the organisational structure is concerned, the IAU is part of the agency in which it is set up and is directly responsible to the Chief Executive of that agency. Operationally, IAUs receive directives and supervision from the Financial Management Unit in the Ministry of Finance.

The Government of *Malta* is proceeding with the gradual introduction of internal audit in major Ministries. By July 1993, initial training programmes were complete and the first teams of internal auditors were deployed in four Ministries. The Ministry of Finance established a Central Audit Policy Unit and draft Audit Standards were completed.

In *Trinidad and Tobago*, it is increasingly accepted that the internal audit should be clearly distinguished as a separate career path, that training of up-to-date methodologies should be provided, and that senior positions should require the holders to have an appropriate professional qualification.

Following these developments, the Government is considering the introduction of Audit Committees, modelled on the best private sector practices, into the public services, while at the same time introducing computer audits to secure the integrity and reliability of management information systems.

In the *UK*, there is no statutory obligation for government departments to conduct internal audits; however, failure to do so may result in criticism by the Public Accounts Committee of the House of Commons in Parliament. Permanent Heads of Department are personally accountable to Parliament, and the internal audit is an important source of information and advice.

In 1981, the Public Accounts Committee criticised the general standard of internal audit in government and charged the Treasury to ensure that standards were improved. The main causes for concern included:

* the audit of computer systems was inadequate;

* a lack of personal skill and management within the audit;

* inadequate personnel policies; and

* inadequate direction from the centre.

In 1983, the Government Internal Audit Manual (GIAM) introduced standards for the internal audit. This manual was updated in 1988 and again in 1994. Comprehensive training programmes for internal auditors were introduced, together with a Basic Training Standard set out in GIAM.

The Treasury Internal Audit Development Division was set up to ensure compliance and in 1985 was established as a separate division. Reports are circulated and principal finance officers receive a letter containing detailed observations. The Head of the Government Accountancy Service and the Chief Accountancy Adviser subsequently write to Permanent Heads of Departments asking for confirmation that any necessary action has been taken.

Other useful material (current as of 1996)

Civil Service of Malaysia – A Paradigm Shift, Kuala Lumpur (MAL)

Provost, L. The Changing Role of Internal Audit. Institute for International Research. Internal Audit Conference, Wellington, 1992 (NZ)

The Internal Audit in the Public Service. Management Leaflet No. 14. State Services Commission, Wellington, 1986 (NZ)

Government Internal Audit Manual. HMSO, London, 1988 (UK)

Government Information Systems Audit Manual. HMSO, London, 1993 (UK)

6.3.3 Introducing accrual-based accounting

Traditionally, public service organisations have used cash accounting systems which only recognise transactions when cash is received or paid, and in which financial results are reported on the basis of differences between cash received and cash paid.

While cash-based accounts give an accurate view of an entity's cash flows, accrual-based accounts give a fuller picture of the operations and overall financial position. *Accrual-based accounting* relates activities to the period in which costs are incurred or revenue is earned, regardless of when or whether money changes hands. It keeps track of assets and liabilities, and records changes in their values.

Accrual accounts therefore differ considerably from cash-based accounts. For example, accrual accounts:

- show as assets, the value of amounts due but not yet paid to the government for goods and services supplied or for taxes levied during the period;

- show as liabilities, the value of amounts due but not yet paid by the government for goods and services supplied, or for taxes refundable during the period;

- report non-cash assets, such as buildings, state highways and military equipment, and reflect changes in their value through depreciation and revaluation;

- include non-cash liabilities, such as accumulated employee leave entitlements and unfunded pension liabilities; and

- show certain changes in the value of the government's financial assets and liabilities due, for instance, to exchange rate movements.

All of these items would have been omitted or ignored under cash accounting. However, accrual reporting should not be seen as replacing cash reporting. The latter reveals flows affecting the government's liquidity and financing requirements. The two systems are complementary and data from both are relevant to assessments of financial performance.

The context for change

In the context of pressure to improve effectiveness within the public service changes, reform of financial reporting systems is fundamental in order to encourage accountability and delegation, and to provide up-to-date information to assist management decision taking and resource allocation.

Cash accounting systems do not consider the depreciation of capital assets, interest on capital, or internal charges, all of which are at the core of accrual accounting.

Accrual-based accounting systems, based on both balance sheets and operating statements:

- reflect the true financial state of an organisation;

- establish accurately the resources used;

- indicate the extent to which costs are recovered;

- permit the calculation of the return on capital; and

- generally provide means of setting efficiency targets and other indicators.

Some of the advantages of accrual accounting can be illustrated by considering the choice which a government might face between paying higher public salaries immediately, and providing greater employee pension benefits in the future. A decision to increase those benefits instead of salaries would be reported differently under cash and accrual accounting frameworks.

Under cash accounting, higher pension benefits might appear artificially attractive even if they ultimately cost more because the cost is unreported until the year in which the liability is actually paid. Experience has shown that this offers a false sense of sustainability and makes it harder to ensure that sufficient resources are available when the obligations finally have to be met.

Under accrual accounting, by contrast, the cost of higher pension entitlements would be reported as employees accrue the benefits (that is, as they work and earn the eventual pension) possibly years before the benefits are paid out. An increase in the future liability during a given period is reported as an expense, and the accumulated sum of such liabilities appears in the balance sheet.

Accrual reporting thus gives a clear view when financial implications extend beyond a year and encourages a longer-term focus in decision making. It also facilitates more meaningful assessment by Ministers and legislators of the performance of government entities (including departments), and of managers responsible for them.

Reasons for caution

The introduction of accrual accounting is a major administrative step, strongly dependent on the availability of appropriate accounting skills. It can only be part of a comprehensive, integrated series of financial reforms aimed at improving accountability and achieving value for money. It is particularly associated with capital charging and reforms to the budgetary process, such as end-of-year flexibility and delegated budgetary responsibilities.

In moving towards accrual accounting, two fundamental issues have to be addressed: the establishment of an opening balance sheet; and the combination of all the diverse types of public sector agencies under the same accounting standards.

The establishment of an opening balance sheet will highlight the absence of systematic records of asset values, including buildings, liabilities and receivables, and capital; the calculation of which is time-consuming and contentious. Many departmental accountants, trained under a cash-accounting regime, will need extensive re-training to undertake this task.

On the question of common accounting standards, different departments with different characteristics may argue that special circumstances require the adoption of special rules. A multitude of special rules will subsequently present difficulties in managing an already complex system.

The introduction of accrual-based accounting will require extensive modification and updating of most management information systems.

The challenges of utilising accrual-based accounting systems for the public service are such that strong support will be necessary from the national professional accounting body.

Achieving change

There are two possible strategies available: the modification of the existing cash-based accounting systems or the introduction of a new tailor-made system.

The existing cash accounting system can be adapted to include accruals and non-cash items, such as capital costs, rentals and superannuation. Supplementary accruals-based information can be produced by memorandum-based trading accounts and capital-asset registers.

This approach may be more practical in large departments where the design and implementation of a completely new system might not be practical within a reasonable time scale.

The introduction of accrual accounting is dependent upon the national accounting profession having established a body of generally accepted accounting practice. The underlying principles and standards must be applied consistently over time and backed up by quality audit assurance.

The questions to be considered prior to adoption of accrual accounting are as follows:

1. Is the accounting system ready for accrual accounting?

This broad issue can be divided into a number of subsidiary questions:

- Has an adequate time frame been established to convert the accounting system from a cash-based to an accrual accounting system?
- Has the Chart of Accounts been revised for accrual accounting?
- Is the fixed asset information available for accrual accounting?
- Have the overhead allocation policies been established for reporting on each significant activity?
- Are the administrative procedures for operating the accounting system defined and efficient?
- Is the existing accounting software likely to present any difficulties in adopting accrual accounting?

2. Do the users understand accrual accounting?

- Has an education programme been established to improve the understanding of accrual accounting statements?
- Are the objectives of introducing accrual accounting clearly established?
- Which groups within the organisation should be included in the education programme?

3. How is the accrual accounting information to be presented and used?

- Will accrual accounting be used for monthly internal management reporting as well as periodic external reporting?
- Will budgeting and management planning use accrual accounting?

The introduction of accrual accounting requires good project planning that addresses the conceptual, technical and educational issues involved. A project timetable and regular monitoring is required, as well as the active involvement of senior staff. Without this involvement, they will neither understand nor use the financial statement prepared on an accrual basis.

Examples of change

New Zealand was one of the first countries to provide government and public sector financial reports which include a balance sheet of assets and liabilities and an accrual-based operating statement of income and expenses.

The introduction of accrual-based accounting was seen as a wide-ranging financial management reform aimed at improving public sector efficiency. The main thrust of these reforms has been towards achieving an output orientation. Key elements of the initiative were delegating decision making, increasing accountability, and improving financial reporting, including through the introduction of accrual accounting.

The Public Finance Act, 1989, required all departments to have an accrual-based accounting system in place within a two-year time frame (before July 1991). In fact this objective was achieved within 18 months, i.e. by January 1991, and in the 1994/5 Budget Estimates, all Crown entities were required to submit accounts prepared on an accrual basis.

The key issues, preparation of an opening balance sheet and determination of accounting standards, were resolved as follows:

* The issue of the balance sheet was resolved by requesting all departments to prepare and maintain a register of major capital assets and liabilities. This exercise included valuations of all main assets and liabilities which were subsequently agreed.

* On the question of accounting standards, the strategy was to use the standards outlined in the Generally Acceptable Accounting Practices of the New Zealand Society of Accountants. The advantages of this were that it avoided the Treasury having to determine precise accounting rules, thus saving time, and it enabled private sector resources to be used.

In the long term, the use of similar rules in both private and public sectors encourages openness and comparison.

In the *UK*, "core non-commercial" elements of the public sector traditionally presented accounts on a cash basis.

However, with the introduction of delegated budgetary responsibilities and the emphasis on efficiency in resource allocation, and in achieving value for money, together with the creation of Executive Agencies under the Next Steps initiative, the need for a refinement of existing accounting arrangements was recognised.

In November 1993, the Chancellor announced the decision, in principle, to introduce resource-based accounting to all non-commercial departments.

Other useful material (current as of 1996)

From Problem to Solution. Commonwealth Strategies for Reform. Managing the Public Service. Strategies for Improvement No. 1. Commonwealth Secretariat, 1995 (ComSec)

McCulloch, B. Accounting and Management Reforms in New Zealand Government. In Administrative and Managerial Reform in Government: A Commonwealth Portfolio of Current Good Practice. Proceedings of a Pan Commonwealth Working Group Meeting held in Kuala Lumpur, Malaysia, 19-22 April 1993. Commonwealth Secretariat, 1993 (ComSec)

The Manager's Deskbook Third Edition. Treasury Board of Canada, 1993 (CAN)

McNally, G. Preparing Accrual-Based Financial Statements, New Zealand Society of Accountants, Public Sector Convention, 1989, Wellington (NZ)

Scott, G. & Ball, I. Financial Management Reform in the New Zealand Government. The Treasury, Wellington (NZ)

Putting It Simply – An Explanatory Guide to Financial Management Reform. The Treasury, 1989, Wellington (NZ)

Efficiency and Effectiveness in the Civil Service. HMSO, London, 1982 (UK)

Financial Management in Government Departments. HMSO, London, 1983 (UK)

Better Accounting for the Taxpayer's Money: Resource Accounting and Budgeting in Government. HMSO, London (UK)

6.4 Focusing on Outputs

6.4.1 Achieving an output orientation

The New Zealand Public Service provides a useful definition of an output:

"An *output* is an identifiable good or service supplied outside an organisation. In the case of government departments, outputs include goods and services for Ministers, other departments, the public and the private sector. Possible types of output include policy advice, the administration of regulations, the provision of services, the production of goods and the administration of grants and benefits. It is important that departments are able to define their outputs in terms of quality, quantity, cost and time."

An output orientation entails moving the focus of accountability towards the goods or services actually produced rather than on the production processes.

In its most developed form, an output orientation requires the restructuring of departmental budget estimates and financial reports so that they are presented in terms of the goods and services produced. More generally, an output orientation is a focusing of managerial concern on the goods and services produced by the public service, while recognising that many financial and reporting systems still concentrate on staff and financial inputs almost exclusively.

This entry describes the issues addressed by the Public Service of New Zealand in restructuring its budget processes; however, this radical development may not be considered appropriate or feasible in other settings.

The context for change

The degree of precision in the specification of outputs varies according to the use to which the information is to be put. The uses of output information are:

* parliamentary accountability;
* Ministerial decision making concerning output purchasing; and
* internal management decision making.

Output-based management may be adopted for various reasons:

* *To improve the capacity of government to scrutinise the output of departments.* Specification of outputs represents a significant improvement in the standard of information available to government.
* *To improve managerial performance.* Associated with the introduction of outputs is the removal of detailed input controls. This gives managers greater freedom to make decisions on the mix of inputs necessary to ensure resources were used to best effect.
* *To enhance departmental accountability, allowing a much clearer statement of what is expected.* The specification of outputs allows Ministers to make more meaningful decisions about what they wish to purchase. It is also easier to judge the efficiency and effectiveness of departmental activity and make meaningful comparisons of performance between departments and the private sector.

Overall, the rationale for an output focus is that it allows a more effective and acceptable relationship between Minister and department. Heads of departments can be held accountable for performance in the delivery of services at an output level, allowing Ministers to assume greater responsibility for the ultimate consequences of government programmes, the outcome.

Reasons for caution

The development of an output orientation rests on a complex set of pre-conditions:

- Output management emphasises increased delegation of responsibility to managers, and the concomitant liberalisation of many financial controls by allowing financial decisions to be taken at departmental or line-management level. Other forms of control are required.

- The existence of a cadre of trained managers, willing, able and qualified to take such responsibility, is an essential prerequisite. The absence of such a cadre will prejudice the success of any reforms.

- Output orientation is intended to deliver increased accountability. It is essential that the appropriate financial reporting systems are in place, both for evaluation and, in view of the liberalisation of financial controls, to permit the strengthening of other forms of control.

- Emphasis on outputs and, in consequence, on performance, will be challenging to managers who have previously seen the public service as based on hierarchy and have taken a procedural view of activities. Confidence-building is essential.

- The implementation of an output-based management system is dependent on the definition of outputs, and the measurement procedures or performance indicators to be applied when evaluating them. It is essential that definition and measurement procedures are clearly understood and are highly practical.

Achieving change

The basic pre-conditions for introducing output-based estimates are:

- departmental accounting systems are able to operate the new procedures;
- the outputs must be aggregated in meaningful clusters; and
- key stakeholders, including Ministers and heads of departments, must recognise the value of the changes.

The introduction of a formal public service system of estimates and reports based on outputs is achieved in a series of stages. It is not realistic to attempt to convert all departments to an output regime at once. Some departments, because of the nature of the services provided, for instance policy advice, are likely to need time to convert.

Departments which receive revenue from third parties, in exchange for particular outputs, also need to be separated into two groups: those where such revenue is immediately directed to a consolidated fund; and those which retain this revenue as part of their appropriation. In principle, identification of outputs and conversion to an output orientation will be easier in the latter.

The outputs themselves must be defined. These will have to be agreed between the department and the central authority driving the reforms, normally the Ministry of Finance. Clearly, output costs will need to be specified with accuracy and precision. In particular, output specifications should include measurable performance indicators, which reflect both volume and quality. Once the specifications have been agreed, the outputs can be included as part of departmental estimates.

Examples of change

In *New Zealand*, the Treasury played a pivotal role in the shift towards an output focus. Departments developed their initial set of outputs through the following steps:

- The department would meet with the Treasury to work through the basic issues.

- These were followed by detailed discussions both with the Treasury and within the department by a steering group reporting to senior management. These discussions would continue until both the Treasury and department agreed on an output specification.

- The agreed specifications were vetted by a quality control panel of senior central agency officials, the purpose of which was to oversee all outputs and develop consistent specification approaches across all departments.

- When cleared by the senior officials, the department would seek endorsement from the Minister, and the Treasury would submit a recommendation to the Minister of Finance that the outputs be issued for inclusion in the Department's annual estimates.

Departments operating under an output orientation are now required to formally produce an annual purchase agreement with their Minister which sets out in considerable detail the exact composition of each output.

In 1990, the Government of *Malaysia* introduced the Modified Budgeting System (MBS). The objective of the MBS is to improve the budgetary process, particularly in relation to accountability, the allocation of resources, and the implementation of programmes by government agencies.

MBS stresses the relationship between inputs, outputs, and the impact of a particular programme or activity. Under this system, government agencies are required to determine their achievement targets in terms of outputs and the impacts of every programme or activity for which there are "programme agreements" between the agency and the Federal Treasury.

In *South Africa*, the Government has introduced the Medium-Term Expenditure Framework which requires departments to link expenditures systematically to strategic aims and, as part of a move away from incremental budgeting of the past, departments will be required to establish clear outputs and priorities, together with key performance indicators, clear monitoring procedures and business plans.

Other useful material (current as of 1996)

Development Administration Circular No. 3. Manual on Micro-Accounting System (SPM) Malaysia, 1992 (MAL)

Scott, G. & Ball, I. Financial Management Reform in the New Zealand Government. The Treasury, Wellington (NZ)

Putting it Simply – An Explanatory Guide to Financial Management Reform. The Treasury, 1989, Wellington (NZ)

Bushell P. Specifying Organisational Outputs, New Zealand Society of Accountants Conference, 1989 (NZ)

Efficiency and Effectiveness in the Civil Service. HMSO, London, 1982 (UK)

Financial Management in Government Departments. HMSO, London, 1983 (UK)

6.4.2 Delegation of financial management

Delegation of financial management is one of the areas of broad strategic choice relating to reforms in government financial management.

Delegation of financial management is taken to involve the transfer of authority for certain financial decisions from central government to departments, sections and agencies. The move to shift more empowerment to the managers is based on a belief that decisions are likely to be more effective and lead to greater value for money if made by the people directly responsible for the provision of goods and services.

Delegation of financial management is one of a number of reforms designed to promote increased accountability and value for money in the public service. It is associated with the introduction of an output orientation, the liberalisation of financial controls, and, in particular, reforms to the budgetary process.

A budget will normally detail expected revenues and expenditure, and can be separated into revenue and expenditure budgets. In the public service, budgets are part of the appropriation procedures when departments outline expenditure plans on which appropriations from public funds are made.

The budget is also an instrument of control. Approval of a budget often determines and fixes the department's operations for the period. Traditionally, public sector organisations have not been allowed to divert expenditure from approved to other purposes, and, at the end of the period, unspent funds are normally returned to the centre. Delegation of financial management is designed to rectify weaknesses associated with this lack of flexibility.

The context for change

As the activities of government have widened and become increasingly complex, the importance of accountability for, and efficient management of, public resources is being recognised.

Reforming the financial management process includes a move towards output-based management, and increased accountability of managers with accompanying liberalisation of budgetary controls. The delegation of financial management is a key element of this procedure.

Delegation of financial management is designed to free departmental managers from the constraints resulting from rigidities in the classification of accounts and in financial management procedures. With increased flexibility and authority to both change budget formats and execute virements between activities under a particular programme, managers will be in a position to take prompt action in the face of changing circumstances, needs and technology.

Reasons for caution

Liberalisation of the budgetary process can render existing financial controls and reporting systems inadequate, enhancing the prospects of unauthorised expenditure.

In order to obviate this danger, changes in the budgetary process must be accompanied by appropriate improvement in control agencies through improved financial reporting and auditing procedures, as described elsewhere in this Portfolio. If reform of the budgetary process is part of a comprehensive plan to reform financial management, then increased liberalisation of controls will be necessarily accompanied by increased accountability and responsibility on behalf of managers.

Achieving change

Delegation of financial management will only achieve success if it is part of a comprehensive and mutually-supporting set of reforms in financial management, of which activity-based costing, output orientation, increased accountability and achieving value for money are central.

Prerequisites for successful delegation include:

- the existence of a central responsible body with the authority to drive the reforms through, and insist on compliance and the resources to offer advice, assistance and training;

- the co-operation of managers and other staff responsible for implementation. This co-operation can be assured through consultation, the empowerment of managers through liberalisation of controls, the availability of appropriate training and, perhaps, a system of rewards for excellence;

- the concomitant development of a comprehensive management information system which permits the accurate recording of transactions, and the subsequent preparation of reliable and informative financial reports.

Any liberalisation of detailed controls must be accompanied by a strengthening of both the internal and external auditing systems.

Delegation of financial management is not only in relation to expenditure. Delegation also has an impact on budget-setting. Traditionally, budgets are developed incrementally. Officers in charge of established programmes justify spending incurred in one year, and develop the proposals for the following year as a series of relatively minor amendments. The underlying spending in question is accepted as necessary.

With the introduction of "zero-based" budgeting, every agency has, on presentation of every budget, to justify the programme entirely as if it were new. This discipline encourages a critical and innovative approach, facilitating output orientation and frequently leading to changes in budgetary procedures.

Examples of change

In 1990, the Government of *Malaysia* introduced the Modified Budgeting System (MBS). MBS is not a simple budgeting system but an integrated and comprehensive management system which involves strategic management, performance measurement, and control systems. It has had important repercussions on the budgetary process itself.

By concentrating on outputs and performance, and on expenditure targets, less emphasis is placed on the "line-item" level, permitting a greater degree of flexibility in financial management. For example, the Controlling Officer in an agency or department is permitted to carry out virements between activities without reference to the Federal Treasury.

In *New Zealand*, the comprehensive measures to implement financial management reform were designed to place increased accountability on management for organisational performance, accompanied by a number of measures designed to encourage output and performance-based management. The latter, in effect, liberalised regulations designed to control financial operations.

In *Singapore*, the Block Vote Budget Allocation System (BVBAS) was introduced in 1989. BVBAS is a computerised system; one of its features is to give Ministries a generous measure of autonomy in the management of voted funds, thus encouraging managers, in this case Permanent Secretaries, to manage more flexibly.

In *Lesotho*, since 1987, the Ministry of Finance has been involved in a new financial management approach for the government. Part of this programme includes a new, less controlled and more decentralised budget system. Eventually this process of decentralisation will enable managers to be responsible for their own budget control.

Other useful material (current as of 1996)

From Problem to Solution. Commonwealth Strategies for Reform. Managing the Public Service. Strategies for Improvement No. 1. Commonwealth Secretariat, 1995 (ComSec)

Budget Flexibility: Carryover Provisions between Financial Periods. MAB-MIC Publication Series. Australian Government Publishing Service, Canberra, 1994 (AUS)

The Manager's Deskbook. Third Edition. Treasury Board of Canada, 1993 (CAN)

Financial Management Manual for Managers and Senior Mangers in the Lesotho Government, 1993 (LES)

Scott, G. & Ball, I. Financial Management Reform in the New Zealand Government. The Treasury, Wellington (NZ)

Putting It Simply – An Explanatory Guide to Financial Management Reform, The Treasury, 1989, Wellington (NZ)

Fiscal Responsibility Act: A Brief Overview. Treasury Briefing Note. New Zealand Treasury, Wellington, 1994 (NZ)

Efficiency and Effectiveness in the Civil Service. HMSO, London, 1982 (UK)

Financial Management in Government Departments. HMSO, London, 1983 (UK)

6.5 Improving Management Systems

6.5.1 Restructuring and classification of accounts

Restructuring and classification of accounts is one of a number of reforms designed to promote improved financial management, increased accountability and value for money in the public service. It is particularly associated with reforms to the budgetary process.

The budget is the formal expression of expected or estimated financial activity for a particular period. A budget will detail expected revenues and expenditure, and is prepared when departments outline expenditure plans on which appropriations from public funds are made.

The line-item approach, specifying in detail activities to be undertaken during the budget period, and the pressure to maintain comparability year by year, encourages rigidity in budget formats and in the classification of accounts.

The context for change

The budgetary process is a key financial tool in financial management and control. It is an extremely flexible document which can be easily adapted to changes in circumstances and to different time scales. This means that it is appropriate to both capital projects and to operating or running costs.

Budgets can be expressed both in terms of inputs and outputs, and facilitate the measurement, evaluation and comparison of organisational or project performance. At the end of the budget period, or at any convenient point within it, planned objectives or outputs can be compared with actual performance, and variance analysis techniques applied.

However, without periodic review and reform, the budget can become an inhibiting factor. The line-item approach becomes fixed and leads to undesirable inflexibility. When controls simply measure or check attainments against planned activities, the process can become more important than the objective it was intended to achieve.

Without increased flexibility and authority to change budget formats, managers will not be in a position to take prompt action in the face of changing circumstances, needs and technology.

Restructuring and classification of accounts in which the existence, number and order of the budget items is changed to encourage innovative thinking and to reflect changing circumstances, is a key element in reforming the budgetary process. It must be seen in the context of:

- *delegation of budgetary responsibilities* – a liberalisation of financial controls giving managers authority and flexibility to move funds from one part of a programme to another, in effect "transfers" between items of expenditure within programmes or departments; and,

- *an emphasis on outputs* – the costed goods and services which the budget enables departments to produce.

Reasons for caution

If budgeting formats are subject to change in different periods, comparison and variance analysis exercises become increasingly difficult. This difficulty can be reduced if the focus of the budget becomes based on outputs and performance rather than on the activities undertaken.

The budget should not be simply a process of listing requirements. It should be also be a management tool linked to internal auditing procedures within departments.

In general, improving the budgetary process should be closely allied to changing the style of management in the public sector from a focus on processes to an output orientation, with emphasis on delegation to, and accountability of, managers.

Achieving change

Any radical change to the structure and classification of accounts will require co-operation, support and input from both the Ministry of Finance and operating departments.

To secure these, a Committee should be set up on which the Treasury and Public Accounts, Ministry of Finance or analogous bodies, operating departments, and other interested jurisdictions are represented.

As it is likely that no single classification system will provide for all coding requirements, a multiple-classification system, with multiple levels of detail within each classification should be developed from the outset.

The effectiveness of any system will depend on individual transactions being properly identified. This will require, as a minimum, a two-fold classification linked to an integrated coding system which requires each transaction to be identified both by nature and source.

The two-fold classification will:

- **identify the nature of transactions** – This classification should provide a breakdown of all of the transactions of each Ministry and department, and each cost centre, to the level of basic line objects where the operations, processes, services, projects, tasks, etc., are identified. These should identify, at various levels of aggregation, the purposes for which funds are spent to achieve their objectives or the sources of revenues received.

  This will provide a coded listing of accounts which are used to record revenue, recurrent expenditure, capital expenditure and below-the-line transactions. Each of these account types should be divided into categories, and these are further divided into standard objects.

  Each standard object consists of a number of line objects, which are the lowest level at which all expenditures are coded, and are therefore the building blocks of the standard object and category classification.

- **identify responsibility for accounts** – The organisational classification ranges from the highest level of managerial responsibility and identifies who is responsible and accountable for spending public funds.

  The organisational classification culminates in a Ministry or departmental vote, which provides the basis for the vote structure by which the legislature appropriates funds.

  At the top of the structure is the Ministry or department which is identified in the estimates by means of a recurrent vote and which is divided into a number of cost centres.

A cost centre is defined as a major programme or activity of a Ministry or department and can be further divided into responsibility centres. A responsibility centre is a sub-section or division within a major programme or activity where there is a manager who is accountable for a budget.

Any new system should be piloted in a sample department prior to implementation. Full implementation should be preceded by the publication of a coding manual with extensive explanatory notes, and by an intensive training programme for departmental accounting officers.

The introduction of a new structure of accounts will have to be accompanied by the development of management information systems based on the new format and should be accompanied by a strengthening of both the internal and external auditing systems.

Examples of change

In *Kenya*, the Office of the Accountant General, under the Treasury, is responsible for developing and evaluating the appropriate accounting systems and procedures to facilitate efficient financial management in Ministries and departments.

The Accountant General is therefore responsible for the planning, co-ordination, design, implementation and control of accountancy systems in the Civil Service, which, together with the accompanying financial regulations, are constantly reviewed and updated.

In *Malta*, the accounting system had been modified to the point where there was no longer an underlying structure that addressed the reporting needs of operating departments, Ministries, the Treasury or the Legislature. Accounting codes were not well understood, nor were they applied consistently, and the resulting financial accounts were generally unreliable for management information services. The boundaries between major types of expenditures depended on local circumstances where the decision to identify a particular financial transaction as operational and maintenance, as special expenditure, or as capital expenditure, was flexible and often arbitrary.

To resolve this problem, a Committee of Advisors was established comprising representatives from both the Treasury and Public Accounts process in the Ministry of Finance, operating departments, and other jurisdictions.

A multiple-classification system, with multiple levels of detail within each classification was developed. A two-fold classification was linked to an integrated coding system which required each transaction to be identified both by nature and source. The two-fold classification consists of a chart of accounts classification to identify the nature of transactions, and an organisational classification to identify responsibility of accounts.

The new system was piloted in a sample department prior to implementation, which was fully implemented in the 1993 Estimates. Full implementation was preceded by the publication of a coding manual with extensive explanatory notes and an intensive training programme for departmental accounting officers.

Development of management information systems based on the new format was concomitant with the design of the new system, and was implemented in February 1993. Codes for recording and reporting transactions according to the new chart of accounts and organisational codes will be used in the Departmental Accounting System.

Other useful material (current as of 1996)

Current Good Practices and New Developments in Public Service Management. A Profile of the Public Service of Malta. The Public Service Country Profile Series: No. 6. pp. 119–122. Commonwealth Secretariat, 1995 (ComSec)

From Problem to Solution. Commonwealth Strategies for Reform. Managing the Public Service. Strategies for Improvement No. 1. Commonwealth Secretariat, 1995 (ComSec)

6.5.2 Introducing flexible budgeting

Flexible budgeting describes the procedures under which departments are enabled to carry forward part or all of the funds allocated to them in a particular period.

In most Commonwealth countries, established financial management practices include the principle that resources, particularly those used for administration running costs or ongoing programmes, are allocated until the end of the financial year, after which any excess or unspent funds are returned to the central authority.

The context for change

One consequence of the growth in public expectations and the consequent pressure on the resources of the public service has been the introduction, in the public services of many Commonwealth countries, of a range of public management reforms, emphasising the need for increasing cost-effectiveness and improving the quality of outputs. Liberalisation of the regulatory and control functions under which public sector resources are used, combined with strengthened accountability for results, has been a key device for improving efficiency.

Traditionally, funds unspent by the end of the year are forfeited and returned to central funds. One of the more deleterious effects of this is the encouragement it offers for spending surges at the end of the financial year as departments seek to disburse unspent funds, resulting in poor purchasing practices.

By allowing excess or unspent funds, or a proportion of them, to be carried forward, managers are encouraged to seek value for money by timely, well-planned and appropriate purchasing.

Reasons for caution

The forfeiting of excess funds at the end of the financial year was intended to discourage departments from seeking resources in excess of their requirements. It is arguable whether the inability to carry over funds has provided a significant downward pressure on the demand for funds, but the concern must remain that allowing flexible budgeting removes one aspect of financial discipline.

Flexible budgeting allows the possibility of concealing known areas of potential savings, with a view to establishing or creating resources to be used for other possibly unauthorised purposes at a later date. Amongst such other dangers, the practice of retaining excess funds in departments can be a misuse of public resources which, if not held by a department, might have been put to alternative uses or returned to the taxpayer in the form of reductions in taxation.

The practice of end-of-year flexibility is contingent on the introduction of other reforms in financial management, in particular, reforms of the budgetary process and of the financial reporting systems. Where implementation is feasible, the introduction of accrual-based accounting enables management to assess precisely the degree of underspend.

An overall prerequisite to the introduction of this reform is the existence of a cadre of managers willing and confident to undertake the range of financial reforms of which end-of-year flexibility is only one.

Achieving change

End-of-year flexibility must be part of the package of financial management reforms which include the general liberalisation of control features to permit a degree of freedom in the application of funds to specific projects. If managers are permitted to make transfers under particular circumstances, then carrying forward funds from one year to another follows naturally.

Commonwealth experience indicates that the principles underpinning the procedures for such flexibility are:

- underspends should first be used to offset overspends in other areas before any carry-over is permitted;

- carrying forward administrative and running costs is to be discouraged;

- carrying over of any funds must be justified in terms of clearly set out criteria;

- the pattern of funds carried over must be monitored in order to give guidance to departments or managers who are allowing project slippage to develop consistently; and

- external and internal audit procedures must be strengthened to reflect the greater flexibility provided to departments.

While technically, the introduction of end-of-year flexibility is through simple legislative procedure and regulatory changes, in most cases it has been preceded by pilot programmes and introduced in stages.

Accrual-accounting systems assist in focusing attention on the medium and longer term, rather than on the present accounting period, encouraging managers to think beyond putative deadlines for expenditure.

Examples of change

In *Australia*, carry-over provisions were introduced as part of the running-cost system in 1987-88. Key features of the scheme are:

- the amount of running costs to be carried over is restricted to a limit defined in percentage terms (e.g. 3 per cent in 1990-91); and

- borrowings must be paid back before further borrowings are allowed.

Experience indicates that use of the facility was considerably less than originally anticipated, and a number of best practice areas are suggested:

- The facility is devolved to the appropriate programme together with the authority to spend and certainty about future years' allocations.

- Financial planning and management should be at programme level on the basis of firm forward estimates.

- Formal planning and reporting systems should include a Board of Management or similar mechanism to oversee budget allocations, performance and outcomes.

- Systematic and ongoing training for programme managers.

In *Malaysia*, there are two types of budget: an operating budget, and a development or capital budget. A Department's operating budget consists of two items: Charged Expenditure authorised by the Federal Constitution, which does not require annual appropriations from Parliament; and Supply Expenditure, which requires annual appropriations voted by Parliament.

The development or capital budgets are administered through Development Funds created under the Development Funds Act 1966. They are approved by the Economic Planning Unit of the Prime Minister's Office and controlled by the Ministry of Finance. The mechanism for administration of development projects is associated with the management of five-year plans, and provides for the review of all annual plans and budgets at half-yearly, or more frequent intervals, when requests for funds are submitted. This system in itself is extremely flexible and in effect ensures the existence of end-of-year flexibility.

Operating budgets are subject to the Financial Procedures Act which stipulates that any funds appropriated for a particular process should be surrendered to the Consolidated Fund if not spent in the period for which they were granted.

In *Canada*, under the reformed budget regime introduced in 1993-94, departments were originally authorised to carry forward two per cent of their operating budget from one fiscal year to the next; a provision which has been increased to five per cent. Procedures were based on a pilot scheme which operated successfully in 1992-93.

The entitlement to carry forward is granted automatically, based on lapses reported in the Public Accounts. Capital funds amounting to five per cent of a capital vote can also be carried forward subject to acceptable justification to the Treasury Board and affordability considerations.

In the *UK*, in principle, money voted for one specific year has had to be spent during that year; if it is not spent, it has traditionally been forfeited. To minimise this restriction, there are now two specific end-of-year flexibility schemes covering capital expenditure and running costs.

In the first scheme, in operation since 1983, departments have been allowed to carry forward into the next financial year any underspending of eligible capital expenditure. Departments have been encouraged to delegate end-of-year flexibility to line or project management level.

The scheme allows for a roll-over of five per cent to be carried over, but any capital underspend must first be used to cover any overspend in other parts of a cash limit. Roll-over in subsequent years is possible subject to strict rules and ceilings.

The Running Costs Scheme, introduced in 1988, is also intended to assist departmental management and budgeting; carry-over is limited to one-half per cent of the year's running cost limit or £50,000, whichever is the greater, and as with capital, any underspend must first be used to offset any excesses elsewhere in the budget. The percentage limit may be revised upwards.

In *South Africa*, the Government has introduced the Medium-Term Expenditure Framework (MTEF) which gives departments more stable resource allocations, projected for five years, which are linked to a rolling-planning process. One of the aims of MTEF was to facilitate the introduction in 1996/7 of multi-year budgeting.

Other useful material (current as of 1996)

From Problem to Solution. Commonwealth Strategies for Reform. Managing the Public Service. Strategies for Improvement No. 1. Commonwealth Secretariat, 1995 (ComSec)

Budget Flexibility: Carryover Provisions Between Financial Periods. MAB-MIC Publication Series. Australian Government Publishing Service, Canberra, 1994 (AUS)

Fiscal Responsibility Act: A Brief Overview. Treasury Briefing Note. New Zealand Treasury, Wellington, 1994 (NZ)

Scott, G. & Ball, I. Financial Management Reform in the New Zealand Government. The Treasury, Wellington (NZ)

Putting It Simply – An Explanatory Guide to Financial Management Reform. The Treasury, 1989, Wellington (NZ)

Efficiency and Effectiveness in the Civil Service. HMSO, London, 1982 (UK)

Financial Management in Government Departments. HMSO, London, 1983 (UK)

The Manager's Deskbook. Third Edition. Treasury Board of Canada, 1993 (UK)

6.6 Financial Management

One component of the holistic approach to Knowledge Management is the reforms relating to *Financial Management*. Financial records arise from transactions or events. These transactions or events relate to customer service interactions and are important measures of performance. Records are fixed, have authority, are unique and are authentic. They are an important part of public sector accountability.

Government is accountable to its citizens and the rendering of accounts to public scrutiny is critical to achieving accountability requirements. The keeping of these records is fundamental to public administration and is critical to financial management. Financial records are the product of doing business and they provide evidence that:

- resources have been received, committed or spent;

- assets have been acquired or disposed; and

- agencies have liabilities.

These records also form the basis for the preparation of annual financial statements. Effective financial management systems provide managers and politicians with the means to:

- monitor and manage resources; and

- strengthen accountability.

Financial management systems need records as inputs to generate outputs. Financial management is the umbrella under which institutions process transactions. Components of financial management systems are often regulatory and scrutinised by the Public Accounts Committee; the Auditor General and the Ministry of Finance. Components of the system also include budgeting, accounting, and internal audit. Information management is central to financial management and includes:

- receiving information;

- processing information; and

- managing information.

These processes constitute the procedural control framework of the organisation whereas support services to financial management include information and communication technology (ICT), human resources and knowledge management.

New Zealand, for example, as part of its reform efforts has specifically focused on financial management. In fact, accountability was built into the system and was not an afterthought. In some countries, the trend has been to move from "making managers manage" to "letting managers manage", by holding them accountable for what they do, spend and accomplish. This has not been the case in New Zealand, where making the manager responsible for his/her performance has been a guiding principal. This is an effort to improve the efficiency and quality of public services. New Zealand gives managers enormous freedom to act, but they closely monitor their financial and substantive results. The most distinctive features of the New Zealand approach to reform have been:

- performance and purchase agreements;

- appropriation of resources by output classes;

- a split between funds voted to Ministers and money provided to departments; and

- accounting and budgeting on an accrual basis.

The concern in other countries is that not enough attention is paid to accountability whereas in New Zealand the complaint is that the cost of maintaining the accountability regime is too high.

There needs to be a balance, however, between whether accountability has more to do with:

- a purchase than with ownership;
- producing outputs than with the overall capacity of the departments; and
- managers meeting targets than with public programmes being effective.

This is aggravated by the distinct focus on outputs.

CAPAM, in its continuing role in providing information to government officials, academics, and senior managers has developed a curriculum for Financial Management and Control. The six components of the programme include;

1. Setting the Framework

- Reforming financial management systems focuses on the protection and maintenance of assets along with purchasing in terms of value for money. Other aspects include accountability, budgetary processes and change drivers such as rates of return, cash limits and output-based management.

- In order to achieve value for money, governments must consider three concepts:
  1. minimising the costs of resources (Economy);
  2. increasing outputs (Efficiency); and
  3. increasing impact (Effectiveness).

2. Improving Planning and Budgeting

- To achieve strategic orientation, the public sector must set and define the budget process in terms of strategic plans and objectives; set purchase agreements in relation to outputs; develop budget initiatives (impact analysis); and approve budgets with a view for the next two years.

- In order to link short, medium and long-term plans, governments will need to put into place change drivers such as ten-year fiscal projections; a budget process that spans a three-year cycle; and strictly defined priorities and outputs. The system cannot be so rigid that decision makers are not able to change priorities and mix outputs within approved baselines.

- The budgetary relationships between centres and departments should be such that they can negotiate between themselves yet determine and agree upon outputs. In addition, Chief Executives should have in place purchase agreements that define key results.

3. Improving Management of Inputs

- The introduction of capital charging includes the ability to define government debt and equity capital; calculate charge rates linked to the capital base and the introduction of accrual-based accounting

- Improving estate management relies on obtaining an objective and informed view of the department's asset base; increased management performance in terms of physical assets; a review of asset inventory to determine validity and the need for or surplus of assets; and the cost of maintenance.

- Two basic approaches to improving asset management include the ability to communicate that poor purchasing leads to unnecessary and uneconomic acquisitions; and that the focus on spending for asset creation needs to shift to the use and management of assets to support the efficient provision of services

- Procurement is the overall process of acquiring goods and services to meet customer needs. Improvements in the procurement process, with the emphasis on value for money, is a key mindset in achieving cost effectiveness and improving the quality of outputs.

4. Improving Management Information

- The introduction of accrual-based accounting differs considerably from cash-based accounts. Accrual accounts show:
  - as assets, the value of amounts due but not yet paid to the government for goods and services or taxes levied;
  - as liabilities, the value of amounts due but not yet paid by the government for goods and services or taxes refundable;
  - reports on non-cash assets; and
  - the inclusion of non-cash liabilities.

- The restructuring and classification of accounts is one of a number of reforms designed to promote improved financial management, increase accountability and value for money. It allows managers to be creative in organising their budget process and accounts for reporting. Managers must however be able to identify the nature of their transactions and who is responsible for accounts before creating the new structure of accounts.

- Introducing flexible budgeting allows managers to carry forward part or all allocated funds into another period. Traditionally unspent funds are reallocated into a central fund. By allowing carry-overs this allows the manager the flexibility to make timely well-planned and appropriate purchasing decisions.

- Using activity-based costing allows government to trace individual costs back to the primary activities which led to them being incurred. It also allows for the tracking of indirect and fixed-cost items.

5. Improving Management Systems

- The achievement of an output orientation means moving the focus of accountability towards the goods and services actually produced rather than on the production process. Government needs to adopt an output orientation to improve the capacity to scrutinise the outputs of departments; improve the managerial process; and enhance departmental accountability through clearer statements of expectations.

- Delegation of financial management and control empowers managers to be more effective and leads to greater value for money. This is achieved if the people directly responsible for the provision of goods and services are given that authority.

6. Improving Financial Accountability

- In order to improve financial reporting, reports need to: be in accordance with generally accepted accounting practices (GAAP); be prepared on an accrual basis; include performance measures; and done on a regular, scheduled basis; be GAAP-based and include audited financial statements.

- By strengthening internal audits, management can be assured that there is objective reporting on ongoing infrastructure changes and on the effectiveness of allocated resources. The appropriateness of outcomes should not be part of an internal audit.

- Through the strengthening of external audits, taxpayers can be assured by an independent authority as to the integrity of public finances and also ensure that value is being achieved in public spending.

Other useful material (2nd edition)

International Records Management Trust, "Principles and Practices in Managing Financial Records: A Reference Model and Assessment Tool". London, U.K., March, 2001

Schick, Allen, "The Spirit of Reform: Managing the New Zealand State Sector in a Time of Change". A Report prepared for the State Services Commission and the Treasury, New Zealand, Wellington, New Zealand, 1996.

CAPAM Curriculum, "Financial Management and Control". Toronto, Canada, 2002.

6.7 Auditing and e-government

The transformation from traditional government to e-government will be one of the most important policy issues of this century. It runs to the heart of how governments operate and interact with the community. Auditing is a central management function that ensures this accountability to citizens and their representatives. This is particularly important as governments enter increasingly complex service delivery arrangements which have been made more possible through e-government innovations and technologies.

Accountability is a relationship between two parties. The contract is between the public and those who have been elected. The concept is fundamental to the democratic system. It establishes the right of all citizens to know what government intends to do and how well it has met those objectives or goals. The real issue for the auditing function is accountability. The simplest explanation of accountability is the requirement to answer to somebody for something. Therein lie the seeds of possible confusion, conflict and often public recrimination.

Auditing is essential because the general public wants to be assured that whatever is done in their name is done properly. That is, it is done according to the law and with reference to the community standards of economy and probity at the time. Democratic societies are at least entitled to that assurance. There are at least two basic elements to this accountability question:

1. What does the public expect? and

2. How does it satisfy itself that its expectations are met?

The public asks: Wasn't someone looking after things to make sure that those responsible were doing what they should have been? Where were the auditors? Where were the regulators? Why didn't they prevent it?

The context for change

First, public discontent is most often expressed at times when emotions are running high. That is, we often hear about a concern only after something has gone seriously wrong. The second point is that there is a great deal of public confusion about the role and power of the auditing function.

Auditors are required to maintain the principles which guide their actions and decisions. However, the reality is that the environment in which they operate is constantly changing, which means they need to adjust to those changes and even be part of them.

In reviewing the performance of Commonwealth agencies, it is relevant for the auditor to examine the implementation of any decision plus the advice provided to Ministers by the relevant agencies in the course of government consideration of a policy decision. Is the advice in accordance with relevant policies and does it represent value for money? In many Commonwealth countries there has been a move beyond value-for-money audits to more comprehensive performance audits. This is a particularly important shift in light of the challenges e-government presents. A performance audit can provide a strategic overview and evaluation of the current positions of the public sector in their implementation of e-government.

The primary goal of the auditing function is to contribute to the improvement of accountability and performance in the public sector. Currently, the audit function is working through the following lines of business:

- attesting to the reliability of the financial statements of the government;
- assessing the quality of the government's service plans and reports;
- examining how the government manages its key risks; and
- supporting legislators in the use of information regarding government performance.

New approaches

We can expect to see an emergence and consolidation of new modalities of accountability in the evolving public/private interface and in the context of e-government. One example is the so-called Triple Bottom Line (TBL). The current construct of accountability in the business world, including government operations, is on the threshold of a major paradigm shift. Public and other stakeholder expectations in an increasingly globalised business and communications environment will provide the drivers for a shift away from a traditional input-output based model of accountability towards a focus on economic prosperity, environment quality and social justice.

TBL goes beyond the current orthodox focus on financial performance, the utilisation of inputs, the disposition of outputs, and probity to also take into account the environmental and social consequences of business activity. This view is supported by the passage of "right-to-know" legislation.

TBL reporting could lead to changes to the manner in which public sector organisations report performance and discharge their accountability to their citizenry. The concept of sustainability requires new definitions of performance and the re-articulation of organisational goals. An important aspect for the public sector is the management of reputations, which is an all-pervasive issue for performance assessment. A degree of "trust and confidence" is essential for a sustainable future, particularly where the general public is placing some value on corporations meeting broader environmental and social goals. The situation is reinforced where there are increasing partnerships between the public and private sectors.

There is still a long way to go before TBL reporting has the rigour that characterises financial bottom-line reporting. In these circumstances there is also a particular challenge for those responsible for auditing this form of reporting, particularly where the evidential links are limited. This is an additional challenge for performance measurement and the qualitative assessment of government programs and services.

All public sector organisations are required to be transparent, responsive and accountable for their activities. Citizens are entitled to know whether public resources are being properly used and what is being achieved with them. Consistent, clear reports of performance and publication of results are important to record progress and exert pressure for improvement. Such transparency is essential to help ensure that public bodies are fully accountable and is therefore central to good governance overall. E-government will assist in the distribution of reports and the publication of results. E-governance will allow for citizen input or feedback related to these reports and results.

There are implications of the changing nature of accountability and with the greater involvement of the private sector in the provision of services to, and in particular for, the public sector. This phenomenon has been variously described, under many headings, for example new public management, the purchaser-provider model and entrepreneurial governance. The latest emphasis has been on Public-Private Partnerships (PPP) for service delivery. The changing environment goes further with the greater emphasis on partnering and networking, between and across organisations, involving all levels of the government and sectors of the economy.

Reasons for caution

Put simply, the challenge becomes to identify who is accountable for what. There is a continuum of accountability relationships between the electorate, Parliament, the Government and the public service. However, the ongoing difficulty is to define such relationships in a credible manner that is acceptable to all those parties. Fundamentally, the clearest accountability goal is adherence to the rule of the law.

The challenges for the audit function include a range of issues associated with the greater involvement of the private sector in public sector activities, including notions of partnership; collaboration; networking; and the notion that e-government activities are of growing importance to agencies within the public sector.

Other issues to which the Auditor needs to form opinions and advise on in this e-government environment include:

- contract management;
- record-keeping in a more networked environment;
- privacy and security versus openness and transparency in both the public and private sectors;
- administrative law considerations in a contractual framework;
- equity law and natural justice;
- values and ethics; and
- governance issues.

The objective should be to recognise these challenges and find a balanced framework to ensure that auditing can contribute to improvements in accountability related to e-government programmes and initiatives. The United Kingdom government for example expressed concern that an over-emphasis on accountability would stand in the way of an appropriate risk management environment in which innovation could flourish.

The Public Audit Forum (UK) responded by stating that:

"Public sector managers are of course responsible, as stewards of public resources, for assessing and managing the risks associated with innovation and increased flexibility, and for ensuring the proper conduct of public business and the honest handling of public money while pursuing innovative ways of securing improvements in public services. It remains important to ensure proper accountability but this must not be approached in a rigid way which might mean missing opportunities to deliver better value for money."

The Forum outlined that auditors will respond to this new environment positively and constructively by:

- adopting an open-minded and supportive approach to innovation; examining how the innovation has worked in practice; and the extent to which value for money has been achieved;
- supporting well thought through risk-taking and experimentation; and
- providing advice and encouragement to managers implementing modernising government initiatives by drawing on their audit work in this area and by seeking to identify and promote good practice so that experience can be shared and risks minimised.

In these ways, it is believed that auditors can support and encourage worthwhile change, while providing independent scrutiny and assurance and fulfilling effectively their statutory and professional responsibilities.

Another challenge is the assessment of the performance of regulatory bodies which pose particular problems for the public auditor. As a general rule, their activities are usually highly technical in nature, and the organisations themselves are sometimes the only source of credible audit expertise.

Risk management

The debate about the responsibilities of external auditors and audit committees has raised the audit profile in both the private and public sectors. The importance of risk management has also entered the management framework in many public sector organisations. Within an audit framework, the suitability of the risk management and an overall governance framework to provide accurate and timely information on key risks is a central issue of control. As such, it is of considerable strategic and operational interest for any audit committee and external audit.

In particular, risk management must address:

- the need to buy expertise (related as much to the range of skills within the Office as to the need for an extended knowledge of the corporate world);
- the quality of data that is gathered – given the size of the project, it is not audited data, but relies on the data supplied by agencies;
- the range of diagnostic tools available and their relative strengths and weaknesses;
- the differences between the environments in which the individual agencies must operate;
- the size and complexity of the project management task; and
- the need to achieve and maintain co-operation with the agencies concerned.

Benefits can flow from a risk management exercise through to policy makers, public sector managers and audit authorities. The benefits can include:

- clear specific criteria for future audit activity and other avenues of assessment;
- credible information on which to base decisions on whether to perform functions in-house or to contract out;
- where functions are to be contracted out, clear and credible performance criteria to be included in tender and contract documentation;
- performance evaluation standards for management to help identify under-performance and reward excellence;
- the benchmarks developed through this method are already being used in other jurisdictions, leading to greater uniformity of performance expectations; and
- in the context of service charters mentioned elsewhere they can help provide for more credible communication with clients or citizens.

In New South Wales, Australia, the Audit Office has developed a "Better Practice Guide" which is designed to assist agencies and government to meet the challenges of exploiting benefits and managing risks with e-government. The Guide specifically focuses on issues at the baseline agency level – the frontline staff and managers. The purpose of the Guide is to assist government Ministries/departments/agencies in being "e-ready". Managing the transformation to e-government will not happen by chance or overnight. It will be difficult and it will require a careful and managed effort.

The 'Guide' includes:

- better practice principles;
- risks to be managed;
- a checklist on performance; and
- HELP references.

The content in the Guide is organised into eight subject areas:

1. Leadership and Governance;
2. Funding;
3. People;
4. Legal;
5. Customer Readiness and Accessibility;
6. Privacy;
7. Security; and
8. Technology and Information Management.

The public sector can leverage off the experience and approaches taken by the private sector in many areas of benchmarking and performance management. However, there are requirements in the public sector environment which are different and need to be treated as such. Partnership arrangements have to recognise this reality and adjust to it. It is not a one-way street. Auditors can facilitate both the understanding and resolution of management, accountability and performance issues.

Opportunities can be taken to be more responsive and improve performance while minimising risk. Fundamentally, good governance arrangements increase:

- participation;
- strengthen accountability mechanisms; and
- open channels of communication within, and across, organisations.

Well-structured governance frameworks will enhance the development of suitable networks and partnerships and facilitate risk management. Private sector frameworks may provide guidance for public sector organisations. By using such frameworks, the public sector can be more confident about delivering defined outcomes and being accountable for the way in which their results are achieved.

Other useful material (2nd edition)

Barrett, Pat, "The Role of Watchdogs in the New Era of Partnerships." International Public Administration Australia National Conference – Beyond Traditional Boundaries, Sydney, Australia, 2001.

The Audit Office of New South Wales, "e-government: Using the Internet and Related Technologies to improve Public Sector Performance." Auditing E-Government Report, September, 2001. www.audit.nsw.gov.au

The Audit Office of New South Wales, "Performance Audit Report – e-government- Executive Summary." Auditing E-Government Report, September, 2001. www.audit.nsw.gov.au

The Audit Office of New South Wales, "Better Practice Guide: e-ready, e-steady, e-government." Auditing E-Government Report, September, 2001. www.audit.nsw.gov.au

Office of the Auditor General of British Columbia, "Service Plan 2002/03 – 2004/05." www.bcauditor.com

Tennessee Valley Authority, "The IIA Government Auditors Forum." Presentation at the International Internal Auditing Forum, June, 2001. www.oig.tva.gov

Desautels, Denis, L., "Public Sector Auditing in Canada and Shifting the Audit Focus to Results." Address Notes by the Auditor General of Canada to the Institute of Public Administration Canberra, Australia, 1997. www.oag-bvg.gc.ca

7.0 Improving Policy Making

7.1 Policy Development

7.1.1 Enhancing policy analysis

Policy analysis refers to the entire range of activities through which policy is developed and provided. In ideal terms, this starts with an appraisal of the options before consulting with interested stakeholders and subsequent decisions and implementation. This ideal cycle is completed with the evaluation and reappraisal of policy outcomes.

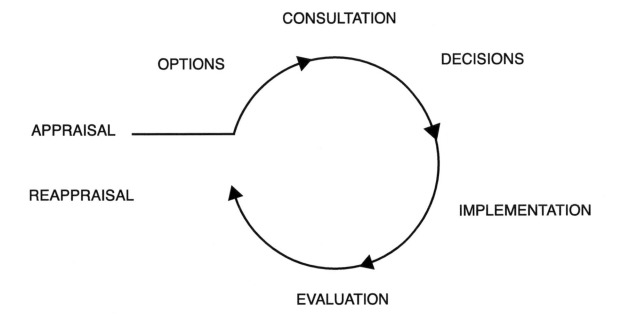

Policy-making cycle

Policy analysis is not a one-dimensional activity. Political imperatives and changing circumstances do not always allow for measured consultation, and evaluation is clouded by conflicting objectives contained within the same policy. Determining policy is a political prerogative, but the policy analysis process is fundamentally constrained by the ability of the public service to conceive and implement policy options. Improving that capacity implies a review of structures and systems within the public service, but equally it requires an improvement to the context within which the public service operates. In particular, it requires an improvement in the partnerships that the public service can establish to ensure fresh thinking in policy appraisal, and informed support though consultation.

The context for change

The pressures for policy change are growing. Continuing fiscal difficulties and growing consumer demands have placed governments under pressure to do more with less. The global spread of new ideas about how government should operate, the breadth of its role, and the style of its management and structures, have accelerated the pace of innovation. Few areas of social or economic policy remain constant.

Within that climate of accelerating change, the difficulties faced by the public service are increasing in some key areas.

- Policy appraisal

In identifying appropriate policy options at a time of rapid change, a balance must be maintained between innovation and consolidation. In preparing policy options for political consideration and for consultation:

- public service experiences in implementing current policies must inform the debate without constraining it to simply more of the same;

- innovations must be considered without allowing untested novelty to overwhelm experience;

- cross-cutting implications for other policy areas, which are themselves also facing rapid change, must be assessed.

- Consultation

The White Paper or equivalent consultative stage must ensure that policy options have credibility for stakeholders and affected groups. While acceptability to stakeholders is a complex and largely political judgement, credibility is a function of adequate research, coherent assessment of the capacity of the public service to administer the policy change, and a clear understanding of international policy trends. This last point is of particular significance in relation to donors and lending institutions and is one impetus for the publication of this Commonwealth Portfolio.

- Advising on policy selection

Aligning fast-changing policy developments across different sectors presents particular challenges. Recent managerial changes within the public service, with departments and units more single-mindedly pursuing business objectives, adds to the challenge of co-ordination.

Reasons for caution

Policy analysis is not an easily defined and well-bounded activity. In focusing on the need to strengthen the policy analysis capacity of the public service, there is a risk of policy overload resulting from the accumulation of too many policy directives with inadequate consideration of implementation difficulties. Discredited initiatives form a poor foundation for further policy developments.

A strengthened policy analysis capacity can result in a faster flow of policy proposals, when what is required is a more targeted and more considered series of initiatives.

Enhancing policy analysis capacity will highlight existing tensions between officials and politicians, particularly where these relate to inconsistent political leadership. Focusing on the policy analysis capacity of the public service may expose existing areas of difficulty.

Achieving change

There are four elements to any strategy for enhancing policy analysis capacity:

1. Identify policy as an output

In developing business plans and in agreeing objectives, Ministries, departments and other units within the public service must recognise policy analysis as an important output with identified targets concerning quality and timeliness.

2. Strengthen central policy analysis bodies

Policy co-ordination requires a central body, capable of identifying policy developments across sectors and departments. Traditionally, this has been achieved by strengthening the offices of the Prime Minister or President, or the Cabinet machinery. Corresponding changes at Ministerial level include the establishment of parliamentary committees. Such bodies take a particular responsibility for monitoring that policy developments are in line with the overall national plan.

3. Improve the climate of policy debate

Policy analysis requires a mix of consolidation and innovation, of respect for existing public service perspectives, and of conviction that outputs can be improved. The balance can only be achieved by establishing an open climate of policy debate in which private and NGO sector interests, academic bodies and service providers can contribute to a broadly-based discussion.

4. Improve skills

There are particular skills required for public policy development:

- benchmarking approaches which assess the trade-off between price and quality in the purchase of policy advice;

- application of analytical tools; and

- the use of quality indicators to monitor policy outputs.

Enhanced policy analysis capacity may require systematic staff exchanges between policy units to share current approaches, and more specific training in qualitative and quantitative policy analysis.

Examples of change

In *Malaysia*, at the national level, policy analysis and evaluation is undertaken by the Economic Planning Unit of the Prime Minister's Department. The Macro and Evaluation Division of this Unit evaluates the impact of government policies on the quality of life and on the economy.

In *New Zealand*, in July 1991, the Minister of State Services directed the State Service Commission to review the provision of policy advice from government departments. One outcome was the handbook entitled, Policy Advice Initiative – Opportunities for Management, designed primarily for use by policy managers as a reference source and as a quick tool for assessing particular policy issues. Efforts to improve the quality of policy advice are ongoing.

In *Tanzania*, Policy Analysis and Research Units have been created in all Ministries in order to assemble all policy-oriented personnel in one organisational unit in a Ministry.

A particular initiative in improving policy analysis and co-ordination in *Trinidad and Tobago* has been the establishment of Standing Committees. Cabinet has established four Standing Committees for Energy, Agriculture, Tourism and Industry, and Services, to advise on sectoral policies and to oversee and co-ordinate the development of major projects on these sectors. These committees are chaired by the Prime Minister and comprise a mix of Ministers, senior public servants and private sector personnel with expertise and interest in these areas. The relevant Ministries function as the Secretariat for the Committees.

Within the *UK* Government, policy analysis and evaluation is being given greater emphasis and more systematic attention as part of the Financial Management Initiative and the drive to improve Civil Service management and accountability generally. They form one aspect of a broad stream of management changes introduced in recent years. Recent developments that reinforce the importance of policy evaluation work include:

- the top-down approach in the Public Expenditure Survey;
- the more strategic relationship between the Treasury and departments; and
- fundamental reviews of programme expenditure.

Other useful material (current as of 1996)

Strategic Planning and Performance Management in the Public Service, Report of a Regional Workshop for the Small States of the Caribbean, Antigua, 29 May-2 June 1989. Commonwealth Secretariat, 1989 (ComSec)

Enhancement of Public Policy Management Capacity in Africa: Report of the High-Level Working Group Meeting, Mahe, Seychelles, 24-27 September 1990. Commonwealth Secretariat, 1990 (ComSec)

From Problem to Solution: Commonwealth Strategies for Reform. Managing the Public Service, Strategies for Improvement Series: No.1. Commonwealth Secretariat, 1995 (ComSec)

Review of the Purchase of Policy Advice from Government Departments. State Services Commission, 1991, Wellington (NZ)

The Policy Advice Initiative – Opportunities for Management. State Services Commission, 1992, Wellington (NZ)

Efficient and Effective Policy. AIC Conferences, June 1993, Wellington (NZ)

Managing Quality Policy. AIC Conferences, March 1994, Wellington (NZ)

HM Treasury, Policy Evaluation: A Guide for Managers. HMSO, London, 1988 (UK)

HM Treasury, Economic Appraisal in Central Government: A Technical Guide for Government Departments. HMSO, London, 1991 (UK)

7.1.2 Enhancing policy co-ordination

All governments face the issue of how best to co-ordinate their business. One particular mechanism for *enhancing policy co-ordination* across government found in many Commonwealth governments is the Cabinet Office System.

The Cabinet Office serves Cabinet and the network of Cabinet committees which between them consider and endorse government policies. Departments with significant policy initiatives are required to clear them through the appropriate committee. The secretariat support is provided by the Cabinet Office. There is generally also a network of official committees serviced by the Cabinet Office, dealing with the day-to-day cross-departmental co-ordination of policy.

The Cabinet Office and similar systems are designed to ensure that all policies are carefully examined for possible cross-departmental implications (including public expenditure implications) before they are endorsed. Committee membership is drawn from a wide range of departments, including all those with a direct interest in the area of policy in question.

The context for change

At a time of rapid and accelerating social and economic change, weaknesses in policy co-ordination can be seen by:

- policy conflicts and inconsistencies;
- abrupt reversals or changes in policy; and
- wasted resources.

Policy co-ordination is weakened by:

- lack of trust between the senior policy makers, including the political leadership and the other paticipants in the policy arena;
- lack of clear definition of organisational roles among co-ordinating institutions;
- conflicting agendas of line Ministries and departments;
- an over-emphasis on confidentiality and a weak climate of policy debate with little opportunity for participation from private and NGO sector interests, academic bodies, and service providers.

Reasons for caution

Over ambitious policy co-ordination mechanisms can result in policy paralysis. Cabinet Office or other mechanisms for co-ordination must impose a framework on proposals which identify the anticipated outcome of the policy initiative – What is to be achieved by when? At what cost? and How are the results to be monitored? Although essential, this is a demanding agenda for line Ministries preoccupied with pressing operational problems.

Co-ordinating units must ensure that their work is pro-active, providing a facilitating service to the line Ministries from which proposals are originating, ensuring that the limited capacity of the unit is not overstretched. Policy co-ordinating units do not only have negative responsibilities for preventing policy conflict, they have a positive responsibility for ensuring continuing flows of high quality policy advice.

Achieving change

Strategies to improve policy co-ordination cover the following areas:

- The primary responsibility for good co-ordination lies with the department initiating a Cabinet paper. Departments should ensure that they consider all the implications for other government agencies and consult them at the earliest opportunity when preparing a Cabinet submission.

- The actual process of consultation needs to be tailored to the complexity of the issue, the resources available, and the deadline to which departments are working.

- When the views of other departments are summarised, this must be done accurately.

- Departments should certify, generally using a set form, to the satisfaction of their Minister, that they have consulted all government agencies with an interest in the issue and that the views of those organisations are reflected properly in the paper.

- The role of Cabinet or other parliamentary committees must be clear and focused.

Examples of change

In *Australia*, the roles of Cabinet Committees have been clarified and focused to enable Government Ministers collectively to assess developments without an overload of detail.

The *Kenyan* Government has set up an Efficiency Monitoring Unit in the Cabinet Office with a mandate to study and advise the government on problems encountered during the implementation of development policies, programmes and projects, suggesting remedial measures, and carrying out the necessary follow-up. This Unit recommends to the implementing Ministries or departments and ultimately to the government, the use of the most cost-effective methods of implementing development programmes and projects, and suggests improvements in the existing methods of monitoring their implementation.

In *New Zealand*, significant improvements have been made in policy co-ordination. The single Department of The Prime Minister and Cabinet (combining the policy advice role of the Prime Minister's Office and the Cabinet servicing role of the Cabinet Office) was created in 1990 as a means of improving policy co-ordination. A number of Officials Committees are also in operation to service virtually all the key Cabinet Committees. The practice of having departmental officials attend most Cabinet Committee meetings has the advantage of allowing officials greater understanding of Ministerial objectives and expectations.

In *Trinidad and Tobago*, the Cabinet has established four standing committees in the priority areas of Energy, Agriculture, Tourism and Industry, and Services, to advise on sectoral policies and to oversee and co-ordinate the development of major projects in these sectors. The private sector/public sector combination on these Committees is intended to facilitate the exchange of ideas between the two sectors, enhance co-operation with respect to policy development, and improve the implementation of major projects.

Other useful material (current as of 1996)

Enhancement of Public Policy Management Capacity in Africa: Report of the High-Level Working Group Meeting, Mahe, Seychelles, 24-27 September 1990 (ComSec)

From Problem to Solution: Commonwealth Strategies for Reform. Managing the Public Service. Strategies for Improvement Series: No.1. Commonwealth Secretariat, 1995 (ComSec)

Ongoing Reform in the Australian Public Service: An Occasional Report to the Prime Minister by the Management Advisory Board. Australian Government Publishing Service, Canberra, 1994 (AUS)

Manual. 1991, New Zealand Cabinet Office, Wellington (NZ)

The Problems of Policy Co-ordination: The New Zealand Experience. Governance. Boston, J. January 1992 (NZ)

7.2 Communicating Policy

7.2.1 Improving policy presentation

Policy presentation and consultation with the public is achieved through:

- paid publicity and advertising campaigns;

- press and information services which respond to media interest and provide appropriate briefings; and

- personal communication from key officers addressing meetings and stakeholders with an interest in new developments.

The broad purpose of policy presentation strategies is:

- to create and maintain an informed public;

- to harness all suitable publicity methods; and

- to sound out public opinion on policy changes and service developments.

At a time of rapid change both in policy objectives, and in the machinery of the public service, policy presentation strategies assume a particular significance.

The context for change

The responsibilities of the public service are changing rapidly. Governments are less involved in direct service provision, and more in regulatory oversight. The public service is increasingly judged on the basis of explicit service standards rather than on its adherence to traditional methods of operation. Partnerships with private sector organisations and NGOs are being strengthened.

The public is being asked to relate to a public service which has changed its structures, systems, and responsibilities significantly in a short time. At this time of rapid change, communication with the public regarding new policy directions is particularly crucial.

Reasons for caution

Policy presentation requires more than simple announcements. Strategies for responding to the media and for communicating with the public must pay attention to the need for follow-up. Unless the policy presentation strategy can deal promptly and accurately with media criticism, and with the need for longer-term information and sensitisation campaigns, little will have been gained.

Achieving change

Improvements in policy presentation strategies require:

- the involvement of information officers at an early stage in policy formulation;

- a strengthened professional information resource, with trained staff capable of managing shifting relationships with the media;

- channels of communication which provide information officers with a good understanding of emerging developments throughout the public service;
- the management of targeted information distribution lists; and
- comprehensive monitoring of relevant media for comments on government policy.

Poor policy presentation is more easily identified than good practice. However, policy presentation is made possible, if not guaranteed, by ensuring that information officers have the capacity to manage:

- press notices, briefings, and conferences;
- interviews with Ministers;
- photo calls;
- the production of articles to go out over the Minister's name; and
- paid publicity campaigns.

Examples of change

In *Canada*, each department is responsible for putting in place its own communications group and for ensuring good communications with its public. In addition, some co-ordination on communications issues is provided by a Communications Consultation Secretariat within the Privy Council Office. Policy guidance is provided through an Information, Communications and Security Division within the Treasury Board Secretariat. Communications activities must meet Treasury Board guidelines on "no-frills" publishing which calls for the streamlining of Government publishing and the creation of a uniform "look" for materials. It aims to achieve information products that are economical, well designed, environmentally sound, and that communicate effectively.

Amongst the various types of communication is the Federal Identity Programme intended to achieve clear and consistent identification of its institutions and to assist the public in recognising and gaining access to federal programmes and services.

In *Kenya*, the Ministry of Information and Broadcasting is responsible for gathering and disseminating information in the public service through such media as television, Kenya News Agency, radio, Kenya Gazette and the newspapers. The Offices of the President and Vice-President both have Press Units to cover day-to-day official functions. In each Ministry, press releases are issued by either the Permanent Secretary, the Minister, or any other officer authorised by the Permanent Secretary. The government requires each Ministry or department and Civil Servants to act as public relations agents of the government in the day-to-day operations.

In *Malaysia*, the Ministry of Information is generally responsible for policy presentation. Public Relations Officers from the Department of Information under the Ministry are stationed in various Ministries and departments to ensure that official news and information are released through press releases; press conferences, interviews with Ministers and/or senior officers, and special launchings.

The Government of *Trinidad and Tobago* has recognised that to improve policy presentation a Communications Strategy is needed which outlines objectives, targets and means. This Strategy focuses on three issues:

- the circulation of information to the relevant sections of the public;
- in a hostile media environment. the development of "an alternative system" of information dissemination, i.e. an alternative to the national media; and
- the institution of mechanisms to receive specific feedback from the public.

Other useful material (current as of 1996)

From Problem to Solution: Commonwealth Strategies for Reform. Managing the Public Service. Strategies for Improvement Series: No. 1. Commonwealth Secretariat, 1995 (ComSec)

A Guide to Good Communications Management. Treasury Board Secretariat, March 1992 (CAN)

The Manager's Deskbook. Third Edition. February 1993. Treasury Board of Canada (CAN)

Treasury Board Manual. Communications Volume, available from Supply and Services Canada (CAN)

Planning Information Products: Effective, No-Frills Publishing Practices. Treasury Board Secretariat, November 1993 (CAN)

Alternative formats: Access for All. Government of Canada, December 1993 (CAN)

7.3 Political and Administrative Roles and Responsibilities

A critical issue in modern democratic governance is how to establish the appropriate mix of roles and responsibilities or interface between bureaucracy and elected officials or between politicians and Civil Servants in policy development. Historically the interface between bureaucracy and democratic rule has long been turbulent, ambiguous and controversial. Getting the relationship right is vital for effective government and for better delivery of services to the people.

The need to define management roles, the desire for improved support services for decision makers (politicians) and the quest for meaningful and effective allocation of duties and responsibilities among public officials, have all been central and critical to efficient government.

The formal relationship under discussion is specifically between the elected official (Minister) and senior Civil Servant variously known as Permanent Secretary, Principal Secretary, Deputy Minister, Director General, Chief Director, etc. The core issues in the formal and functional relationship in policy making are managerial influence, power, authority, responsibility and accountability. Traditionally and in the Westminster type of government, the Minister is responsible for policy development while the Permanent Secretary is responsible for management and the implementation of policy.

The implementation of government reforms and new policy requires that the two sets of officials develop a meaningful and positive interface, which contributes to the achievement of government goals, objectives and policies. The fundamental questions that are often raised in this interface relate to the right mix of relationship, the critical factors that can contribute to a more meaningful and effective political administrative interface, role differentiation and the implications for service delivery to citizens.

The context for change

Improving the interface in policy development and management is predicated upon the need to respond effectively and efficiently to the:

- emerging problems and issues in the management of administrative reforms of the public service;

- need to re-define the roles and responsibilities of the Minister and the Permanent Secretary in an attempt to meet the expectations of the public or consumers of public policy;

- identification of policy and administrative boundaries between elected and appointed officials; and

- development and sharing of the best practices, processes and procedures of enhancing the interface.

The roles and relationships between politicians and Civil Servants have to be clearly delineated. One of the most recent developments in the interface is the introduction of political or special advisers to the Minister. This added layer of officials has been seen in many countries as necessary in order for the politician to implement public policy with a mixture of advice from bureaucrats and a political party official who is not elected but serves at the pleasure of the Minister.

Redefining the management roles between the politician and the bureaucrat within the public service is a key strategy in improving not only efficiency in government but also delivery of service by the state. Redefining management roles and clarifying boundaries between bureaucrat and politician in a democracy seeks to address the following concerns:

- The growing prominence and power of bureaucracy poses important problems in a democracy because it means that non-elected officials have greater opportunities to influence policy, potentially in ways that disregard public preferences. This in turn makes the task of elected officials especially important since they must oversee the bureaucracy, infuse it with democratic preferences and make it accountable to democratic process;

- The formulation of an appropriate mix or optimal mix between elected and non-elected officials becomes important because it determines the extent to which the policy machinery of government reflects predominantly the preferences and values of elected officials or the preferences and values of public servants that are not elected;

- The conflict between politics and administration derives from more than the growth of the administrative state and the increased knowledge and skills needed to deliver modern government services. The different values, perspectives and concerns of politicians and public servants fuel the conflict that often arises between them. The values emanating from democratic politics and elected officials include responsiveness, accountability, short term perspective, revitalisation or modernisation, power, conflict, compromise and change. These contrast with the values of bureaucracy, which include non-partisanship, professionalism, continuity, expertise, experience, problem-solving, long term perspectives and effectiveness; and

- The pressures on the state to respond to the needs and demands of the public, to respond to market forces and to comply with rules. Citizens are demanding new approaches to good governance, better and more effective and efficient methods of service delivery, conflict management and improving skills and knowledge with which to deliver the services.

Reasons for change

Improving the functional relationship between the politician and the public servant has been driven by:

- the demands for change in policy development and public management practices in order to improve service delivery;

- the need to change organisational structures to adapt to the social, political and economic environment within which public management operates. Within the public service reform agenda, particular attention is given to openness, accountability and good governance whose dynamics are based on leadership skills and purposeful goal-setting;

- the political and administrative changes that are taking place sometimes without precedents and sometimes without rules, or codes of conduct;

- the new skills, knowledge, technology and information required for leadership;

- the political and economic liberalisation programmes resulting in the transformation of practices, behaviour patterns and the demands from a larger public for better quality of service. Paralleling these changes, civil society has a desire to participate in the formulation of public policy and new forms of managing conflicts. Both have brought to the fore the need to draw boundaries and build bridges between bureaucracy and elected officials;

- the problems of maintaining a politically neutral Civil Service in a highly political atmosphere and occasional fears of politicisation of Civil Services. Also the contrary, the bureaucratisation of the politician; and

- political interference in administrative matters.

Achieving change

In terms of achieving the "right" relationship between elected officials and bureaucratic officials, the Commonwealth experience suggests there are promising approaches: redefining and clarifying both managerial and policy roles.

Redefining managerial roles

Commonwealth experience indicates that in redefining management roles and delineating the political and administrative boundaries in policy development and management:

- Clear distinction must be made on the separation of powers between politicians and public servants;

- Principles should be formulated to guide the allocation of functions and responsibilities of Ministries of Public Service or Personnel;

- Roles of political advisers should equally be made clear to both the politician and public servants to avoid conflict and duplication of functions;

- Functions of Cabinet Secretaries or the Head of the Civil Service are to be clearly defined; and

- Boundaries between policy making and implementation should be clearly separated.

These guidelines are based on the following fundamental principles:

- Elected officials bring with them authority endorsed by the democratic process in which parliamentary elections are held periodically. They also bring the skills of political leadership and the ultimate responsibility to account to the legislature for what has been done or not done;

- Appointed officials bring proven ability, knowledge and experience, and status derived from being appointed on merit. They have an obligation to put their ability and knowledge to work in support of the Minister and the responsibility to account either directly or through senior officers, to the relevant Ministers, to parliament or provincial legislature as required and to the public for performance of their departments.

A more recent development in the political and administrative interface is the appointment of political advisers by Ministers. The appointment of political advisers is a tactic used by Ministers to achieve greater political responsiveness from the bureaucracy. The rationale for this strategy is that the persons appointed directly by Ministers are more likely to work to further the political goals of the Minister, thus achieving a greater degree of responsiveness from the bureaucracy.

In the United Kingdom, for example, in 2001, each Minister was allowed to have two political advisers on staff. They are political appointments by the Minister and are not Civil Servants (although they could be Civil Servants on leave of absence). Nor are they party political appointments. Political advisers are of two types:

1. Expert advisers who give briefings with which a Minister may check or challenge official advice.

2. Generalist advisers mainly as political aides-de-camp.

Many governments based on the Westminster model tend to develop a protocol of good governance in which codes of conduct for Ministers and Civil Servants are established. The codes should be seen in the context of the duties and responsibilities of members of the executive wing of government, which are generally set out in a handbook. The codes and guidelines vary from one country to the other.

Role of the Minister:

- Provide vision and policy direction;
- Oversee and monitor policy implementation;
- Secure Cabinet support or resources;
- Represent the Ministry in Cabinet;
- Account publicly for the performance of the Ministry;
- Take collective responsibility for Cabinet decision; and
- Be a change sponsor.

Role of the Permanent Secretary:

Three basic roles of the Permanent secretary:

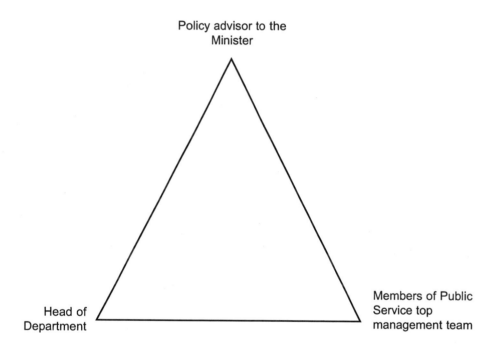

Other Significant Roles:

- Inform and advise elected officials accurately;
- Implement policy and Ministerial decisions efficiently and effectively;
- Be fully accountable to the Minister;
- Co-ordinate, control, manage and communicate with other departments;
- Be a change agent and utilise all relevant sources of data and advice so as to give the Minister the broadest possible bases for policy considerations;
- Manage finance, human resources, technology and other resources;

Both the Minister and Permanent Secretary must fulfil these roles in complex accountability environments. Both have multiple accountabilities and both are involved in the agenda setting stage of the policy making process.

Minister's Environment and Agenda Setting

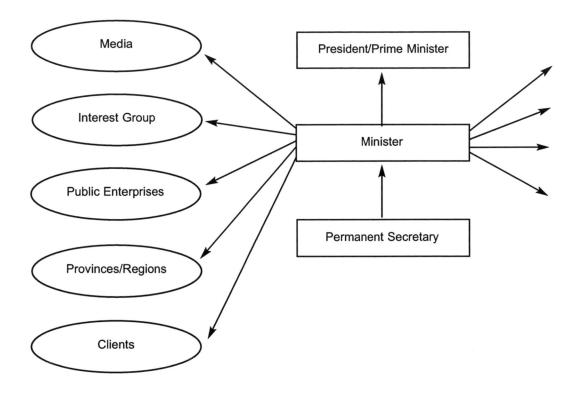

Permanent Secretary's Environment and Agenda Setting

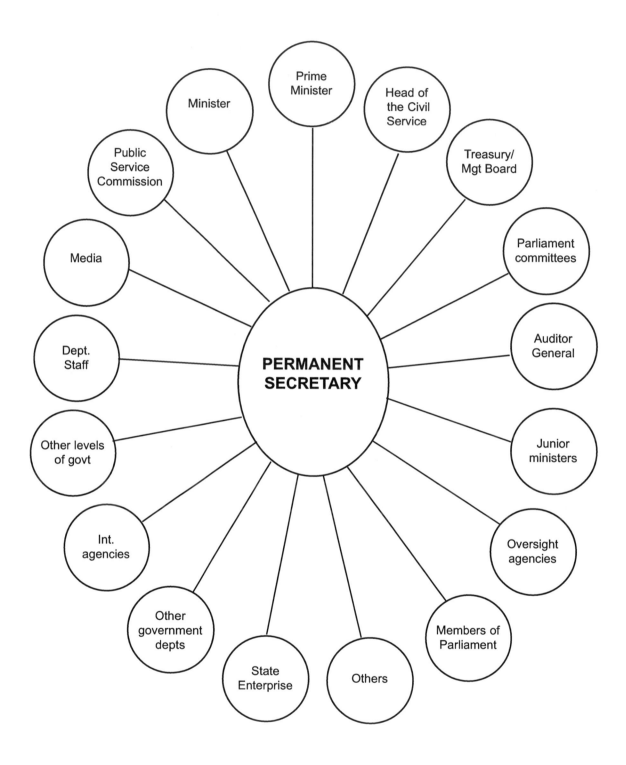

Role of the Cabinet Secretary:

- Provides, as the Prime Minister's or President's Permanent Secretary, advice and support to the Prime Minister on a full range of responsibilities as head of government;

- Provides support and advice to all Ministers and oversees the provision of policy and secretariat support to Cabinet and Cabinet Committees;

- Is responsible for the quality of expert, professional and non-partisan advice and service provided by the public service to the Prime Minister;

- Is Chairperson of a committee of Permanent Secretaries; and

- In some countries, has a say in the careers of Permanent Secretaries as the Prime Minister is usually guided by his or her advice in the nomination of Permanent Secretaries.

Skills for the Permanent Secretary

- Communication skills: ability to present a case clearly and effectively;

- Negotiating skills: crucial for presenting department's case in negotiating with other Ministries especially the Treasury;

- Administrative skills: to get through the huge volume of paperwork e.g. delegation;

- Skills of decision: knowing when to act or when to accept advice;

- Interpersonal and management skills; and

- Strategic vision and strategic management skills.

Who measures the performance of the Permanent Secretary?

The performance of the Permanent Secretary is measured differently in different countries. In some countries the Public Service Commission does most of the performance appraisal that would result in promotion, transfer, and dismissal. While in other countries, performance measurement is done by both the Public Service Commission and Cabinet Secretary and recommendations are forwarded to the Prime Minister. More recently and notably in Canada and the UK, the Cabinet Secretary, in consultation with the Minister of a given Ministry, processes the performance of the Permanent Secretary. In Canada the appraisal has seven basic elements:

1. The Clerk of the Privy Council (Cabinet Secretary) first meets with the Permanent Secretary to discuss objectives for the upcoming period. The objectives upon which measurement is based are divided into three categories for future evaluation: departmental objectives, corporate objectives and leadership and human resource management objectives;

2. At the end of the period, the Permanent Secretary prepares an assessment of his or her performance against the objectives agreed earlier. Performance is measured on a five-point scale;

3. The Cabinet Secretary meets with appropriate Minister to discuss the performance of the Permanent Secretary;

4. The Cabinet Secretary meets with certain other key officials, including the Head of the Public Service Commission and the Head of Treasury Board to solicit views;

5. Based on these interviews, the dossier of the Permanent Secretary is brought before a committee of senior officials to discuss and assess his or her performance;

6. Based on the assessment of the committee of senior officials, the Prime Minister makes a final decision with respect to promotion, demotion, etc, and in consultation with the Clerk of Privy Council makes decisions regarding performance pay; and

7. The Cabinet Secretary meets with the Permanent Secretary to review the comments and decisions made as well as to discuss objectives for the coming year (Peter Larson, 1999).

Role of Political Advisers

- Can, unlike Civil Servants, advise the Minister from a political party perspective;
- Can handle relations with the party, write briefs on departmental policies for government backbenchers and deal with constituency matters;
- Can act as an unofficial channel between their Minister and the press;
- May help the Minister with public appearances; and
- Within the departments they comment on papers going to the Minister and advise him or her on political rather than administrative dimensions of policies and feed in new ideas.

Developing the management relationship

A few governments, on being elected into office, opt for a series of activities geared to preparing Ministers and parliamentarians for office as well as to improving the relationship with appointed officials. The interventions take the following forms:

- A three day orientation programme for all parliamentarians which focuses on issues such as the legal environment of the public service, approaches to managing Ministers, media relations and the parliamentary system;
- Cabinet holds a series of teambuilding activities, which focus on managing relationships with the Civil Service, and the performance of Ministers;
- Ministers submit regular reports on the performance of Ministries in the achievement of objectives; and
- Governments conduct retreats for Ministers, Permanent Secretaries and chief executives of public enterprises.

Some countries organise orientation courses for Ministers in order to ensure a smooth transition upon being elected into office. The key objectives of the orientation programme are to enhance the Ministers' understanding of:

- The key dimensions of a Minister's job;
- The party programme;
- How to structure a Minister's office, notably the appointment of Ministerial staff members;
- The policy-making process, including the structure of Cabinet and Cabinet Committees;
- The proper relationship between a Minister and the professional public service;
- How to deal with the media and lobbyists; and
- How to achieve a balance between work and family.

Management programmes for Permanent Secretaries

Many countries have placed emphasis on developing senior and top managers in the Civil Service. Some countries have put in place conditions which must be met before an official is promoted to a Permanent Secretary. One such condition is that the official should have attended minimum courses on management designed by a national management training institute. In general courses for Permanent Secretaries have included the following competencies:

- Intellectual competencies: the cognitive capacity and creativity of a Permanent Secretary to understand and respond in a strategic manner to the complexities of management in the public sector;

- Future building competencies: capacity to see beyond the single departmental issues to the larger context of public management development;

- Management competencies: Permanent Secretaries must be action-oriented individuals who have the intellectual capacity to anticipate and cope with the short, medium and long term consequences of their strategies. Permanent Secretaries must also understand the inner workings of government, the public service and key players. Teamwork is also an important management competency;

- Permanent Secretaries must be capable of effectively interacting with public and private sector individuals, supervisors, peers and subordinates. They must have excellent interpersonal skills; and

- Personal competencies: must have the ability to sustain high energy levels and resist stress under the ongoing pressures of protecting the public interest.

Political and administrative interface challenges

The challenge is to:

- Develop agreement on goals and roles;

- Build trusting and productive relationships;

- Recognise that management styles will differ;

- Recognise that Ministers often come to their jobs with no relevant training or experience;

- Develop an interface characterised by integrity, professionalism, openness and learning; and

- Identify boundaries between policy formulation and management.

Possible approaches to facilitating the interface

- The strategic planning process: the process facilitates the establishment of a shared vision and clear objectives of the Ministry;

- Regular meetings: regular meetings between elected and appointed officials would provide opportunities for dialogue and feedback and provide a forum within which the relationship could be developed and improved;

- A system to evaluate Permanent Secretaries: a clear and objective system of measuring the performance of a Permanent Secretary could improve the relationship;

- Management development of Permanent Secretaries: the identification of appropriate competencies and skills for Permanent Secretaries ought to provide a basis for their selection and training. Appropriately equipped Permanent Secretaries could go a long way towards ensuring that they play their part in nurturing a healthy and productive relationship;

- Coaching and mentoring: both Ministers and Permanent Secretaries could benefit from systems of coaching and mentoring; and

- Development of codes of conduct: clearly stated codes of conduct for both Ministers and Permanent Secretaries and guidelines for their conduct could also be useful in facilitating the interface.

Examples of facilitating the interface

In the *UK*, the Government established a new Centre for Policy Management Studies (CAMPS) as part of imparting managerial and leadership skills to top Civil Servants;

In *Grenada*, the Commonwealth Secretariat facilitated a weekend intervention that included the Prime Minister and his Cabinet colleagues, and all Permanent Secretaries and all political advisers. The Commonwealth Secretariat has also facilitated such seminars in *St.Kitt's & Nevis*, and *St Lucia*;

The *Barbados* Government also utilised a retreat setting to bring together parliamentarians and senior public servants for focus on, among other issues; the appropriate relationships between elected and appointed officials;

In 1998, *Swaziland* held a retreat for Ministers and Permanent Secretaries to discuss political and administrative interface problems;

In *Sierra Leone*, after the democratic elections, the Commonwealth Secretariat and Department of International Development (DIFD) facilitated a retreat for Ministers, Permanent Secretaries, and Chief Executive Officers focusing on policy management and improving their relationship;

In 2000, the *Bermuda* Government had a two-day retreat for Ministers and Permanent Secretaries facilitated by Commonwealth Secretariat officials; and

In 2001, *Namibia* held a retreat for Ministers and Permanent Secretaries on development.

Other useful material (2nd edition)

Dunn, D. Politics and Administration at the top: Lessons from Down Under, Pittsburgh Press, 1997.

Agere, Sam (ed) Redefining Management Roles. Improving the Functional Relationships between Ministers and Permanent Secretaries. Managing the Public Service Strategies for Improvement Series: No 10, Commonwealth Secretariat, 1999.

Draper, G. The Caribbean Experience, 1999. CAPAM Practice Knowledge Centre.

James, Simon, The British Experience, 1999. CAPAM Practice Knowledge Centre.

Larson, Peter, The Canadian Experience, 1999. CAPAM Practice Knowledge Centre

Plowden, W. Ministers and Mandarins. Institute for Public Policy Research, 1994.

Civil Service Reform: Report to the Prime Minister from Sir Richard Wilson, Head of the Home Civil Service, published by Cabinet Office (UK)

CAPAM High Level Seminar for Cabinet Secretaries. Cambridge University UK. A report by Sandford Borins, Sept 1997.

Eddie Teo, Permanent Secretary (Prime Ministers Office) Singapore 2000.

Dennis Osborne, Governance, Partnership and Development, 1999.

Kevin Theakston, Permanent Secretaries: Leadership as Conservation 1999

Rudy B Aneweg, Advising Prime Minister, 1999.

Wade Mark, The New Public Administration: A re-examination of the political and administrative interface: CAPAM Biennial Conference 1998, Malaysia.

John Hilligan, Comparing Relations between Politicians and Public Servants in four countries: Transformation or Re-affirmation CAPAM Biennial Conference 1999, Malaysia.

Canadian Center for Management and Development: Treasury Board: The Leadership Network, 2000.

APPENDIX

i) Useful Commonwealth Websites

COMMONWEALTH REFERENCE	URL
1. South African Government Online	www.gov.za
2. South African Government Information	www.polity.org.z/nguindex
3. Uganda Revenue Authority	www.uganda.co.ug/home.html
4. Prime Minister's Office – Mauritius	Ncb.internet.mu/pmo/index.html
5. The Republic of Namibia	www.grnnet.gov.na/intro.html
6. Public Service & Merit Protection Commission – Australia	www.psmpc.gov.au
7. Singapore Government Online	www.gov.sg
8. eCitizen: Government Services – Singapore	www.ecitizen.gov.sg
9. eCitizen Singapore	www.ecitizen.gov.sg/main.html
10. Government of Malta	www.amgnet.mt/welcome
11. Federal Government of Australia	www.fed.gov.au/ksp
12. Government of Canada	www.canada.gc.ca/howgoc/howeind_e.
13. The Republic of Ghana	www.ghana.gov.gh/sitemap.html
14. Government of Saint Lucia	www.stlucia.gov.lc
15. International Institute of Administrative Sciences	www.iiasiisa.be/iias/aiace.html
16. New Zealand Official Development Assistance (NZODA)	www.mft.govt.nz/nzoda/nzoda.html
17. The World Bank Group	www.worldbank.org
18. Transparency International	www.transparency.org
19. Departments of the UN Secretariat	www.un.org.depts/
20. HM Government – UK Online	www.toolbar.e-envoy.gov.uk
21. Welcome to the DfID Website	www.drif.gov.uk/main_content.html
22. UNPAN – Global Online Network on Public Administration and Finance	www.unpan.org
23. The World Bank Group – Administrative and Civil Service Reform	www.worldbank.org/publicsector/ civilservice/index.html
24. European Foundation for Management Development	www.efmd.be/main.html
25. The Australian Government's Overseas Aid Programme	www.ausaid.gov.au
26. Canadian International Development Agency	www.acdi-cida.gc.ca

COMMONWEALTH REFERENCE	URL
27. Commonwealth Business Council	www.cbcd.to
28. Commonwealth Broadcasting Association	www.cba.org.uk
29. OECD	www.oecd.org
30. International Headquarters of the Royal Commonwealth Society	www.resint.org
31. Commonwealth Heads of Government Meeting	www.chogm2001.net
32. National Library of Australia	www.nla/gov/au/oz/gov/federal.html
33. Commonwealth Local Government Forum	www.clgf.org.uk/pages/wavl.html
34. Commonwealth Parliamentary Association	www.comparlhg.org.uk
35. Commonwealth Writers Prize 2002	www.commonwealthwriters.com
36. The Commonwealth Foundation	www.commonwealthfoundation.com
37. The Commonwealth Institute	www.commonwealth.org.uk
38. The Commonwealth of Learning	www.col.org
39. The Commonwealth Secretariat	www.thecommonwealth.org

ii) Overview of CAPAM's Practice Knowledge Centre© (PKC)

Since its inception in 1994, CAPAM has been developing a database of documents and materials concerning excellence in public sector administration and management. CAPAM holds this evolving collection of materials under the title "Practice Knowledge Centre"© or PKC.

These materials are gathered from the 27 CAPAM Affiliates, from the 80 CAPAM Institutional members, from CAPAM pan-Commonwealth, regional and country-based conferences and seminars, and through CAPAM's membership spread through 80 countries worldwide.

CAPAM has been using these documents as teaching materials in the CAPAM Senior Public Executive Seminar, a programme delivered on both a customised in-country basis and on an annual "generic" basis. Since 1995, CAPAM has sent a selection of these materials, on a quarterly basis, to CAPAM Institutional members and Affiliates as part of its service to these members.

The materials have been divided into the following broad **subject** categories:

A. Overview of Public Sector Reform

B. Human Resource Management and Development

C. Organisational Change and Partnerships

D. Information Systems and Standards of Service

E. Financial Management and Control

F. Policy Development

A brief overview of the materials that comprise each subject collection follows. Please note that the collection of documents included within each subject area is continuously augmented and recorded in the PKC database. Also note that <u>all</u> of the submissions to the CAPAM International Innovations Awards Programme, to date held in 1998 and 2000, are available through the PKC.

A. Overview of Public Sector Reform

By far the largest collection of articles in the CAPAM PKC falls within the category of "Overview of Public Sector Reform". The 430 documents under this subject heading include case studies, (such as A Case Study of Program Review in Agriculture and Agri-Food Canada), proceedings of conferences, (such as the National Symposium on Civil Service Reform in Tanzania), a commentary on the new Public Service Act in Australia and whether the Act represented an end to the Westminster tradition as presented at a conference in Australia, and speeches such as that given by a senior South African provincial public servant concerning the sub-national governments in that country. Within this topic there are also papers on the sub-topics **ethics and corruption**, and the **political administrative interface**.

The articles, speeches, case studies and other documents on this subject are drawn from such diverse sources as: the Public Service Commission of Australia; CAPAM Institutional Members; the African Association for Public Administration and Management; the CAPAM Biennial conferences held in Malaysia in 1998, in Malta in 1996, and in Canada in 1994; the conference celebrating the 50th anniversary of the journal *Public Administration and Development* (PAD) held in 1998; and the journal of the Public Management and Policy Forum of the United Kingdom.

The materials in this section of the PKC are used to support a module in the CAPAM Senior Public Executive Seminar on this precise topic. The module sets out the rationale for reform (why, what, how, when, etc., together with the principles and criteria which will govern the reform process in its particular setting) and outlines the reform process.

B. Human Resource Management and Development (HRM&D)

The HRM&D section of the CAPAM PKC contains over 200 recent articles and speeches, the vast majority of which were written within the last two years. They cover such topics as leadership challenges for the public sector, reward strategies, motivation of public sector chief executives, and gender management. Within this topic, there is a sub-section devoted to the sub-topic **performance measurement** and one to **benchmarking**. Many of the pieces in this section are written by senior public sector executives, with some contributions from academics in the public sector management field, and, in addition to those from the Commonwealth, this subject category features a number of articles on experiences in the United States.

The HRM&D materials support the module of the same name in the Senior Public Executive Seminar. That seminar sets the context for change, sets out the nature of the public service sector as a service industry – heavily reliant on the knowledge, skills, behaviours and performance of public servants, identifies the scope to improve performance, and outlines recent developments and trends in HRM&D which seem to be producing worthwhile results. It also discusses the role of central agencies in encouraging and initiating reform.

C. Organisational Change and Partnerships

In this part of the CAPAM PKC, over 200 documents relate current experience in adapting organisational structures to meet the needs of the end of the 20th Century. Under the single title "Organisational Change and Partnerships" are grouped articles, speeches, and case studies on topics ranging from alternative service delivery to linking government services through single-window operations to decentralisation, privatisation, and contracting out. A sub-theme within this section deals specifically with emerging practices of **partnership**: with the private and non-governmental sectors and between levels of government. Most of these materials were prepared within the last two years.

The CAPAM Senior Public Executive Seminar module on this topic provides a background to organisational change, noting that public administrations are being forced to reconsider the way they relate to society, to question their role in the economy, and to review the way they function.

The module makes the link between an organisation's purpose and its actual practices, the main thrust being that the structure of the organisation needs to more clearly match the functions and tasks that it has to deliver.

D. Information Systems and Standards of Service

The experience of a number of countries in introducing information systems into organisational design and programme delivery are covered through the 120 documents contained in this section on "Information Systems and Standards of Service" in the CAPAM PKC. Documented is the introduction of cellular telephone technology in Bangladesh to improve local public service delivery, quality improvement through information technology in Malaysia, the use of websites for government transactions in Canada. All of this practical experience is covered through articles, speeches and case studies. Similarly, improving customer service is the subject of several papers: from India on improving public health through municipal works, from Canada in service to business, and from South Africa in battling crime.

The Information Service and Standards of Service module within the Senior Public Executive

Seminar covers the basic capabilities of information technology and its limitations, familiarises participants with the principles of information resource management, and provides an overview of strategic planning for IT to meet government's long and short-term programme objectives. It also covers the need to differentiate between the opportunities IT provides to implement *new* services and modernising *existing* services through process re-engineering. This module also deals with the challenges of bridging the gap between senior officials and the IT community.

E. Financial Management and Control

The "Financial Management and Control" section of the CAPAM PKC, containing over 70 documents, includes several overview pieces on increasing value for money, an article on improving reports on financial management to parliament, a retrospective on dealing with fiscal challenges, and as well as a full report on modernising the comptrollership function in government. Two subtopics covered under this subject heading are **accrual accounting** and **performance measurement**.

The CAPAM Senior Public Executive Seminar module on Financial Management and Control deals with such issues as engaging non-specialists in understanding financial management reforms, managing the risks in changing basic financial management systems, and breaking financial management into a series of management tasks for example: financial planning and decision making, preparation of budgets, delegation and control, procurement, etc.

The materials in this section are equally divided between those written by practitioners and those prepared from a more academic viewpoint.

F. Policy Development

The "Policy Development" section of the CAPAM PKC contains approximately 70 pieces written by practitioners about modernising the policy process. A speech by a senior official in the United Kingdom exhorts its audience to develop structures, processes and leaders for the modernisation of policy development. A paper by a senior World Bank official situates the need for reform of policy development within the overall context of public sector reform. A Minister from New Zealand writes about the relationship between the politician and the senior official in designing policy to meet outcomes. Within this section of the PKC, a subsection is devoted to the political administrative interface as it relates to policy development.

The CAPAM Senior Public Executive Seminar module on Policy Development deals with the changing environment, alternative models of policy making that are inclusive and multi-sectoral, creating sustainable policy, and mechanisms for assessing policy capacity among government departments and agencies.

Accessing the Materials in the PKC

Each item in the CAPAM PKC has an individual record. Each record contains, *inter alia*, its title, author, year of publishing or release, CAPAM topic and sub-topic, subject country (where applicable), format (speech, article, book etc.), and, perhaps most importantly, a 100- to 250-word abstract.

The PKC is readily searchable through any combination of these fields.

For more information about the CAPAM PKC contact:
CAPAM
1075 Bay St., Suite 402
Toronto, Ontario, Canada M5S 2B1
tel: +1 416 920 3337
fax: +1 416 920 6574
e-mail: capam@capam.ca
website: www.capam.comnet.mt

iii) CAPAM International Innovations Awards Programme

In 1998, CAPAM launched the first CAPAM International Innovations Awards Programme. Through the International Innovations Awards Programme, CAPAM has endeavoured to expose Commonwealth countries to varying perspectives on public sector innovation, to promote excellence in public administration and management and to further strengthen communications and exchange among member countries.

Since its inception in 1994, CAPAM's overall mandate has been to enhance Commonwealth co-operation to improve managerial competence and organisational excellence in government. CAPAM exchanges experiences on new developments and innovations in management in governments by building networks among senior public officials (both elected and appointed), academics and the private and non-governmental or voluntary sectors. Through these networks, CAPAM provides rapid access to information on best practices in government administration. The biennial International Innovations Awards Programme is one of the prime mechanisms CAPAM has developed to access and disseminate innovative practices in this field.

The theme of the CAPAM International Innovations Awards Programme varies. In the 1998 and 2000 Awards Programmes, the theme was "Service to the Public". In 2002, it was "Innovations in Governance." Innovators throughout the Commonwealth made over 400 entries to these three programmes.

A representative jury of 10 internationally recognised practitioners, advisors and academics, knowledgeable in the fields of public administration and management, and well-versed in international economic, social and cultural contexts, reviews the Awards submissions and selects 10 finalists. Selection of the Award winners takes place after each of the finalists presents their submissions to the jury. The finalists are also asked to introduce their innovations during a Plenary session to the delegates at the CAPAM Biennial Conference. During the Closing Ceremony of the CAPAM Biennial Conference, the winners of the gold, silver and bronze awards are announced.

Each Awards Programme is launched one year in advance of the CAPAM biennial Conference. The deadline for submissions to the programme is approximately six months before the Conference.

Winning submissions and those of the finalists are profiled in a Special Edition of the quarterly CAPAM newsletter, *Commonwealth Innovations*, as well as on the CAPAM website. A summary of the all submissions with a contact name and address, is included in both places to ensure maximum opportunity to investigate innovations that might be applicable in other jurisdictions. The summaries of the submissions remain on the website for ongoing reference.

All submissions are eligible for participation in the CAPAM International Innovations Cascading Programme, a joint CAPAM Commonwealth Secretariat initiative that encourages the appropriate replication of innovations in other jurisdictions.

Awards Programme entrants must be CAPAM members – either individual or institutional members – of good standing. If not a member, the Awards submission must be accompanied by an application for CAPAM membership.

To inform yourself about the CAPAM International Innovations Awards Programme, please contact CAPAM or visit the CAPAM website.

CAPAM Contact Details

CAPAM
1075 Bay St., Suite 402
Toronto, Ontario, Canada
M5S 2B1
tel: +1 416 920 3337
fax: +1 416 920 6574
e-mail: capam@capam.ca
website: www.capam.comnet.mt